JUMP START
Your Day

With A Smile, Story, Scripture & Saying

A. Daniel Goldsmith

JUMP START YOUR DAY
With A Smile, Story, Scripture & Saying
by A. Daniel Goldsmith

Cover photo taken by: Ron Blair
Cover photo: The Matthew Carter family and Joy Bean

Printed in the United States of America

ISBN 9781498436410

Unless otherwise indicated, scripture quotations are taken from The New King James Version Copyright © 1982 by Thomas Nelson, Inc.; The Message (MSG). Copyright © 1993, 1994, 1995, 1996, 2000, 2001, 2002 by NavPress Publishing Group; The New International Version (NIV). Copyright © 1973, 1978, 1984, 2011 by Biblica, Inc.; The New Living Translation (NLT). Copyright © 1996, 2004, 2007 Tyndale House Publishers, Inc.; The Living Bible (TLB). Copyright © 1971 by Tyndale House Publishers, Inc. Used by permission. All rights reserved.

www.xulonpress.com

INTRODUCTION

In 2010 I published a book entitled *Jokes, Quotes & Anecdotes Made Especially for Citizens with Seniority.* I received many encouraging comments, some with a joke and a note: "For your next book." After several such comments, I started asking myself some questions. "Should I consider publishing another book? I've been '39' years old for several decades. Would I live long enough to finish such? What kind of book should it be?" Someone told me that they read a page from my book to their spouse each evening. Another said that they read a page in the morning. A lady told me she was enjoying the book and read a couple of pages before going to bed, discovering that she slept better. I don't guarantee that, but it worked for her. Some dear friends in Michigan said that they used it along with their devotions. With these and other comments, I thought maybe a book with a daily slice of humor would be the way to go.

Jump Start Your Day is a book with a daily *smile*, a *story*, a *scripture* and a *saying*. It has been said that: "A smile is the lighting system of the face, the cooling system of the head, and the heating system of the heart." So may this book give you a smile, a cool head and a warm heart.

Let me say that the jokes are nearly all about people. You may identify with some of the happenings. Rather than saying "a certain man, a little girl" or "an elderly lady" 300 plus times, I chose to use a variety of names for most of the jokes. I trust that no one is offended if your name is used in a joke. A name was never used about anyone that I knew in a similar situation. They were simply randomly chosen.

Since many jokes have similar themes, you will notice that there are similar comments, appearing more than once.

Additional copies for sale at **www.xulonpress.com/bookstore**, or at a Christian Book Store, online book supplier, or as an e-book.

DEDICATION

I was born and raised in a family that loved the Lord and loved to laugh. Times were tough in the 1930's. It was the Great Depression. There was unemployment, little cash and empty pantries. Though there were times when my parents had to do without, there was never any shortage of love and laughter in our home.

As a father, I did my best to pass on those two *loves*. Now, as a grandparent, thinking about loving the Lord and loving to laugh, I want to dedicate this book to my five grandsons, Joshua, Austin, Zachary, Quinton, Griffin and to my first grand-daughter, Kacie, Joshua's wife. It is my prayer that you and future grand-daughters and all who follow will "love the Lord your God with all your heart, with all your soul, and with all your mind." Matthew 22:37

It is also my hope that as you grandchildren journey through life you will be able to capture and enjoy the experiences which life will bring your way, enabling you to turn some of them into times of fun and laughter." Love, *Papa*

ACKNOWLEDGEMENTS

I t was Charles Swindoll who said: "The closest a man can come to understanding childbirth is by writing a book."[1] I did not publish this book without help. I want to thank those who assisted me with the birth of this book.

First, I thank my wife for her patience, especially in the last several months while I spent many hours at the computer. Without her support and encouragement, this book would never have become a reality. Also she gave the book its name: *Jump Start Your Day.*

Secondly, I want to express my gratitude to James Chuang and Jack Diamond for their suggestions and valuable input. I am grateful to Paul Redekop for the two volumes, limited editions, of *one-liners* which he compiled and gave to me. Don Dirks promptly responded whenever I needed help with my computer and sending the completed manuscript to Xulon Press.

Who would ever want to proof read these many pages? Well I found a very willing friend who graciously agreed to do so and actually said that he enjoyed the task. Henry Hooge spent many hours meticulously reading every word of the manuscript, making note of spelling, punctuation and grammatical errors while offering corrective measures and suggestions. Thank you Henry. By the way, Henry didn't proof-read these introductory pages, so don't blame him.

I want to acknowledge those who frequently passed on a joke or a humorous story, plus the friends that willingly submitted an endorsement.

To all of these I express my deepest gratitude. Thank you!

Dan Goldsmith

April 2015

ENDORSEMENTS

"We all love to laugh and most of us even agree that humor is good medicine. *Jump Start Your Day,* however, shows us something else. It demonstrates how wonderfully effective good humor can be for making a point and helping us to see things just a bit differently than we did before. And somehow, it makes us enjoy the whole process. I can't think of a better way to point our minds toward truths worth reflecting upon, one each day, than by introducing each with a humorous story that points the way. I highly recommend this book by Dan Goldsmith."

Dr. Paul Chamberlain,
Director; Institute of Christian Apologetics, Professor of
Apologetics, Philosophy & Ethics, Trinity Western University,
Langley, BC

"Dan Goldsmith has been my Spiritual Father for the past four decades. What I remember most from our relationship is his prayerfulness and his keen sense of humor. Both enriched my ministry. His prayer was used of God to open many doors and his sense of humor helped me to build pleasant platforms to reach out. You will love Dan's second book, *Jump Start Your Day*, because it successfully combines the pleasant daily smile and in-depth daily reflection. This format reminds us that our God is always fun loving and seriously involved in our daily affairs."

Rev. James Chuang,
serving as missionary for 40 years with C&MA
and with Open Doors International,
Hong Kong

"Rev. Dan Goldsmith is a long time friend and pastor. As a single man, he boarded at my parents place for his first church posting. Years later our families connected again when he became our pastor. We could always count on Dan giving us a humorous moment. We read his first book from cover to cover and got a chuckle each page. I am sure this one will be even better."

Willis Creighton,
Senior Development Officer, Global Action,
Mesa, AZ

"I cut my teeth in pastoral ministry under Dan's tutelage. With a love for laughter and for people, he helped me to see back then the importance of relational engagement that probes the humorous side of life as a gift for all. Who among us doesn't take on far too often the weighty and burdensome challenges that life delivers? I can only benefit from a jump start to my day, a tonic moment of unscripted laughter, where humor, truth and reality converge releasing anticipation that God is indeed in control and so thoroughly delights in our thorough enjoyment of Him. I really want to laugh with God a lot more!"

Rev Brem Frentz,
Vice President of Global Ministries
The Christian and Missionary Alliance in Canada,
Toronto, ON

"My husband Brad and I both enjoyed Dan's first book. It contained some of the best of Christian humor, both clean and funny. This new book is very appealing with a funny story or joke for each day, followed by creative and practical applications for daily living. It will put a smile on your face and will cheer your soul."

Ruth Hartt,
retired missionary, and pastor's wife
ministering to Spanish congregations,
Renton, WA

"Dan's daily readings are like multi-faceted gems that elegantly reflect the love of the Almighty. He has provided an anchor-point in Scripture, illustrated with a real life story, punctuated with humor and capped off with a quote from a master. They are a breath of fresh air that will put a smile on your face all year long."

Mark L. Maxwell,
President & CEO of Prairie Bible Institute,
Three Hills, AB

"My wife and I have known the Goldsmiths for many years. They have had a consistent testimony for Jesus Christ. Dan's book, *Jokes, Quotes & Anecdotes* has been a very interesting book for Shirley and me. I am sure his new book, *Jump Start Your Day* will be a blessing to many people."

Rev. Bill Jackson,
Bible teacher and speaker on
"Tribal Trails Television Ministry."
Goodfish Lake, AB

"If you like *Laughter: The Best Medicine* from *Reader's Digest,* you'll delight in Dan Goldsmith's humor. But there's a catch. Dan wants you to go deeper. His comments grab your mind. His nuggets ground you. And his tidbits rivet the heart. Once you're hooked you won't want to *jump-start your day* without it!"

Dr. J. Allen Thompson
President, International Church Planting Center, Inc.
Cumming, GA

"The 'weaving together' of humor and Biblical principles is a great way to impress truth upon the minds and hearts of listeners. What some may think to be ponderous theology can be quickly made into understandable truth by well-timed, appropriate lightness through a 'pun with a purpose.' There is a 'funny side to life' and to be reminded of it helps us see ourselves as we are, and adds strength to numbers of Biblical principles. My college confrere, Dan Goldsmith, offers us a 'harvest of humor' that is down-to-earth and 'up-to-date.' I heartily recommend *Jump Start Your Day*. This book will do just that!"

Dr. Barry Moore,
Evangelist, Barry Moore Ministries
London, ON

"Some speakers are blessed with a rich sense of humor. The rest of us rely on Dan's delightfully rich treasure troves of humor and stories for any occasion. And if you see yourself as more of a reader than a speaker, Dan's latest collection of anecdotes and quotes will brighten and bless the darkest of days with its daily dose of lively humor, keen insights, and inspiring truths."

Rev. Norm Morrison,
Executive Pastor,
Sevenoaks Alliance Church,
Abbotsford BC

"The Bible says that a merry heart does good like medicine. This volume from my dear friend Dan Goldsmith will go a long ways toward delivering a lot of merriment to the reader. I have known Rev. Dan since 1949, when we were classmates in Bible College; I have profited immensely from his fellowship, including a hilarious joke countless times. His sound commitment to the truth of God's Word ensures that the humor is of the highest quality."

Dr. Gerald Wheatley,
Retired Pastor and College
professor of Bible and Theology
Lee's Summit, MO

January 1
Are You Accountable?

Today's Smile: Megan had been gaining weight for months and the Christmas season did not help any. So New Year's Day she sat down and wrote out a few New Year's resolutions. One of her resolutions was to lose weight. That evening, after writing out her list of resolutions, she phoned her friend Kim and said, "I've made some New Year's resolutions. My big goal is to lose thirty pounds this year. I started dieting today but I realize that I will need to be accountable to someone. Would it be alright if I phone you when I have the urge to go to out and get a burger, fries and a milkshake?"

"That would be fun," replied Kim, "I love burgers, fries and milkshakes. Anytime you feel like having a burger, fries and a milkshake just give me a call and I'll go to Dairy Queen(R) with you!"

Today's Comment: Do you make New Year's resolutions? Maybe you call them goals. Resolutions are easy to make, but hard to keep. If we fall by the way and break them, that's not the end of the world. Let's get up and start again.

How many times have we made losing weight a goal? Maybe we endeavored to spend more time with our children, or visiting our parents. Many people have made a resolution saying that they were planning to read through the Bible in a year, memorize scripture, or spend more time in prayer, yet often those resolutions were broken.

If we are really serious this year about our resolutions or goals, maybe we need to be accountable to a friend. That way we have a little incentive to stick with it. If you're serious about setting goals for this year why not pray that God will guide you to a friend to whom you can be accountable.

Today's Golden Nugget of Truth: "I don't mean to say that I am perfect. I haven't learned all I should even yet, but I keep working toward that day when I will finally be all that Christ saved me for and wants me to be." Philippians 3:12 (TLB)

Today's Philosophical Tidbit: "A New Year's resolution is something that goes in one year and out the other." Author Unknown

January 2
Who Is In Charge?

Today's Smile: It was the beginning of the New Year and Tory decided that he was going to let his employees know once and for all who was in charge. He was very upset over the Christmas break realizing that he had been unable to get his employees to do their work properly. Furthermore, there was very little respect for the fact that he was the one who assigned them their duties and paid their salary. So early on the morning of the second of January he was there at the office before any of his employees arrived and he put up a sign where everyone would see it. In bold letters it said, "I AM THE BOSS!"

That sign seemed to help a little and some of his staff appeared to show some improvement. A couple of his employees apologized for their slipshod work and he felt that maybe that sign would eventually help everyone to know who was in charge.

Returning from lunch with one of his supervisors, he found a memo on his desk which his secretary had placed there which read, "Your wife phoned and said she wants her sign back."

Today's Comment: Who is the boss in your house? I read about a young brother and sister that were playing together. The little boy was telling the sister what to do and where to go. She had had enough, so turned to him and said, "Who do you think you are. . . my husband?"

The Bible does not use the word *boss*. It speaks about roles and responsibilities which if carried out by Spirit filled partners makes for a harmonious marriage. If you're married and the relationship is a little out of tune, this is a good time of year to start afresh. Pray today that the Lord will be in charge, with husband and wife fulfilling their particular roles harmoniously.

Today's Golden Nugget of Truth: "Wives, submit yourselves to your own husbands, as it is fitting in the Lord. Husbands, love your wives and do not be bitter toward them." Colossians 3:18, 19

Today's Philosophical Tidbit: "The kind of music that couples should have in their homes is domestic harmony." Author Unknown

January 3
Costly Mistakes

*T*oday's Smile: While Jared was standing in line at the bank, he developed a bad case of hiccups. With each step towards the teller, his hiccups worsened. Upon reaching the teller, and barely able to speak between hiccupping, he handed her his Visa bill, which he wanted to pay out of his account, and also requested, as best he could, $200.00 cash. The teller proceeded to pull up his account with the computer. She paused a few seconds and then looked at Jared and said, with a bit of a concerned look on her face, "I am sorry, but you do not have enough money in your account to cover your Visa, nor can I give you $200.00 cash."

"Insufficient funds? Why I deposited a check for $2,000.00 last Friday. Are you telling me the truth?"

"She grinned. "I'm just joking," said the teller." She continued to process his account, and just before she gave him his cash she said, "And did you notice that your hiccups are gone?

Today's Comment: A similar thing happened to me several years ago. I intended to keep the statement to prove my story, but accidentally shredded it. Anyhow, I deposited a check for around $1,500.00, and then I told the teller that I wanted to pay my Visa bill, which was not a very big amount. The teller looked at me and said, "I'm sorry, Mr. Goldsmith, but you are overdrawn and there are not sufficient funds to pay your bill."

"But, I just deposited my check. That's much more than my bill. How much am I overdrawn?" I don't remember the exact dollar and cent figure, but the teller said it was over $399,000.00. "$399,000.00," I said, "but I only have an overdraft of $1,000.00." I laughed. I thought that was so crazy. When the teller investigated further it was discovered that I had written a check a few days earlier for $40.00 and the clerk had entered $400,000.00 instead of $40.00.

We all make mistakes. My dad used to tell me that's why they put erasers on the end of pencils. Some mistakes can easily be erased, and laughed off. Other mistakes may prove costly. Receiving wrong information may cause serious problems. Driving the wrong direction may cause an accident. Taking the wrong medicine may cause death. Believing the wrong interpretation of scripture may lead into a Christ-less eternity. Let's pray today that we will be careful where we go, what we hear, what we say, what we do and what we believe.

Today's Golden Nugget of Truth: "Beware lest anyone cheat you through philosophy and empty deceit, according to the tradition of men, according to the basic principles of the world, and not according to Christ." Colossians 2:8

Today's Philosophical Tidbit: "We feel foolish when we make mistakes, but we can become wiser when we learn from our mistakes." A. Daniel Goldsmith

January 4
Do The Children Understand

Today's Smile: Gwen was a single mother and she and her son Bernie regularly went to the First Baptist Church on their Sunday School bus. This particular Sunday, there was a slight blizzard, and Gwen was fighting a cold, so Bernie went on the bus without her. When he came home after the church service, Gwen asked him what he learned in Sunday School, and also what the pastor talked about. Bernie replied and said, "Well, last Sunday the teacher told us we would be learning about the Holy Spirit today, but the lesson this morning was something about getting a quilt. And mommy it was really cold in the sanctuary. The pastor said that they were having problems with the furnace, so I didn't hear everything that the pastor said in the service. I think he said his Bible text was "Many are cold and a few are frozen."

Well, Gwen figured out the pastor's sermon. That was Matthew 22:14, "Many are called, but few are chosen." But the Sunday School lesson? What was that about? So she phoned Johnny's mother and she said that Johnny had told her the same thing, something about quilts. She had phoned the teacher. The teacher said it was about the Holy Spirit, John 15:26, "But when the Comforter is come, Whom I will send. . ."

Today's Comment: Do you have children, grandchildren? Are you teaching young children in Sunday School? How often have you checked to see that they understood what you said? Back in the 1960's when it was acceptable to pray the Lord's Prayer in the public schools, I had in my congregation an elementary school teacher who gave his students an assignment. Having recited the Lord's Prayer since starting school, he asked students in grades 4, 5, 6, and 7 to write out from memory as much of the Lord's Prayer that they could. He gave me several excerpts from his students work. Here are just a few: "Other Father how art in heaven. . . Father witch art. . . How loud be his name. . . How will be thy name. . .Halo be thy name. . .Halibut thy name. . . It will be non on earth. . . Forget our trusd basses. . . Give us our daily breath. . .And forgive us all the days of our life. . ."

So sad, but it was true. Let's pray today that what we are saying is what these young children are hearing and understanding.

Today's Golden Nugget of Truth: "And these words which I command you today shall be in your heart; you shall teach them diligently to your children. . ." Deuteronomy 6:6, 7

Today's Philosophical Tidbit: "Every home is a school. What do you teach?" Author Unknown

January 5
A Wrong Assumption

T oday's Smile: The president and owner of a manufacturing company made a surprise tour of his company. As he walked through the warehouse he noticed that a young man was standing by a stack of pallets doing absolutely nothing. This angered the owner and he said to the young man, "How much do you make a week?"

The young man said that he usually made about $800.00 each week. The owner pulled out his wallet and gave him $800.00 cash and said to him, "Now leave, and don't you ever come back here again." Without saying a word, the young man put the money in his pocket and quickly left.

The owner then walked over to the warehouse manager, who was staring at the owner, and asked the manager, "How long has that young fellow been working here?"

The manager replied, "Sir, that fellow doesn't work here. He had just delivered some pizza for our lunch break and Pete went to collect the money from the other fellows so he could pay him."

Today's Comment: We may judge a person by their clothes, their hair, or maybe other outward appearances. I remember when the church receptionist informed me that a man had come into the church and wanted to speak with me. I walked out into the reception area to invite him into my office. When I saw him, my first thought was here is another person who wants a financial handout. As I engaged in conversation with him, I quickly realized that I was wrong in my assumption. This man had come for spiritual help. As a young person he had received the Lord Jesus as his personal Savior, but had wandered far from the Lord.

Before the man left my office, he had prayed and recommitted his life to the Lord. A few weeks later, he asked if I would meet with his wife. She wanted what he had. The two of them began to walk the spiritual journey together and continued to grow in their spiritual lives.

How often do we jump to conclusions? We make a judgment call from the appearance of things. It is so easy to take action without knowing all the facts. Let's pray that we get the facts before we begin to give orders or take action.

Today's Golden Nugget of Truth: "Don't jump to conclusions. There may be a perfectly good explanation for what you just saw." Proverbs 25:8 (MSG)

Today's Philosophical Tidbit: "Jumping to conclusions is very poor exercise." Author Unknown

January 6
Don't Walk In The Dark

*T**oday's Smile:* Lester had received a book as a Christmas gift. It was all about fishing, but since it was winter in North Dakota, he decided to study all the tips about ice fishing. He read that the primary tool used to drill holes in the ice is a tool that looks like a long corkscrew with sharp blades attached to the bottom. He found a sports shop that sold one, so he made a purchase.

He set off early one cold January morning. The sun doesn't rise very early in North Dakota in the winter so he considered himself fortunate to find ice so close to home especially since it was still quite dark.

He got out his brand new auger and started drilling. He had barely got started when he heard a voice saying, "You won't find any fish there." He thought maybe he was imagining that he had heard someone and so kept drilling. Again the voice said, "You won't find any fish there." He thought maybe it was a voice from heaven giving him guidance.

"Is that You, God?"

"No," said the voice, but this time the voice sounded very stern and very close. "I am the manager of this ice skating rink."

Today's Comment: How many of us have tried to work in the dark? It is so easy to take a wrong step or make a wrong turn when we're in the dark. We have a friend who walked out of a room in an unfamiliar dark hallway and fell down a flight of stairs.

When it comes to our spiritual relationship with God, let's not walk in the dark. We are to walk in God's light, not in the light of our own conscience or what we think is best. Charles H. Spurgeon, a great preacher of the 19th century said: "Sons of light must not have fellowship with deeds, doctrines, or deceits of darkness. . . In judgment, in action, in hearing, in teaching, in association, we must discern between the precious and the vile, and maintain the great distinction which the Lord made upon the world's first day. . . 'And God divided the light from the darkness'." Genesis 1:4

Pray today that the Lord will lighten our pathway.

Today's Golden Nugget of Truth: "But if we walk in the light, as He is in the light, we have fellowship one with another and the blood of Jesus Christ His Son cleanses us from all sin." First John 1:7

Today's Philosophical Tidbit: "Man has never invented a device that will produce darkness. Darkness is the absence of light." - A. Daniel Goldsmith

January 7
All One In Christ Jesus

T^{oday's Smile:} Bev was an obstetrics nurse at a large city hospital in a multi-cultural area of the city. One day, while she was waiting for a new mother to be transferred to her division, she checked the chart and assumed, by the last name, that this new mother was of European descent.

When the new mother was wheeled in, Bev was surprised to see that this young lady was Asian. As Bev was checking her patient, the new mother said that she was Chinese and her husband's ethnic heritage was Czech. After a short pause, she quipped, "I guess that makes my children Chinese Czechers!"

Today's Comment: What is your nationality? Does it really matter what your ethnic background is? We all came from Adam and Eve. We are one people, human beings. Then why can't we get along? The only answer that I know is that sin has marred our relationship with God as well as our relationship with fellow members of the human race. All the wars and fighting and killing, etc are because of the sinful nature of man. When we get right with God, we can then begin to accept one another. Jesus Christ is the only One that can restore a peaceful relationship.

Pray that the Prince of Peace will be acknowledged and accepted in our community, church, country and world.

Today's Golden Nugget of Truth: "There is neither Jew nor Greek, there is neither slave nor free, there is neither male nor female: for you are all one in Christ Jesus." Galatians 3:28

Today's Philosophical Tidbit: "Those at war with others are seldom at peace with themselves." Author Unknown

January 8
Know All The Answers

*T**oday's Smile:* Nick had been doing well on a quiz program. He had been able to answer every question directed at him. He was now down to the last question which was worth $50,000.00. He was given the choice of a category and he selected the category on American History. The host reminded Nick that if he gave the correct answer he would walk away with $50,000.00 but if he did not come up with the correct answer he would only receive $10,000.00. "Are you ready?" the host asked Nick.

Nick nodded with a cocky confidence; after all he had answered every question so far with a correct answer. "Nick," said the host, "your question, like all final questions, is a two-part question. However, you may choose to answer the second part of the question first. If you get the second part right you double your cash win to $100,000.00. Which part would you like to take a stab at first?"

Nick was now appearing to be a little nervous. His self-confidence, which had been so noticeable in previous questions, was no longer evident. After a few seconds, he said: "Well, I think I'll go for the second part of the question."

"OK," said the host, "I'll ask you the second half first. If you answer correctly, the game is over and you win a $100,000.00. If you are wrong you will receive $10,000.00." There was a deathly silence in the audience. "Here is your question, Nick. In what year did it happen?"

Today's Comment: Have you ever met a Mr. Know-It-All, or a Mrs. Know-It-All? They are people that have an answer for every question and an opinion on every subject. A friend told me about having coffee with several others on a regular basis. One of his friends monopolized the conversation every time they met. Finally, my friend told this talkative friend of his, "Would you please shut up and let someone else talk!"

I heard about a woman who said of her marriage, "I wanted to marry Mr. Right. I just didn't know that his first name was 'Always'."

What about you and me? Do we know what we sound like in the ears of others? Maybe we need to stop sometime and let someone else contribute a few words. They may actually have a point to make that we've never heard before. God may want to speak to us through someone else. Let's pray that we will be led by the Spirit of God when we speak with others.

Today's Golden Nugget of Truth: "Let your speech always be with grace, seasoned with salt, that you may know how you ought to answer each one." Colossians 4:6

Today's Philosophical Tidbit: "It isn't so much what we say as the number of times we say it that makes us a bore." Author Unknown

January 9
Follow The Directions

T oday's Smile: Penny was a veterinarian. She often diagnosed her own health and would sometimes take some of the horse medicine that she had at her clinic. However, this time, she was really ill and decided to go see her family doctor.

Dr. Sawchuk checked her blood pressure, eyes, ears, throat, her heart beat, asked her all the usual questions about symptoms, how long had she been experiencing the pain and discomfort, etc., when Penny interrupted him: "Hey Doc," she said, "look, I'm a Vet. I don't need to ask my patients these kinds of questions. I can determine what's wrong by simply looking at them. Why can't you?"

The doctor nodded in agreement, looked her up and down and wrote out a prescription which he handed to her and said: "Get this filled, and if that doesn't restore you to good health, we'll have to have you put down."

Today's Comment: Have we ever asked for some advice and then quickly proceeded to supply the answer? If we go to a doctor, counselor, pastor, friend or spouse and ask for some advice, we should be courteous enough to let them respond, and give us the counsel or advice that we have asked.

The same is true when we go to the Lord in prayer and ask that He would reveal His will to us, that He would guide us in the decisions that we need to make today. Pray that we will follow through on what He prescribes for us.

Today's Golden Nugget of Truth: "Listen to counsel and receive instruction, that you may be wise in your latter days." Proverbs 19:20

Today's Philosophical Tidbit: "The best advice is only as good as the use we make of it." Author Unknown

January 10
Will It Hurt Someone

Today's Smile: Bruce was in the locker room of a private club, along with several other men, having just finished a good work-out. Someone had apparently forgotten their smart phone which was on the bench beside Bruce. When it rang he picked it up and answered it.

"Honey, it's me. Are you still at the club?"

"Yes," answered Bruce.

"Good, I'm at Cherry Hill Mall, two blocks away." I just saw the most beautiful mink coat. It's absolutely gorgeous. May I buy it?"

"How much does it cost?" asked Bruce.

"It's only $3,895.00. If you buy it this week you get an 18 karat gold necklace for 50% off. May I buy that too?"

"If you like them go ahead and buy them. That will be an early Valentine's Day gift." said Bruce.

"Oh, you're such a sweetie. Just for that I'm going to buy two tickets for us to Hawaii. There is a bargain price on all this week. Airfare from L.A. with seven nights, breakfast included in a five star hotel in Honolulu and it is only $2,199.00 for the two of us. Is that O.K?"

"I guess we could use a break," said Bruce.

'Oh thank you thank you thank you. I love you."

When the call had ended, Bruce held up the smart phone and asked, "Do any of you fellows know whose phone this is?"

Today's Comment: Have we ever met a "practical" joker? Most of us have. Probably some readers of this book may qualify for that description. Unfortunately some so called practical jokes are not always practical and have had serious consequences. *Mirriam-Webster Dictionary* defines the word practical as "likely to succeed and reasonable to do or use." Many so-called practical jokes are not reasonable.

The most publicized practical joke in recent years was the prank played by a couple of radio personalities at an Australian FM radio station, when they posed as Queen Elizabeth and Prince Charles and phoned the King Edward VII hospital in London where Kate, the Duchess of Cambridge, was being treated for morning sickness. The news reported that two days later, the nurse who took the call, was apparently so humiliated that she died from what appeared to be a suicide.

We pray about all kinds of things. I wonder, have we ever prayed before engaging in a practical joke? Probably not. Prayer might be a good idea. Enjoy your practical joke, but make sure that it is practical.

Today's Golden Nugget of Truth: "A merry heart makes a cheerful countenance, but by sorrow of the heart the spirit is broken." Proverbs 15:13

Today's Philosophical Tidbit: "Genuine humor is always kindly and gracious. It points out the weakness of humanity, but shows no contempt and leaves no sting." Author Unknown

January 11
No Discipline Makes A Delinquent

Today's Smile: Fulton J. Sheen has told of an incident in his life when he was riding the subway and stood up to offer his seat to a lady who was standing, holding onto a strap. The lady appeared somewhat surprised for she had seldom seen any man do such. "Why did you do that?" the lady asked Father Sheen.

Thinking that the lady would not understand the fact that this is what a man should do, simply replied by saying, "Madam, I tell you ever since I was a little boy I have had an infinite respect for a woman with a strap in her hand."

Today's Comment: I realize that the methods used for discipline have changed. In my school days, the principal had a strap in his office and administered the same. That is no longer the case. My Dad had a razor strap which hung on a hook in the kitchen. Many parents today have resorted to other ways of disciplining. Some limit TV time, curtail the child's activities and some seek to reason with their child. My Dad called the strap the "gentle persuader." When the occasion arose, he used it for a purpose other than sharpening a razor. It was used to "sharpen" us children. Seeing it every day as it hung in the kitchen was usually sufficient reminder for us to behave.

Whatever form of discipline that you use, pray that it will be effective and that God will help you to raise a child or children that will honor their parents and glorify their God.

Today's Golden Nugget of Truth: "Train up a child in the way he should go, and when he is old he will not depart from it." Proverbs 22:6

Today's Philosophical Tidbit: "A boy is like a canoe, he behaves better if paddled from the rear." Author Unknown

January 12
I Want My Way Now

T oday's Smile: A fellow was on trial for first degree murder and if found guilty would be electrocuted. His brother having carefully studied the faces of the members of the jury thought maybe he would approach one of the members and offer to pay him $10,000.00 if he could convince the other members to bring in a charge of manslaughter.

The jury was in meeting for several days and finally returned with a verdict of manslaughter. After the trial, the brother of the convicted man went to the irresponsible juror's house and thanked him for a job well done. True to his word, he handed the man $10,000.00 cash.

The juror responded by saying that it was not easy trying to convince the rest of the jury to change the charge to manslaughter. They all thought that his brother was not at all guilty and should be set free.

25

Today's Comment: Long before digital cameras and when colored slides were popular, I wanted to buy a Kodak® slide projector. I made a hasty decision one night before Christmas and made the purchase. Four days later, Christmas Sunday, one of the elders presented a Christmas gift to us, a gift from the congregation. What was it? The identical projector, a Kodak slide projector.

Have you ever worked hard for something, only to find out that things would have been far better if you hadn't got involved? We can become so obsessed with wanting our will or our way and wanting it now that we mess things up. This is especially true if one has to scheme or connive or cheat. If we have to go that route to make things happen, then it is the wrong route. We need to pray for patience, trusting in the living God.

Today's Golden Nugget of Truth: "And He gave them their request, but sent leanness into their soul." Psalm 106:15

Today's Philosophical Tidbit: "The trouble with people today is that they want to get to the promised land without going through the wilderness." Author Unknown

January 13
Kind Remarks

*T**oday's Smile:* Betsy invited some old friends and also Carol, a relatively new friend to her house for dinner. Carol was a photographer and she took great pride in her work and wherever she went she would take samples of her photography.

As they were sitting around the table, following a most delicious meal, Carol passed some of her photos around for all to see. As the guests were complimenting Carol on her work, Betsy, the hostess, exclaimed, "Wow, these are really nice photos, you must have a very expensive camera."

Carol did not really appreciate that remark but kept her thoughts to herself, until they all moved from the table to the living room and one by one were thanking Betsy for the lovely meal. At this point Carol verbalized her thoughts and said, "Thank you Betsy for such a wonderful meal, you must have a great set of pots and pans."

Today's Comment: Have we ever stopped to analyze what we have said when making a compliment? What we say may sound different to the hearer than what we thought we were saying. We have probably all said something to a person thinking that they knew well what we meant. We meant it as an compliment. They took it totally out of context and were offended. So let's be careful how we phrase our compliments.

My mother wrote the following words in my autograph book when I was about ten years old. "Before you speak ask yourself, is it kind, is it true, is it necessary." If we would follow that advice regularly, our words should not be coming out the wrong way. Pray that our words will be kind, true and necessary.

Today's Golden Nugget of Truth: "Let it be the hidden person of the heart, with the incorruptible beauty of a gentle and quiet spirit, which is very precious in the sight of God." First Peter 3:4

Today's Philosophical Tidbit: "Don't forget that appreciation is always appreciated." Author Unknown

January 14
Free Advice

*T**oday's Smile:* A doctor and a lawyer were both invited to a dinner reception. During the evening, there were several people that stopped by to chat briefly with the doctor. The lawyer noticed this and said to the doctor, you must have a lot of friends. I saw several people chatting with you this evening. It must be nice to be so well known and respected."

"No," replied the doctor, "they were not personal friends. They are people that know that I am a doctor and want some medical advice. I don't know how to stop this. Do you have any advice?"

The lawyer responded and told him, "I tell you what I do. If anyone speaks to me at a function like this and asks for advice, I send them a bill in the mail." The doctor thought that was a good idea and decided that he would act upon the lawyer's advice.

Later in the week, the doctor's secretary placed his mail on his desk. He was surprised to see that there was a letter from his new lawyer friend that he had met at the dinner. He was even more surprised when he opened it and discovered that it was a bill!

Today's Comment: Are we guilty of asking for help at inopportune times? Lawyers, doctors, counselors, pastors, professors, and many more appreciate some time when they can enjoy fellowship and interaction with friends without having to be responding to questions which should be addressed at other times.

Our Lord Jesus Christ desired times without people around Him asking questions. He sought a quiet place, often in the mountains, where He could be by Himself and pray to His Father in heaven. So let us permit and pray that others will have the pleasure of such moments. Let's leave our questions for a more convenient time or arrange for an appointment.

Today's Golden Nugget of Truth: "And He said to them, come aside by yourselves to a deserted place and rest a while. For there were many coming and going and they did not even have time to eat." Mark 6:31

Today's Philosophical Tidbit: "Being married is the best way to get some free advice." A. Daniel Goldsmith

January 15
Rejoice With Those Who Rejoice

*T*oday's Smile: Three Lutheran ministers, who were friends of the Roman Catholic parish priest, were invited to attend a mass so they would have a firsthand experience as to how the Catholics worshipped. They arrived a little late and the pews were all filled with parishioners. So they stood at the back of the church.

The priest noticed them standing there as he was about to begin the mass. He whispered to one of the altar boys and asked him to get three chairs for his Lutheran friends. The altar boy did not hear what was said as the priest did not want everyone to hear. So the priest spoke again, this time a wee bit louder, and said: "Three chairs for our Lutheran friends."

The boy was a bit perplexed but dutifully stepped up to the altar rail and loudly proclaimed to the congregation, "Three cheers for the Lutherans! Hip hip hoorah, hip hip hoorah, hip hip hoorah!"

Today's Comment: Do you rejoice when the Bible believing church down the road is growing faster than the church where you attend? If we are part of the family of God we should be encouraged to see that people are being reached with the gospel by whatever means. You probably know of communities, as I do, where the Christians in one church will have nothing to do with the Christians attending the church across the road. That is not the Christian spirit. If we looked at the church as God sees it, we should be able to give three cheers and rejoice in what God is doing in another church. People are receiving Christ as their personal Saviour. In this we should be rejoicing. Let's pray for our neighboring churches that God will give them a great ministry.

Today's Golden Nugget of Truth: "For where there are envy, strife, and divisions among you, are you not carnal and behaving like mere men? For when one says, 'I am of Paul,' and another, 'I am of Apollos,' are you not carnal?" First Corinthians 3:3, 4

Today's Philosophical Tidbit: "Biblical orthodoxy without compassion is surely the ugliest thing in the world." Francis Schaeffer

January 16
How To Manage Money

Today's Smile: Holly was in grade ten and had secured her first job working on Saturdays as a clerk at a fast food restaurant. Prior to this her only income had been from baby sitting and she had always been paid in cash. Now that she was receiving a check at her place of employment, her father went with her to open her first bank account. He took her to the City Bank, where he and his wife had accounts. He showed Holly how to make a deposit and write a check and do her own banking.

It was a big day when she went on her own and deposited her second check. Again a third and fourth check was deposited and since she did not qualify for a credit card, she paid most of her bills either with cash or by writing checks.

After three months of working at her new job, she came to her father with tears in her eyes and said, "That bank, which you and Mom have been doing banking with, and where you introduced me to the manager and helped me open my account, is in big trouble."

"What do you mean, honey? They are one of the largest banks in the city. There must be some mistake," said her father.

"Well," said Holly, "the bank just returned one of my checks with a note that said, 'Insufficient Funds'."

Today's Comment: A regret that I have, as I look back over my eight decades plus, is that I was not taught early in life how to budget and handle money. I've never lacked financially, but I have envied those people who learned early in life how to budget and live within the same and not have to rely on loans or credit cards.

May I say that if you have young children, or are just starting out on married life, get some help and learn how to manage your finances and how to help those who are under your care. And don't forget to tithe and teach your children how to tithe and pray that they will continue to give to the Lord's ministry when they are no longer under your roof.

Today's Golden Nugget of Truth: "The rich rules over the poor and the borrower is servant to the lender." Proverbs 22:7

Today's Philosophical Tidbit: "Some people spend money they don't have, to buy things they don't need, to impress people they don't like." Author Unknown

January 17
Humble Beginnings

Today's Smile: My friend Jack shared with me that back in the 1940's a new pastor was installed at the church where he and his parents and his siblings attended. The morning after his first Sunday, the new pastor needed to get some work done on his old car. In his search for a repair shop, the new pastor ended up meeting Jack's father, who was a mechanic and owned and operated a service station and auto repair shop.

Fifty years ago and more, most pastors had a very meagre salary. A manse or parsonage was usually provided for living accommodation. To supplement the pastor's salary, parishioners, and particularly the farm folks, gave the pastor and his family eggs, milk, cream, vegetables and sometimes some meat.

Well, there were also some other perks. The new pastor was hoping this mechanic would take pity on him and so said to Jack's dad, "I'm the new pastor in town. I need to have some work done on my old car, but I don't have a lot of money. I hope you don't charge too much because I'm just a poor preacher."

"Yes, said Mr. Schroeder, the mechanic, "I know you're a poor preacher. I heard you preach yesterday morning."

Today's Comment: Well, I need to add that the mechanic and the pastor had a big laugh over this encounter and became the best of friends forever after.

I remember when I accepted my first pastoral ministry. I had two small churches about fourteen miles apart. I was young and single. My only preaching experience was the few times I preached during my college years and now I found myself being a pastor. I learned after my first Sunday that the board chairman of each church got together and discussed my sermon. You see, I did not preach for a call, I was appointed. One chairman asked the other, "Well, what do you think of our new pastor?"

The other chairman responded by saying, "What choice do we have?" Let me say that I was warmly received and encouraged, even though those early sermons preached needed a lot of improvement.

The great preachers of today were once young and all preached their first sermon. "Billy Graham's first sermon was preached in Palatka, Florida to 40 people. He had four borrowed sermons and preached all four in eight minutes."[1]

So today I offer a special thanks to all the elders and deacons' boards and parishioners who opened their arms to a young pastor who was just beginning. We had to start somewhere. May I say, keep encouraging your pastors, young or old. Most older pastors have weathered a few storms, but the young ones haven't. Pray for those young pastors and give them a word of encouragement now and then.

Today's Golden Nugget of Truth: "I was with you in weakness, in fear, and in much trembling." First Corinthians 2:3

Today's Philosophical Tidbit: "A word of encouragement during a failure is worth more than an hour of praise after success." Author Unknown

January 18
Teach Us To Number Our Days

Today's Smile: Abe resided in a Jewish nursing home. He had been a resident of the home for 17 years. The home put on a big party for him as he celebrated his 105 birthday. He was known and loved by all of the residents. The head nurse was interviewing Abe at his party and one of her questions was to what he owed his longevity.

Abe replied, "I was only married to one wife. I ate kosher food; worked hard all my life and I did all of my Jewish exercises."

"But," said the head nurse, "Levi on the 3rd floor did exactly what you did. He married only one wife, he ate kosher food, worked hard all of his life, did all of the Jewish exercises and yet he died at 77. How come?"

Abe replied, "I guess that Levi didn't keep it up long enough."

Today's Comment: Death is no respecter of persons. A friend may have eaten proper food, exercised daily, lived a stress free life and died at a young age. Another may have been careless with their diet, lived as a couch potato and lived much longer. How come, we ask? I don't have the answer. All I can say is that our days are numbered and only God knows the number. I visited a friend in hospital who was full of cancer. He was resting in the Lord and he said to me, "One thing I know for sure, I'll die on time, not a day early and not a day late." Let us pray that we will be ready when our day comes.

Today's Golden Nugget of Truth: "So teach us to number our days that we may gain a heart of wisdom." Psalm 90:12

Today's Philosophical Tidbit: "Plan as though you had many years to live, but live as though today were your last day." Author Unknown

January 19
An Honest Day's Work

*T**oday's Smile:* Nicole was applying for a receptionist job at a fairly large accounting firm. Mike and Brendon were the two accountants assigned to interview her. They were both amazed with her unusual qualifications.

"So tell us," Mike said as they were about to conclude the interview, "do you have any other skills that you think would be worth sharing with us?"

"Actually, I do," replied Nicole in a modest sort of way. "Last year I had three short stories published in a couple of national magazines and I have finished my first novel which has just gone to press."

"That is amazing," said Mike, "but I was thinking about skills that you could apply at work during office hours."

"Oh," said Nicole as she explained enthusiastically, "Those were all written at work during office hours."

Today's Comment: One of the hardest summer jobs that I had when I was a college student was working for an auto parts plant. The company had two sites in the city. I was not at the main plant but at the plant where we received our orders for parts on the hour. When our orders were filled, we had nothing to do until the next set of orders arrived. The boss simply said to us, who were pickers, "look like you're working." I would much rather had been working than acting like I was fulfilling orders.

If you are an employee and your employer has no work for you, that is one thing. That is your employer's fault. However, I know that there are those who cheat on their employer when they should be working. Are you an employee? Do you use your employer's time for personal reasons when there is work for you to do? If our working hours are not totally committed to doing the assigned work, then we are guilty of stealing. Pray that our lives as Christians will be above reproach and that we will do an honest day's work.

Today's Golden Nugget of Truth: "Servants, do what you're told by your earthly masters. And don't just do the minimum that will get you by. Do your best. Work from the heart for your real Master, for God. . ." Colossians 3:22 (MSG)

Today's Philosophical Tidbit: "A successful man continues to look for work after he has found a job." Author Unknown

January 20
Life Beyond Age Sixty-Five

Today's Smile: A university professor and an eighty-five year old man were seated side by side on a flight from Cape Town, South Africa to London, England. The professor wanted to talk, but the older man was tired and wanted to sleep. The professor asked the gentleman if he would like to play a game. The senior man politely declined.

The professor persisted. He said that the game he had in mind was a lot of fun. The professor said: "I will ask you a question, and if you don't know the answer, you pay me $10.00. Then it's your turn to ask me one, and if I don't know the answer, I will pay you $100.00." The man perked up at this offer and agreed to play the game.

So the professor asked the first question. "What is the distance from the earth to the moon?" It had been a good many years since the eighty-five year old had been in school and he had no idea what the distance was. So he handed the professor $10.00.

It was the senior's turn. He asked the professor, "What goes up a hill with three legs, and comes down with four?" The professor didn't respond immediately but took his laptop and began to search to see if he could find the answer. He sent out e-mails to some of his fellow professors and old classmates and some of his students. After a couple hours of searching, he handed the man one hundred dollars. The man put the money in his wallet and pulled the blanket up over him and was about to go to sleep.

The professor was going crazy not knowing the answer and shook his fellow passenger. "Tell me, what goes up a hill with three legs and comes down with four?"

The wise old senior said, "I don't know," pulled out his wallet and handed the professor a ten dollar bill and settled down again for a sleep.

Today's Comment: Seniors may be older in years, but many of them still have their "smarts." They have a wealth of knowledge and experience. Pick their brains sometime and find out for yourself.

Ronald Regan was president of the United States of America when he was in his 70's. Benjamin Franklin invented bifocals at age 79. Strauss was still composing music after his 80th birthday. Verdi wrote the famous *Ave Maria* at age 85. Bev Shea, the soloist with the Billy Graham Association, was still singing after reaching his 100th birthday. Want to know something else? I started this book when I was in my 80th year.

I should add that a few weeks ago my wife and I visited a lady who was celebrating her 105th birthday. She has a sharp mind and a good sense of humor. With a smile on her face, she told us that she started over when she reached her 100th birthday, and now that she is five again she was going to go to kindergarten and learn how to use the computer.

Don't rule the seniors out of your life. Pray for them. They may have the answer that you've been looking for.

Today's Golden Nugget of Truth: "They shall still bear fruit in old age; they shall be fresh and flourishing." Psalm 92:14

Today's Philosophical Tidbit: "It's easier to have the vigor of youth when you're old than the wisdom of age when you're young." Richard Needham

January 21
Laugh At Our Mistakes

*T**oday's Smile:* John and Betty decided to move to Northern Ontario when they retired. They found a nice two bedroom house in a small community and were enjoying their retirement. They purchased some of the things they had heard about which their kids owned; a computer, I-pod, and smart phones. They were settling down to life in the north but were also able to communicate with their children and grandchildren with all their new toys.

One day, John went ice fishing with his new neighbor. He left early in the morning. Along about 8:30am Betty sent a text message to John. It read: "Windows frozen. What should I do?"

John texted back, "Spray some de-icer or splash some hot water on them."

About ten minutes later, Betty sent a text: "Done that. Now the computer has completely quit working!"

Today's Comment: How many times have we said something to a person, be it our spouse or child or someone else, and they totally misunderstood us and then responded and said, "Oh, I thought you meant. . .?" It happens all the time. Utter confusion!

How do we respond to such confusion? We can get mad and say, "Why weren't you listening?" Or we can laugh and apologize for not being more specific. It helps if we can laugh at our mistakes and move on. Let's not be too hard on ourselves or the other person. It makes for better relationships. Perhaps we should pray that we can see the humor in it all and move on. No reason to cry over spilled milk.

Today's Golden Nugget of Truth: "Brethren, I do not count myself to have apprehended; but one thing I do, forgetting those things which are behind and reaching forward to those things which are ahead." Philippians 3:13

Today's Philosophical Tidbit: "Seeing humor in life's blunders won't hurt your eyes, but it will brighten your day." A. Daniel Goldsmith

January 22
Is Your Mind In Gear

Today's Smile: Ernie worked for the state governor. He dragged himself into the house and barely made it to his favorite chair before he dropped exhausted. His sweet caring wife was right there with a freshly baked cookie, a cup of coffee and of course an inquisitive mind. As they sat drinking their coffee, his wife said, "Sweetheart, you look beat. What's wrong? Are you not feeling well?

"No! There is nothing wrong with me. It has just been one terrible day at work today," said Ernie. "I think it is the worst day that I have ever experienced since I started working for the government. The computer system broke down early this morning and all of us, including the governor, had to do our own thinking."

Today's Comment: Do some of you remember when we had to use our brain more? Some of you will remember memorizing the mathematical tables. You had to use your brain when adding or subtracting. I am sure that many of you reading this have had an experience where you gave the clerk a ten dollar bill and a quarter for an item which cost five dollars and fifteen cents. You were expecting the clerk to give you a five dollar bill and a dime for change. What did the clerk do? First there was a puzzled look, and then he/she reached for the calculator to figure out how much change you were to receive.

If you are having a similar problem, try doing some simple math without the use of a calculator. Better still, if you want to stimulate your mind, memorize a poem or some verses of scripture. If you memorize a scripture, pray that God will bring it to mind at a time when you can share it with someone in need.

Today's Golden Nugget of Truth: "So I turned my mind to understand, to investigate and to search out wisdom and the scheme of things. . ." Ecclesiastes 7:25 (NIV)

Today's Philosophical Tidbit: "A lot of people work, but their minds are unemployed." Author Unknown

January 23
Are We Clearly Communicating

Today's Smile: The new minister was single and only 26. He had an earned a PhD degree, of which he was very proud, and always signed his name Doctor L.E. Slowden. In attempting to become better acquainted with their new minister, an older couple in the church invited him to dinner. They received a note from him acknowledging their invitation. Since they could not read his writing, they did not know whether he was accepting their invitation or not. The husband said, "Why don't you take the note to the corner pharmacy. Pharmacists are expert at reading doctors' hand writing no matter how bad it is."

So the lady took the note to the pharmacist. After looking at the note for a few seconds, the pharmacist took it to the back. Within five minutes he came back out with a bottle of pills and said to the lady, "There you are ma'am. Take one with each meal as instructed and if you have any re-actions contact me immediately."

Today's Comment: Can others read what you write? Most handwriting has been replaced by printed materials produced by computers, and other electronic gadgets. My father, who would have celebrated his birthday today, born in 1909, had to leave grade 8 because my grandfather said he had to get a job as he was only a working man's son. That did not stop Dad in his pursuit of knowledge. Dad was a student. By the time he was 50 he had a library of some 4,000 books, took several correspondence courses, one of which earned him a Bachelor of Theology. That was put to good use. Five years before retiring he became the pastor of a country church and continued that for ten years beyond his retirement.

My Dad worked for over thirty years in the main office of a major auto parts plant, often filling in as office manager when the manger was away. There were two other fellows, together with Dad, doing the same work. They both were university graduates. Dad wasn't. He only went as far as grade eight. How did Dad attain to such a position? His handwriting! He started working there by unpacking boxes containing auto parts. He was promoted to a back order office, and soon after to the main office. His printing and writing which were done to perfection, earned him his promotions.

Today, fewer people than ever do any handwriting. We telephone, we type, we text. Handwriting is a lost art. You would probably never get a promotion today because of your handwriting. However, we are still communicating with others. Whatever way we communicate, may the recipients understand our message. Pray also that we will be good communicators of the truths of God's Word.

Today's Golden Nugget of Truth: "See with what large letters I have written to you with my own hand." Galatians 6:11

Today's Philosophical Tidbit: "If our handwriting is an extension of our personality, what kind of person are we?" A. Daniel Goldsmith

January 24
First Responders

*T*oday's Smile: It snowed for days and days in the Rocky Mountains of Colorado. Brent and Mitt were volunteers with the Red Cross and along with the government search and rescue crews would sometimes assist when there was a heavy snowfall in the mountains. One day they were asked if they could help. An airplane had spotted a cabin where the snow covered the windows and doors and only the roof was showing, but obviously someone was inside because of the smoke seen billowing up from the chimney.

The fellows were prepared. They had a 4 by 4, snowmobile, snow blower, picks and shovels. They followed the instructions given to them, and managed to find the cabin. The smoke was still coming out the chimney. Sure enough, the windows and doors were covered. The two of them went to work. They worked as fast as they could removing the snow, eventually reaching the door. When they knocked on the door, an elderly bearded man answered. Brent said, "Sir, we are from the Red Cross. . ." Before he could finish, the man said, "I'm sorry fellows, but I made my annual donation four weeks ago when I was in town."

Today's Comment: Thank God for our paramedics, our doctors and nurses, our firefighters, our law enforcement men and women, the Red Cross, The Salvation Army, World Vision, Samaritan's Purse and all others who assist in times of emergency.

My wife and I were the recipients of emergency help. In 1970 we were in a serious auto accident near Banff, Alberta. Our car was a total write-off. One of the paramedics told me later that he said to his partner, when he saw our car, "We're going to be picking up bodies." The help that we received that afternoon was unbelievable.

Prior to the arrival of the paramedics, two different nurses stopped at the scene of the accident to wash the cuts and apply bandages. An off duty medical doctor from Calgary was there with a prepared report on his assessment of us ready to give to the paramedics. An off duty Royal Canadian Mounted Police officer directed traffic. A Roman Catholic priest knelt down beside me and asked if there was anything that he could do. We have been eternally grateful for all who came to our rescue and for the many years we've had since then. Pray today for those who tend to our physical needs and well-being in times of crisis.

Today's Golden Nugget of Truth: "We then who are strong ought to bear with the scruples of the weak. . ." Romans 15:1

Today's Philosophical Tidbit: "There is no better exercise for strengthening the heart than reaching down and lifting people up." Author Unknown

January 25
Do You Know Your Neighbor

Today's Smile: Trevor and Darla were touring the British Isles. They had had a most enjoyable three weeks and were nearing the end of their trip. They were in a small village in the far north of Scotland when they experienced car problems. They spotted a little store. Trevor went in and asked the clerk whether they had any mechanics in the village. The clerk turned and called his son, who was busy stocking shelves, "Alastair, do we have any mechanics here?"

"I can't think of any Dad," replied Alastair. "We have McCauleys, McAlisters, McCallums, McCormacks and McDonalds but I don't know of any Mechanics."

Today's Comment: How well do we know our neighbors or fellow church members? I visited a church which seated about 1,200 people. I knew an usher in that church and so I asked another usher if he had seen Frank, my usher friend, that morning. He replied by saying, "I don't know Frank."

I responded and said, "Well, he has been an usher here for years."

"Oh, he must usher on the other side of the church." I was puzzled that the ushers didn't know one another. Don't they ever meet together? Anyhow, we can be guilty of staying in our own little group and never reach out to greet or meet someone else. It's not too late to make another new year's resolve. Let's pray that in the next few days we will connect with someone in our community or church that we can befriend.

Today's Golden Nugget of Truth: "Give each other the handshake of Christina love. Peace be to all of you who are in Christ." First Peter 5:14 (TLB)

Today's Philosophical Tidbit: "You may only be someone in the world, but to someone else, you may be the world." Author Unknown

January 26
An Embarrassment

Today's Smile: Buzz and Audrey invited their new neighbors to come for a dinner. The new couple were not accustomed to being in a home like that of Buzz and Audrey. Buzz and Audrey were quite well off and the other guests included the mayor and his wife along with the manager of City Bank and his wife.

When they had finished their dessert and were still sitting around the dining table, the conversation drifted to music and discussion about different composers. They talked about Beethoven, Strauss and Mozart. The new neighbor lady, attempting to be a part of this conversation said, "Oh, Mozart. You are so right. I love that man. It was only yesterday morning that I saw him getting on the number four bus to Coney Island."

There was an immediate hush and everyone looked in her direction. Her husband was mortified. As soon as they began to move into the living room, he whispered to her and said, "We need go home and right now!"

They thanked their host and hostess for the dinner and apologized for leaving so soon. They quickly headed for their house. As soon as they were in their place, she turned to her husband and said, "You are angry about something that I said."

"Angry!" he said, "I've never been so embarrassed in all my life. You said you saw Mozart getting on the number four bus to Coney Island. You idiot! Don't you know that the number four bus doesn't go to Coney Island?"

Today's Comment: Do we embarrass others by what we say? Maybe we have been an embarrassment and didn't know it. We all have probably had those times when we have spoken much to the embarrassment of our parents, spouse, children or grand-children. I've conducted many funerals and heard many humorous stories about the deceased saying or doing something that caused a family member or members to be embarrassed. Those stories make for a good laugh at a memorial service, but were probably not laughable at the time that they happened.

Perhaps a more sobering question would be to ask whether we have ever been an embarrassment to the church, the gospel message or to other Christians. Our prayer should be that we would not say or do the wrong thing. I do not want to be an embarrassment to the truth of the Gospel and I'm sure that you share that sentiment.

It's better not to chime in on a conversation unless we know the subject and are certain that what we speak is factual and truthful. The problem is that we often speak before we think. Pray today that we will stop, listen and think before we speak.

Today's Golden Nugget of Truth: "The heart of the godly thinks carefully before speaking; the mouth of the wicked overflows with evil words." Proverbs 15:28 (NLT)

Today's Philosophical Tidbit: "In the days of the Old Testament it was a miracle if a donkey spoke, but times have certainly changed." Author Unknown

January 27
Children Are An Heritage

*T*oday's Smile: Nori was born and raised in Japan. He immigrated to the United States, at the age of 32, to work as a chef with a large Japanese restaurant in San Francisco. When he was interviewed for the job, he met with the owner and the management team which asked him many questions about his experience in the food business and some of his specialties. They also wanted to know something about his family.

In response to his place of birth, he indicated that he had been born and raised in Hiroshima. He began his career in Osaka working first at a fishmonger's and then at a sushi restaurant. When he was twenty-five years old he got a job at a large Japanese restaurant in Tokyo.

When he shared something of his family, he indicated that he had four siblings, three brothers and one sister. "Where and when did you meet your wife?" asked the owner.

"I met Akari when I was working in Osaka. Akari was a waitress." Nori said. "We've been married for nine years."

"And do you have some children?" one of them asked.

"No," he said, still struggling with many English words and thinking he knew the right word, said, "Akari is inconceivable." There were a few smiles which made him realize that he had said the wrong thing. Seeking to correct his mistake he said, "I guess I should have said that she is impregnable." This time they all laughed and he tried to correct his answer again by saying, "Akari is unbearable."

Today's Comment: My heart goes out to those couples that long to have a family and yet the wife is unable to conceive. Some couples have found doctors and medical treatment that have helped. Some have conceived in answer to special prayer. Some couples have been led to adopt. Pray today for godly parents raising children. The temptations facing our children and youth seem to be increasing year by year. Parents need the wisdom from above. Pray also for those who desire to have children but cannot do so.

Today's Golden Nugget of Truth: "All your children shall be taught by the Lord, and great shall be the peace of your children." Isaiah 54:13

Today's Philosophical Tidbit: "If raising children was going to be easy, it never would have started with something called labor." Author Unknown

January 28
Don't Waste Time

Today's Smile: Ryan was a restless sleeper. He tossed and turned most of the night and would eventually drop off to sleep about four o'clock in the morning. The result was that he did not hear his alarm, therefore arrived late at work. This went on for weeks to the point where his boss was so frustrated with him that he said, "Unless you go to your doctor and get some help, you're finished as of the end of the month."

Well, that smartened Ryan up. He visited his family doctor and asked if the doctor would give him some sort of medication that would help him get to sleep quickly and have a good night's sleep.

The first night he decided to double the prescription, which is not a good idea. However, he got a good night's sleep and woke up a few minutes before the alarm. He had a shower, a good breakfast and was raring to do a full day's work. He got to work early, and who should he meet first, but his boss. "Boss," he said, that pill that my doctor prescribed really worked. I had the best sleep in years and I never woke up once. It really worked well.

"I'm glad," said his boss, "but where were you yesterday?"

Today's Comment: How punctual are we? When I was 18 years old, I started working for a radio station as a disc jockey, spinning the records. I worked a total of three long summers which paid for my Bible College training. For those readers who do not know what a record is, they were vinyl discs containing music or spoken words, speeds varying from 33 ½ rpm's to 78 rpm's with diameters ranging from 7 inches to 15 inches.

Since being punctual at the radio station was so important, the owner/manager of the station offered a good behavior bonus each week to each staff member, providing we were on time for work. That instilled in me the habit of striving to be on time for appointments. Time is a treasure which we should value. We ought not to waste it or take advantage of other peoples' time. Pray that if you are constantly late, that God will help you to learn to be punctual. Oh, by the way, I never missed a pay check without the good behavior bonus added to it.

Today's Golden Nugget of Truth: "To every thing there is a season, and a time to every purpose under heaven." Ecclesiastes 3:1 (KJV)

Today's Philosophical Tidbit: "Time wasted can never be recalled, reused or recycled." A. Daniel Goldsmith

January 29
Are We Tithers

Today's Smile: The church treasurer decided not to seek re-election and so a new treasurer was elected to serve for the coming year. The church was in a farming community, with the new treasurer serving as manager of the local grain elevator. He agreed to accept the position under two conditions. First that no treasurer's report would be given during the first year, and second that no questions would be asked about the finances for that year. The people were a little surprised by his requests but knew the man to be a man of integrity and so agreed to his requests.

At the end of that year he gave his report. It stated that the church indebtedness of $285,000.00 had been paid in full. The minister's salary had been increased by 10%. Money given to missions had gone up by 200%. There were no unpaid bills and there was a cash balance in the bank of $17,234.15.

The congregation was stunned. "How were you able to do that? Where did the money come from? Did some rich member remember the church in his will?" There were numerous questions.

The treasurer quietly responded by saying: "Most of you bring your grain to my elevator. During the past year that I have been treasurer, I have simply deducted ten percent from the price of your grain, and gave it to the church on your behalf. It appears that none of you even missed it."

Today's Comment: That is not the usual method of giving a tithe, but it worked. Many have argued the question whether or not we are required to give a tithe in our dispensation of grace. Whether you agree or disagree, we ought to strive to give at least a tithe (10%) or more. We've often been told that if every church member would give a tithe, the local church and the world of missions would have no lack of funds. Pray that God will help us all to give cheerfully at least ten percent to the work of God.

Today's Golden Nugget of Truth: "But this I say, He who sows sparingly will also reap sparingly, and he who sows bountifully will also reap bountifully." Second Corinthians 9:6

Today's Philosophical Tidbit: "Do your giving while you're living, so you're knowing where it's going." Author Unknown

January 30
Chronic Complainers

*T*oday's Smile: Phil was fed up with the rat race of society. He was always on the go. Always at meetings, or work, always noise, talk, people. The smart phone was constantly ringing, text messages, e-mails, memos, etc. He was tense, angry, frustrated and sick, tired of his life. Several times a week he drove by a monastery. He thought maybe that was the solution to life.

He made an appointment to see the Abbot. He explained his life to the Abbot and stated that he had been thinking that maybe he should become a monk. The Abbot was impressed with Phil and told him that at this particular monastery he had to take a vow of silence. There was to be absolutely no talking. No one would talk to him and he would not talk to anyone. "However," said the Abbot, "at the end of two years you will be permitted to say two words. Is that the kind of life you want?"

"Yes!" replied Phil. He returned a month later and agreed to the vow of silence and became a monk. Two years quickly passed and the new monk had done well. He appeared before the Abbot and was granted the privilege of saying his two words.

"Think carefully what you want to say," said the Abbot.

The monk spoke his two words, "Bed hard!" He returned to his ministry of reading, meditating, prayers and manual labor around the monastery. At the end of another two years, he again appeared before the Abbot and was given the opportunity to say two more words, "Food bad!" said the monk.

After another two years had passed, the privilege was again granted to the monk to speak two words. Without hesitation he said, "I quit!"

"Well," said the Abbot, "it's about time. You've been here six years and every time you open your mouth to speak, you complain."

Today's Comment: Are you a complainer? There are chronic complainers. They criticize everyone and everything. You know before they speak that they will be complaining about the weather or the government, or a friend or a family member or the church. Nothing is ever right. Reminds me of the deacon whom I heard about who was a constant complainer. He came late one night to the deacon's meeting and as he walked in the door he said, "I don't know what you've been discussing, but I'm against it." Pray that no one will look at you as being a complainer.

Today's Golden Nugget of Truth: "Do all things without complaining and disputing." Philippians 2:14

Today's Philosophical Tidbit: "Look on the bright side. You'll feel better and so will those around you." Author Unknown

January 31
Reading The Word Of God

*T*oday's Smile: Willis was pastor of a little country church. The members of the church took turns cleaning the church and getting the old wood stove fired up for Sunday. It was the Tucker family's turn to clean the church and get the fire started. So they went to the church Saturday evening and took their three young sons with them. The oldest boy helped a bit, but the two youngest mostly played. This particular Saturday night the two young boys found the pastor's Bible on the pulpit and got a little mischievous.

They found some glue and glued some of the pages together. Sunday morning, the pastor was reading in the book of Exodus. The last part of that first page which he read was: ". . .and he gave Zipporah his daughter to Moses." He turned the page and continued reading, "the length one hundred cubits, the width fifty and the height five cubits, woven of fine linen thread. . ." He stopped, took off his reading glasses and looking at the congregation said, "In my 42 years as pastor, I don't ever remember reading that description of Moses wife. It just goes to prove that we are fearfully and wonderfully made."

Today's Comment: Some people like to get guidance from the Bible, by simply flipping the pages and pointing to a verse. I would not argue that some probably have received some guidance, or comfort that way, but it is not the recommended way.

You've probably heard the old story of one that used this method. Thumbing the pages, he pointed to Matthew 27:5 where it is speaking of Judas, "He threw down the pieces of silver in the temple and departed, and went and hanged himself." He didn't like that so he turned several pages, pointed to Luke 10:37, "Then Jesus, said to him, Go and do likewise." That was a bit too much so he closed his eyes and turned to the Old Testament. When he looked there staring him in the face was Song of Solomon 8:14 "Make haste, my beloved. . ."

Here are nine helpful rules for reading the Bible, written by Jason Jackson. "Read it regularly, analytically, systematically, persistently, completely, reverently, expectantly, fervently, and collectively."[1] Pray that these nine simple guidelines would be practiced in our daily Bible reading.

Today's Golden Nugget of Truth: "This Book of the Law shall not depart from your mouth, but you shall meditate in it day and night, that you may observe to do according to all that is written in it. For then you will make your way prosperous, and then you will have good success." Joshua 1:8

Today's Philosophical Tidbit: "If you have the Spirit without the Word, you blow up. If you have the Word without the Spirit, you dry up. If you have both the Word and the Spirit, you grow up." Don Lyon

February 1
When You Can't See Ahead

T *oday's Smile:* It was snowing heavily when Carmen finished her job at the office. As she started to leave her work place, the snow starting blowing to the point that it was almost impossible to see the road. She was very pleased when she managed to spot a snow plow. She remembered what her Dad had told her concerning driving in a snow storm. "If you catch up to a snow plow," he said, "simply stay behind the same and you will be safe."

Well, she was feeling pretty lucky to have spotted a snow plow so quickly. It was not moving very fast, but that was alright with her, she just stayed behind and followed it at every turn. She had been following the plow for about ten minutes, when the snow plow stopped and the driver got out and came back to her car. "Are you alright?" he asked. "I see that you have been behind me for the past several minutes."

"I'm fine, thank you," she replied. "Why do you ask?"

"It's fine with me if you want to follow me, but I just want to let you know that I've just finished the Wal-Mart® parking lot and now I am going across the street and do the Sears® lot."

Today's Comment: We are like a lot of other people in that none of our children or grandchildren live close by. When we do not see them or talk with them on the phone, we manage to keep track of them with Face Book and texting.

Today we read the comments which our daughter recorded on Face Book. She lives in a mountainous part of interior British Columbia. Their house is on an acreage at an altitude of 4,000 feet. Here are her words: "I know sometimes snowy roads can be treacherous but tonight on my way home there were no cars in sight and I was able to just enjoy the beauty of the trees weighted down by snow. Just as I was about to make my ascent up a hill, I met the sanding truck coming towards me at the bottom. Perfect timing for the rest of the drive. Just another reason to always enjoy the beauty in your life now and not worry about the road ahead. God's already got it covered."

Are you worried about the future because you can't see ahead? As my daughter Sharilyn said it so well, "God's already got it covered." Trust Him for what lies ahead, and pray that we will follow with Him one step at a time.

Today's Golden Nugget of Truth: "Has thou entered into the treasures of the snow?" Job 38:22 (KJV)

Today's Philosophical Tidbit: "Stop telling God how big your mountain is and start telling the mountain how big your God is." Author Unknown

February 2
Every Day Is Special

*T*oday's Smile: Douglas sat at the breakfast table, and in his usual form was reading the morning newspaper, paying no attention to his wife. Finally, his wife Lucy said, "I bet you don't know what day today is?"

He put down his paper, gave her a big smile and a kiss on the cheek, and assured her that he certainly did know what day it was.

At work he had his secretary order a dozen roses to be sent to his wife. He asked one of the interns to go to the nearest drug store, purchase a five pound box of chocolates and deliver them to his wife. In the early afternoon he phoned his wife and told her that she did not have to fix dinner as he would be taking her out for their evening meal.

Together they enjoyed a wonderful evening of fine dining. Once at home he devoted his evening to his beloved wife and they had a good long chat, talking about the nearly thirty years that they had been together, and all of the fun times that they had enjoyed with their family. Eventually they began to retire for the evening. As they were about to bed down for the night, she turned to her husband and said, "Honey, I want to thank you for the most enjoyable *Ground Hog's Day* that I've ever had."

Today's Comment: Maybe you have had the same experience that we have had, receiving an anniversary or birthday card in a month other than the right one. A couple of friends planned a surprise luncheon for my wife's 75th birthday. I found out about it a few days before the event, and one of the ladies said to me, "It is her 75th birthday, isn't it?" Well, the long and short of it all is that my wife had over thirty lady friends surprise her on her 74th birthday. They laughed, observing that according to the Chinese tradition way of reckoning that she is 75. So in spite of the wrong year, they enjoyed the occasion.

For the child of God, every day is a special day, not just birthdays, anniversaries or special holidays. At my stage of life, I thank God for every day. It is a gift from God. Let's pray that we will rejoice, make the most of today and give thanks for it.

Today's Golden Nugget of Truth: "Oh that men would give thanks to the Lord for His goodness, and for His wonderful works to the children of men." Psalm 107:21

Today's Philosophical Tidbit: "Gratitude to God should be as regular as our heartbeat." Author Unknown

February 3
A Forgiving Spirit

oday's Smile: A business executive had a meeting the next morning in the city of Omaha, Nebraska. He boarded the bus in Des Moines, Iowa and told the driver that he was a very sound sleeper and since the bus arrived in Omaha in the middle of the night that he would sleep past his destination unless someone wakened him. So he gave the bus driver a twenty dollar tip in advance and made him promise that he would make sure he was awakened and got off at Omaha.

Well, when the executive awakened he discovered he was in Lincoln. He was furious. He grabbed the bus driver by the collar and said, "You are the worst of the worst when it comes to being a dependable bus driver, and I'm going to report you to the company and I trust you never drive a bus again."

"Well, I am terribly sorry for disappointing you and failing to wake you up. Here is the twenty dollar bill that you gave me and I will see that you get a full refund for your ticket. I realize that you are very angry with me, but not nearly as much as the man that I put off the bus in Omaha."

Today's Comment: Did you ever reprimand or punish someone for something that they did, and you found out later that you did it to the wrong person? I have two sons and one daughter. The boys were boys and they were disciplined when they disobeyed, so was the daughter. One day I disciplined the wrong boy. It was not Dan Jr that had done wrong, it was Brian. When I found out what I had done, I apologized. To the credit of my son Dan, he forgave me. As for Brian, it was his lucky day

Do we have what it takes to forgive family or friends when we have been wrongly accused? God will give us the grace and we will be the stronger for it when we forgive those who have wronged us. Pray that we will not hold a grudge or an unforgiving spirit when treated wrongfully.

Today's Golden Nugget of Truth: "For if you forgive men when they sin against you, your heavenly Father will also forgive you." Matthew 6:14 (NIV)

Today's Philosophical Tidbit: "When a deep injury is done us, we never recover until we forgive." Alan Paton

February 4
Complain Or Commit

Today's Smile: Edwin was riding the Marta, the transit system in greater Atlanta. A man and woman, who he sized up as a husband and wife were seated next to him. The man was well dressed and his wife was magnificently dressed wearing very evidently expensive jewelry. As Edwin listened, the woman was doing all of the talking. She was complaining about everything. She was complaining that their car would not start that morning and she had to ride the Marta. She complained about the weather. The world news was upsetting her. The breakfast that they ate at a fast food restaurant before boarding the Marta was not agreeing with her. She was still complaining about the previous night when they were babysitting a grand-daughter and the baby threw up on her. She carried on and on.

Finally Edwin thought for a bit of diversion that he would try to engage them in conversation. He directed his question to the man. "What part of the city do you live in?" He learned that the couple lived fairly close to where he lived. He learned also in further conversation that the man had been born in Alpharetta, just a few miles away and lived in the greater Atlanta area all his life. "What about your wife? Was she raised here?

"No," said the man. She was born in Louisiana. We met in university here in Atlanta, got married and have been here ever since, even though my wife hates this city."

52

"Does she have a job?" asked Edwin.

"Yea, she is in the manufacturing business. She manufactures her own unhappiness."

Today's Comment: Do you know people like that? Constantly complaining. Nothing is ever right. Always unhappy. We dare not offer to help fix matters for them. Why? Well, they would tell us that we don't understand. It's always been that way and always will be. They would be happier, or should I say more miserable, if you would just let them be. They have no peace. They don't want our help.

Unhappy people are everywhere. There may be some who are part of your family circle, your community, your workplace. Maybe you have one or more in your church. It may take some time to change them from being a complainer to being a complimentary person. Some people try to help such individuals; to encourage them to be more positive in their thinking. Well, that may work for some, but I believe that help is needed outside of themselves.

That help is only in the eternal God. If you know people like that woman, God can give a peace, with a change of attitude and action. The Word of God, the Bible, is food for the soul. It is a power, the power of God. When its truths are accepted and applied, lives can have a different outlook on life. The end result is that nothing will offend. Pray for any you know today that fit the above description. Pray that they will seek help in the Word of God and the God of the Word.

Today's Golden Nugget of Truth: "Those who love your laws have great peace of heart and mind and do not stumble." Psalm 119:165 (MSG)

Today's Philosophical Tidbit: "Men and automobiles are much alike. Some are right at home on an uphill pull; others run smoothly only going downgrade. And when you hear one knocking all the time, it's a sure sign that there is something wrong under the hood." Author Unknown

February 5
Take Care Of Yourself

*T*oday's Smile: Young Casey had an ear infection and so his mother took him to the pediatrician. Beatrice was very impressed with the way in which the doctor directed his comments and questions to her young son. When he asked Casey if there was anything that he was allergic to, Casey nodded and whispered in the doctor's ear. With a smile on his face, the pediatrician wrote out a prescription and handed it to Beatrice. She tucked it into her purse without even looking at the prescription.

On their way home they stopped by the pharmacy to have it filled. They waited while the prescription was being filled. When the pharmacist handed her the bottle of pills, he commented on the unusual food-drug allergy that Casey had. Beatrice was puzzled and did not know what he meant. So he showed her the label on the bottle. As per the doctor's instructions, it read: "Do not take with broccoli."

Today's Comment: Do you turn up your nose at broccoli? It's good for you and so are a lot of other veggies. Our body is the temple of the Holy Spirit and as such we should strive to do our best to care for it. Nutritionists tell us that we should have five servings of fruits and vegetables each day with a serving being about one half cup. They contain fiber and lots of vitamins and vegetables. A good diet proved beneficial for Daniel, Shadrach, Meshach and Abednego (Daniel 1:15, 16). Whatever their diet, it proved one thing that these young Hebrew boys knew God desires that we should take care of our bodies. Pray that we will not defile our bodies with that which is not good for our health.

Today's Golden Nugget of Truth: "But Daniel purposed in his heart that he would not defile himself with the portion of the king's meat, nor with the wine which he drank. . ." Daniel 1:8 (KJV)

Today's Philosophical Tidbit: "Most kids think a balanced diet is a hamburger in each hand." Author Unknown

February 6
Jesus Is Coming Again

*T*oday's Smile: Pastor Grant was preaching from the last chapter of Revelation, Revelation 22:12 "Behold I come quickly." He lost his place in his sermon and remembered that he had been taught in seminary that if you ever lose your place when you're preaching to simply repeat yourself one or two times for emphasis and it may give you enough time to get back on track.

So he repeated the verse, "Behold I come quickly." He still couldn't remember what he was to say next, so with great gusto and enthusiasm, he launched forward and said, "Behold I come quickly!" This time he fell off of the platform and landed in the lap of an elderly lady sitting in the front row. Embarrassed, he stood up and sincerely apologized to the lady. "I hope that I didn't hurt you. I am so sorry, lady."

"That's alright," said the dear lady, "I should have been prepared. You told me three times that you were coming."

Today's Comment: The Lord Jesus Christ told us that He is coming again. This truth, which my Dad obviously had never heard or had never registered in his thinking, was expressed by Dr. Charles E. Fuller on the *Old Fashioned Revival Hour* radio broadcast. Dr. Fuller said, "The Lord is coming again and He could come before this broadcast is finished." It was not long after that remark that my father prayed to receive the Lord Jesus Christ as his personal Savior. If the Lord should come today, would you be prepared to meet Him? If not, pray, surrendering your life to the Lord Jesus Christ. He could come before you finish reading this page.

Today's Golden Nugget of Truth: "Men of Galilee, why do you stand gazing up into heaven? This same Jesus, who was taken up from you into heaven, will so come in like manner as you saw Him go into heaven." Acts 1:11

Today's Philosophical Tidbit: "His appearing will be with such suddenness that it will catch unawares all who are unprepared." Lehman Strauss

February 7
Character Traits

Today's Smile: Darren and Dora were seated around the table enjoying dinner together with their three sons, Nathan, Griffin and Cameron. They always enjoyed these times together. It seemed with work, with the boys' schools, sports involvement, church activities, etc. they were all either coming or going. So Darren and Dora made it a priority to spend a little more time around the dinner table relaxing and interacting with their three young sons.

On this particular night, the conversation got around to discussing traits which parents pass down to their children. Darren said, "Nathan has my eyes, Griffin has my creativity, and Cameron has his mother's intelligence."

Cameron spoke up and asked, "Daddy, what's intelligence?"

Today's Comment: When we look at our families, we will agree that there are similar physical and character traits that appear among family members. You may have physical features that resemble your father or your mother. Your daughter may be an artsy-craftsy person like one of you. Your son may be very studious, like one of his parents. How often have you heard it said, "He is a chip off the old block?"

If there is one character trait that we trust is passed down to the next generation it is that they have a deep love for God and His Word. This is by far the best of all traits. Pray that we might demonstrate a deep love for the things of God, and have children that follow in our footsteps.

Today's Golden Nugget of Truth: "You shall teach them to your children, speaking of them when you sit in your house, when you walk by the way, when you lie down, and when you rise up." Deuteronomy 11:19

Today's Philosophical Tidbit: "Train up a child in the way he should go, but make sure you go that way yourself." Author Unknown

February 8
Pray Without Ceasing

*T*oday's Smile: In the early 1980's I was listening one day to radio station KMBI, Spokane, WA. Dr. Charles Swindoll was preaching at the *Founder's Week* at Moody Bible Institute in Chicago. I recently read this story in one of his books, *Laugh Again*.

He told how that on a previous visit to MBI that he had received a note from a lady who said: "I love your sense of humor. Humor has done a lot to help me in my spiritual life. How could I have raised 12 children starting at age 32 and not have had a sense of humor? I married at age 31," she said, and "I didn't worry about getting married. I left my future to God's will. Every night I hung a pair of men's pants on the bed. Knelt down and I prayed this prayer, 'Father in heaven, hear my prayer, grant it if you can, I've hung a pair of trousers here, please fill them with a man.' He did."

Pastor Swindoll went on to say that he fit that story about the lady and her note into his sermon the next Sunday. Three weeks later, he had a phone call from one of the ladies in his church who did not hear this sermon and this story. The Sunday that he shared this story only her husband and son were present to hear. The lady said, "Pastor, I'm a little concerned about my son and I'm not certain what to say or do. For the past two or three weeks he has had a bikini hanging at the foot of his bed."[1]

Today's Comment: Sounds like a rather unique prayer request. I believe every prayer can be unique. We are exhorted in scripture not to use "vain repetitions" (Matthew 6:7). Neither do we need to have formal prayers. We are encouraged to come as we are. It is always a delight and privilege to hear a new Christian pray. They don't have all the jargon or pious prayers that some of the rest of us have. Is there a prayer request that you would like God to hear? He loves it when we ask Him, not only for the big things, but the little things. Yes, He even delights when a young person prays that God will guide to bring the right spouse into their life.

Today's Golden Nugget of Truth: "Call to Me, and I will answer you, and show you great and mighty things which you do not know." Jeremiah 33:3

Today's Philosophical Tidbit: "To pray is the greatest thing we can do, and to do it well, there must be calmness, time, and deliberation." E. M. Bounds

February 9
Praying Expectantly

*T*oday's Smile: A grade three Sunday School class of boys was given time in class to write a brief letter to a missionary in Africa. They had heard this missionary speak in the Sunday morning service a year ago and had been praying for him in their Sunday School class ever since. The teacher said to the class of boys, "Mr. Brandon is a very busy person, so don't expect him to answer all your letters."

That did not deter some of the boys from asking questions just the same. Lane wrote and asked if Mr. Brandon had ever ridden on an elephant. Andy asked if he had ever had a snake in his house. Others asked a variety of questions, like what games boys their age played; did the young boys go hunting; did they eat yams every day. However, not everyone asked questions. Christopher, having heard the teacher say that the missionary is a very busy person, wrote and simply said, "Mr. Brandon we are praying for you, but we don't expect an answer."

Today's Comment: Is that the way we pray? Have our prayers become a mechanical routine? A formality? Do we really expect God to answer? We should pray in faith, believing and expecting God to accomplish His plan and His purposes. God does answer prayer, though sometimes it may not be the way that we thought it should be or what we wanted. He still answers. He knows what is best and He wants the best for us. So let's keep on praying expectantly.

Today's Golden Nugget of Truth: "But without faith it is impossible to please Him, for he who comes to God must believe that He

is, and that He is a rewarder of those who diligently seek Him."
Hebrews 11:6

Today's Philosophical Tidbit: "Wonderful things happen to us when
we live expectantly, believe confidently, and pray affirmatively."
Author Unknown

February 10
Display Of Arrogance

*T*oday's Smile: A young girl, fresh out of university, appeared on
a quiz show. The prizes were very appealing. Some of the prizes
included vacations in the Caribbean, Spain, Indonesia and Great
Britain. Luxury cars were also given away, plus large amounts of cash.

The university graduate had already won a trip to Spain, a Cadillac,
and now with her final question she was going for $75,000.00. The
host asked the following question: "Which one of the following birds
does not build its own nest, a cardinal, a cuckoo, an eagle or a robin?"

"That's easy," responded the young girl. "It is the cuckoo!"

"You're absolutely right," responded the game's host. "Here's
your check for $75,000.00."

As she was leaving the studio, one of the other contestants ran over
to this graduate and asked, "How in the world were you so confident
and responded with the correct answer so quickly?"

The young girl said, "Everyone knows that cuckoos don't build
their nests. They live in clocks!"

Today's Comment: There are a lot of people who appear to be very
clever, but behind the veneer, are really not all that intelligent. The
world is full of people who think they are someone, when they are
not. I remember as a young person meeting a student from a particular school whose air of superiority and pride made me think that I
would never want to attend that school. I am so thankful that I did
not let that one student deter me, for the student of which I speak
and the school that he attended was one of the schools from which
I graduated.

Pray that we might not cause another to stumble.

Today's Golden Nugget of Truth: "When pride comes, then comes shame; but with the humble is wisdom." Proverbs 11:2

Today's Philosophical Tidbit: "Some people get so caught up in their own holiness that they look at the Trinity for a possible vacancy." John MacArthur

February 11
Committed To Each Other

*T**oday's Smile:* Elmer, who was very shy and had never ever had a girlfriend, or even a date, met this most beautiful young lady at a church social. He saw her the next Sunday at church saying but a few words to her. He looked for her again the next week and the next and the next. After chatting with her briefly after the morning church service for about ten Sundays, he mustered up enough courage to ask her for a date. Well, that date happened and a second and third and they continued to date for nearly a year.

Although Elmer had never ever hugged her or kissed her, he thought that he should maybe read a book that would give him some help in this area. After all, he thought, I should hug her and kiss her when I propose to her. So he went to the library and looked at the shelves of books. He didn't know what such a book would be entitled, but after searching for an hour and a half, he saw what he wanted, it was entitled, *How To Hug*.

He took the book off of the shelf and went over into the corner where several people were reading the daily newspapers. Not wanting anyone to see what he was reading, he picked up a newspaper and used it as a shield so no one would see the book. When he opened the book, he found to his surprise that he had volume seven of an encyclopedia with facts indexed from "How" to "Hug."

Today's Comment: That story reminds me of the boy who when the teacher asked him to tell her the chemical formula for water, responded by saying, "H I J K L M N O." When she asked what on earth he was saying, he answered and said, "Yesterday you told us it was "$H_2 O$."

Well, most of us never had lessons or read a book on how to hug or how to kiss. Somehow or other it seemed to come naturally. When I courted my wife, Leona, there were very few books out there from a Christian perspective that gave pointers or helpful hints regarding courtship and marriage. Few pastors offered pre-marital counselling. We didn't have any.

I remember the first "tool" that I had to offer young couples in pre-marital counselling. I had about four pages of mimeographed material which a pastor friend shared with me. Later we had books, temperament tests, video series, DVD's and many more. Sadly of all those helps which are available today, marriages are still falling apart.

What is the answer? The one solid step or commitment that couples need to make today is to be wholeheartedly committed to the Lord and then to each other. Pray that God would help us to be committed to Him first and then to each other.

Today's Golden Nugget of Truth: "For this reason a man shall leave his father and mother and be joined to his wife, and the two shall become one flesh. So then, they are no longer two, but one flesh. Therefore what God has joined together, let not man separate." Matthew 19:5, 6

Today's Philosophical Tidbit: "A hug is a roundabout expression of love." Author Unknown

February 12
Demonstrate Love

Today's Smile: Wendell phoned his girlfriend and began to pour out his love and affection for her. "Sweetheart," he said, "you mean all the world to me. I am so glad that Sue introduced us. I just want to be with you all the time. I hope that you know how much I love you. I love you so much that I would fight wild beasts to be by your side. I would tread on broken glass just to hold your hand. I would swim the ocean just for one hug. I'd do anything to be able to look into your eyes and tell you how much I love you. I'll pick you up tomorrow night at 7:00pm providing my car will start and the road is not covered with snow."

Today's Comment: Many people talk about their Christianity and what they would do for the Lord. They say that they're going to pray more. They're going to read the Bible every day. They're going to share their faith with their neighbor the next time they get together for coffee. But do they? No! Their words are empty. They say one thing and do another. Pray that God will help us, as Christians, to walk the talk.

Today's Golden Nugget of Truth: "Greater love has no one than this, than to lay down one's life for his friends." John 15:13

Today's Philosophical Tidbit: "You may do your best to describe love, but it is much better to demonstrate love." A. Daniel Goldsmith

February 13
Meaningful Dreams

*T**oday's Smile:* The alarm rang and woke up Andrew and Courtney. As they were dressing, the young wife told her husband about her dream. "I was just dreaming," she said, "when the alarm rang that you gave me the most beautiful pearl necklace for *Valentines Day*. What do you think it means?"

"I am sure you will know tonight when I get home from work," he said. When Andrew came home he discovered that his wife had prepared a nice candlelight dinner with all his favorite foods, roast beef, mashed potatoes, gravy, Yorkshire pudding, peas and carrots, topped off with apple pie and ice cream. After the dishes were put away, the two of them went into the family room and sat by the fireplace.

They chatted away recalling some of those surprise dates that he took her on. Andrew had a funny, but rather warped sense of humor so he was still surprising Courtney in ways she least expected. This time was no different. He presented, to his wife, a small package. She eagerly took off the ribbon and wrappings. She stared. Much to her disappointment, this was another one of his weird jokes. There was a book entitled, *The Meaning of Dreams*.

Today's Comment: My name is Daniel, but I've never been able to interpret any dreams. Many of my dreams are about being late for a preaching appointment. My wife's dreams are getting lost on a university campus. We smile at them and move on. However, in the day in which we are living, we continually hear about people in countries where the public preaching of the Gospel is banned. The Lord, in His sovereign way, is speaking to many people through dreams and visions. This is often a prelude to meeting someone who shares God's Word with them and many times a turning point in their life whereby they surrender whole heartedly to the Lord.

Pray today that many more who sit in spiritual darkness will be spoken to by a vision or dream, not one about a pearl necklace, but that which will lead them to repentance and faith in the Lord Jesus Christ, becoming part of the body of Christ, the family of God, the church.

Today's Golden Nugget of Truth: "But you are a chosen generation, a royal priesthood, a holy nation, His own special people, that you may proclaim the praises of Him who called you out of darkness into His marvelous light." First Peter 2:9

Today's Philosophical Tidbit: "The best gifts are tied with heartstrings." Author Unknown

February 14

Unending Love

Today's Smile: Several girls in a Christian College gathered together for prayer. As they prayed and poured out their hearts in praise and thanksgiving to their Heavenly Father, one of the girls prayed, "Lord give us pure hearts." Another prayed, "Lord give us clean hearts." A third girl boldly prayed, "Lord please give us 'sweet' hearts." With that all the girls, together, said "Ah MEN!"

Today's Comment: My father passed away on *Valentines Day* 1999 at the age of 90. He was predeceased by my mother, three years earlier. At the memorial service, my brother David said that he pictured Dad arriving at the gate of heaven, and the gate keeper turning and saying, "Ada (my mother) there is a gentleman here to see you and he has a dozen roses for you."

On this *Valentines Day* our hearts and minds are focused on love of family and friends. Some may have a special friend for the first time. Others may be celebrating 67 years of a wonderful marriage, as did my parents. Some of us may be reflecting upon the happy days enjoyed with our parents or spouse or with children, or a close friend. They are no longer with us. Death has separated us. Others may have gone through a painful divorce. God's love for you and me has never wavered. His love remains constant. Thank God today that we can rest in His everlasting love, a love that will never cease to embrace us.

Today's Golden Nugget of Truth: "Yes, I have loved you with an everlasting love; therefore with loving kindness I have drawn you." Jeremiah 31:3

Today's Philosophical Tidbit: "The love of God cannot be earned, but it can be spurned." Author Unknown

February 15
Don't Wait Another Day

Today's Smile: Vern had been hospitalized for some days and his doctor had popped in nearly every day to check on him and update him on his progress. Things were not going all that well for Vern and the doctor missed one day. However, the next day he visited Vern early in the morning.

"Vern," he said, "I have some good news and some bad news. What would you like to hear first?"

"Tell me the good news," said Vern.

"The good news is you only have 24 hours to live."

"That's the good news!" exclaimed Vern. "What's the bad news?"

"The bad news is I was supposed to tell you this yesterday morning."

Today's Comment: We may not have a 24 hour notice of death. We may not have any notice. I had a friend who was riding as a passenger in their car which his wife was driving. She had gone only a few miles from home when she noticed her husband suddenly slumped up against the passenger door. She took one glance at him, turned around and headed back to the city and to the hospital. Her husband had died of a heart attack.

We are not promised tomorrow or another minute. Have you come to the place in your spiritual life where you know for certain that if you died today, you would go to heaven? Don't wait another day. God is only a prayer away.

Today's Golden Nugget of Truth: "Prepare to meet your God. . ." Amos 4:12

Today's Philosophical Tidbit: "Heaven is a prepared place for a prepared people." D. L. Moody Read Appendix "A"

February 16
Put The Cookies On
The Bottom Shelf

*T*oday's Smile: Shane was seeking to set up a branch office for his company in Charleston, South Carolina. He bumped into John Paul, an old classmate of his that he had known in university. As they chatted a bit, Shane asked John Paul if he had a job.

"I've got better than a job," replied John Paul, "I'm an orator."

"What do you mean by that?" asked Shane.

"Well," said John Paul, "if y'all should ask me what two plus two is and I tell you that it is four, that's conversation. But if y'all should ask me what two plus two is and I say: When in the course of human events it became necessary to take the numeral of the second denomination and add the figure two, then it can be said without any fear of contradiction that the result inevitably is four. That's oratory!"

Today's Comment: When I heard that story I was reminded of the old story that speaks of an orator reciting Psalm 23. He spoke flawlessly and received a great applause. When the applause had subsided, an old retired pastor, who was well on in years, made his way to the podium. He indicated that he would like to recite some scripture. To the surprise of all, he began reciting Psalm 23. When he finished, there was no applause, but there were few dry eyes. The orator stood to his feet and addressing the audience again said, "I know the Psalm, this dear gentleman knows the Shepherd."

Simple truths are sometimes spoken in such a manner that we do not understand what is being said. Early in my pastoral ministry, I was encouraged to preach my sermons so that a junior high student would be able to understand the same.

Let's pray that as we share the gospel with others it will reach the heart of the young and the old alike not just the head.

Today's Golden Nugget of Truth: "Then the Lord answered me and said, write the vision and make it plain. . ." Habakkuk 2:2

Today's Philosophical Tidbit: "It is better to put the cookies on the bottom shelf, than to put them so high that one must use a step ladder." Author Unknown

February 17
Walk The Talk

Today's Smile: My neighbor's oldest boy had been driving for about four years. He was twenty-one, had a good paying job, and had purchased a late model car. As a young man, he became extremely impatient whenever a slow driver was in front of him. One night, on his way home from work, there was a very slow cautious driver in front of him. When the traffic light turned yellow, the gentleman in front suddenly applied his brakes and came to a stop. The young man did not appreciate that. He figured that they both could have made it through the light. He started honking the horn. He wound down his car window and yelled at the man in front of him, cursing and calling him names.

The young man was unaware that directly behind him was a police officer in an unmarked car. When the light turned green the officer turned on his siren and lights, indicating the young man was to pull over. Once the young man produced his driver's license and his car registration, the officer went back to his car to verify that the papers were accurate. He returned giving back his license and papers and then explained to him, that the reason that he had stopped him was because he saw the Christian fish logo, and a couple of bumper stickers which read, *What Would Jesus Do?* and *Follow Me To Sunday School.* He said, "I thought by your actions and words that maybe you had stolen a car."

Today's Comment: Do we walk the talk? Do our actions match up to our profession of faith? Too many followers of Christ are inconsistent in their Christian walk. They can spout off pious platitudes in church on Sunday, but when it comes to living the Christian life Monday through Saturday, they are no different than their non-Christian neighbors.

My mother used to often quote the words of Edgar A. Guest: "I'd rather see a sermon than hear one any day. . .And the best of all preachers are the men who live their creeds, for to see good put in action is what everybody needs. . ." There is much more to that poem. However, I've quoted sufficiently to remind us all that we should be living the Christian life and walking the talk, rather than pretending to be a Christian. Pray that Christ will be seen in us today!

Today's Golden Nugget of Truth: "But no man can tame the tongue. It is an unruly evil, full of deadly poison. With it we bless our God and Father, and with it we curse men. . .Out of the same mouth proceed blessing and cursing. My brethren, these things ought not to be so." James 3:8-10

Today's Philosophical Tidbit: "If you are a Christian, even your dog should know it." Author Unknown

February 18
What's My Name

*T*oday's Smile: A woman was pregnant and went into a coma in the delivery room just as she was about to give birth. She came out of her coma three weeks later and asked the doctor about the baby.

"You had twins," said the doctor, "a boy and a girl and they are both fine. They had to be registered and so your brother named them for you."

"Not my brother! He's an idiot! What did he call the girl?"

"Denise," the doctor replied.

"That's not such a bad name," said the mother. "What did he call the boy?"

The doctor said, "Denephew."

Today's Comment: The age old question has been asked, "What's in a name?" I learned early in life that my name Daniel means "God is my Judge." With that in mind may we remind ourselves that we will some day stand before God, the Judge. There are two judgments. One is the Judgment Seat of Christ, at which Christians will stand. Will we hear God say "Well done good and faithful servant?" Or will we hear Him at the Great White Throne Judgment, the judgment of non-Christians, say: "Depart from Me, I never knew you?"

The name of Jesus makes all the difference as to where we will stand. Where we stand at the time of judgment depends on whether we have taken our stand here and now crossing over into God's camp. Do we bear His name today? It is a sweet name; a beautiful name; a wonderful name; a precious name. It is a name above all names. Pray that we will exalt His name today!

Today's Golden Nugget of Truth: "Therefore God also has highly exalted Him and given Him the name which is above every name, that at the name of Jesus every knee should bow. . ." Philippians 2:9, 10

Today's Philosophical Tidbit: "A man has three names: the name he inherited, the name his parents gave him, and the name he makes for himself." Author Unknown

February 19
Judging By Appearance

*T**oday's Smile:* Chester was a rookie police officer. He was out for his second day and was riding in a cruiser with an experienced partner who was training him on the job. They were approaching the downtown center of the city when a call was received asking that they disperse a crowd of people that appeared to be loitering, for no reason, at one of the main intersections. The older officer let Chester be in total command of this situation in order to see how he would handle it.

They arrived at the intersection where about twenty people were standing and blocking most of the sidewalk. He stopped the cruiser and using the P/A speaker ordered the crowd to disperse and move on. The crowd did not move but simply stared at the officers. Chester then, with a more firm and authoritative voice said: "Get moving and now!"

He waited. Slowly, one by one, the people began to move on, but all the time staring at the officers. When Chester was satisfied that it was no longer a crowd of people, he drove on and headed for their coffee break. He was pretty proud of his accomplishment and turned to his partner and instructor and asked, "Well, how did I do? Did I pass?"

The veteran officer could hardly get the words out of his mouth. He broke into a belly laugh and eventually said, "You did an excellent job, especially since those people were at a bus stop waiting for their bus."

Today's Comment: How many times have we acted without having all the facts? We've formed an opinion by what we heard, judged someone by their appearance and believed what we read as being the truth.

A story is told about a couple who attended a musical concert. The music was superb. The audience was very enthusiastic in their applause. A lady was seated next to them. Not once did this lady applaud. They wondered why she was not more appreciative of the music. They became quite judgmental. When the performance ended and they all stood to leave, the couple noticed that this dear lady only had one hand.

We can be so prone to judge and form our opinion of another when we do not know all of the facts. Let's not be quick with our judging or criticism.

Pray that God will forgive us for judging by appearance without knowing the facts.

Today's Golden Nugget of Truth: "Do not judge according to appearance, but judge with righteous judgment." John 7:24

Today's Philosophical Tidbit: "A man's judgment is no better than his information." Author Unknown

February 20
Do Your Homework

Today's Smile: Amanda was in her first year of teaching a grade four class. She was working hard to keep ahead of her students. One day she was teaching her young students about the solar system. Judy, who was a very bright student, and seemed to be ahead of her classmates in many subjects, asked her teacher, "When did they discover the Comet Ison? My Daddy was telling me about it last night."

Amanda answered Judy by saying, "That is a very good question Judy. I don't know the answer. Where do you think we could find that answer?"

Judy, somewhat surprised said, "You don't know the answer! I thought teachers knew everything!"

Well, Amanda smiled and was just about to say that learning is a life-long process. She was going to share some ideas as to where, as a class, they could probably find the answer. She was interrupted by a boy who shouted from the back of the room, "How could she know? She's only a fourth grade teacher."

Today's Comment: When a question has been asked and I did not know the answer, I have tried to find the answer. It has been made much easier in recent years with the advent of the internet and its trillion bits of information.

Since retiring and sitting in a Bible class, I asked the teacher a question to which he responded, "Dan, why don't you find an answer and share it with us?" I did. It resulted in a most uplifting and informative study of God's Word. I later shared it with the class.

Do you have a Bible question? Maybe we should do a study on our own before asking. It is amazing what we learn when we begin to dig in and have a personal study time. Pray that we will be better students of God's Word.

Today's Golden Nugget of Truth: "These (the Bereans) were more fair-minded that those in Thessalonica, in that they received the word with all readiness, and searched the Scriptures daily to find out whether these things were so." Acts 17:11

Today's Philosophical Tidbit: "The goal of Bible study is not just learning, but living." Author Unknown

February 21
Don't Seek Revenge

*T*oday's Smile: Alex was a letter carrier and often had to ward of some mighty ferocious dogs as he delivered the mail. The day finally came, when the dog won the battle and got a good chunk of Alex's left leg. Alex was hospitalized and the doctor eventually had to inform him that he had rabies. At that time, there was no reliable cure for the same. His doctor told him that there was little that they could do and that he might not make it. He suggested to Alex that he should consider writing his will or revising it, if he had one.

Later that day, before leaving the hospital, the doctor popped in to see how his patient was doing. He found Alex sitting up and writing. "I see that you have followed my advice and are working on your will. You're a good man," said the doctor.

"This ain't no will, doctor. This is a list of all of the people that I want to bite before I die."

Today's Comment: I'm sure that you've heard someone utter the words, "I'll get even with you," or "You're going to pay for this!" Trying to get even or fighting back is the natural response.

A young teenage girl, who was one of our baby-sitters when our children were small, was brutally murdered as a young mother. My wife and I attended her memorial service and heard her father say that he forgave the young man that murdered his daughter. That was a supernatural response. He and his wife began to pray for this young man. In due time, this murderer became a born again Christian while in prison.

We may never be faced with the decision to say that we forgive a murderer, but let's pray that God will grant to us the grace and the spirit of forgiveness when some wrong is done to us.

Today's Golden Nugget of Truth: "Beloved, do not avenge yourselves, but rather give place to wrath; for it is written, 'Vengeance is Mine, I will repay,' says the Lord." Romans 12:19

71

Today's Philosophical Tidbit: "Any man can seek revenge; it takes a king or a prince to grant a pardon." Arthur J. Rehrat

February 22
Church Of The Open Door

*T*oday's Smile: Anthony had recently graduated from seminary and had assumed the pastoral position of a fairly small congregation in a new urban area. One Sunday, early in his ministry, his homiletics professor from the seminary wanting to hear his student preach arrived unannounced. The professor told his former student later, that he was very encouraged by the way that he led the service and much impressed by his sermon. "However," he said, "You need to be more creative with your sermon titles. I noticed that on the marquee out in front you just said, 'Sermon number three from the book of Mark'. You need to put something on that sign that if a bus load of people should drive by they would want to get off of the bus and come in and hear you preach."

Anthony thought that was good advice. He thanked his professor and the next week spent some time pondering what he should call his sermon. The marquee read, in large letters, "There's a Bomb on Your Bus!"

Today's Comment: What attracted you to the church where you attend? The music? The pastor's preaching? Children's program? Youth? Senior's ministry? Friends? Or did you experience a loss? Divorce? Death of a family member or friend? Desired friendship? Hungry to know God? There are a multitude of reasons why people seek out a church.

Does your church meet the needs of those who are looking for a church? I am reminded of the story of a young man in his early twenties who wandered into a very conservative church one Sunday morning, no shoes on his feet, wearing jeans with holes and a dirty T-shirt. His hair had not been combed. Since the church was full to capacity, he walked up the center aisle and sat on the floor in front of the first pew. The members were a bit uncomfortable looking at the young man who seemed very much out of place.

A deacon, well into his eighties, wearing a three piece suit slowly made his way from the back of the sanctuary toward this young man. There was total silence except for the deacon's cane clicking on the floor as he made his way to the front. The deacon, with great difficulty lowered himself to the floor and sat beside the young man. The pastor had stopped his preaching as everyone watched what was happening. Everyone was choked with emotion. When the pastor gained control of himself he said, "What I was about to preach you will never remember. What you have just seen, you will never forget.

Give newcomers time. Let's be more accepting. Pray that God will use us in reaching out to them in love, not with a set of rules.

Today's Golden Nugget of Truth: "I was hungry and you gave Me food; I was thirsty and you gave Me drink; I was a stranger and you took Me in." Matthew 25:35

Today's Philosophical Tidbit: "They may forget what you said, but they will never forget how you made them feel." Carl W. Buechner

February 23
Feeding The Mind

*T**oday's Smile:* Kristi complained to her mother that her stomach was hurting. "Your stomach is hurting because it is hungry," said her mom. "You got up and started to play with your dolls and didn't eat any breakfast. Your stomach is empty. You need to put something in it and then you will feel better." Well, after Kristi had something to eat, she went with her mother to do some shopping. First, they stopped at a bank as her mom had to cash a couple of checks.

As the teller was waiting on her mother, Kristi heard them talking and she heard the teller say to her mother that her head was really hurting. Kristi, remembering what her mother had told her early that morning said, "Your head is hurting because it is empty. You need to put something in it."

Today's Comment: What is an empty-headed person? A few synonyms for empty headedness are: brainless, silly, skittish, stupid, know-nothing, unschooled, uneducated, illiterate and many more.

The sad truth is that many people are filling their minds with all the wrong stuff. Television, magazines, music and the internet are means through which the mind may be destroyed, or the same may be used to take in some spiritual nourishment. Which will it be? In reference to filling our minds with that which corrupts, someone has said "Garbage in, garbage out."

Oh that we might be careful what we permit to enter our minds, what we read, what we view, and what we hear. Pray also that children and grandchildren will feed on that which is wholesome and healthy for the spirit, soul and body.

Today's Golden Nugget of Truth: "Don't copy the behavior and customs of this world. . ." Romans 12:2 (TLB)

Today's Philosophical Tidbit: "Let no picture hang on the walls of your imagination that you wouldn't hang on the walls of your home." Author Unknown

February 24
Don't Repeat It

Today's Smile: Great preparation had gone into the upcoming evangelistic crusade for a small town. Several pastors and churches had united and worked for over a year to bring in a well-known evangelist for a week of meetings. The meetings were to run from Sunday to Sunday.

On the Friday prior to the opening night, a dinner was held to which the co-operating pastors were invited. Many dollars had been spent on a lot of advertising, radio, television, newspapers, billboards etc. Reporters, representing the local media, were also invited to the dinner and had agreed to give the crusade one added bit of promotion in their Saturday news.

The evangelist won the hearts of all who were present and everyone was excited about the opening meeting on the Sunday evening, everyone except for one reporter. He was a substitute for the reporter from the local newspaper. The newspaper reporter that they had been dealing with was a Christian and very supportive of the crusade. This reporter was not a follower of Christ and was intent on painting a negative picture about the evangelist.

When the evangelist spoke, following the dinner, he expressed his thanks to all the pastors for their hard work, and special thanks to the media for their co-operation. He talked about the week ahead of them and then gave a brief devotional. In his devotional comments, he used a couple of excellent stories to illustrate his point. In so doing, he politely asked the reporters that they not publish these stories as he would use them again during the week.

Well, the newspaper reporter found what he wanted. The next day the newspaper had a story on the dinner meeting and information about the coming week of meetings. The reporter wrote: "The evangelist told some stories last night that cannot be printed."

Today's Comment: Are we guilty of saying things to a few that we would not want to have published or made public? I have been appalled by the number of Christians that forward e-mails, tell stories and say things for which they should be ashamed. Long before I published my book *Jokes Quotes & Anecdotes - Made Especially for Citizens With Seniority,* I sought to find a book of humor that I could give to a patient in the hospital to lift his spirits. What I found contained a fair bit of sacrilegious and suggestive material. That was what motivated me to publish my first book of humor.

Pray that we will not be guilty of saying things that we would be embarrassed to have printed or repeated.

Today's Golden Nugget of Truth: "Out of the same mouth proceed blessing and cursing. My brethren, these things ought not to be so. Does a spring send forth fresh water and bitter from the same opening?" James 3:10, 11

Today's Philosophical Tidbit: "If you wouldn't write it and sign it, don't say it." Earl Wilson

February 25
A Productive Life

*T*oday's *Smile:* The employees of a large manufacturer of high end furniture were overjoyed when the CEO of the company had been given an early retirement. He did very little besides play golf, and was not very approachable and seldom in his office.

With a bonus check in hand, he went to the bank to cash the same. He was so eager to cash his check that he had forgotten his wallet and all identification, including his bank card. The teller apologized and said that she could not cash his check without his card or some identification.

"I have been the CEO of the furniture manufacturer across the road. You know who I am," said the CEO.

"Yes sir, I know who you are, but with all of the regulations and monitoring of the banks because of impostors and forgers, etc, I must insist on seeing some ID."

"Ask your manager, and some of these tellers, they all know me."

"I am sorry," she said, "but these are the bank rules and I must follow them. The only thing that I can do for you is if you can prove that you are who we think you are then I will be able to cash your check. For example, Tiger Woods came in here one day without any ID. To prove that he was Tiger Woods he pulled out his putter and made a beautiful shot across the bank stopping on a quarter which was on the floor. On another occasion Andre Rieu didn't have any ID, but he had his violin and played that classic *Greensleeve'*." We knew that was Andre and we cashed his check. Sir, what can you do to prove that it is really you/"

The CEO stood staring at the floor for quite some time. "You know," he said, "my mind is a total blank. There is nothing that comes to my mind. I can't think of a single thing that I have done. I don't have a clue."

"OK," said the teller, "would you like the amount of your check in large bills or small bills?"

Today's Comment: Are we living productive lives? If you're still pursuing an education or are in the work force, are you giving your best? For others like myself, retired, are we couch potatoes or are our senior years purposeful? What about our volunteer ministry in the church, or some benevolent ministry? When people look at our lives, whether we are in school, on the job or retired, may they see someone who is wholly committed to doing their best. Pray that a tribute given to any of us upon our departing from this life may it be that of commendation and not criticism.

Today's Golden Nugget of Truth: "His lord said to him, 'Well done, good and faithful servant; you have been faithful over a few things, I will make you ruler over many things. Enter in the joy of your lord'." Matthew 25:23

Today's Philosophical Tidbit: "The fellow who considers himself a big gun, will probably soon be fired." Author Unknown

February 26
The Gospel According To You

*T*oday's Smile: A new monk arrived at the monastery and was assigned to help some other monks copying out the old canons and laws of the church by hand. He soon noticed that the other monks were not copying from the original manuscripts but were simply copying from copies that had been copied from other copies. So he spoke to a senior monk and questioned this practice pointing out that if one of the monks had made one simple error that it would be copied without correction.

The senior said, "Well, we have been copying from copies for centuries, but I think you have a good point. I'm going downstairs and look at some of the original manuscripts which are stored in a vault and see if we have made any errors."

Hours passed and the senior monk had not returned and so this junior monk was worried that maybe he had fallen. He went downstairs to see. He found him banging his head against the wall and wailing at the top of his voice. When the young man asked him why he was crying, the senior monk blurted out between his cries, "We made at least two mistakes. We've been writing out the word 'celibate.' That wasn't the original word. Somewhere along the line the original word had three 'E's'. The second 'E' was replaced with the letter 'I' and then later a monk omitted to copy the letter 'R'. The word was 'celebrate'."

Today's Comment: The Holy Bible has been translated over the years into many languages and also many English translations. We are thankful for all those who have translated the Bible and have been diligent in their study to see what the original Greek and Hebrew copies have said. Pray today for all those who continue to be involved in Bible Translation and are seeking to put the Bible in the language of many tribes and cultures. Pray that their translations may be correct and not mislead anyone. Pray for those who are receiving a copy of the written Word of God for the very first time.

Our lives are a translation of the Word of God. May we not be misleading people by our life-style. Pray that our translation of God's Word into action will be blameless.

Today's Golden Nugget of Truth: "All Scripture is given by inspiration of God, and is profitable for doctrine, for reproof, for correction, for instruction in righteousness, that the man of God may be complete, thoroughly equipped for every good work." Second Timothy 3:16, 17

Today's Philosophical Tidbit: "There are a number of splendid translations of the Bible. However, the most effective is its translation into the lives of people. Author Unknown

February 27
A False Assurance

*T*oday's Smile: Paul had moved from Idaho to be near his daughter in Victoria, British Columbia. He hadn't been in Victoria long before he found a Tim Hortons® coffee and donut shop. They are scattered across the Canadian landscape. He had heard that there were a few Tim Hortons that were springing up in the United States. There were about a dozen states on the Atlantic coast and Great Lakes area that had a Tim Hortons but none in Idaho. His daughter introduced him to some of the retirees that lived in their area, and soon he was at Tim Hortons every weekday morning at 10:00 having coffee and a donut with his new found friends.

Tim Hortons had a contest going called "Roll Up The Rim To Win." When one finished drinking their coffee they would roll up the rim of the paper cup and it may say "Play Again," or if you were fortunate you might win a free coffee, or donut, or a Tim Hortons gift card worth $100.00, or a $5,000.00 gift card, or it might be a brand new Toyota Corolla®. Well, Paul hit the jackpot. He rolled up the rim of his cup and started to scream, "I've won a motor home! I've won a motor home! I've won a motor home!"

One of the girls serving coffee, said "That's impossible, sir. Our biggest gift is a car." That did not calm down Paul. He still kept making it known to everyone that he had won a motor home.

Finally the manger went over and told Paul, "I'm sorry sir, but you're mistaken. You couldn't have possibly won a motor home because we don't have that as a prize."

"No," said Paul, "it is not a mistake. Here look at my cup. He handed his cup to the manager and he read: "W I N A B A G E L."

Today's Comment: You've probably received mail or a phone call from some company or organization, saying that you have been selected to win a big prize, maybe a car, a home, a cruise or millions of dollars. On the strength of one of those letters, an elderly couple in one church, where I was senior pastor, shared with me that they had won a million or more. They were telling everyone that they had won, based on one of those letters which thousands and thousands of people receive. The truth is they never won the prize, but they were convinced that it was coming, no matter what anyone told them.

In a similar way millions of people have misread or have been mislead into thinking that they have won a place in heaven. Some so called pastor or Bible teacher has given them a false hope and assurance that they will go to heaven. After all, they say they live a good life and that's what counts. Well, they are mistaken. Christ alone is our only hope of life everlasting, and without Him we lose.

Don't base your hope of everlasting life on a false notion. Likewise pray that your family and friends will know the truth and not be misled by some false teacher.

Today's Golden Nugget of Truth: "But evil men and impostors will grow worse and worse, deceiving and being deceived." Second Timothy 3:13

Today's Philosophical Tidbit: "The father of lies is working to destroy the saving sanctifying truth that God has given to us in His Word and in His Son." John MacArthur

February 28
Explanation Needed

*T*oday's Smile: A new flight attendant was on her first long flight but there was a layover before making the return trip. To complicate matters, she had seldom been away from home or travelled very far, let alone ever spend a night in a hotel. When they arrived at their destination, she went along with the other attendants and the pilots. They all stayed in a hotel only a couple of miles from the airport.

The next morning when she had not shown up in the lobby of the hotel at the appointed hour and their shuttle was soon to arrive to take them all to the airport, the captain phoned her and asked, "Are you alright? You need to be in the lobby soon. We're leaving in about five minutes."

Well, she was crying and through her tears she managed to tell him, "I can't find my way out of this room. There are three doors in here," she sobbed, "one is the bathroom, one is the closet and the third one has a sign on it that says *Do Not Disturb*."

Today's Comment: It is interesting to see young people today, and some much older that have all kinds of facts and figures in their mind. They can easily solve a calculus mathematical challenge, or know the names of all of Henry the VIII's wives, but don't know how to use a can opener, or perform some other simple chore or task.

As I look back on life there are a lot of things that I was not taught or given a lesson in but I learned by watching and seeing it done. We all too often take for granted that our children or grand-children know certain things because they are so common place. They could or should have learned it by watching us or listening to instructions.

However, the truth is that some of these matters did not register in their thinking, when we assumed that they did. Assumptions!

Is the same not true of biblical matters? The gospel is so simple that even a child can understand and respond, and so we have assumed that all our family or friends understand, when in actual fact they have not. So let's pray that those around us know the simplicity of the gospel. Perhaps an explanation is needed.

Today's Golden Nugget of Truth: "Declare His deeds among the peoples, make mention that His name is exalted." Isaiah 12:4

Today's Philosophical Tidbit: "How many family members and friends are headed for a Christ-less eternity because many Christians that are around them assume that they are followers of Christ?" A. Daniel Goldsmith

February 29
A Smile On Your Face

*T**oday's Smile:* Bryce met Cindy at the company Christmas party. He never ever dated her but since that party he had phoned her every night. Finally, February 29th came. It has been known that in some parts of the world it is acceptable for a girl to do the proposing on the 29th.

So Cindy phoned Bryce on February 29th and said, "Bryce, since it is leap year and since you've been calling me every night now for over two months, I propose. . ."

Bryce interrupted and said, "Cindy, with my salary, I am in no position to be thinking about marriage."

"I know that," said Cindy. "That's why I am calling. I thought that I would propose that you stop calling me and give some other fellows the opportunity to phone and maybe even go on a date."

Today's Comment: Dating in our culture usually leads to marriage. Would you ever think of choosing February 29th as a day for a wedding? My paternal grandparents did just that. Daniel and Elizabeth Goldsmith were married in Lowestoft, England, February 29th, 1904. Grandpa said that Grandma was the only girl that he had ever dated.

As I remember them today, it is with thankfulness for my heritage. They were God fearing people and also had a gift for humor, especially grandpa. As children we always delighted in having him tell some of those crazy things that he did as a young person growing up in England. He always made us laugh. I think that my love of humor not only comes from my father, but also from my grandpa Goldsmith.

I hope that this little book that I've put together is putting a daily smile on your face and your family. When you share some of these pages with your friends may it contribute to a little more laughter in their lives.

Pray that we might bring a smile to someone's face today.

Today's Golden Nugget of Truth: "A merry heart makes a cheerful countenance. . ." Proverbs 15:13

Today's Philosophical Tidbit: "As your hands help to give you a clean face, so your heart helps to give you a smiling face." A. Daniel Goldsmith

March 1
Prison Ministry

*T*oday's Smile: The neighbor's uncle had been imprisoned for fraud. Upon his release from prison he told the neighbor about his first day in prison. After having been admitted and given his cell, it was lunch time and he was taken to the chow hall. He was given a seat beside a prisoner whose nickname was "Light Fingers." He learned that Light Fingers was also serving time for fraud. As they were just about finished eating, a prisoner stood to his feet and yelled out "43." The hall erupted in laughter. Then another prisoner stood and called out "23." Again the fellow prisoners were doubled over in a hilarious laugh. So the new prisoner asked his new friend what they were laughing at. "Well," said Light Fingers, "some of us have been here so long that we've heard the same jokes over and over again, so we came up with the idea of numbering them. When the joke number is called out, we remember the joke and so that's why we are laughing."

So the neighbor's uncle decided that in order to introduce himself and get acquainted with his new friends, he would call out a number. "Give me a joke number," he asked Light Fingers. Having been given a number he stood to his feet and shouted, "Number 69." There was dead silence. He turned to Light Fingers and asked, "What happened? Nobody laughed at my joke."

"Well," said Light Fingers, "some people know how to tell a joke and some don't."

Today's Comment: Most prisoners are serving time because they committed a crime, which was contrary to the law of the land. However, there are many people, men and women who are imprisoned in our world today, not because they committed a crime, but because they love Jesus. They may have invited people to their home to study the Bible, gave a New Testament to a neighbor, or simply been found with Christian literature in their home. These people are not sitting around in prison telling jokes, they are sharing the gospel.

Many stories are related in a daily devotional book entitled: *Daily Inspiration From The Lion's Den.* These imprisoned believers look upon their time in prison as their "prison ministry." Many stories are told of those imprisoned who share the good news of the gospel and scores of prisoners come to faith in Christ. I read of one evangelist that served time in three different prisons and led over 400 fellow prisoners to the Lord.[1]

Pray for those who are imprisoned for fraud, for theft, or for murder, pray that they will find Christ in prison. Pray also for the many that are imprisoned because of their faith and their love for the Lord Jesus Christ. Pray that in their "prison ministry" they will be able to lead many others to a saving knowledge of who Jesus Christ is.

Today's Golden Nugget of Truth: "But let none of you suffer as a murderer, a thief, an evildoer, or as a busybody in other people's matters. Yet if one suffers as a Christian, let him not be ashamed, but let him glorify God in this matter." First Peter 4:15, 16.

Today's Philosophical Tidbit: "We have to pray with our eyes on God, not on the difficulties." Oswald Chambers

March 2
False Humility

Today's Smile: Gerald and Tyler were seminary students. They were from the same home church and had been buddies since they were in grade five. It was midterm exam time and the two fellows had heard from upper class men that Professor Todd had always given the same exam every midterm. The question on the midterm was to write their analysis of the Sermon on the Mount. So they studied hard and were well prepared for their test.

The morning of their exam, their professor handed out the test papers and the question was "Trace the Three Missionary Journeys of the Apostle Paul." Obviously, the professor had got wind of the fact that he needed to change the exam from what it had previously been.

Gerald wrote his name on the paper and turned it in. That was all. Tyler was writing furiously and filled several pages. The two friends met in the cafeteria at noon. Gerald said, "I didn't know that you were so knowledgeable about Paul's journeys. All I did was sign my name and turn in my paper. What were you writing about?"

Tyler said, "Well, I wrote 'I do not feel worthy to analyze the missionary journeys of the great apostle Paul, so I would like to write about the Sermon on the Mount'."

Today's Comment: Tyler obviously was using a false humility as an excuse not to answer the question. We've all met people who pose as being humble, but in reality they are proud as a peacock. Pretending to be humble is really a manifestation of pride. People who are humble don't talk about it. I read the story recently about a deacons' board that gave their pastor a gold medal which read: "Our pastor manifests a true spirit of humility." The deacons took it away from him the next week when he wore it to church.

Let's pray that we will walk humbly with our God.

Today's Golden Nugget of Truth: "Let another man praise you, and not your own mouth; a stranger, and not your own lips." Proverbs 27:2

Today's Philosophical Tidbit: "Humility is a thing which must be genuine; the imitation of it is the nearest thing in the world to pride." Charles H. Spurgeon

March 3
Looking On The Bright Side

Today's Smile: Dean and Duane were twin brothers. They were as opposite as day and night when it came to their personalities. Dean was a total pessimist and Duane a total optimist. The worried parents took them to see a psychiatrist.

In an attempt to brighten his outlook on life, the psychiatrist took Dean, the pessimist, to a room filled with toys. Since the psychiatrist had his office in his house, which was on a small acreage on the edge of town, he took Duane, the optimist, out to the barn. In a corner of the barn was a big pile of horse manure which the doctor planned to spread on his field in the Spring. He left Dean in the room full of toys and Duane in the barn with the manure.

After chatting with the parents for about twenty minutes, he went back to check on the boys. He looked in on Dean with all of the toys. He was still standing just inside the room crying like a baby. "What's the matter?" the psychiatrist asked, "Why aren't you playing with some of these toys?"

"I'm afraid that I will break them," said Dean. The doctor took him back to his parents and then proceeded out to the barn. As he approached the barn he heard Duane laughing his head off. When the psychiatrist opened the barn door, there in the corner was Duane digging in the manure with his bare hands and throwing it in the air.

"What are you doing, Duane?" asked the doctor.

"With this big pile of manure there's got to be a pony in here somewhere," said the boy.

Today's Comment: Are you a pessimist or an optimist? I read about a schoolboy who brought home his report card. Most of the grades were very poor. When he handed it to his father, the father took one look at it and then looked his son in the face and asked, "And what have you to say about this?"

The son, looking unashamedly said, "One thing for sure Dad, you can be proud of me. You know I haven't been cheating!" That's optimism if there ever was such.

Being optimistic and looking on the bright side of life is good medicine. You'll have fewer ulcers and also be a joy to others. You might also be willing to get your hands dirty now and then.

Since we have a hope beyond the grave, pray that our lives will demonstrate an optimistic and contented outlook.

Today's Golden Nugget of Truth: "Do not sorrow, for the joy of the Lord is your strength." Nehemiah 8:10

Today's Philosophical Tidbit: "A pessimist is someone who feels badly when he feels good for fear he'll feel worse when he feels better." Author Unknown

March 4
Taste Your Words

Today's Smile: Elsie and Lorinda were born and raised in the same small town. They attended elementary school and high school together. They both got married and had their first child about the same time. They often went together for coffee, pushing their infants in a stroller.

The inevitable happened when Elsie's husband was transferred to Sao Paula, Brazil. A few years later, Lorinda and her husband and family moved to Topeka, Kansas. In the moves, addresses were lost so they were no longer in contact with one another. In due time, they were able to reconnect with the help of a mutual friend. Elsie was able to secure Lorinda's phone number and placed that long distance call which was a big day for both of them.

Well, Elsie had been a big talker and always so excitable. Her brain always ran ahead of her mouth so that on more than one occasion she put her foot in her mouth. This call was no exception. She could not wait to tell Lorinda all that had happened during their years of silence; she began in high gear.

"Lorinda" she said, "so many exciting things have happened to me in these last several years since we moved to Brazil. I hardly know where to begin. For one thing, last year I had my teeth all taken out and a stove and refrigerator put in."

Today's Comment: Some people are always putting their foot in their mouth, but I never heard before about putting a stove and a refrigerator in it. A wise sage of old exhorted us to "taste our words" before we speak. It is so easy to blurt out words without thinking what they sound like or how they will impact our hearers.

Pray that God will help us today to "taste our words" before we speak and say only those words which are kind, true and necessary.

Today's Golden Nugget of Truth: "Let the words of my mouth and the meditation of my heart be acceptable in Your sight, O Lord, my strength and my Redeemer." Psalm 19:14

Today's Philosophical Tidbit: "Put your mind in gear before you take your mouth out of park." Author Unknown

March 5
Are You Listening

*T*oday's Smile: Several denominations use a greeting, some at the beginning of the service and some in their liturgical reading, which dates back centuries ago. The pastor speaks to the parishioners and says, "The Lord be with you." The parishioners respond by saying, "And also with you."

One Sunday the sound system wasn't working very well. The pastor stepped up to the pulpit and said, "There's something wrong with this microphone."

True to their custom and in keeping with tradition the congregation responded, "And also with you."

Today's Comment: Do we listen? Do we really listen to our parents, children, grand-children? Do we listen to our superiors? What about our spouse? Or are we so pre-occupied that our mind is a thousand miles away so we are not giving our full attention? It could not be any better illustrated than by Charles Swindoll's written statement.

Dr. Swindoll writes: "Some years back, I was snapping at my wife and children, choking down my food at mealtimes, and feeling irritated at those unexpected interruptions through the day. Before long, things around our house reflected the pattern of my hurry-up style.

"After supper one evening, the words of one of our daughters gave me a wake-up call. She wanted to tell me something important that had happened to her at school that day. She hurriedly began, 'Daddy-I-wanna-tell-yousomethin'-and-I'll-tell-you-really-fast.'

Realizing her frustration, I answered, 'Honey, you can tell me . . . and you don't have to tell me really fast. Say it slowly.'

I'll never forget her answer: 'Then listen slowly'."[1]

Pray that we will be good listeners, especially to our children and grandchildren. If we're too busy to listen to them now, they will be too busy to talk to us in a few year's time.

Today's Golden Nugget of Truth: "So then, my beloved brethren, let every man be swift to hear, slow to speak, slow to wrath; for the wrath of man does not produce the righteousness of God." James 1:19

Today's Philosophical Tidbit: "A lasting gift to a child is the gift of a parent's listening ear." Author Unknown

March 6
A Slip Of The Tongue

*T*oday's Smile: Billy Graham's "most uproarious flub occurred at the Memphis Crusade in 1951. The police chief had asked Billy to help promote a traffic safety campaign for the city. Before 30,000 plus hearers Billy pointed to a neon sign behind him on the platform. It read *150 Days*. Billy dramatically singled out that sign and announced, 'You see this sign back here? That *150 Days?* That means there have been 150 days without a fertility.'

"There was soon a swelling tide of laughter. Dr. Robert G. Lee, world-renowned clergyman, almost fell off the platform in hysterics. Cliff Barrows cupped his hands and in a stage whisper, blurted out, 'fatality, man, fatality'!"[1]

Today's Comment: How often have you been thinking one thing and said something else? No matter what our age, we hear people all the time say something which is not what they intended to say. One of our pastors, Lyle Magnus, recently was preaching and in the course of his message said, "I never cease to be amazed at how a caterpillar turns into a buffalo. . . I mean butterfly."[1] Though he assured us that he did not plan to say buffalo, it came out of his mouth and the congregation responded with laughter. I heard a pastor friend preaching one Sunday morning about Jonah. He talked about Jonah being "down in the whale of a belly." While we snickered, he never knew what he said until after the service.

We can smile at these bloopers and move on. However, when it comes to sharing God's truth pray that we will speak the truth and not mislead people with some false statement.

Today's Golden Nugget of Truth: "For we all stumble in many things. If anyone does not stumble in word, he is a perfect man. . ." James 3:2

Today's Philosophical Tidbit: "The tongue is in a wet place and slips easily." Author Unknown

March 7
Running From A Bear, Meeting A Lion

Today's Smile: Kent and Candace were at the Phoenix airport awaiting their flight home. The two of them were dressed in a heavy parka, scarf, gloves, wearing heavy boots ready to head home to winter on the Canadian Prairies. An older couple, standing close by were intrigued by their manner of dress, especially the wife. Most of the people in the terminal were wearing shorts, sandals and a summery top.

It was too much for this older woman. She was so curious that she turned to her husband and said, "Look at that couple with all those heavy clothes. I wonder where they are flying?"

The husband, not taken by Kent and Candace's apparel nearly as much as his wife simple responded to her and said, "How would I know?"

"Well, you could go ask them, couldn't you?" she said.

"I don't really care how they are dressed. If you're curious as to where they are going, why don't you go and ask them," he countered. She decided to do just that and walked over to the couple and said,

"Excuse me but I've noticed the way you're dressed and I am curious as to where you're going?"

Kent replies, "Saskatoon, Saskatchewan."

When the woman had rejoined her husband, he said, "O.K. now that you are satisfied, where are they going?"

She replied, "I don't know, dear. They don't speak English."

Today's Comment: I want to pay tribute once again to the host of Christian missionaries that encompass our globe. Most of them speak two languages, some three and four or more. Oh how they need our daily prayers. They speak about our Savior, the Lord Jesus Christ, as being the Son of God, the Prince of Peace, the giver of eternal life. Many who hear their message and receive Christ as their personal Savior are imprisoned, tortured, some being brutally murdered. The Christian's churches are being destroyed. Their houses are being burned. Their children are being kidnapped. Others are running for their lives, but often meet up with a more violent enemy. They have nowhere to turn, but God.

Pray today pray for "the persecuted church," and the missionaries that are seeking to help, encourage and keep focused on our precious Lord. I might add, that some of the missionaries are being forced out, leaving their respective countries to return to their homeland.

Today's Golden Nugget of Truth: "Finally, dear brothers and sisters, we ask you to pray for us. Pray that the Lord's message will spread rapidly and be honored wherever it goes, just as when it came to you. Pray, too, that we will be rescued from wicked and evil people, for not everyone believes." Second Thessalonians 3:1, 2 (NLT)

Today's Philosophical Tidbit: "He is no fool who gives up what he cannot keep to gain that which he cannot lose." Jim Elliot

March 8
My Way Or God's Way

*T*oday's Smile: Bud was many pounds overweight and decided that it was time to shed some of these excess pounds. He found a diet that he liked and was doing marvellously well. He even changed his driving route to the office to avoid being tempted to go into his favourite bakery. One morning he arrived at the office with a half dozen donuts, cherry filled, chocolate coated, glazed, etc. He was severely reprimanded by his fellow workers. However, he was undeterred.

"These donuts," he explained are very special. "I accidentally drove by my baker friend's shop and there in the window was a display of fresh donuts. I felt that this was no accident, so I prayed, 'Lord, if you want me to have a half dozen of those delicious donuts, please let me have a parking place directly in front of the bakery.' Sure enough," he continued, "the fourth time around the block, there was the parking spot that I had asked for."

Today's Comment: Have we ever sought to answer our prayers in the way that we want it to be answered? Do we pray that God would direct our steps, and then do it our way? God's way is perfect. He has a plan for our life.

Dr. Charles Stanley in speaking on the subject of *Seeking God's Will* has shared seven words that pertain to finding God's direction for our lives. Those seven words are: "Cleansing, surrendering, asking, meditating, believing, waiting and receiving."[1] I would like to add one more word, the word "obeying." If we've committed the matter to Him and laid it "on the altar," let's not take it back and do it our way.

Let us pray for God's guidance; then let's do as the hymn simply says, "Trust and Obey."

Today's Golden Nugget of Truth: "And do not be conformed to this world, but be transformed by the renewing of your mind, that you may prove what is that good and acceptable and perfect will of God." Romans 12:2

Today's Philosophical Tidbit: "Potters work with the clay; they don't fret over it or ask permission to remake the clay into whatever they wish." Dr. Charles Swindoll

March 9
One Size Does Not Fit All

Today's Smile: A Memory Therapist stopped and filled up his gas tank at a new Gas Bar on his way home from the clinic. When he arrived home he realized that he had forgotten to put the gas cap back on. He had placed it on top of the car while he filled the tank. Now it was gone. Since it was not too far back to the station, he rode his bicycle back, retracing his route looking for the lost cap. He didn't find it,

He thought that he was probably not the first one to lose a gas cap, so he rode back and forth to the station three times, in the hopes that he might find someone else's gas cap. Sure enough, he found another cap, and it fit perfectly.

In relating his experience to his wife, he told her how he had lost the gas cap on his way home, but with his riding back and forth, he found another one which he figured was much better. "Honey," he said, "I took that cap, placed it on the opening to the tank, and it was a perfect fit. And do you know what? This one is even better than the one we had. This one locked!"

Today's Comment: Sometimes, what appears to be better than what we have or had, is not always so, especially when we don't have a key to unlock the cap. It is so easy to fall for something that we think is better. We need to be careful when looking for a replacement. What we see may not be what we need.

The same is true about the many religions and different faiths that abound. Some sound like they might fit us to a tee; just what we want. Compare with the Bible. Is it sound? Is it true? Does it match up with what God says in His Word? Not all that appears right is right, but God's Word is always right.

There are so many things in life, including the spiritual realm, that appear like the right thing. Pray that you will always have spiritual discernment.

Today's Golden Nugget of Truth: "If anyone teaches otherwise and does not consent to wholesome words, even the words of our Lord Jesus Christ, and to the doctrine which accords with godliness, he is proud, knowing nothing, but is obsessed with disputes and arguments over words, from which come envy, strife, reviling, evil suspicions, useless wranglings of men of corrupt minds and destitute of the truth, who suppose that godliness is a means of gain. From such withdraw yourself." First Timothy 6:3, 4, 5

Today's Philosophical Tidbit: "Not all educated people are intelligent." Author Unknown

March 10
Little Ears Are Listening

Today's Smile: Jody was a single mom but was always on the look out for newcomers at church. She worked full time at an insurance office. She did her best to care for her young son and daughter. However at least once a month she put a roast in the oven before going to church inviting a new family to come for dinner.

It was that time of month again when Jody put a roast in the oven and baked a couple of lemon pies. On this occasion she had invited a new young family with two children the ages of hers. With two young children, having worked ten hours overtime that week, along with her sister visiting with her for two days, Jody was worn out wishing that she had waited another week before inviting company. However, she was going to stick to her commitment.

Once they were seated around the table, Jody thought it would be nice to have her five year old son, the man of the house, give thanks for the food. "But Mommy," said her son Cody, "I don't know what to say."

"You'll do O.K. son, just say what mommy said this morning at the breakfast table."

With that Cody bowed his head and said, "Oh Lord, why on earth did I invite these people here on a day like today."

Today's Comment: That is a good reminder that we need to be careful what we say when there are little ears that are listening. When I was pastor in Vernon, BC, I had a radio ministry three mornings each week at 9:40am. My wife was taking night courses one winter, and the instructor shared with the class that her preschooler was taking

God's name in vain. His speech often included the name "Jesus." Then she continued and said that she blamed it on that radio preacher, none other than me, for I was always talking about Jesus.

Well, I doubt that I taught the little fellow to use profanity. I rather think that he heard it in his home. What words do our children or grand-children hear when we open our mouth? Would we be embarrassed if little ones repeated to others, what they heard us say?

Are our words uplifting or downgrading? Are they glorifying God? Pray that the Lord will help us to taste our words before we speak.

Today's Golden Nugget of Truth: "You shall not take the name of the Lord your God in vain, for the Lord will not hold him guiltless who takes His name in vain." Exodus 20:7

Today's Philosophical Tidbit: "What is in the well of your heart will show up in the bucket of your speech." Author Unknown

March 11
Use Your Hands

Today's Smile: Three students, Pierre from France, William from England and Luigi from Italy were studying at a university in The Netherlands. During their school break the three of them decided to explore a couple of countries in Asia. Pierre, George and Luigi were Christians and one of the countries that they visited during their break was not entirely friendly towards Christianity. They were not thinking when they entered the country and each of them was in possession of a Bible.

They were detained at the border, handcuffed and one by one interrogated. Pierre was the first one to be taken and questioned. He was investigated for five minutes and answered all of the questions. Next William, the English chap was questioned. His questioning also lasted five minutes. Finally Luigi, the Italian, was called in. He was detained for thirty-five minutes.

When they were all released once again on their way, Pierre and William asked Luigi why it took him so long. "Well, he said, "I didn't answer any of their questions."

"Why didn't you answer?" William asked, "We could have been on our way sooner."

"I wanted to, but I couldn't move my hands!"

Today's Comment: Many dispute these statements, but I did some research and found that the Italians and Jews are notorious for talking with their hands. There are a couple of other countries that rank a good second. I read a blog by a Jewish student who said, "I know I talk with my hands a great deal; it's a source of much entertainment around here. In fact, I took a couple of TV classes in college where I couldn't talk with my hands. It drove me nuts." Well, some of the rest of us do our fair share with hand gestures, too.

There are, however, people who must use their hands in order to communicate - the deaf. Thank God for those who do signing and communicate the gospel to deaf people. Many churches have a person that does signing so that those who are hearing impaired may share in the service. I have a friend in Arizona who is deeply involved in a signing ministry. Every year he and some of his family and friends attend an annual gathering of the hearing impaired. They use this event as a time to share the gospel with many who come from throughout the country.

Let's not take our hearing for granted. Thank God that we are blessed with the ability to hear. If you are hearing impaired, thank God for those who communicate with you, and for all who share the gospel message by way of signing. Pray today for signing ministries.

Today's Golden Nugget of Truth: "You shall not curse the deaf, nor put a stumbling block before the blind, but shall fear your God: I am the Lord." Leviticus 19:14

Today's Philosophical Tidbit: "Everything has its wonders, even darkness and silence, and I learn whatever state I may be in, therein to be content." Helen Keller

March 12
Tell Those Who Don't Know

*T*oday's Smile: The story is told about a humorist who was invited to speak at a college. When he got up to speak, he asked the audience if they knew what he was going to talk about. They indicated that they did not know. With that, he said, "I do not know what I am going to speak about either," and walked off of the stage.

He was invited back. He asked the same question as to whether they knew what he was going to speak about. This time they all raised their hands indicating that they knew what he was going to say. "If you know what I am going to say," he said, "I won't waste my time talking." Again he walked off of the stage.

Well, he was asked to make a third appearance. Would you believe that he asked the same question again? "How many of you know what I am going to talk about?" This time the audience was divided. About half of the students raised their hands to say that they knew what he was going to say, and the rest indicated that they did not know what he was going to say. "Then," said he, "will those that know please tell those who don't know and then all will know." Once again he walked off of the stage.

Today's Comment: That in a nutshell is the great commission given to every follower of Christ. We, who know the Lord, are to tell those who do not know Him. The Lord desires that all men everywhere should hear the good news and then all will know.

I am sure that someone told you about the Lord, even as I was told. Pray that God will help us to share with those who do not know the Lord that they too will come to understand who He is and receive Him as their Saviour and in turn tell others.

Today's Golden Nugget of Truth: "And He said to them, Go into all the world and preach the gospel to every creature." Mark 16:15

Today's Philosophical Tidbit: "As Christians, we daily occupy some kind of pulpit and preach some kind of sermon." Author Unknown

March 13
Keep Your Ears And Eyes Open

Today's Smile: It was spring break for Ethan's high school so he spent a weekend with his grandfather. On Sunday he went to church with his grandfather. The pastor was five minutes into his sermon, when his grandfather dozed off to sleep and began to snore loudly. It was disrupting everyone around him. Ethan nudged him, spoke to him and shook him, but could not get him to wake up. It was so bad that the pastor stopped, looked down at Ethan and said, "Would you please wake up your grandfather."

Ethan replied by saying, "Pastor I've tried every way imaginable. I can't get him to wake up. Why don't you try something? You put him to sleep."

Today's Comment: Pastors are sometimes blamed for putting people to sleep. I know all about it. I've experienced it.

In the days when reel to reel recorders were the in thing, a parishioner loaned me his recorder for a few days. I did not own such and so I decided to record a Sunday morning service. I was so excited about this. I had never before heard myself preach a sermon. So after lunch that Sunday, I turned the recorder on, lay down on the couch and began to enjoy the service. I heard the congregational singing, the choir, the announcements, the prayers. I heard the scripture reading and the introduction to my sermon. I woke up as I was pronouncing the benediction.

If you tend to sleep during the pastor's sermon, maybe going to bed earlier Saturday night, or a good cup of coffee Sunday morning may help. We should not only pray for the pastor and his ministry, but we should pray that we will go to church alert and expecting to hear from God. If we were to have an audience with a King or Queen, President or Prime Minister would we let ourselves fall asleep? Let's not blame the pastor. Let's pray for the pastor.

Today's Golden Nugget of Truth: "He who has ears to hear, let him hear!" Mark 4:9

Today's Philosophical Tidbit: "I have learned more when I was listening, then when I was talking." A. Daniel Goldsmith

March 14
A Christian's Lifestyle

*T*oday's Smile: The Reverend Turner, priest at a nearby Anglican Church was walking home one night when a thief produced a gun and demanded his money or his life. As the priest reached into his pocket to hand over his wallet, the thief noticed that this man wore a clerical collar. "I'm sorry Reverend; I see that you are a priest. Keep your money, I'll let you go."

The Reverend Turner was pleasantly surprised by the thief's unexpected response. So in turn the Reverend offered the thief a chocolate bar. "No thank you, Reverend, I gave up chocolate bars during Lent."

Today's Comment: There are many who profess to being a Christian, while their life style is far from becoming a follower of Christ. What makes us different than our neighbors who make no profession of being Christian? Do we think differently? Do we act differently? Do they see anything different about the way we live? The Bible is very clear in its teaching that we should live a life that reflects the character of God.

I recall a young couple who began attending a church where I was the senior pastor. The husband had not attended church for years. The young man shared with us that he was raised in a Christian home, but what he saw as a young person and the way some of the leaders in the church acted, their lifestyle, etc. turned him off and he left the church.

Pray that our lives today show to those around us that we are true disciples of the Lord Jesus Christ.

Today's Golden Nugget of Truth: "Therefore everyone who hears these words of mine and puts them into practice is like a wise man who built his house on the rock." Matthew 7:24 (NIV)

Today's Philosophical Tidbit: "What you are speaks so loud that the world cannot hear what you say." Author Unknown

March 15
A Manager Of God's Property

*T*oday's Smile: A little country church was faced with some major repairs to their church building. They didn't have sufficient funds in their general account and so the Board of Deacons agreed to establish a special fund for the repairs.

The first Sunday that this special fund was presented to the congregation, the chairman of the Deacons Board shared with the congregation details concerning some of the items that needed repairing. He mentioned that the restrooms, the nursery, the roof and several other areas needed some upgrading. Pointing to the ceiling, he indicated that there were a few places where the plaster was loosening and someday a piece would fall and maybe injure someone. He challenged them and said, "We need men and women who will give at least five thousand dollars towards the much needed repairs of our church building."

Would you believe that at that precise moment, a piece of plaster fell from the ceiling hitting one of the wealthiest members in the church? It shocked the man and though the chairman was not asking for a verbal response, this man spoke out and said, "I'll give five thousand dollars."

A split second later, an elderly lady who was only ever able to give "the widow's mite" shouted out, "Lord hit him again!"

Today's Comment: What does it take to motivate us to give to the work of the Lord? Will someone have to hit us on the head or do we give out of love for our Lord and His Church? Do you realize that the Bible teaches that God is the owner of everything? A couple of verses you may wish to look at are Psalm 50:10-12 and I Corinthians 10:26. We really don't own anything. We came into the world with nothing, we leave with nothing.

We are stewards of His property. We are the managers. That means that our decisions about how we spend money, what we give and what we keep is basically how we are managing God's property. Someone has said that financial stewardship is, "Using God-given abilities to manage God-owned property, to accomplish

99

God-ordained results." Pray that we will be good managers of God's property.

Today's Golden Nugget of Truth: "The earth is the Lord's and all its fullness. The world and those who dwell therein." Psalm 24:1

Today's Philosophical Tidbit: "God doesn't look at just what we give. He also looks at what we keep." Randy Alcorn

March 16
Prayer Requests

*T*oday's Smile: A man went to his pastor and asked if he would pray for his floatin kidney. "Floatin kidney," asked the pastor, "why would you ask me to pray for a floatin kidney?"

"Well," said the parishioner, "I heard you praying for 'loose livers' last Sunday and thought maybe you would pray for my floatin kidney."

Today's Comment: Have you ever looked at the prayer sheet at your church, or listened to the requests that are most often voiced in a prayer meeting? What are they? They are usually requests for physical healing.

* Please pray for my aunt who has terminal cancer.
* Pray for my son, he fell playing basketball and has a broken leg.
* Pray for my brother who is having heart surgery.
* Pray for my father who is covered with a rash which is very itchy.

Are we praying for the salvation of the lost; for that wayward niece; for the distribution of the scriptures; for the gospel message which goes out by means of radio, television and the internet; for our missionary friends? There is so much more. How often have we prayed for a revival to start in our church?

There is nothing wrong with praying for physical needs. I do it every day. It just seems that it has become the number one priority when it comes to prayer requests. Those pastors and Christians who are a part of what we call "the persecuted church" are not so concerned with praying for their physical needs and comforts. They pray that they may be found faithful to the end.

Yes, and I would add that I believe we should pray for "loose livers" - those who profess faith in God, but walk far from Him.

Today's Golden Nugget of Truth: "Call to Me, and I will answer you, and show you great and mighty things which you do not know." Jeremiah 33:3

Today's Philosophical Tidbit: "We are more interested in keeping the saints out of heaven than we are in keeping the lost out of hell." Dr. Adrian Rogers

March 17
Beware Of Sham Rocks

Today's Smile: Patrick O'Malley had been dating Chloe for a good two years. He decided that St. Patrick's Day was a good time to pop the question and ask her if she would marry him. So he picked a nice fine dining room just out of Belfast, which had a coastal view. They reminisced about their romance and all the good times that they had. Just before indulging in their desert, Patrick asked Chloe to marry him. She was quick with her response, mingled with tears of joy.

He pulled from his pocket a sparkling diamond ring and put it on her finger. Her parents had gone to bed by the time she got home that night, but the next morning she was up bright and early waiting in the kitchen to greet them when they came for breakfast, and show them her prize. Whether it was a good thing or bad, Chloe's father was a jeweler. He examined it closely and saw that it wasn't a real diamond. Chloe called her fiancé that morning and arranged to meet him for lunch. As soon as they were seated, she flung the ring at him and said, "You are nothing but a cheapskate. Of all the low down tricks! My dad looked at this and said that it is a fake diamond. What do you mean by all of this?"

"Sweetheart," he smiled, "I thought it was the Irish thing to do. I did it in honor of St. Patrick's Day. I gave you a sham rock."

Today's Comment: We live in a day that is full of deceitfulness. Many of you have probably received letters, phone calls, e-mails, etc. posing as being for real, when they are a scam. A fellow had received three telephone calls from individuals who claimed to be with Microsoft® and said that they had received some of his documents and would like to fix his computer. When the fourth call came, the wife took the call and told the caller that she did not own a computer. That was the truth. The husband had a computer but not the wife. They never had any more such calls.

I heard of a lady who got her first computer. Four days after purchasing the same, she received a similar call. Unfortunately, being a novice at computers, she complied with the caller's instructions and the result was that they trashed her computer.

A friend of ours received a phone call saying that we recommended their Bible study. That was not true either. The supposed Bible study was a hook from a false cult. Pray that we will not be misled by that which poses as being real, but is a sham. That also goes for false teachers of the Word of God.

Today's Golden Nugget of Truth: "He who works deceit shall not dwell within my house; He who tells lies shall not continue in my presence." Psalm 101:7

Today's Philosophical Tidbit: "On Christ the solid rock I stand, all other rocks are sham rocks." Author Unknown

March 18
I Have A Song To Sing

*T*oday's Smile: Ralph loved ministering to the smaller churches and the country churches. He was a travelling evangelist and together with his wife, who was an accomplished pianist, they went from church to church conducting a week of meetings. One night the host pastor announced that the prison quartet would be singing the following night. Ralph was unaware that there was a prison nearby, but looked forward to hearing the same.

The next evening, four men from the church came to the platform and the pastor introduced them. "This is our prison quartet," he said, "they're always behind a few bars and looking for the key."

Today's Comment: When I was a student at Columbia International University in Columbia, SC one of my Christian Service assignments was teaching Bible in an elementary school. There were several of us fellows that would teach a class once a week. At the close of our school year we were invited to take a school assembly. The Dean of Men, from CIU, was to be the speaker and four of us teachers put together a quartet, plus our pianist.

On our way to the school, which was in another city, we came up with the idea of singing a song which we had not practiced, but we knew by memory. We practiced in the car and guessed at what key it was in.

Just before the Dean was to speak, we sang this particular song. Since we had no time to practice at the school, the pianist played the introduction in the key which we thought it was in. Well, it was pitched way too high. We struggled through the first stanza and some of the children began to snicker. By the time we made it through the chorus, the entire assembly had broken out into laughter. With that, we stopped and sat down. The Dean stood to his feet. We were the perfect introduction to his message. He began by saying, "Before I received Christ as my personal Savior, I was like that quartet, all out of tune."

Life without Christ is a life which is out of tune. One may try to act like they have a song in their heart, but many of those songs are sad songs. You might agree that some of the world's songs sound like they have no tune.

Music is a blessing and Christians, whether on key or off key, can sing from their heart. I trust that you have a song to sing today, a song that will lift your spirits and glorify your God. And let me add that if you have the gift of music, pray that your singing will bring glory to God and not yourself.

Today's Golden Nugget of Truth: "Let the Word of Christ dwell in you richly in all wisdom, teaching and admonishing one another in psalms and hymns and spiritual songs, singing with grace in your hearts to the Lord." Colossians 3:16

Today's Philosophical Tidbit: "In my heart there rings a melody, there rings a melody of love." Elton Roth

March 19
Happy With Your Work

*T*oday's Smile: It was 7:30 in the morning and Jonathan was still in bed. His mother went into his room and pulled the covers off of him and said, "Wake up, son. It is time that you were up, dressed and getting ready for school."

"Aw Mom, I don't want to go to school."

"Give me two good reasons why you don't want to go to school."

"Well, yesterday Pete threw chalk at me and hit me in the eye, and Annie put a thumb tack on my chair, I didn't see it and sat on it. Mom, I don't like school and I don't want to go. I'm always being picked on by others."

"That's no reason to stay at home. Now come on and get out of that bed!"

"Mom, give me two good reasons why I should go to school."

"Well, for one, you're 47 years old, and for another, you're a teacher!"

Today's Comment: Do you enjoy your job? There are a lot of people that go to work every day and really don't find joy or satisfaction in what they do. They do what they do because there is a pay check at the end of the week or twice a month. That is so sad. We spend a lot of years on the job. How is it with you?

I am so thankful that I have enjoyed my work. In 1958 I became a pastor of two small churches in northern Alberta. I retired from full-time ministry in a church of over a thousand. I never got rich in dollars and cents, but I am indeed rich. I've rejoiced with people on the birth of a child. I have had young children hug me in the lobby. I have had a ton of fun with young people. I have celebrated with couples at their wedding. I have walked with people through the challenges of life. I have prayed with the sick in their time of weakness. I have pointed the sorrowing to the God of all comfort, and led the sinner to the Savior. What a privilege, and what a joy! An added benefit was studying God's Word as I prepared to share the same, and getting paid to do it all. Need I say that I found great fulfillment and satisfaction in my work?

Pray that your employment is fulfilling and that you can get up in the morning with a spring in your step and a peace in your heart knowing that you are where God wants you to be.

Today's Golden Nugget of Truth: "I have learned in whatever state I am, to be content." Philippians 4:11

Today's Philosophical Tidbit: "The choices we make and the objectives we have are what breed contentment or discontentment." Charles Swindoll

March 20
May My Living Not Be In Vain

*T*oday's Smile: The bookkeeper's wife was getting a bit concerned about her mother who was getting on in years but also was becoming quite forgetful, unable to think clearly or make small decisions. The next time that she visited her family physician she asked him, "How can you tell when a person needs to be placed into a nursing home? My siblings and I think that we need to be looking into a place for my mom."

The doctor said, "One simple test that you can do is to fill the bathtub with water and then give your mother a teaspoon, a teacup and an ice cream bucket and ask her to empty the bathtub."

"That sounds like a good test. I guess that the normal person would use the bucket," she said.

"No," said the doctor, "a normal person would pull the plug. When do you want a bed?"

Today's Comment: I am so thankful that my mother and father were clear in their thinking till the day they died. The same was true of my wife's parents. The night that my Dad died, he was lying on his bed, conversing with my brother. He shared how much he loved his family. Since my brother was looking after Dad's financial affairs and his banking, Dad inquired of David whether checks had been written for his tithe. Furthermore, Dad even related a funny incident that happened several years prior. However, that is not always the case with many older people. Their mind wanders. They can't think clearly. They become confused.

May God help us to be understanding, patient, loving and caring. It is not their fault that their mind is failing. Pray today for those with memory problems, and thank God that we still have functioning minds.

Today's Golden Nugget of Truth: "Assuredly, I say to you, inasmuch as you did it to one of the least of these My brethren, you did it to Me." Matthew 25:40

Today's Philosophical Tidbit: "Every day, try to help someone who can't reciprocate your kindness." John Wooden

March 21
How Well Do You See

*T**oday's Smile:* An elderly gentleman was asked to appear in court as a witness to a burglary. The defending lawyer asked, "Mr. Peters, did you see my client commit this burglary?"

"Yes sir," said Mr. Peters. "I saw him with my own eyes take the lawnmower."

The lawyer posed another question to Mr. Peters. "Mr. Peters, you know this theft happened at night. Are you sure that you saw my client take the lawnmower?"

"Yes sir," said Mr. Peters. "I saw him do it."

The defending lawyer said, "Mr. Peters, you are 87 years of age and your vision is probably not as good as it used to be. How far can you see at night?"

Mr. Peters replied, "I can see the moon. How far away is that?"

Today's Comment: We can see the moon. What else? What is our vision like? Do we see people with needs? People who are lonely? People who need a helping hand? People who are discouraged? Do we see people who are sitting in spiritual darkness? Is there someone in your circle of friends that would appreciate a letter of encouragement? I know letters are almost a thing of the past, but if we have a computer why not send an email. Don't send the worthless trivia that abounds, but a personal note, or maybe make a phone call. There are so many around us that need a spiritual lift. Do we see them?

Pray that God will open our eyes to see what He sees.

Today's Golden Nugget of Truth: "But whoever has this world's goods, and sees his brother in need, and shuts up his heart from him, how does the love of God abide in him? First John 3:17

Today's Philosophical Tidbit: "I don't care how much you know until I know how much you care." Author Unknown

March 22
Sometimes The Truth Hurts

*T*oday's Smile: Six year old Susie was invited by her grandmother to go shopping with her as she wanted to buy a new dress. They went to four different stores and finally grandma found just what she was looking for, a bright yellow dress. Susie waited for her just outside the fitting room. When her grandmother came out modelling the dress, looking in the mirror, she said to Susie, "Well honey, what do you think? Does it look good on me?

"Oh grandma," said Susie, "it looks real good on you. It looks just like the big yellow school bus that I ride!" Grandma didn't buy the dress.

Today's Comment: We are encouraged to speak the truth, but sometimes the truth hurts, not because it isn't true, but the way we speak it. One might say, "You have a face that would stop a clock!" But how much better to say, "When I look into your face, time stands still." Same thing said in two different ways.

How well do we speak the truth in husband/wife, parent/child, sibling/sibling relationships or at school, work place, community or church, etc? Do we speak the truth in a confrontational way, or in a gentle way, constructive or destructive manner? Pray that God will keep us from lying about issues and help us speak the truth with boldness and gentleness.

Today's Golden Nugget of Truth: "Therefore, putting away lying, let each one of you speak truth with his neighbor, for we are members of one another." Ephesians 4:25

Today's Philosophical Tidbit: "The truth hurts most when you step on the bathroom scale." Author Unknown

March 23
Do You Love The Family Of God

*T*oday's Smile: At the corner of Main Street and Center Street were three churches. Unfortunately, these three churches did not see eye to eye. There was no interaction or fellowship with one another. The members of each of these churches seemed to have a negative attitude towards the other two.

One Sunday, a newcomer to town decided that he would seek out a church where he could worship. Having had a bit of a problem finding a parking place, he was a few minutes late. As he approached the intersection where the three churches were located, he heard the church nearest to him singing that old familiar hymn, *Will There Be Any Stars In My Crown?* The congregational singing was beautiful. However, it was a very old church building and he did not fancy walking up the flight of stairs to the main door. So he crossed over to another church which had a level entrance. As he did, he heard that church singing, *No Not One, No Not One!* He thought to himself, that doesn't sound very Christ-like. When what should he hear emanating from the third church, but *Oh, That Will Be Glory For Me!*

Today's Comment: Unfortunately, in some churches there is a divisive spirit. Within the family of God and the family of churches, there should be no animosity. We are not to be competitive, or critical. The church is not the building, though we may refer to the building as the church. The church is made up of people like you and me.

Let's examine our hearts and see to it that we have love for our fellow Christians, and not hatred. We may have a different style of worship. We may differ on some interpretations of scripture. We may dress differently. If we are agreed on the basics, that we are all sinners and that Jesus Christ is the only way to God and eternal life, then let us encourage each other. If there is hatred let it be hatred of sin.

I've always been impressed by a pastor, who in his pastoral prayer, prays for other churches in the same city. Let's pray that we will demonstrate genuine love for the family of God.

Today's Golden Nugget of Truth: "By this all will know that you are My disciples, if you have love for one another." John 13:35

Today's Philosophical Tidbit: "To love the whole world may be a big chore, but what about the Christian who lives next door?" Author Unknown

March 24
Thank God For Generous Givers

*T**oday's Smile:* The CEO for the one and only mill in the small town was approached by a representative of the community center asking if he would be willing to contribute $30,000.00 towards the building of a new arena. Everyone in town knew that the CEO had money, at least more than the majority of the town's people.

He responded by saying, "I know that most of you think that I have a lot of money. Well, I do have a bit, but did you know that we had to place my mother in a costly nursing home in the city? Did you know that my brother-in-law died of a massive heart attack leaving his wife, my sister, with five children, penniless and without insurance? Did you know that my son, who is a very compassionate person works for a recovery house and his income is far below the national poverty level? And did you know that my youngest daughter is working two jobs trying to save enough money to go to college in a couple of years? If I don't give a penny to any of them why should I give to a new arena?"

Today's Comment: Maybe today's smile wasn't very funny. Upon reviewing the same, I think I should have deleted it, but I didn't. Why? Well, not all rich people are stingy. Thank God for men and women who consider it their ministry to make money and share the same. Schools, churches, missionary organizations, etc. have benefited from many generous gifts given by the financially rich, as well as the "widow's mite."

As a twelve year old boy, I heard R. G. Letourneau, the inventor and manufacturer of some mighty big earth moving equipment. Mr. Letourneau was known for giving away 90% of his income and living off of 10%. It made quite an impression on me as a young boy. I read two biographies written about him. You may say that he had a lot more than you do. That may be true, but the point is he didn't spend the 90% on himself like many do. I know several people who I would consider to be in a good financial position. They have money and they are very generous. The question is not how much do we give, but how much do we keep for ourselves. Pray that our giving will be in line with our professed relationship with God.

Today's Golden Nugget of Truth: "The Lord does not look at the things man looks at. Man looks at the outward appearance, but the Lord looks at the heart." First Samuel 16:7 (NIV)

Today's Philosophical Tidbit: "Give not from the top of your purse, but from the bottom of your heart." Author Unknown

March 25
Keep Focused

Today's Smile: The introduction of a speaker should be informative. A good introduction is a work of art. Evangelist Barry Moore tells of a time when he was introduced by a friend. The friend began by saying that he had heard that Barry had started to do some preaching. In fact Barry had been invited to do an evangelistic sermon in a nearby country church. Continuing, he stated that Barry was nervously pacing the floor awaiting the congregation to arrive. Twenty-five minutes after starting time there was only one elderly farmer sitting in the back row. No one else had come. Barry went to the gentleman to ask what he felt they should do. His answer was cogently couched in an illustration from the farm.

The farmer, pausing momentarily, said "Well, sir, if I called the cows and only one came, I'd shore feed her." With this gracious rebuke pulsating in his mind, Barry proceeded to preach for over an hour on every Biblical subject he could think of trying to show the old gentleman that he had been prepared. As the story teller continued, he said, "Barry met the farmer as he left the building. He thanked him for coming and foolishly asked if he'd enjoyed the service. His answer, 'Well, sir, if I called the cows and only one came, I sure wouldn't unload the whole load!'

Today's Comment: I heard a couple of speakers who spoke the same afternoon. The first speaker captivated the audience. He gave a warm, personable presentation, often punctuated with humor. The speaker that followed him had good content, but appeared more focused on the teleprompter than the audience.

When we talk with someone, are "we all there?" Is our attention on the person with whom we are conversing or addressing or are we looking beyond that person? The same holds true when talking to God. Are we focused on the person of God, or is our mind wandering all over the map?

When we are praying, let's be focused on our praying. Let's give our undivided attention to God.

Today's Golden Nugget of Truth: "But you, when you pray, go into your room, and when you have shut your door, pray to your Father who is in the secret place; and your Father who sees in secret will reward you openly." Matthew 6:6

Today's Philosophical Tidbit: "Whatever is your best time of day, give that to communion with God." Hudson Taylor

March 26
How's Your Driving

Today's Smile: Bubba stopped every Tuesday and Thursday at the Wayside Café on highway 32 for lunch. He delivered produce to small grocery stores, and was dearly loved by all who knew him. No one had ever seen him get mad. He was just an all round nice guy.

One Tuesday, he stopped for lunch at the Wayside and ordered his favourite Tuesday lunch, a two patty hamburger with all the trimmings, plus French fries, onion rings and a large Pepsi. On this particular Tuesday, three tough looking motorcyclists stopped in at the café. One of the cyclists grabbed his hamburger off of his plate. Another took his Pepsi, and the third one walked off with the plate of fries and onion rings. Bubba stood up, walked over to Heidi, the cashier, paid for his meal and left. Heidi waved and watched him as he calmly climbed up into the cab of his truck and drove off.

"Well," said one of the cyclists, "he's not much of a man. He didn't even put up a fight. The big sissy!"

"No," said Heidi, "and Bubba is not much of a truck driver, either. He just drove over three motorcycles."

Today's Comment: How's your driving? Recently my daughter reminded me of a day when I drove her to school. She was in about grade 2, and of course I was much younger and a little more foolish. The city roads were covered with fresh fallen snow. The sand trucks and snowploughs had not yet reached some of the streets and I was entertaining my daughter by trying to spin the car on the slippery roads. Well, one spin went out of control and I ended up on someone's front yard.

Driving a car is often a real test of our faith. I've seen a few angry drivers in my life-time; drives screaming at pedestrians or at young people playing on the road; drives honking their horn because I stopped too soon or didn't start quickly enough when the traffic lights changed. We've all been tail-gated only to have the driver pass and then slow down in front of us. It takes patience to sit behind the wheel of a car or truck. I often have to smile when an impatient driver passes me and three other cars in order to get ahead, and then we all meet again at the next traffic light.

If you're an impatient driver, ask God for His patience. Pray that we will demonstrate our faith today when driving a car.

Today's Golden Nugget of Truth: "For as the body without the spirit is dead, so faith without works is dead also." James 2:26

Today's Philosophical Tidbit: "We are good at showing our faith and love for God when we pray and kneel. Let's show that same faith and love for God when we steer the wheel." A. Daniel Goldsmith

March 27
Failure May Be
Your Road To Success

*T**oday's Smile:* Miss Merritt was receiving auditions for the "Dense Award" skit that would be presented by her grade six class to the parent teacher's spring meeting as part of the entertainment. She wanted four boys for an impromptu quiz in which the parents would ask any question they wanted and the boys would respond with a dumb answer. So in her auditioning she was asking each of them two test questions in order to see what kind of dumb answer they would give. She already had selected three boys and was now interviewing the last one.

"OK Alvin, here is the first question. How many days are there in a week that start with the letter 'T'?"

"That's easy," said Alvin. "There are two."

"Very good. What are they?"

"Today and tomorrow," he said.

"That would be a good answer. Here's another question. How would you answer this one? How many seconds in a year?"

Again Alvin was quick with an answer. There are twelve. January 2nd, February 2nd, March 2nd, April 2nd, May 2nd etc. . ."

"How is it," she asked, "that you boys are quick with dumb answers to good questions but you're mighty slow with good answers in class?"

"Miss Merritt, why don't you try giving us dumb questions, then maybe we could give a smart answer?"

Today's Comment: At Prairie Bible Institute we had a method of study called "Search Questions." We had a book of questions and had to find the answer in the Bible, without the help of commentaries, etc. We would then be called upon to share our answer in class. As it happened, the first Bible class that I had with L. E. Maxwell, who was the first principal of the school, I was called upon by Mr. Maxwell to answer question #3. I stood, shared my answer, and he graciously commented and said, "That's a good answer, but it doesn't answer the question."

There is a popular phrase which I'm sure you've all heard, "There is no such thing as a dumb question, only dumb answers." I think that the desire to learn also includes failure. So if you present a wrong answer, don't be discouraged. It was Thomas Edison who said "I've not failed; I've just found 10,000 ways that won't work." A failure spurred him on and there are 1,093 patents to his credit.

In 1923, Babe Ruth broke the record for the most home runs in a season. That same year he broke the record for more strike outs than any other player in Major League Baseball. A wrong answer should serve to help us learn. Learn from our mistakes. Of course it would be good if we learned from the mistakes of others, too.

So if you feel like a failure, you've given a dumb answer, keep going; learn from past failures! I have long since forgotten Mr. Maxwell's question and my answer. That was in September 1951. I've learned much since that day.

Pray that we will keep learning from our mistakes.

Today's Golden Nugget of Truth: "And the Lord, He is the One who goes before you. He will be with you. He will not leave you nor forsake you, do not fear nor be dismayed." Deuteronomy 31:8

Today's Philosophical Tidbit: "Champions of faith are people who have learned from their failures." Author Unknown

March 28
Honesty Is The Only Policy

*T**oday's Smile:* Lisa and her friend stopped at a fast food restaurant where each of them bought a hamburger and a cold drink. Once they were seated and about to take their first bite, Lisa exclaimed, "Do you know what? That clerk forgot to take my money. I never paid for this. I am going back and pay for this before I eat."

"Why bother," said her friend. "The clerk forgot, so why don't you just forget it and enjoy your free meal?"

"No," said Lisa, "I've always found that honesty is the best policy." With that she went back to the counter and told the clerk, "You failed to charge me for my meal."

"Oh yea, you got the hamburger and root beer, the same as your friend. Let's see, that was $4.29 with the tax." So Lisa handed him a five dollar bill and paid for her lunch.

When she rejoined her friend, she said, "I told you that honesty was the best policy. I gave that clerk a five dollar bill and he gave me change for a ten."

Today's Comment: I read four different websites about the honest stand which Chelsee Richard, a high school golfer from Bloomingdale High School in Brandon, Florida took. Chelsee lost her chance to win the 2004 state championship because of her honesty. I quote from one of those sites:

"In the qualifier for the state finals, Chelsee hit her tee shot on the second hole into the rough. Without knowing it, she played another golfer's ball out of the rough and finished the hole. On the third hole, she realized what she had done. The rule is that a golfer must declare on that hole, they hit the wrong ball before putting the ball into the hole, or they are disqualified.

Chelsee drew strength from her favorite Bible verse, Philippians 4:13 - 'I can do all things through Christ who strengthens me.' She reported her error, a painful ending to her senior season and her dream of going to State. She said: 'With my faith and with God, being honest was the most important thing to me, and that's what is going to advance on throughout my life, being honest and making the right choices'."[1]

Thank God for the Chelsees in our world. Honesty is the best policy, even if it does hurt. Pray that we will be honest in all of our dealings.

Today's Golden Nugget of Truth: "A good man is guided by his honesty; the evil man is destroyed by his dishonesty." Proverbs 11:3 (TLB)

Today's Philosophical Tidbit: "Telling the truth, when you know there is a great cost, will make you richer in the end." A. Daniel Goldsmith

March 29
Lead By Example

Today's Smile: A seminary professor was leading a group of seminarians on a tour of Israel. He had shared with his students the parable of the good shepherd and had explained to them that they would probably see shepherds leading their sheep, as they did when Jesus was on earth. "Shepherds," he said, "always lead their sheep, walking in front of them in case they should face any dangers, and that way he can protect his sheep."

It was only a few moments after sharing this with his students, that the bus rounded a corner and there in front of them was a man, but he wasn't leading the sheep as the professor had shared, he appeared to be chasing them. The professor got out of the bus and went over to the man who was behind the sheep and said, "I always thought that shepherds in this part of the world led their sheep and were out in front. I just finished telling my students that this was so."

"You're absolutely right," said the man, "but you have to know the difference. I am not a shepherd, I'm a butcher!"

Today's Comment: If you're a pastor, a Sunday School teacher, a care group leader or a shepherding elder or any other Christian leader, strive to be a shepherd who leads your sheep. This also applies to parents and the children, the little lambs that God has entrusted to us. Let's be good parents. Good leaders. Godly leaders. Let's set the right example for those who are following. Let's not act like a butcher who is about to kill the flock.

There are pastors and parents and other leaders who are always condemning, criticizing and complaining about their congregation or their children. Seek to be complimentary, constructive and compassionate. Pray that we will be in front of the flock, leading by example, rather than driving from behind.

Today's Golden Nugget of Truth: "Shepherd the flock of God which is among you, serving as overseers, not by compulsion but willingly, not for dishonest gain but eagerly; nor as being lords over those entrusted to you, but being examples to the flock." First Peter 5:2, 3

Today's Philosophical Tidbit: "As a leader, are you pushing, pulling, or leading?" Author Unknown

March 30
Reach For The Top

*T*oday's Smile: Roy was on his way into town to buy some groceries and get a supply of chicken feed. A couple of miles down the road, he remembered that his old friend Johnny had sold his farm and he saw the new owner standing out in the field. He slowed down, glancing at the new owner and wondered why he was just standing there in the field. He stopped his truck, got out and walked out into the field to greet him and welcome him to the neighborhood.

"Hi! My name is Roy. I live one mile down the road and I heard that you were to be moving in soon. Welcome to life on the Prince Albert Road."

"Well, thanks for stopping by. I'm Konrad. My wife and I just moved in two weeks ago. We are sure enjoying the country air and the quietness."

"Where did you move from?" asked Roy.

"We've been living in town. I've really never lived on a farm before. I was born and raised in town and have my own painting business. I still have that, but bought this farm in order to qualify for the *Nobel Peace Prize*."

Roy was a little puzzled by Konrad's response. "I don't understand. You say you bought this farm so that you could qualify for the Nobel Prize? Explain."

"Well I heard that they award the prize to people who are out standing in their field!"

Today's Comment: Academy Awards, some say that the Oscars are the same, others disagree, whatever, they are given for excellence in movie making, best picture, best director, best actor, etc. Grammy Awards are given in appreciation for music contributions to American culture. The Commissioner's Trophy is awarded in baseball. Many Gold, Silver and Bronze medals are earned at Olympic sports. Canadian football has its Grey Cup. There are so many awards and trophies for many and varied achievements that I could fill many pages listing them all. Awards ranging from a cup earned in some child's club to the Nobel Peace Prize are all given in recognition for achievements or accomplishments.

What about the prize mentioned in the Bible? The Bible teaches us that we who have received the Lord Jesus Christ as our personal Lord and Savior will someday stand before the Judgment Seat of Christ. Rewards or awards will be presented at that time. My prayer is that we might run the race, a spiritual race here and now on this earth, so that when that time shall come, we will hear the Lord say, "Well done, good and faithful servant." Pray that we will strive today for that crown which God wants to give to us.

Today's Golden Nugget of Truth: "Do you not know that those who run in a race all run, but one receives the prize? Run in such a way that you may obtain it." First Corinthians 9:24

Today's Philosophical Tidbit: "I long to accomplish a great and noble task, but it is my chief duty to accomplish small tasks as if they were great and noble. Helen Keller

March 31
How Will I Be Remembered

*T**oday's Smile:* Miss Jones was known to nearly everyone in the small town. She was born and raised there and lived all her life in the house in which she was born. She was also the oldest resident in the town and had never married.

Well, Miss Jones died and the town wanted to do something special for her. Since she had no living relatives, some friends of hers had put some money together to have a nice tombstone placed over her grave. Dennis, who owned Superior Memorials, had agreed to do the lettering on the stone. However, since Miss Jones had really never done anything outstanding or noteworthy or had any known vices, he was at a loss to know what epitaph to write on the tombstone.

One morning he was having coffee at the town's most popular coffee shop. Many of the business and professional people gathered there usually around mid-morning. This particular morning he sat at a table with his friend Dudley, who was the owner and publisher of *The Chronicle* the town's newspaper. "Hey, Dudley," said Dennis, "I've got a problem and you have a few editors that might be able to help me."

"What's your problem," asked Dudley.

"I agreed to do the lettering on Miss Jones' tombstone. I need some ideas as to what to put on her tombstone."

"Well, I'll tell you what," said Dudley, "I'll ask the first editor that I see when I get back to the office to write something for you." True to his word, the first editor that he saw back at the office was Chris, the sports editor.

It didn't take long for Chris to write something for the tombstone. This was his submission to his boss.

"Here lie the bones of Nancy Jones, for her life held no terrors, She lived in peace, she died in peace, no hits, no runs, no errors."

Today's Comment: What will your family engrave on your tombstone? "Margaret Workizer's epitaph, Trefyffrin Township, Chester County, PA says: "Verses on tombstones are but idly spent, the living character is the monument."

I have a collection of epitaphs written on various tombstones around the world. Some are humorous and some are thought provoking.

In Nantucket, MA: "Under the sod and under the trees, lies the body of Jonathan Pease, He is not here, there's only the pod, Pease shelled out and went to God."

Billy Sunday, Forest Park, IL: "I have fought a good fight, I have finished my course, I have kept the faith." Second Timothy 4:7

Ruth Bell Graham, Charlotte, NC "End of Construction - Thank you for your patience."

Fanny Crosby, Bridgeport, CT, "She hath done what she could."

Dwight L. Moody, Bridgeport, MA, "He that doeth the will of God abideth forever."

Martin Luther King, Jr., Atlanta, GA "Free at last, free at last, thank God Almighty I'm free at last."

Pray that our tombstone will be a testimony to all who pass by.

Today's Golden Nugget of Truth: "Precious in the sight of the Lord is the death of His saints." Psalm 116:15

Today's Philosophical Tidbit: "A life well lived is a life well spent; with Jesus in your life we'll know where you went." A. Daniel Goldsmith

April 1
A Fool Says There Is No God

*T**oday's Smile:* A Methodist pastor, Bob, and a Jewish rabbi whose name was Abram were neighbors. They had been neighbors for five years and though they differed concerning the person of Jesus Christ and the New Testament scriptures, they got along well. They often had a coffee together.

A new family moved into their neighborhood, and the pastor and rabbi were anxious to welcome this new family. Their first attempt was to invite the new neighbor to join them for coffee. They learned that their new neighbor was an investment officer and did a lot of his work on his computer in his home. They detected a different accent discovering that he had moved from Australia. The three of them shared information as to where they were born, grew up and something about their family.

The topic finally got around to Bob and Abram's occupations. The new neighbor discovered that he was having coffee with a couple of religious leaders. He told his two new religious friends that he was an atheist and that he always was irritated to think that many religions had special holidays. "You," he said turning to Bob, "have Easter and Christmas, and you," addressing Abram, have your special holidays. Why can't we atheists have a recognized holiday?"

The Methodist pastor, biting his lip and trying to be nice, said, "You've had your holiday for years."

"Oh, when is that? I am not aware of any atheist holiday at least we did not have one in Australia."

Bob said, "The atheist holiday is the same day every year, the first of April."

Today's Comment: We may smile at the Methodist pastor's response, but an atheist does not believe in the existence of God. April 1st is known as "April Fool's Day." For centuries there have been those who have held strongly to the belief that there is no God. Saying that there is no Pacific Ocean does not make that ocean non-existing. Saying there is no God does not alter the truth that there is a God. Only a fool says there is no Pacific Ocean and only a fool says there is no God.

Pray that the eyes of many who deny the existence of God may be opened to see and know that there is one true God and someday we will all stand before Him.

Today's Golden Nugget of Truth: "The fool has said in his heart, there is no God." Psalm 53:1.

Today's Philosophical Tidbit: "An atheist defies the God he claims doesn't exist." Author Unknown

April 2
Be Not Deceived

*T*oday's Smile: A young man named Hugo bought a donkey from an old farmer for $100.00. The farmer agreed to deliver the donkey in a couple of days. When the farmer arrived at Hugo's place, he noticed that the donkey had died enroute. "Sorry son, but I see that I have some bad news. I loaded the donkey earlier this morning and it is in my truck, here, but I see that it is dead."

Hugo replied, "Well that's OK. Just give me my money back."

The farmer said, "I can't do that son. I've already spent it."

Hugo said, "OK then, just unload the donkey and leave it with me."

The farmer asked, "What are you gonna do with a dead donkey?"

Hugo said, "I'm going to raffle it off."

To which the farmer exclaimed, "You can't raffle off a dead donkey!"

Hugo, with a big smile on his face, said, "I sure can. You watch me. I just won't tell anybody that it is dead."

A month later the farmer met up with Hugo and asked, "What happened with that dead donkey?"

Hugo said, "I raffled it off selling 500 tickets at two dollars a piece and made a profit of $798.00."

Totally amazed, the farmer asked, "Didn't anyone complain that you had stolen their money because you raffled off a dead donkey?"

Hugo replied, "The only guy who discovered that the donkey was dead was the fellow who won. When he came to claim his prize, I told him that it had died. So I gave him his $2 back plus $200 extra. That's double the going value for a donkey, and he went away thinking that I was a great guy."

Today's Comment: In my last full-time pastoral ministry before retiring, I was pastor to seniors at Sevenoaks Alliance Church in Abbotsford, BC. I cautioned the seniors not to get taken by all of the scammers and fraudulent phone calls, letters and emails. In spite of that, one dear lady who was approaching ninety fell for a telephone caller that said he was an investigator and in doing a check on her bank, needed her to take $300.00 cash out of her account and give to him so that he could follow through with his investigation. She met him, gave him the $300.00 and never saw him again.

We continually receive telephone calls and e-mails where they say they are checking our credit cards. It is a sad story when we hear of people being sucked in by these deceivers. What is far worse are the many false teachers and deceivers that prey on people with their "doctrines of devils."

As I trust that you would be careful with telemarketers, even so be very careful with those who claim to teach the Bible but are not teaching the truth of God's Word, but heresy. Pray that you will be so immersed in the Word of God that you will be able to know right from wrong.

Today's Golden Nugget of Truth: "Beloved, do not believe every spirit, but test the spirits, whether they are of God; because many false prophets have gone out into the world." First John 4:1

Today's Philosophical Tidbit: "You can fool all the people some of the time, and some of the people all the time, but you cannot fool all the people all the time." Abraham Lincoln

April 3
The Day Of Resurrection

Today's Smile: A very zealous young preacher set out to win his first convert to the Lord. He came upon a farmer busily working in his field. Being concerned about the farmer's spiritual life, the preacher stopped and asked the farmer, "Are you laboring in the vineyard of the Lord, my good man?"

Not even looking at the preacher and continuing his work, the farmer replied, "Naw, these are soybeans, not grapes."

"You don't understand what I'm asking," said the preacher. "Are you a Christian?"

With the same amount of disinterest as his previous answer the farmer said, "Nope my name is Jones. You must be looking for Jim Christian. He lives a mile south of here."

Undaunted, the determined young preacher tried again asking the farmer, "Are you lost?"

"Nope! I've lived here all my life," answered the farmer.

"Are you prepared for the resurrection?" the frustrated preacher asked.

This caught the farmer's attention and he asked, "When's it gonna be?"

Thinking he had accomplished something the young preacher replied, "It could be today, tomorrow, or the next day!"

Taking a handkerchief from his back pocket and wiping his brow, the farmer remarked in a monotone voice, "Well, I'm terribly busy sowing these soybeans right now, so please don't mention it to my wife. She don't get out much. If she hears about it she'll want us to go all three days!"

Today's Comment: Are you prepared for the first resurrection? There are two resurrections, the first one will be when Christians are raised from their graves and those Christians which are alive on earth will be caught up with them and meet the Lord in the air. The second resurrection is when the non-believers are raised and will stand before the Great White Throne judgment.

Which resurrection will you be a part of? If you have received the Lord Jesus Christ as your personal Lord and Savior you will be raised at the first one. The second resurrection is to eternal damnation. If you are not ready for the first resurrection you need to pray right now and invite the Lord to be King on the throne of your life.

Today's Golden Nugget of Truth: "The hour is coming in which all who are in the graves will hear His voice and come forth, those who have done good, to the resurrection of life, and those who have done evil, to the resurrection of condemnation." John 5:28, 29

Today's Philosophical Tidbit: "Our Lord has written the promise of the resurrection, not in books alone, but in every leaf in springtime." Martin Luther

April 4
Lying Compounded

*T*oday's Smile: Teresa was sharing with her friends at the Weight Watchers® meeting. She had worked hard towards her goal and had already lost 23 pounds. She told them that she decided to make her husband and two sons a coconut cream pie. She had not been doing much baking since joining Weight Watchers as she knew a pie would be a big temptation for her. However, she thought that she should not be punishing her family because she was on a diet. So she made the pie and watched her three men consume three quarters of it.

The next morning, Teresa kept looking at the remaining quarter. She wanted to sample it but told herself, "No!" Then she thought that they would never miss a little sliver of the pie. She gave in and took a sliver, and then another sliver. Having made a cup of coffee for herself, she soon realized that she had eaten the remaining quarter. She told her friends at Weight Watchers that she was so upset with her lack of willpower and knew that her husband would be very disappointed with her.

Her friends tried to cheer her up and let her know that most of them had succumbed to the temptation to eat more than they should. Put it behind and move on. Then someone asked, "What did your husband say when he found out?"

She started to laugh and said, "He never found out what I did. I made another pie and ate three quarters of it!"

Today's Comment: We may have committed an act of disobedience which led to a second act of disobedience and third. There may be times in your life when you look back and recall how you committed a sinful act and then lied about it, denying that you did such. One sin often leads to another. Don't you feel a great relief when you confess your sin or sins? The burden has been lifted. The Lord in His mercy is a forgiving God.

No matter how deep we've gone in sin, Christ is waiting to forgive and forget if we will but confess to Him. He will cleanse us. Pray that God will help us refrain from committing that first sin, and the second and the third.

Today's Golden Nugget of Truth: "Be sure your sin will find you out." Numbers 32:23

Today's Philosophical Tidbit: "If you don't avoid the hook, you'll end up on the hook." Dr. James Kennedy

April 5
Evaluating Yourself

Today's Smile: A woman went to her family physician for a check-up. As the nurse was beginning to take her vital statistics, she asked the woman how much she weighed. "I weigh 125 pounds," she said. The nurse pointed to the scale which showed that the woman was 173 pounds.

The nurse asked her if she knew how tall she was and how much she weighted. "I am 5'9". She measured 5'1".

The nurse then took her blood pressure and said, "Your blood pressure is extremely high. It is 168 over 93."

"Well, what do you expect? Of course it is high," said the patient. "When I came in here I was tall and slender and now I am short and fat!"

Today's Comment: There are people who have a great inferiority complex. They are so hard on themselves and say they can't do this or that, etc. Then there are those who are really stuck on themselves. They gloat over all of their accomplishments and love to brag about themselves. When they walk into the room and enter into conversation it is usually what they have done or what they are doing.

Putting ourselves down or exalting ourselves is not what we should be doing. We need to accept ourselves the way God made us. We all have differing gifts and abilities; we are not all the same. We are each fashioned according to God's plan and are special in His eyes. L. E. Maxwell used to say, "After God made you, He threw the pattern away." There is only one you. Pray that we will be that special one that God planned we should be, bringing glory to God our Maker.

Today's Golden Nugget of Truth: "Be honest in your estimate of yourselves, measuring your value by how much faith God has given you." Romans 12:3 (TLB)

Today's Philosophical Tidbit: "Too many people overvalue what they are not, and undervalue what they are." Malcolm Forbes

April 6
God Forgets

*T*oday's Smile: The coffee shop had closed a few minutes earlier. Bill helped the boss count the cash and place it in the safe. He then checked his pockets for his keys but they were not there. A quick search in the shop revealed nothing. Suddenly he figured that he must have left the keys in the car. Frantically he headed for the parking lot. Sure enough, his car was gone. His wife had scolded him many times for leaving the keys in the ignition. Well, once again he did it.

Bill immediately phoned the police and told them what had happened. He gave a description of his car and the license number. He reluctantly phoned wife. "Honey," he stammered. I did it again. I left the keys in the car and the car has been stolen."

There was a slight pause. His wife said, "Bill, have you forgotten that I dropped you off at work?"

"Oh, I forgot. I'm sorry. Honey, will you please come and pick me up?"

"Yes, dear, but I may be a few moments because I may have to convince the police that I have not stolen your car."

Today's Comment: Though I am in my 80's, I still have a fairly good memory. There are times when I may not be able to recall some names; I've forgotten to pick up that jug of milk on the way home, or make a phone call. However, I take courage when some that are younger than me tend to have a bit of a problem remembering things.

I am thankful that God has promised to remember, but He has also promised to forget. The Bible has many examples where God remembers. He remembered Noah. He remembered His covenant with Israel. He remembered Hannah, etc. He says in Isaiah 49:15 "Surely they may forget, yet I will not forget you."

However, He also says He will not remember. He will not remember our sins. How encouraging. He forgets them. Someone may remind us of wrong doings, but God will forget them. So take courage. As a child of God we have a great future. Pray that we will not dwell on past sins and failures. Let's forget them. God has forgiven us and He forgets them.

Today's Golden Nugget of Truth: "Their sins and their lawless deeds I will remember no more." Hebrews 10:17

Today's Philosophical Tidbit: "If God were not willing to forgive us, heaven would be empty." Author Unknown

April 7
Encouraging One Another

Today's Smile: A young widow and her three small children were staying away from Sunday School at a small Community Church. They had been quite regular in their attendance, but had not attended for a long time. So some of the ladies from the church visited the home to find out why this family was not attending. They discovered that the children did not have any decent clothes and the mother was too embarrassed to send them. So the ladies group quickly took care of that problem providing the family with some nice new clothes.

After a month or so when the children had still not shown up for Sunday School, these ladies contacted the family again to see why they had not been coming. The mother very sweetly thanked them for the clothing and said, "The girls looked so nice in their new clothes that I decided to send them to the Presbyterian Church Sunday School."

Today's Comment: Do we express our appreciation and thanks for those gifts and acts of kindness that people do for us? I sometimes wonder how many times has there been when I failed to thank a giver for their tokens of love and their kind acts. I hope that I have not failed in this area too many times.

When I was a senior pastor, I did what several pastor friends did, I had a little card printed and placed in the church pews entitled *Encouragement Card*. It was blank except for the name of the church together with the words from Hebrews 10:25 "Encouraging one another." Our members used these cards, as they were prompted by the Spirit, to write a note and give to a fellow member. I have kept many of those cards that I received and they still give me a lift. If you write a note to a brother or sister in Christ, pray that it will be a great encouragement to them.

Today's Golden Nugget of Truth: "And one of them, when he saw that he was healed. . . fell down on his face at His feet, giving Him thanks. . . Jesus answered and said, 'Were there not ten cleansed? But where are the nine'?" Luke 17:15-17

Today's Philosophical Tidbit: "Thankfulness could well be the finest sentiment of man, and also the rarest." Author Unknown

April 8
It Pays To Advertise

Today's Smile: The Bishop contacted the rector of All Saints Church and said that he would be in that area in a couple weeks time and would like to preach on the Sunday morning. When the appointed Sunday arrived, the bishop led in the Bible readings and delivered his sermon. Only five people showed up for the morning service. After the service, the bishop asked the rector whether he had advertised that he would be coming.

"No," said the Rector, "I forgot, but it seems like the word got out."

Today's Comment: The smallest audience that I ever preached to was in the Muskoka region of Ontario. For a few days, just prior to assuming my first pastoral ministry in Alberta, I was at Pioneer Camp in the Muskoka Lakes area. One of the leaders at the camp asked if I would preach at a small country church on the Sunday afternoon. I agreed to do so.

I arrived before anyone else did. When the first couple showed up, I asked the man who would be leading the meeting, making the announcements, etc. All my questions were answered and we waited for the people to arrive. We waited, and waited. Finally, he said to me, "I don't think anyone else is coming, so we had better start." Well, we didn't sing any hymns. There were just the three of us. As this couple sat in the first or second pew, I stepped over close and shared a few scriptures and thoughts, and had prayer with them.

That church probably didn't advertise. Many churches don't. I always did. I used the newspapers to advertise our church services, and in two pastoral ministries, the church printed a four page tabloid newspaper that was distributed to thousands of homes in the area of our church. So whether your church advertises in newspapers, radio, etc., the best advertising is what parishioners do. Those involved with some of the great evangelistic crusades have told us that a high percentage of people that have received Christ at their meetings have come because an individual invited them.

Pray that our lives will advertise to the world that a personal relationship with God is what they need.

Today's Golden Nugget of Truth: "Be ready to give a defense to everyone who asks you a reason for the hope that is in you." First Peter 3:15

Today's Philosophical Tidbit: "You have been saved out of the world and then sent back into the world to witness to the world, and that's the only business in the world you have in the world, till you're taken out of the world." Adrian Rogers

April 9
Coming And Going

*T**oday's Smile:* As the Jones family was leaving church, little Danny asked his mom and dad if he could go back and talk with the pastor. "Why sure, Danny, we'll just wait here in the car for you."

The pastor was still shaking hands with the last of the parishioners. Danny patiently waited. When the pastor saw him he asked, "What can I do for you Danny?"

"I was listening to you preach this morning and you told us that our bodies were made from dust."

"That's what I said," responded the pastor.

"And you also said that when we die our bodies go back to dust."

"That's what the Bible teaches us," said the pastor.

"Well pastor," said Danny, "I think that you should come over to our house this afternoon and look under my bed. There is a lot of dust there and I think maybe someone is either coming or going."

Today's Comment: We may smile when we hear what young children comprehend or what they take in from what we teach or preach. However, one thing for sure, every day people are coming or going. They are being born and they are dying. The statistics which I read at the time of this writing stated that in a given day, worldwide, there are approximately 353,000 births and 153,000 deaths. Dr. A.B. Simpson wrote the words to the hymn *A Missionary Cry*. The first few lines of stanza one says: "A hundred thousand souls a day are passing one by one away in Christless guilt and gloom. . ."

We have a message for all ages. It is that Jesus Christ is the Way and all men everywhere need to hear this message, turning from their sin and receiving Christ as their personal Lord and Savior. It's been a joy and privilege to lead young children to Christ, along with youth, middle age, and the elderly, people of all ages. People are coming and going. Pray that we will do our best to share God's truths with them while they are with us.

Today's Golden Nugget of Truth: "I am the way, the truth, and the life. No one comes to the Father except through Me." John 14:6

Today's Philosophical Tidbit: "Jesus is not one of many ways to approach God, nor is He the best of several ways, He is the only way." A. W. Tozer

April 10
Watch Where You Walk

*T*oday's Smile: It was Easter Sunday morning. The morning service began in the little country church with the choir entering from the back of the church marching in perfect step down the centre aisle to the front of the church. The last lady choir member was wearing 5 inch spike high heel shoes. She had forgotten about the hot air register in the middle of the aisle. The heel of one shoe sank into a hole in the register. She realized her predicament. Not wanting to stop the processional, and without missing a step, she slipped her foot out of her shoe and continued to march down the aisle.

The processional continued with clock like precision. The first man following the lady saw her shoe firmly imbedded in the grate, bent over, picked up her shoe but the grate came with it. Still singing, and in step with the rest of the choir he kept walking down the aisle, holding the shoe and the grate.

Everything was still moving like clockwork, the choir still singing, and every member in step. The person behind the man with the shoe and the grate was the youngest member of the choir, a small 12 year old boy. He stepped into the open register and disappeared.

As the choir ended with "Allelujah, Christ arose" a voice was heard shouting, "I'm coming up!"

Today's Comment: One comment could be about the wisdom of wearing five inch spike heels when you are going to be in a processional. The other comment is watch where you're walking. Of greater importance than watching that we don't collide with another person, or fall through a hole, is to take note of our spiritual walk. If we are not careful how and where we walk, we can easily wander off of the spiritual pathway which God would have us walk.

An anonymous author has written five guidelines for walking in step with God. They are: "(1) Give God the first hour of every day. (2) Give God the first day of every week. (3) Give God the first consideration in every decision. (4) Give God the first portion of all your income. (5) Give God's Son, Jesus Christ the first place in your heart." Pray that these five points may be guideposts in our spiritual journey.

Today's Golden Nugget of Truth: "Walk in the Spirit, and you shall not fulfill the lust of the flesh." Galatians 5:16

Today's Philosophical Tidbit: "The Christian walk is much like riding a bicycle, we are either moving forward or falling off." Robert Tuttle

April 11
A Volunteer For Jesus

*T**oday's Smile:* One day a florist went to Billy's Barbershop for a haircut. As he was opening his wallet, Billy the barber said to the florist, "The haircut is free today. I am doing community service all this week." The next morning when Billy arrived at his shop, there by the front door was a dozen roses, a gift from the florist.

The next day, Billy cut a policeman's hair. He pulled out a twenty and Billy said, "No my friend, today's haircut is on me. I'm doing community service all this week." The next morning Billy found a box with a dozen donuts awaiting him, a gift from his officer friend.

A senator came in for a haircut. Before he could find his wallet, Billy said, "Mr. Senator, never mind finding your wallet, this week's haircuts are free. I am doing community service."

The Senator was very pleased with his free haircut. Billy arrived at his shop, the last day he was giving free haircuts and there lined up waiting for free haircuts were seventeen senators.

Today's Comment: Have you been the recipient of a friend or neighbor's kindness? Did they shovel the snow off of your sidewalk this past winter? Are they cutting your grass? What about the numerous times that they have given you a ride to church, or brought food to you when you were sick? There are many people that go out of their way to help a friend or fellow church member. Have we remembered to thank them? Too many good Samaritans are simply taken for granted.

Today may be the day to show some appreciation and thanks to that special person that helped you when you were in need. Pray that you will be guided as to who you should help today.

Today's Golden Nugget of Truth: "But encourage one another daily, as long as it is called today. . ." Hebrews 3:13 (NIV)

Today's Philosophical Tidbit: "Appreciation can make a day, even change a life. Your willingness to put it into words is all that is necessary." Margaret Cousins

April 12
Thankful For Health Care

oday's Smile: A mechanic was removing a cylinder head from the motor of a Harley motorcycle when he spotted a well known heart surgeon in his shop. The surgeon was there waiting for the service manager to come take a look at his bike. The mechanic shouted across the garage, "Hey Doc, may I ask you a question?"

The surgeon, a bit surprised, walked over to the mechanic working on the motorcycle. The mechanic straightened up, wiped his hands on a rag and asked, "So Doc, look at this engine. I open its heart, take valves out, fix'em, put'em back in, and when I finish, it works just like new. So how come I get such a small salary and you get the really big bucks when you and I are doing basically the same work?"

The surgeon paused, smiled and leaned over, and whispered to the mechanic. "Try doing it with the engine running!"

Today's Comment: Have you ever been a patient in a hospital? Had surgery? I've been hospitalized several times in the last twenty years and had surgery four times. I am so thankful for the medical care of which I have been the recipient. I often think of the millions of people suffering in other lands, where they do not have a hospital and oft times no clinic close by. I heard on the six o'clock news just tonight of a clinic in Sierra Leone that said they do not have the medical supplies to treat their sick.

In our western world, we have much to be thankful for when it comes to medical care. Unlike a mechanic, surgeons do their work while we are alive, even if they need some medical equipment to keep us alive.

So, if we are prone to criticize our medical profession or hospitals or having to wait in emergency or for a surgery, we need to stop a moment and remember those who are not as fortunate as we are. Let us pray for them, but also for the medical missionaries that serve and seek to help the millions in other lands. Let's be thankful for what we do have.

Today's Golden Nugget of Truth: "In everything give thanks, for this is the will of God in Christ Jesus for you." First Thessalonians 5:18

Today's Philosophical Tidbit: "Feeling better has become more important to us than finding God." Larry Crabb

April 13
Fountain Of Youth

*T*oday's Smile: Gus and Mandy were getting on in years. They had recently celebrated their 60th wedding anniversary, but they realized that their strength was long gone compared to what they had the day that they were first married. Mandy was beginning to worry more about Gus. He could only walk a short distance with his walker and then he would have to sit for a couple of moments. He had lost all spunk.

Mandy shared with her neighbor lady about her concern for Gus. Victoria, the neighbor, said, "I think I know what you guys should try. One of the couples in our care group at church learned about a new multi-level program. They sell a product called 'Fountain of Youth.' They told us that they have been taking it for about a month and already noticed a big change. Why don't I see if I can get a bottle of the pills for you?"

Victoria had them within a couple of days and gave them to Gus and Mandy. That evening before going to bed, Gus took six of them with a glass of milk. He figured a stronger dose than that recommended should show some signs of making one feel younger faster than just taking one pill.

When Mandy woke up in the morning, Gus was not in bed. She looked in every room in the house and she could not find him. She decided to go outside and see if he was there. She eventually spotted him sitting on the curb at the side of the road. When she got near to him she noticed that he was crying. "What's the matter Gus? Why are you crying?"

Gus responded through his tears, "I missed my school bus!"

Today's Comment: You may wish that you could roll back the years and go back to that point in time when you had a little more energy and could do more than you do today. There are vitamins and energy boosting products that help a bit. However, we need to face it, no matter how old we are, we are all getting older one day at a time so there is little that we can do about it. We cannot stop the clock. So let us make sure that we value every day that we have and that we use it wisely.

Oh, yes and let's make sure that we are prepared for that day when our life on earth will end. What then? Have you committed your life to the Lord Jesus Christ? In Him alone is there life eternal, an everlasting fountain of youth. If you have never received Him, He is only a prayer away.

Today's Golden Nugget of Truth: "For with You is the fountain of life." Psalm 36:9

Today's Philosophical Tidbit: "Many school class reunions today resemble a geriatric convention." A. Daniel Goldsmith

April 14
The Fragrance Of God

Today's Smile: Charlotte dutifully prepared a big breakfast for her husband and two teenage sons. When that was all finished, she then got ready to drive off to a nearby elementary school where she taught a grade three class. This particular morning when she arrived at school, an eight year old boy followed her into the room. He watched as she readied her supplies for the day. "You sure smell good today, Mrs. Black," he said.

"Why thanks, Bobby," she replied, trying to remember which perfume she had squirted on before leaving the house.

"Yeah, you smell like bacon!"

Today's Comment: Do we smell good? I am not referring to perfume or after shave lotion. As followers of God do we have a fragrant aroma? There are fellow believers that we delight to be with. They are sweet, loving and have a positive and bright outlook. They exude the fragrance of God. There are others, who profess to be "born again believers," who, to put it bluntly, "stink!"

Pray that as we interact with people today that they may be attracted to our blessed Lord and Saviour Jesus Christ. Why? Because we smell like God!

Today's Golden Nugget of Truth: "For we are to God the fragrance of Christ among those who are being saved and among those who are perishing." Second Corinthians 2:15

Today's Philosophical Tidbit: "It is impossible to have the fragrance of Christ when we have been playing in Satan's cesspool." A. Daniel Goldsmith

April 15
Be Brief Brother Be Brief

*T**oday's Smile:* Lorin raised cattle on the western plains and was always trying to improve his herd. One day he saw a poster advertising a large livestock auction in nearby Columbus, Nebraska. He was looking for a real good bull to improve his stock and decided to make the 75 mile trip to Columbus. He thought maybe he would ride the bus to Columbus and visit his aging mother for a couple of days. So he told his hired man Jason that if he found the right bull that he would send a telegram to him so Jason could then drive the truck in to pick him up bringing the bull back with them.

Lorin had never sent a telegram before. So he wrote out his message and gave it to the telegraph operator. He wrote, "Jason I bought the perfect bull. It is guaranteed to produce more live calves than the one that we have now. Come as soon as you can and meet me at my mother's. We can then go to the auction yard and pick up the bull. Hopefully you will be here tomorrow."

The telegraph operator told Lorin that he should limit his telegram to ten words or less. "O.K," said Lorin, "I'll just use one word. Write *comfortable.*"

Today's Comment: Now if you didn't get the punch line, read that last word slowly com-for-ta-ble. Probably some of you have never seen a telegram. It was a popular means of communicating messages dating back as far as the mid 1800's. The cheapest telegram was ten words or less.

It was Dwight Moody, the famed evangelist of the 19th century who was asked by a man as Mr. Moody was boarding a train, "What must I do to be saved?" Moody had but a few seconds to answer. He said, "Go home and read Isaiah 53:6. Go in at the first 'all' and come out at the last 'all'." That verse says: "*All* we like sheep have gone astray; we have turned every one to his own way; and the Lord hath laid on Him the iniquity of us *all.*"

My friend Paul, who was a school superintendent, told us that his wife Rose had five words of advice for him whenever he was to give a speech. Those words, today's title, were "Be brief brother, be brief." Pray today that we all can get to the point, whether we're preaching, teaching or simply sharing with another.

Today's Golden Nugget of Truth: "When words are many, sin is not absent, but he who holds his tongue is wise." Proverbs 10:19 (NIV)

Today's Philosophical Tidbit: "We have a head on us for the same reason a pin has - to keep us from going too far." Author Unknown

April 16
God Is With Us In The Detours

Today's Smile: A fire started in some grassland in Southern Saskatchewan. The fire department from the closest town was called to the farm, but the fire was more than they could handle. The chief put through an emergency call to a neighboring hamlet that had a volunteer fire department. Some of the firefighters didn't think that their neighbors would be able to help much, but the chief had already made the call.

The small neighboring volunteer department arrived in a run down old fire truck. These volunteers drove straight towards the fire and stopped in the middle of the flames. They jumped off of their truck and frantically began spraying water all over the place. In a matter of moments they had the flames doused.

The farmer was so impressed with this volunteer fire department's work and so grateful that his farm had been spared, that he presented the volunteer fire department with a check for $3,000.00.

A local news reporter asked the volunteer fire captain what the department planned to do with the money. The captain responded by saying, "Well, I hope it was obvious. The first thing that we are going to do is get the brakes fixed on that stupid old truck."

Today's Comment: Interesting that when things go wrong and don't work the way we want, that they often turn out for our good. How often have you looked back on some breakdown, or a situation, which, at the time, you wondered if God was looking the other way? Maybe you lost your job, but you got a better one. Maybe a boyfriend dropped you, but you met the man of your dreams. Maybe you didn't get that promotion, but then neither were you blamed for the downturn in the business. It pays to remember that God has a plan for our life, even when some of the detours take us through what we see as a big storm or a fire.

Let's pray that we will not be complaining or be bitter towards God when the unexpected and unwanted happens to us. May we remember that God knows what He is doing, even if we don't.

Today's Golden Nugget of Truth: "And we know that all things work together for good to those who love God, to those who are the called according to His purpose." Romans 8:28

Today's Philosophical Tidbit: "God may be doing His greatest work when evil seems to triumph." Author Unknown

April 17
I'd Rather Have Jesus

*T*oday's Smile: Warren and June were madly in love. They had met in their junior year in college and had been seeing one another almost every weekend since. Warren was very vocal about his love for June. He had a diamond on lay away and was making weekly payments, hoping that he could surprise her with the same on the night of their graduation.

They were faithful in their church attendance, and if their schedules did not allow them to meet on a Friday night or Saturday, they were always seated together in church. One Sunday morning, when Warren should have been listening to the pastor's sermon, he was thinking of June. He started thumbing through the hymnal and on page 638 he saw the title, *I Need Thee Every Hour.* He slipped the book on to June's lap and pointed to the same.

June took the book and searched until she found the appropriate response. She turned back to page 506 and handed it to him. Then she pointed out the hymn *I'd Rather Have Jesus.*

Today's Comment: Is the Lord Jesus Christ our first love? The Bible teaches us that God should be first in our lives. All too often we have our priorities mixed up. Sometimes a girl friend is number one, or with some workaholics their business and making money takes the top spot. I am not alone in saying that our priorities should be God first, spouse second, children third and work or ministry fourth.

A pastor friend shared at a pastor's retreat how he realized that his ministry, even preparing sermons, was a high priority so that he had spent very little time alone with God. He wrote about God, talked about God, but seldom talked or listened to God. It is so easy to be busy about God's business and yet not have time for God. Pray that we might have our priorities in the right order?

Today's Golden Nugget of Truth: "But seek first the kingdom of God and His righteousness, and all these things shall be added to you." Matthew 6:33

Today's Philosophical Tidbit: "Don't allow the tyranny of the urgent to blind you to the value of the important." Author Unknown

April 18
I'll Do It For Nothing

*T**oday's Smile:* A fairly well-to-do rancher was impressed with the Christian College that was in his town. Many of the students attended the same church as he did and they were a great bunch of young people. The college was building a new chapel so he decided that he would like to make a donation. He was a free and easy sort of guy and dearly loved by all. His one problem was that he had his own unique sense of humor which was often misunderstood.

One day he stopped by the college and went in desiring to talk with the president. True to his style, he asked the president's secretary if the head hog was at the trough. The president's secretary was taken aback. "Please sir, do not refer to our esteemed president as the head hog at the trough. I think that is very insulting. We refer to him as Dr. John Fox. If you want to see him you need to make an appointment."

"I am very sorry ma'am. I was in town today and I was hoping that I could talk with your president today as I had intended to give him $50,000.00 towards the building of your new chapel."

"Hold on a moment, sir, I see the Big Oinker coming down the hall right now."

Today's Comment: We've all heard it said that "money talks." Surveys have stated that many women are attracted to men by their wealth. Many people like to become friends with people with money. There was a time when volunteers in a community or church were just that, volunteers. Today, it seems that more and more people will offer to help out with a task or ministry if they receive a little money for the same. Are we willing to pitch in and do our part without remuneration?

Thank God for all of those who regularly volunteer and serve cheerfully without any thought of being reimbursed for their service. Maybe it is the janitor in your small church, the choir leader, organist, pianist, Sunday School teacher, youth workers, etc. Let's pray for them today. One or more of them may be feeling a little down or discouraged. Pray that their spirits will be lifted.

Today's Golden Nugget of Truth: "We give thanks to God always for you all, making mention of you in our prayers, remembering without ceasing your work of faith, labor of love..." First Thessalonians 1:2, 3

Today's Philosophical Tidbit: "There are many of us that are willing to do great things for the Lord but few of us are willing to do little things." D. L. Moody

April 19
Get To The Point

T oday's Smile: An eccentric philosophy professor gave a one question final exam after a semester dealing with a broad array of topics. The class was already seated and ready to go when the professor picked up his chair, plopped it on his desk and wrote on the board: "Using everything that you have learned this semester, prove that this chair does not exist."

Fingers flew, erasers erased, pages were filled in furious fashion. Some students wrote over 10 and 12 pages in one hour attempting to refute the existence of the chair. One member of the class, Murray, was up and finished in less than a minute.

A few days later when the grades were posted, some of his classmates asked Murray how he could have received an "A" when he had barely written anything at all.

Murray's answer consisted of two words: "What chair?"

Today's Comment: The wordiest answers and longest speeches do not always get to the point. Such detail often blurs the issue and leaves many wondering just what was said. I knew a pastor several decades ago who was a master at long introductions. He would sometimes take up to fifteen minutes on his introduction. He didn't leave much time for the body of the message. In addressing a subject or in conversation, get to the point.

Sir Winston Churchill made his point when speaking to the Harrow School in October 1941, a boarding school which he attended when he was a young boy. There is far more to his speech than three words, as is so often stated. However, he is remembered for those three words: "Never give in!" He made his point. "Never give in, never give in, never, never, never, never in nothing, great or small, large or petty, never give in. . ."

Pray that we won't take for ever to get our message across. If we take too long, the mind of the hearer(s) may wander off into space.

Today's Golden Nugget of Truth: "I may be unskilled as a speaker, but I'm not lacking in knowledge. We have made this clear to you in every possible way." Second Corinthians 11:6 (NLT)

Today's Philosophical Tidbit: "If you would be pungent, be brief; for it is with words as with sunbeams, the more they are condensed, the deeper they burn." Robert Southey

April 20
Financial Rip-Off

*T**oday's Smile:* Young Reggie overheard his father talking to his mother and said, "We are broke. We have no money." Reggie had been raised in a Christian home, taken to Sunday School and church knowing that God was a loving and caring God. So he sat down writing a letter.

He wrote, "Dear God: My daddy is out of work, my mommy is sick, my little brother fell down the stairs and broke his arm and we have no money for the doctor, and we don't have any money for the rent or for food. Would you please send us $100.00? Thank you, God." Signed: Reggie

The letter, which was simply addressed to God ended up in the dead letter office. The postal worker showed it to his boss, and they decided that they would each put $5.00 in a letter and send it to the young boy. When the boy received the letter, he found two five dollar bills in the letter. He wrote another letter, addressed to God. "Dear God: Thank you for sending the hundred dollars, but next time, please don't send it through Washington, they kept $90.00."

Today's Comment: Well I doubt that Washington, Ottawa, London, Canberra, Wellington or any other capital is going to deduct that much from any donation. They all take a slice of the money you make before you give, but not 90%. Your donation is paid with "after-tax" dollars. However, there are charitable organizations that do take a good chunk of money for salaries and the organization, and non-essentials. You need to check out the organization that you desire to give, making certain that a large percentage of your donation goes to the intended purpose for which you gave.

I recall when I was in my teens and early twenties working at a radio station, that we aired a national religious broadcast where the radio preacher was known to take better than 50% for himself. He stated in his defence that if he took in one hundred thousand dollars and only twenty-five thousand of that went towards the ministry, that the ministry received twenty-five thousand that they would not have received had he not been on the radio. What faulty reasoning.

There are many ministries that are above board willing to make available their financial statement. You can see for yourself where your giving is going. I am sure that you want to be a good steward of what God has entrusted to you. It is impossible to give to every mission or charity. Pray for wisdom as to where you give your money.

Today's Golden Nugget of Truth: "And now I make one more appeal, my dear brothers and sisters. Watch out for people who cause divisions and upset people's faith by teachings things contrary to what you have been taught. Stay away from them. Such people are not serving Christ our Lord; they are serving their own personal interests. . ." Romans 16:17, 18 (NLT)

Today's Philosophical Tidbit: "Beware of the poor little lamb that cries for help, but is a wolf in sheep's clothing." A. Daniel Goldsmith

April 21
Missing An Appointment

*T**oday's Smile:* Ethan and Dawson went to the train station with their friend. Since they were informed that the train was going to be late, the three of them decided to go into the coffee shop and have a light lunch. They talked of old times, sipped away at their coffee while eating their sandwiches.

They were so involved in their conversation that they only heard the final call that the train was about to depart. The three of them got up and started running. When they reached the train, it started to move. The three of them ran alongside of the train and Ethan and Dawson managed to get on the last car. Meanwhile their friend didn't make it. He stopped running and doubled over with laughter. A bystander seeing him laughing uncontrollably asked, "Why are you laughing so hard? You just missed your train."

"That's right," he said, between his laughs. "I did miss my train. What's so crazy is those two friends who caught the train came to the station to see me off."

Today's Comment: You've probably never experienced what these three friends did. However, you may have taken food to your care group when it wasn't your turn, or forgot to bring food when it was your turn. Something similar has happened to most of us. We've turned up at an appointment, only to have the wrong week, or we failed to show up when we did have an appointment. Reminds me of the woman who phoned the newspaper office and complained that the paper boy had not left her Sunday paper. "Sorry, lady," said the receptionist, "today is Saturday not Sunday."

"Oh," said the caller, "that explains why there was no one at church this morning."

Keeping appointments is important. My wife and I each have our own day timer and frequently compare dates to ensure that we both have the same dates written in our book. Do you keep your appointment with God; a devotional time, Bible reading and prayer? You may not have them written on a calendar or in a book, but hopefully they are inscribed in your mind. Pray that we will all be faithful in our daily meeting with our God.

Today's Golden Nugget of Truth: "Then they rose early in the morning and worshiped before the Lord. . ." First Samuel 1:19

Today's Philosophical Tidbit: "Prayer is the key of the morning and the bolt of the evening." Matthew Henry

April 22
Do Not Retaliate

oday's Smile: A state trooper was rushed to the municipal hospital with a ruptured appendix. Surgery was performed that same day. The next morning the surgeon assured the trooper that all had gone well, and that his stay in hospital would only be for another day or so.

Later in the day the state trooper was experiencing pain in his chest. It felt like someone was trying to pull the hair off of his chest. He was worried that maybe he had another problem that the doctor had not shared. He mustered up the strength and courage to pull his hospital gown down far enough so that he could see what was making him so uncomfortable.

Taped firmly across his hairy chest were three wide strips of adhesive tape. Written in large block letters were these words: "Get well soon! From the nurse that you gave a speeding ticket to last week."

Today's Comment: Have you ever had that feeling when you would like to give some one "a piece of your mind?" I must confess that I have written several letters in my head, especially in bed at night. The next morning, when I re-thought what I wanted to put on paper, it didn't seem to be such a big issue. Having given it some rational thought in the morning, I felt it was better left unsaid.

We should pray and give such things time and thought. It is not worth the hassle and hurt feelings that could result. God will work it out His way, and in His time.

Today's Golden Nugget of Truth: "Dear friends, never avenge your-selves, leave that to God, for He has said that He will repay those who deserve it. Don't take the law into your own hands." Romans 12:19 (TLB)

Today's Philosophical Tidbit: "One of the surest marks of good character is a man's ability to accept personal criticism without feeling malice toward the one who gives it." Author Unknown

April 23
How Determined Are We

*T*oday's Smile: Eddie had been hired as a janitor for a local clothing manufacturer. He was punctual and had never ever been late for work. He was very meticulous and kept his area looking spotless. However, the president of the company discovered after a few months that Eddie could neither read nor write. So he fired him.

Eddie took his few dollars that he had saved and bought a mobile popcorn stand. He parked his stand near one of the city parks. He did well. He made an exceptionally good bag of popcorn and sold it at a very reasonable price. He soon had enough money for a second stand. He paid one of his sons to work evenings and weekends. The son did well, and soon Eddie had a third popcorn stand and a fourth and a fifth. In a matter of four years he managed to own and staff fifty popcorn stands in various parts of the city.

One day the bank manager called him into his office and complimented him on the successful business that he had built. In the course of their conversation, the bank manager said to Eddie, "You've done extremely well for an illiterate person, but did you ever think where you would be if you had learned to read and write?"

"Yes," said Eddie, "I've thought of that often over the last couple of years. I would still be doing janitor work over at the clothing factory."

Today's Comment: History tells of many people who did not have a lot of formal education, but with hard work and determination, accomplished what they did and are remembered for their achievements. A couple of examples are George Washington, the first president of the United States, who had no formal college education. Thomas Edison, known for his inventions of the phonograph, microphone, light bulb and many more, had very little formal education. He was self taught. G. Campbell Morgan, a British evangelist, preacher and leading Bible scholar had no formal training for the ministry, yet he preached 23,390 sermons and wrote over seventy books. So don't let lack of education hinder you. Pray that you will live up to your full potential, whether you have several earned degrees or none.

Today's Golden Nugget of Truth: "God chose things the world considers foolish in order to shame those who think they are wise. And He chose things that are powerless to shame those who are powerful." First Corinthians 1:27, 28 (NLT)

Today's Philosophical Tidbit: "Don't give up when you still have something to give. Nothing is really over until the moment you stop trying." Author Unknown

April 24
Taken Out Of Context

Today's Smile: Randy and Allison set a goal, early in their marriage, of someday owning a house in the country. Once they made their final payment for their small acreage they began to build their dream house, as funds were available. The two of them, with some occasional help from a few family members and friends, spent many of their days off, plus vacation days, seeing their house take shape.

After moving into their house, they started to replace the furniture that they had purchased from thrift stores. The day came when the last piece of new furniture, a bedroom suite, arrived.

As Allison opened the door to the two men delivering the same, she excitedly exclaimed, "Finally! I've been waiting for this for eleven years."

One of the men looked at her a bit perplexed and said, "Ma'am, please don't blame us, we only got this order this morning."

Today's Comment: In our excitement we sometimes say things that can be taken out of context and misunderstood by others. You are thinking one thing and your listener is thinking something else in an entirely different context.

This happens often at my age. My wife may tell me something about John. However, I know so many fellows with the name John. I have a son-in-law named John. In one church where I was senior pastor, out of an elder's board of seven men, four of them were named John. If the speaker and the listener are not thinking about the same person, things can surely get mixed up.

There are more serious things then thinking about a different person. The point I want to make is that we wonder how what we say, will sound in a listener's ear. It's like the old story about the barber who, as he was sharpening his razor and desirous of sharing the gospel with his customer, asked him, "Are you ready to die?" If one didn't know what the barber had in his mind one might have jumped from the chair and run away.

Pray that we will be tactful in all of our communicating.

Today's Golden Nugget of Truth: "He who answers a matter before he hears it, it is folly and shame to him." Proverbs 18:13

Today's Philosophical Tidbit: "Wisdom is knowing when to speak your mind and when to mind your speech." Author Unknown

April 25
Take A Short Cut

*T*oday's Smile: Mikala had just graduated from high school, secured her driver's license and had earned enough money to buy herself a car. Since her Dad did not want her wrecking the family car, her older brother had taught her how to drive on an old stick shift car, which had been sitting idle on the family farm for a few years.

She was now the proud owner of a four year old Hyundai Accent. She loved the automatic transmission and found that driving the car during daytime that it worked like a charm. However, once the sun had set and it got dark, it would not move. So as soon as the dealer was open in the morning she drove there and explained to him that the car did not work at night. The mechanic gave it a thorough inspection and told Mikala that he could see absolutely no mechanical problem. "Are you sure that you are using the right gears?" he asked.

"Of course, I'm using the right gears. During the day I use the "D" gear and at night I use the "N" gear.

Today's Comment: Texting is a very popular way of communicating messages. It is a phenomenon which has grown rapidly. I bought a smart phone a few years ago so that I could keep in touch with my children and grandchildren. In sending "texts" we use abbreviations.

If we have been talking about day and night, it is possible that rather than repeat the words we might use "D" and "N." We have become so accustomed to abbreviations, short cuts, acrostics and more. However, there are no short cuts to spiritual growth.

I remember a radio pastor who used to advertise his devotional book which was called *Daily Meditations For Busy People*. Are we too busy to take time to pray, to read God's Word? The spiritual life is a walk. It is a time of growth. When we think of our physical life, we don't go from infancy to adulthood in a few minutes. There is no short cut to becoming a mature adult. Likewise, it takes time to grow into a mature spiritual adult. Pray that you will grow in the Lord by digesting spiritual food and exercising your spiritual gifts.

Today's Golden Nugget of Truth: "Therefore, leaving the discussion of the elementary principles of the elementary principles of Christ, let us go on to perfection, not laying again the foundation of repentance from dead works and of faith toward God." Hebrews 6:1

Today's Philosophical Tidbit: "You never graduate from growth." Author Unknown

April 26
Leaving A Legacy

Today's Smile: Billy Frank was the youngest of four children. One warm Alabama spring morning when his siblings were in school he went for a walk with his grandmother. As they walked along enjoying the sunshine, Billy Frank picked up something off of the ground and started to put it in his mouth.

"Don't do that Billy Frank," said his grandmother.

"Why?" asked Billy Frank.

"Because it's been on the ground and it's dirty, probably has some germs on it and you have no idea where it came from," said his grandmother.

Billy Frank looked at his grandmother in response to her comments, and asked "Grandma how come you know all this stuff?"

His grandma turned to him and said with a smile, "Grandmas know all kinds of stuff. It's on the Grandma Test. You have to know all kinds of things or they won't let you become a Grandma."

The two of them walked along in silence for a minute or two. Evidently Billy Frank was pondering this new bit of information. Suddenly, he turned to his grandmother and said, "Oh, I get it!" he beamed. "So if you don't pass the Grandma Test you have be the Grandpa."

Today's Comment: I am married to a grandmother and I know that she didn't have to write any Grandma Test. The way she became a grandmother and I became a grandfather was that we had children who had children. Many of you reading this are probably grandparents, maybe even great grandparents. Would you agree with me that it is a wonderful stage of life?

Our five grandsons are beyond the infant stage. They are in their teens and twenties. Our oldest grandson is married. However, I remember those years when if they cried or needed some attention, I could simply hand them off to their parents.

As grandparents let's pray for our grandchildren, let's encourage them, and let's model Christ before them. We live in a society that is becoming more and more godless; more secular all the time. Grandchildren need to see that as we near the end of our years, that we have a faith in God that transcends all of the fame and fortune that the world offers.

Pray that we, who are grandparents, pass the grandparents test when it comes to being godly grandparents.

Today's Golden Nugget of Truth: "When I call to remembrance the genuine faith that is in you, which dwelt first in your grandmother Lois and your mother Eunice, and I am persuaded is in you also." Second Timothy 1:5

Today's Philosophical Tidbit: "The duties of Godly grandparenthood falls into four roles: giving a blessing; leaving a legacy; bearing a torch, and setting a standard." Dr. Tim Kimmel

April 27
Children Are A Gift From God

Today's Smile: Michael and Maria had been married for seven years before they had a child. They shared with Evan and Tiffany, who were childless, how Michael had gone to Rome and lit a candle and within a year they had a boy. Evan and Tiffany thought maybe it would be worth a try. So Evan made the trip, by himself, and lit two candles hoping that maybe they could have two children.

Within fourteen months, they had twin girls, a year later they had a son, two years later they had another daughter, and two years later they had triplets. Michael and Maria, who had moved to the west coast soon after their friends had their twin girls, came back for a visit. When they arrived Tiffany was worn to a frazzle trying to manage her brood of seven children, all born within five years. Maria, who had had her hands full raising one child, said, "You shouldn't be trying to look after all these children by yourself. Evan should get you a nanny or someone to help you. Where is he, at work?"

"No, he's not at work. He took the week off. He's in Europe."

"Europe!" exclaimed Maria, "this is no time for a vacation. He should be here helping you."

"Oh he's not on vacation," said Tiffany, "he flew to Rome a couple of days ago. He's gone to blow out the candles."

Today's Comment: I'm certain that lighting a candle half a world away is no guarantee that you'll have a family. Some childless couples have adopted. Others have received medical help and had a child. Some have had pastors, elders and care groups surround them in prayer and have had a child. Other couples have also had medical help and/or prayer, but they did not have a family. You may ask why. I have no answer as to why some had a family and some didn't. God alone has the answer. I can say this though, if God has blessed you with children, love them and bring them up to fear the Lord. If you do not have children you may have a Sunday School class or you're club leader. You may have nieces and nephews. Love them. Seek to help them. Maybe you would choose to sponsor a needy child in some far off land, and correspond with them. There are millions of children in this world that need someone to love them and pray for them. You may be that one.

Today's Golden Nugget of Truth: "Take heed that you do not despise one of these little ones, for I say to you that in heaven their angels always see the face of My Father who is I heaven." Matthew 18:10

Today's Philosophical Tidbit: "If we paid no more attention to our plants than to our children, we would now be living in a jungle of weeds." Luther Burbank

April 28
A Spirit Controlled Life

Today's Smile: Don stopped at Wendy's® and bought a coffee and a big hamburger with fries. The clerk said, that will be $5.27. He put a five dollar bill down and was reaching for some change. The young clerk said, "Listen, I'll give you the senior's discount. That will only be $4.74."

As Don walked out of the restaurant he thought to himself, that young fellow thinks that I am a senior. Why I am only 52. I'm no senior citizen. So he went back in prepared to give the young man a piece of his mind.

The young clerk was smiling and said, while holding up the keys to the man's van, "I knew you would be back. You can't get far without these."

He headed back to his van, slipped the key into the ignition, but he couldn't get it to start. That's when he noticed some purple beads hanging from the rear view mirror and a child's car seat in the back. Well, he quickly made his exit and found his van. When he got back on to the main road, he reached down for his burger, but the burger, fries and coffee were not there. He went back to Wendy's asking whether he had left his food and drink in there. It was not there. As he walked back to his van, a young girl came running up to him holding up a bag and a coffee and said, "Mom said that she thought that maybe you had left these in our van."

The mother came over and said, "That's OK sir. My grandfather does stuff like this all the time. Enjoy your lunch."

Today's Comment: Isn't it interesting that when we are about to speak our mind that we suddenly become aware of our own shortcomings and imperfections. We all do well to look into a mirror before we endeavor to straighten out another person. Before we start interacting with people today, let's take a look in the mirror, the mirror of God's Word and pray that He will help us to have Christ like thoughts, actions and speak words that will glorify Him.

Today's Golden Nugget of Truth: "For if anyone is a hearer of the Word and not a doer, he is like a man observing his natural face in a mirror, for he observes himself, goes away, and immediately forgets what kind of man he was. But he who looks into the perfect law of liberty and continues in it, and is not a forgetful hearer but a doer of the work, this one will be blessed in what he does." James 1:23-25

Today's Philosophical Tidbit: "God has a program of character development for each one of us. He wants others to look at our lives and say, 'He walks with God, for he lives like Christ." Erwin Lutzer

April 29
Tongue Under Control

*T*oday's Smile: Pastor Tony went to his church office on Monday morning only to discover a dead mule in the church yard. He called the police. Since there did not appear to be any foul play, the police referred the pastor to the health department. The health department said that since there was no health threat that he should call the sanitation department. The sanitation manager said he could not pick up the mule without authorization from the mayor.

Now the pastor knew the mayor; he really was not too eager to talk with him. The mayor had a bad temper and was always difficult to deal with, but the pastor called him anyway. So the mayor began as usual to rant and rave at the pastor. He finally said, "Why did you call me anyway? Isn't it your job to bury the dead?"

The preacher paused to gather his thoughts. Though he was not surprised with the mayor's response the pastor was irritated that he could never talk to the mayor without some violent eruption of words. "Yes, Mr. Mayor," said Pastor Tony, "it is my privilege to bury the dead, but I always like to be certain that all of the relatives have been notified."

Today's Comment: Some of us would love to have been that pastor and said those words. However, knowing me like I do, I would have to apologize later. I know. I've been there and I've done that.

Over fifty years ago I was pastor of three small churches. We lived next to one church in a small hamlet. One of the other churches was ten miles away in a rural setting. The third church was 35 miles away. One day a young girl was to sing a solo at the church which was ten miles away from our home and she was hoping that my wife would accompany her at the piano. Leona did not go with me that Sunday. She was in the early stages of her second pregnancy and was experiencing morning sickness. The young girl's father lit into me, complaining that my wife was not there very often. The truth was Leona was there every Sunday except when unwell.

I did not appreciate his remark and I shot back saying that my wife was there as often as he was. That did it. All during the service he sat there looking out the window and when I was greeting people at the door, he looked away from me and would not shake hands. I knew that I had offended him and sought to apologize to him. He simply responded and said, "You know where I live." Well, I did not have the time to go to his house as I had a service at one of the other churches within the next thirty minutes with a third service, 35 miles away that evening. So on Monday, I drove to his place to apologize.

As much as we would love to fire back at people and give them what is coming to them, let us pray that the Lord will set a guard on our lips and enable us to be gracious in our manner of speaking, even when we are tempted to do otherwise.

Today's Golden Nugget of Truth: "A soft answer turns away wrath, but a harsh word stirs up anger." Proverbs 15:1

Today's Philosophical Tidbit: "Kindness consists in loving people more than they deserve." Joseph Joubert

April 30
Keep Short Accounts

*T*oday's Smile: Brady and Dustin were seniors at the Community College. They had a big physics exam coming up on Monday, but instead of studying, they decided to go to Myrtle Beach for the weekend. They came home late Sunday night and were so tired and worn out Monday morning that they both overslept and missed their class. On their way to school, Brady said to Dustin, "Why don't we tell Professor Carl that we had a flat tire and that's why we were late." Dustin thought that was a good idea.

So they told their professor that they had a flat, asking if they could they still write the exam. The professor told them that they could come an hour early the next morning to write their exam.

Tuesday morning they were there bright and early. The professor gave each an exam, and asked Brady to sit at the back of the class and Dustin to sit at the front. The first question was for five points. "Explain the contents of an atom." The second question was worth ninety-five points. "Using two words, which one of the four tires went flat?"

Today's Comment: When I was in high school in the late 1940's, a student function was running late one night, so the janitor entrusted the keys to one of the students asking him to lock up the school. With a handful of keys, he found his way not only into the principal's office but also the storage room where he took one copy of each of the upcoming exams, copied them out selling them to fellow students. When the "not so smart" students started telling the teachers that they found the questions relatively easy, while pulling off high marks, the teachers became suspicious. To make a long story short, they were caught and the appropriate punishment meted out.

Lying, stealing, cheating have all become the norm with many people today. Eventually they will be caught. They may get away with it in this life, but the Bible tells us that all mankind will have to stand before a holy Judge someday. He won't need any witnesses. He will have perfect knowledge. I am thankful that as a young boy I heard these words: "Keep short accounts!" Is there a matter, a sin that should be confessed, and maybe restitution made? Do it now, and pray that we will always keep short accounts!

Today's Golden Nugget of Truth: "He who covers his sins will not prosper, but whoever confesses and forsakes them will have mercy." Proverbs 28:13

Today's Philosophical Tidbit: "You know what you ought to do, why don't you do it?" John Hehl

May 1
Stretching The Truth

T oday's Smile: Richard walked into the boss' office at coffee break time and came right to the point asking his boss for a raise. The boss asked what the reasons were that he felt he should have a raise.

"Well," said Richard, "I've worked for this company for over twelve years. I've done my best and at the moment, I have four companies that are after me. I decided to talk with you first."

"I would love to give you a good size raise," said the boss, "but this is a difficult time with the economic situation being what it is. However, I don't want to start a brain drain with employees going to other companies. I would be willing to give you a couple of fives. Five extra days of vacation, and a five percent raise in pay. How would that be?"

"That sounds great," said Richard. "It's a deal. Thank you, thank you."

"Before you go, Richard, out of interest's sake, I would like to know what the other companies are that are after you."

Richard responded by saying, "The gas company, the water company, the electric company, and the mortgage company."

Today's Comment: Maybe you heard about the little girl who said, "A lie is an abomination unto the Lord and a very present help in time of trouble."

There are times when we are telling the truth, but because our English words convey different meanings, we may be creating a false impression. That is a lie. Let's make sure that we don't hide the truth, even though what we say is true, but the setting may give the hearer a completely different interpretation. Pray that we will always be truthful.

Today's Golden Nugget of Truth: "Deliver my soul, O Lord, from lying lips and from a deceitful tongue." Psalm 120:2

Today's Philosophical Tidbit: "There must be a shortage of truth the way so many folks are stretching it these days." Author Unknown

May 2
Know Your Bible

oday's Smile: A pastor was preaching at a fairly large and prominent church with the hopes that he might become the new pastor. One of the elders offered to give the pastor a quick tour of the church facilities during the Sunday School hour. Before beginning the tour he asked the pastor if there was anything that he would like to see in particular. "Yes," he said, "I would like to pop in on some of the Sunday School classes."

The elder said that their church prided themselves on teaching the Word of God. All of our classes are studying the Bible. They don't spend time playing, or with meaningless talk. So the elder took him to an adult class, and a youth class. The pastor said, "I would like to visit a class of junior boys and ask a question or two."

The elder took the pastor to a junior boys' class. The pastor asked the class: "Who tore down the walls of Jericho?"

"It wasn't me," said one boy. Several other boys indicated that they didn't do it. The elder said to the pastor, "If these boys say they didn't do it, they are telling the truth. They are honest boys, boys with integrity."

"That's fine," said the pastor. Following the service, the elders had a brief meeting with the pastoral candidate.

They told the pastor, "We understand that there has been a problem about some walls being torn down. We have voted that no matter who tore the walls down, we have agreed to rebuild them."

Today's Comment: How well do we know our Bible? Do we read it daily, or do we just talk like we know it when we don't? Did we read it today? What about yesterday? How long has it been since we read it?

Some of you will remember the days when we used to have Bible quizzes quite regularly at our young people's meetings or even some church socials. Bible quizzing was very popular. On one occasion, I was one of four Bible college students on a TV show in Columbia, South Carolina. The show was called, *"Know Your Bible."* I remember a wrong answer which I gave. I can assure you that I know the right answer to that question and have ever since that TV show.

May our goal be to know the Word of God. It is God's instruction manual for mankind. It tells us who God is, how to know Him, and all that He desires to give to us; an abundant and fulfilling life here now plus an eternity with our God and the family of God.

The question we need to ask ourselves is, do we have an appetite for God's Word? Vance Havner said: "Two things make a good meal, good food and a good appetite. And the best preparation for the Bread of Life is a good hearty appetite."[1] Pray today that we will be hungry for the Bread of Life and thirsty for the Water of Life.

Today's Golden Nugget of Truth: "Study to show thyself approved unto God, a workman that needeth not to be ashamed, rightly dividing the Word of Truth." Second Timothy 2:15 (KJV)

Today's Philosophical Tidbit: "The Bible was not given to increase our knowledge but to change our lives." D. L. Moody

May 3
Lost And Found

Today's Smile: A big city lawyer was called in on a case between a farmer and a large railroad company. The farmer noticed that his prize cow was missing from the field through which the railroad passed. He filed suit against the railroad company for the value of the cow. The case was to be tried before the Justice of the Peace in the back room of the General Store.

The defence attorney immediately cornered the farmer and tried to get him to settle out of court. The lawyer did his best selling job, and the farmer finally agreed to take half of what he was claiming to settle the case. After the farmer signed the release, received his check, the young lawyer couldn't help but gloat a little over his success. He said to the farmer, "You know, I hate to tell you this but I put one over on you in there. I couldn't have won that case. The engineer was asleep and the fireman was in the caboose when the train went through your farm that morning. I didn't have one witness to put on the stand."

The old farmer replied, "Well, I'll tell you, young feller, I was a little worried about winning that case myself because that cow came home this morning."

Today's Comment: Did you ever have an experience where you lost an article, only to have it turn up after you had filed for a claim? The cashier, at a grocery store that we often shopped at, noticed at the end of her shift that her diamond ring was missing from her hand. She shared about her loss with some friends of ours. The cashier reported the loss to her insurance company and was paid accordingly. Several months later, our friends were cleaning out their deep freeze when they took out a roast that was still in the plastic bag from the store. When they looked in the bag, there was a diamond ring. Knowing the cashier's story, they took the ring to her. It was her ring and there was great rejoicing.

Over the years, there have been people that I have interacted with, shared the gospel with, leaving them the way I found them. Unrepentant. Unchanged. Some time later, sometimes years later, I meet them again, excited to learn that they repented, they changed, they're now a follower of Christ. What I thought was lost, has been found.

So don't be discouraged if you shared with one or more and saw no change. Pray that the seed that you have sown will someday bear fruit. You may or may not see any change in this lifetime, but someday that one with whom you shared and for whom you have prayed may meet you on the golden streets in glory.

Today's Golden Nugget of Truth: "It was right that we should make merry and be glad, for your brother was dead and is alive again, and was lost and is found." Luke 15:32

159

Today's Philosophical Tidbit: "Jesus came to save the lost, the last, and the least." Author Unknown

May 4
Kind Words

*T*oday's Smile: It had been a long flight, from Detroit, Michigan to London, England. Everyone was weary of the flight, especially young Lance who was with his mother. They were going to visit his grandparents in Liverpool.

After they had disembarked, the flight attendants were checking for items that had been left behind. One of the attendants found a small bag of marbles in a seat pocket. In the bag was a note which said, "Have lots of fun, love, Auntie Marie."

The attendant quickly gave the bag of marbles to the gate attendant hoping that the little fellow would get his bag of marbles before leaving the air terminal. In a matter of moments, the announcement boomed over the public address system, "Would the passenger who lost his marbles on the Delta flight from Detroit, please go to gate number 40."

Today's Comment: We've often referred to someone, because of their actions, as "losing their marbles." Often it is said in jest, but sometimes it may well be said of someone who is getting forgetful. We all go through different stages of life as we age, becoming quite prone to forgetfulness.

Maybe a parent is forgetting more than they remember, but is it kind to be describing such in a belittling manner? The day may come, all too soon, for some of us when we will become forgetful and "lose our marbles." It will be troubling when that happens. Pray that we will be more understanding, caring and kind for those who are aging, while having memory problems.

Today's Golden Nugget of Truth: "Kind words heal and help; cutting words wound and maim." Proverbs 15:4 (MSG)

Today's Philosophical Tidbit: "Kindness is a language that the deaf can hear, the blind can see, and the mute can speak." Author Unknown

May 5
Eaves Dropping

*T*oday's Smile: The census taker was going door to door and came upon a nicely landscaped and what appeared to be a well kept home. Five year old Barbara answered the door.

Barbara told the census taker that her daddy was a doctor but he wasn't home right now. He was at the Municipal Hospital performing an appendectomy.

The census taker was very impressed saying to the young girl, "That is a mighty big word for such a small girl. Do you know what it means?"

"Yes, sir," said Barbara, "two thousand bucks, but that doesn't include the anesthesiologist!"

Today's Comment: Children have ears to hear and they hear what we say when we least expect it. They don't always hear us when we call them or give some instructions, but they are good at eaves dropping. This behooves us to be careful what we say, especially if it is something we don't want repeated. Wouldn't it be rewarding if children picked up those words which are edifying and also glorifying to our Lord? Pray that God will help us so that we do not lead any child astray or cause them to stumble when they overhear our conversations.

Today's Golden Nugget of Truth: "She opens her mouth with wisdom, and on her tongue is the law of kindness." Proverbs 31:26

Today's Philosophical Tidbit: "Speak all kind words, and you will hear kind echoes." Author Unknown

May 6
Learning The Truth

*T*oday's Smile: A young woman with an Irish name was the teacher of a kindergarten in a Massachusetts school. She had taught her class to repeat together the Twenty-third Psalm. As the little voices chorused out, she seemed somewhere to detect a false note. She heard the children one by one, until at last she came across one little boy who was concluding the psalm with the words, "Surely good Miss Murphy shall follow me all the days of my life."[1]

Today's Comment: Some of you will remember the days when in the public school we learned about God and the Bible. It was my privilege in 1982 to attend a weekend celebration for the 100th Anniversary of my elementary school, McKeough School in Chatham, Ontario. I was asked to be one of two speakers at the Sunday morning church service held in the school gym. I was able to share with the audience of 600 plus that I had memorized and learned to recite the books of the Bible in one minute or less in that school. I memorized First Corinthians chapter 13 in that school. I also made the Wordless Book in that school and learned the gospel message that is presented with the same.

That Sunday morning, I shared with the audience the message of the Wordless book. Encouraging aspects were that even though I had graduated from grade eight thirty-seven years earlier, in 1945, I had four of my original teachers in that audience. My grade six teacher came into the principal's office prior to the service and said, "Danny, I'm praying for you." My mother, who had graduated from the same school, played the piano at that service.

A further interesting bit of trivia that I share with you is that at least two of that school's graduates became well known throughout the world. Geoffrey O'Hara, who graduated in the 1890's, was a writer of over 500 popular and patriotic songs, plus hymns. A couple of Geoffrey's well known songs are *K-K-K-Katy, Beautiful Katy* and the music to the hymn *I Walked Today Where Jesus Walked*. I heard Mr. O'Hara when he gave a concert at my high school. The other person was my friend in both grade school and high school. He is Leighton Ford, who is a brother-in-law of Billy Graham, who became an associate evangelist with Dr. Graham and later founded Leighton Ford Ministries

Forgive me for reminiscing. I'm at that age where I find myself reflecting on my life's journey.

Anyhow, let's offer a prayer today for school teachers, both public and private, praying that those who are professing Christians will have a positive impact on the many students that go through their classes.

Today's Golden Nugget of Truth: "One generation shall praise Your works to another, and shall declare Your mighty acts." Psalm 145:4

Today's Philosophical Tidbit: "The highest goal of learning is to know God." Author Unknown

May 7
Sharing With Others

Today's Smile: Sam, Steve and Kelvin had been buddies since their high school years. They decided to take a trip to France. Being devout Roman Catholics, they attended Mass their first Sunday in Paris, even though they did not understand the French language. They managed to stand, kneel and sit when the rest of the congregation did, so it wouldn't be obvious they were tourists. At one point, when the priest spoke, the man sitting next to Steve stood up, and so the three fellows stood. The entire congregation broke into hearty laughter.

After the service these three fellows approached the priest, who spoke English, asking him what had been so funny. The priest said that he had announced a birth in the parish and asked the father to stand up.

Today's Comment: Have you ever tried to communicate with someone when you don't know their language nor do they know yours? Our missionary friends have an abundance of stories concerning their learning a language along with attempts to communicate early in their learning to those around them.

A couple of my missionary friends have shared with me one of their experiences. Jon, a missionary in the Czech Republic told me of his early days when he and his family were invited by another couple to come as a family to their cottage. At the close of a meeting, in his new found language, he said to his friends, "I hope the next time we see each other it will be at your cottage." Every one around them laughed hysterically. What Jon had said was, "I hope the next time I see you it will be naked."

My friend Don, a new missionary in Gabon, West Africa, was giving a morning greeting to those he met. People smiled. He was informed later that he was asking everyone if they had "laid an egg."

Perhaps these flubs should be good reminders to pray today for our missionary friends that are learning a foreign language. They're learning a language so they might be able to communicate the truth of God's Word in that language.

Today's Golden Nugget of Truth: "Go into all the world and preach the gospel to every creature." Mark 16:15

Today's Philosophical Tidbit: "Why should anyone hear the gospel twice before everyone has heard it once?" Dr. Oswald J. Smith

May 8
Incidence Or Coincidence

*T**oday's Smile:* Before the days when expectant fathers were able to be in the delivery room with their wife and witness the birth of their child, there were three fathers-to-be sitting in the waiting room. All three were quite nervous because this would be their first child.

After sitting scanning magazines and conversing with one another and trying to keep one another calm, Melvin's doctor came and extending his hand congratulated him. His wife had just given birth to twins. Melvin was delighted and said that it was quite a coincidence that he had twins because he worked for the Minnesota Twins.

Not long after that another doctor came and greeted Theo and said, "You are to be congratulated, young man, your wife has just had triplets."

"I can't believe it," said Theo, why I work for 3-M, Minnesota, Mining & Manufacturing Company."

No sooner had the doctor told Theo the news that Oliver, having listened to Melvin and Theo's doctors, jumped up and ran out of the room. "What do you think is his problem?" asked the doctor.

Theo said, "Oliver told us that he works for Seven Up."

Today's Comment: There are a lot of things that happen to us that we might say are just coincidental. Most followers of Christ prefer to acknowledge these happenings as God moments or divine appointments. Don't brush off things that occur to us as being coincidental. Even disappointments are not coincidental. It's been said many times that "Disappointments are His appointments."

If we began the day by committing our ways to the Lord, asking Him to guide our steps and direct our paths, then believe that these things are of God. He wants to give the best to us, even though His best may not always appear as something we would consider to be the best. It is the best! Trust God. He makes no mistakes. Pray that if we don't understand what is happening to us today, we can look back in time and see that our steps were ordered by the Lord.

Today's Golden Nugget of Truth: "He who is the blessed and only Potentate, the King of kings and Lord of lords." First Timothy 6:15

Today's Philosophical Tidbit: "A coincidence is when God performs a miracle, and decides to remain anonymous." Author Unknown

May 9
Stewardship Of Time

T oday's Smile: Reuben was sitting on a bench outside of a Dairy Queen® enjoying a chocolate milk shake. As he sat there he looked across the road and there were a couple of men working on the boulevard. One man was digging a hole two or three feet deep, then promptly moving on to dig another hole. The other man a few feet behind was filling in the hole.

Reuben could stand it no longer. As soon as he finished his milk shake he crossed over to the other side of the street and speaking to the man doing the digging said, "I am a little curious. Can you tell me what you guys are doing?"

"Well, we work for the city. Our main work in the spring and summer is to plant trees."

"But," said Reuben, "You are not accomplishing a thing. Aren't you wasting the taxpayer's money?"

"You don't understand, mister," one of men said, leaning on his shovel and wiping his brow. "Usually, there are three of us, Todd, Rodney and me. I dig the holes, Rodney sticks in the trees, and Todd, here, puts the dirt back into the hole. However, today Rodney's sick, but we still have to work."

Today's Comment: How often have we criticized all levels of government for wasting time and money? You've seen workers on a project and it appears that one of them is working while three are looking on. Sometimes when I see three or four people standing talking, I will jokingly ask if it is safety meeting that they are holding. When one asks what is a safety meeting, I simply reply telling them it is when "no one moves and no one gets hurt."

It is easy to see others wasting their time. What do we see when we look at ourselves? Could we have been more productive yesterday? I'm not saying that rest and relaxation cannot be on the agenda for the day, but do we sometimes come to the end of the day asking ourselves the question, "What did I accomplish today?' You've probably heard of the fellow who said, "When I got up this morning I had nothing to do, but by bedtime I only had it half done."

Pray that God will help us be good stewards of the time He has given to us.

Today's Golden Nugget of Truth: "So be careful how you act; these are difficult days. Don't be fools; be wise; make the most of every opportunity you have for doing good." Ephesians 5:15 (TLB)

Today's Philosophical Tidbit: "Do not squander time for that is the stuff life is made of." Benjamin Franklin

May 10
Impressionable Children

*T**oday's Smile:* Miss Brown had been giving her second grade class a science lesson. The lesson was all about magnets. She explained how they made them and what they were made of, then showing them how a magnet would pick up pins, nails and other iron pieces. She explained to the class that the larger the magnet the bigger piece of iron it would pick up. You can have a pocket magnet or have a big crane that has a huge magnet which can pick up several pounds of iron at one time.

It was now time for questions. She began, with a very simple question. She said to her grade two class, "Let's say my name begins with the letter 'M' and I pick up things, what am I?"

A little fellow at the front of the class, said, "You're a mother!"

Today's Comment: A marriage counselor was once asked by a mother, "How many years am I going to have to be picking up my children's stuff?"

He replied with a smile, "Until they leave home." Well, that may or may not be true. I hope for you mothers reading this that your children learn long before they leave home to pick up their things. Maybe you should show today's reading to them.

One thing for sure, when your children have forgotten what the teacher taught in science class, or what you as a parent taught them, your attitude as well as your actions before your children will be remembered forever. I've forgotten much information which my teachers taught or my parents shared with me, but the memory of their lives and the way they acted or responded to me, lingers with me to this day. Remember always, you are making a big impression upon them, a lifetime impression.

My friend Peter shared with me about his grandson. The Sunday School teacher was giving a lesson on the greatness of God. As a little test, she gave the class a Bible word puzzle and asked them to fill in the three letter blank for the following: "No problem is too big for _ _ _." His grandson told his teacher that the answer was "Mom."

When you pray today thank God for godly mothers.

Today's Golden Nugget of Truth: "That they admonish the young women to love their husbands, to love their children." Titus 2:4

Today's Philosophical Tidbit: "An ounce of mother is worth a pound of clergy." Author Unknown

May 11
Honor Thy Mother

*T*oday's Smile: One afternoon Robert came home from work to find the house a total disaster. His three children were outside, still in their pyjamas, playing in the mud, with empty food boxes and wrappers strewn all around the front yard. The door of his wife's car was open, as was the front door to the house.

Proceeding into the entry, he found an even bigger mess. A lamp had been knocked over, and the throw rug looked like it had been thrown up against the wall. In the front room the TV was loudly blaring a cartoon channel, while the family room was strewn with toys and various items of clothing. In the kitchen, dishes filled the sink, breakfast food was spilled on the counter, dog food was spilled on the floor, a broken glass lay under the table, and a small pile of sand was spread by the back door!

He quickly headed up the stairs, stepping over toys and piles of clothes, looking for his wife, and mother of his children. He was worried that she may be ill, or that something serious had happened. He found her lounging in the bedroom, still curled up in the bed, reading a novel. She looked up at him, smiled, and asked how his day went. He looked at her bewildered and asked, "What happened here today?"

She again smiled and answered, "You know every day when you come home from work and ask me what in the world did I do today?"

"Yes," was his incredulous reply.

"Well," said his wife, "today I didn't do it!"

Today's Comment: Well it is that time of year when we pay special attention to mothers. There are all kinds of mothers. They come in different colors, speak different languages, are different sizes also having different dispositions. Some speak out readily, while others seldom speak. Some are musical, some are not. There are so many different kinds of mothers.

As I reflect upon my mother, these traits become evident: she was kind, patient, musical, friendly, hospitable, a hard worker, and above all loving. Some of you reading this may not have such good memories of your mother. My heart goes out to you.

Let's give the honor and respect due to our mothers, not only in May, but always. Most of us don't know what our mothers went through or "put up" with, until we ourselves became parents. If you are a mother, pray that you will be the best.

Today's Golden Nugget of Truth: "You made all the delicate, inner parts of my body, and knit them together in my mother's womb." Psalm 139:13 (TLB)

Today's Philosophical Tidbit: "Throughout the ages no nation has ever had a better friend than the mother who taught her children to pray." Author Unknown

May 12
When You Look At Others

Today's Smile: A young lad went to the lingerie department in a store to purchase a Mother's Day gift for his mother. He bashfully told the clerk that he wanted to buy a half slip for his mom, but he didn't know her size. The lady explained that it would help if he could describe her. Was she thin, fat, short, tall, or what?

"Well," replied the young lad, "she's just about perfect." So the clerk sent him home with a size 34. A few days later the mother went to the store to exchange the gift. It was too small. She needed a size 52.

Today's Comment: The little fellow had seen his mother through the eyes of love, which didn't take into account her exact dimensions. How do you look at people? Do you simply look at their appearance, their size, judging just by what the eye can see?

We need to view people as the whole person. What is their personality like? Are they people of integrity? Are they warm in their love and affection? Some of the best people you know may never have their picture on a magazine cover, but they are people with whom you enjoy fellowship. They are people who will go out of their way to help you.

The prophet Isaiah wrote about the coming Messiah and said: "He has no form or comeliness, and when we see Him, there is no beauty that we should desire Him." (Isaiah 53:2) Yet no one else has demonstrated such love and compassion as our blessed Lord Jesus Christ. Pray that we will be more interested in the life we live, than in just the outward appearances.

Today's Golden Nugget of Truth: "The Lord does not look at the things man looks at. Man looks at the outward appearance, but the Lord looks at the heart." First Samuel 16:7 (NIV)

Today's Philosophical Tidbit: "People seldom notice old clothes, if you wear a big smile." Author Unknown

May 13
Bow Your Heads In Prayer

Today's Smile: Christian was home from university for the summer, meeting up with a new neighbor who had just moved in across the street while Christian was away at school. Wanting to get to know the new neighbor, Christian invited him to a game of golf. As it turned out, the new neighbor was a missionary who had come home for a one year home assignment.

Chatting, while walking between holes, Christian learned about his new missionary neighbor and his service in Nigeria, West Africa was with a denomination unfamiliar to Christian. At the seventh hole the missionary, who had played very little golf, asked Christian what he was going to use on this hole.

"I'm going to use an iron. How about you?"

The missionary replied, "I'm going to hit a soft seven and pray."

Christian used his iron and set the ball down on the green. The missionary topped his ball and it dribbled only a few yards. Christian broke the silence and said, "I don't know about your church, but in my church when we pray we keep our heads down."

Today's Comment: It has been so refreshing in a world which does not pay reverence to Almighty God to see a family in a restaurant bow their heads in prayer before partaking of their meal; to see a sports person bow in prayer before a game; to see high school students celebrating "See you at the pole" bowing their heads in prayer.

Today's reading is a little longer than usual. I want to share with you Pastor Joe Wright's prayer, opening the new session of the Kansas Legislature, January 23, 1996. Everyone expected the usual generalities which had been the norm of previous prayers. Instead they heard Pastor Wright begin his prayer by saying:

"Heavenly Father, we come before You today to ask Your forgiveness and to seek Your direction and guidance. We know Your Word says, 'Woe to those who call evil good,' but that is exactly what we have done. We have lost our spiritual equilibrium and inverted our values.

"We confess that we have ridiculed the absolute truth of Your Word and called it moral pluralism. We have worshipped other gods and called it multiculturalism. We have endorsed perversion and called it an alternative lifestyle. We have exploited the poor and called it the lottery. We have neglected the needy and called it self-preservation. We have rewarded laziness and called it welfare. We have killed our unborn and called it choice. We have shot abortionists and called it justifiable. We have neglected to discipline our children and called it building esteem. We have abused power and called it political savvy. We have coveted our neighbors' possessions and called it ambition. We have polluted the air with profanity and pornography and called it freedom of expression. We have ridiculed the time-honored values of our fore-fathers and called it enlightenment.

"Search us oh God and know our hearts today; try us and see if there be some wicked way in us; cleanse us from every sin and set us free.

"Guide and bless these men and women who have been sent here by the people of Kansas, and who have been ordained by You, to govern this great state. Grant them Your wisdom to rule and may their decisions direct us to the center of Your will. I ask it in the name of Your Son, the Living Savior, Jesus Christ. Amen."[1]

The response to Pastor Wright's prayer was immediate. A number of legislators walked out during the prayer in protest. In six short weeks, Central Christian Church in Wichita, where Rev. Wright was pastor logged more than 5,000 phone calls with only 47 of those calls responding negatively. Paul Harvey aired this prayer on his radio broadcast, *The Rest of the Story* and received the largest response that he had ever had in all of his broadcasting experience, requesting a copy of the prayer.

Pray today for our government leaders that they might turn their hearts heavenward.

Today's Golden Nugget of Truth: "If my people who are called by My name will humble themselves, and pray and seek My face, and turn from their wicked ways, then I will hear from heaven, and will forgive their sin and heal their land." Second Chronicles 7:14

Today's Philosophical Tidbit: "It may be unconstitutional, but I always pray before an exam." A student

May 14
Don't Muffle The Sound

*T**oday's Smile:* A tuba player was hiking in the mountains when he came upon a shepherd that was caring for his flock of sheep. The tuba player stopped and chatted with the shepherd, asking the shepherd, "If I can guess how many sheep you have here, would you let me pick out one and keep it?"

The shepherd agreed, thinking that there was no way that this man would know how many sheep he had. So the tuba player said, "You have 237 sheep." The shepherd was astonished and told the man that he was correct. He did indeed have 237 sheep.

"I'll keep my word," said the shepherd. "Take your pick." The tuba player picked out his sheep, swung it over his shoulders and was about to leave when the shepherd spoke.

"Just a minute, I have a question to ask you. If I guess what you do in your spare time, can I have my sheep back?" The tuba player agreed. "You're a tuba player in a small orchestra."

The tuba player was surprised. "How on earth did you know that?"

"If you take my dog off of your shoulders, we can talk about it."

Today's Comment: I was raised in The Salvation Army and started taking cornet lessons when I was nine years old, switching later to a baritone horn. Our senior class at Prairie Bible Institute had planned a fun night. We put a little orchestra together, so I agreed to play the tuba. I had fun sounding those bass notes at our practice.

When our part in the evening's program arrived, I picked up this big horn and began to play. Well, I tried to play. I could not get a sound out of it. I stopped, all the while the orchestra continued to play, reaching into the bell of the horn to see if I could feel anything.

I felt nothing. So I sat and didn't play. I learned later that some of my "friends" had gone into the auditorium before our meeting, removed the big bell from the tuba and stuffed a scarf down deep, beyond the bell itself. Small wonder I had been unable to reach it.

Today, the message of God's love and His great sacrifice is often muffled or muted. Be it from a pulpit or by an individual, the gospel message is oft times not getting through. There are so many distractions, so many misinterpretations along with so many issues that are hindering the truth from being heard. Pray that in our sharing the truth of God's Word, whether as a pastor or a parishioner, it will be clear and plain.

Today's Golden Nugget of Truth: "For if the trumpet makes an uncertain sound, who will prepare for battle?" First Corinthians 14:8

Today's Philosophical Tidbit: "Sound the battle cry, see the foe is nigh, raise the standard high, for the Lord! Gird your armor on, stand firm everyone, rest your cause upon His holy Word." William F. Sherwin

May 15
Do You Go To Sunday School

Today's Smile: Aaron arrived late for his Sunday School class. The teacher knew that this boy was always on time having never ever been late before. So he asked if there was anything wrong. Aaron replied saying, "No, that he was going to go fishing with his dad, but at the last moment his Dad told him that he should rather go to Sunday School today."

The teacher was quite impressed and so he asked Aaron if his Dad had said anything to him as to why it was more important to go to Sunday School than to go fishing. "Yes," he said. "He told me that he didn't have enough bait for both of us to go fishing."

Today's Comment: Were you raised in a home where fishing was more important than Sunday School? I have been a pastor in two different churches where we picked up children with a Sunday School bus. We found that many parents were very happy to let their children ride our church bus because it gave the parents a morning alone without their children. They could sleep in, watch television, go shopping, or go fishing.

Today let us pray for these types of homes. Pray for the children who come to church without parents. Many receive Christ as their Savior, but have no encouragement at home. Pray that the church families will encourage them, modeling Christ before them. Pray also for their parents, that many of them will be drawn to Christ by noticing a change in their children.

Today's Golden Nugget of Truth: "But Jesus said, 'Let the little children come to Me, and do not forbid them, for of such is the kingdom of heaven." Matthew 19:14

Today's Philosophical Tidbit: "It is extremely difficult to train up a boy in the way the father does not go." Author Unknown

May 16
One Grand Alliance

oday's Smile: The President of the Christian & Missionary Alliance was speaking to the delegates at their Annual Council. In seeking to convey what a great group of people they were, saying that in heaven there are not going to be any Baptists. There will not be any Pentecostals, or Methodists, or Presbyterians, or Lutherans, or Free Church, or Mennonite. He went on to list many more denominations. "No folks, none of those people will be there. We will all be one grand Alliance!"

Today's Comment: Are you proud that you belong to a certain denomination? I've met people who tell me that the church that they attended when younger conveyed the idea that they were the only ones that were right. They used the right Bible; they wore the right clothes; they sang the right songs, knowing for certain that they were going to heaven. As for other denominations, they were questionably looked upon.

I've lived long enough to know that the family of God is made up of people from all denominations along with independents; from those who appreciate a liturgical service to those who have loud contemporary music; from suits and dresses to jeans and cut-offs; from the King James Bible to the latest paraphrased Bible; from premillennial to amillennial. You name it. There are a lot of differences.

If we have received the Lord as our personal Saviour, we are part of the body of Christ, the family of God. Church membership does not guarantee us a place in heaven. We must acknowledge that we are sinners and invite the Lord Jesus Christ into our life. Then, should I say it??? In heaven we'll be one grand Alliance!

Pray today that our love will encompass the family of God no matter what denominational label one wears.

Today's Golden Nugget of Truth: "There is neither Jew nor Greek, there is neither slave nor free, there is neither male nor female, for you are all one in Christ Jesus." Galatians 3:28

Today's Philosophical Tidbit: "Culture changes, churches change, life changes, God doesn't." James L. Wilson

May 17
The Shepherd Is Awake

Today's Smile: Cecil had always been a bird lover. Late in the spring he occasionally went out on the back deck and enjoyed a cup of coffee as the sun was setting. He enjoyed sitting there for an hour or so and watching the stars begin to appear. One night he started hooting like an owl. After about a week of doing this, one night an owl called back to him. Throughout the rest of the summer, he would often go out on the deck; once it was dark Cecil and his feathered friend hooted back and forth with each other. About the time that he figured that he was on the verge of a breakthrough in interspecies communication, his wife was chatting with Amy, the next door neighbor.

"You know," said Cecil's wife, "Cecil spends several nights a week, after sundown calling out to owls."

"That's funny," said Amy, "so does my husband."

What a hoot! It suddenly dawned on them that their husbands were night owls.

Today's Comment: A lot of people are night owls. They stay up late, night after night. Some watch television. Some party. Some read. Some visit. Then there are some that just can't sleep. Strange that today's smile should be next on my list. I just got up. It is 3:45am and I have been awake over two hours with leg pains. We live in a condominium and next to us are three high rise condos. I've noticed that there are far more lights on at 1:00am than there are at 7:00am. Night owls!

I just read a chapter from the Bible, and had a brief time of prayer. You've heard it said that if you cannot sleep try counting sheep. I've also heard that rather than count sheep, why not talk to the Shepherd. The Lord Jesus is the Good Shepherd; He died for us. He is the Great Shepherd; He cares for us. He is the Chief Shepherd; He is coming again.

Problem sleeping? Pray! The Lord is our Shepherd. He is awake.

Today's Golden Nugget of Truth: "I am the good Shepherd. The good Shepherd gives His life for the sheep." John 10:11

Today's Philosophical Tidbit: "Shepherdless sheep and sheep with shepherds are totally different. It is the shepherd who makes the difference. The Lord Jesus is the Good Shepherd." Stuart Briscoe

May 18
How To Get To Heaven

T oday's Smile: Kevin was standing at the corner waiting for the traffic light to change so that he could cross the road. At the same time, a nicely dressed gentleman came along side of him. The man turned to Kevin and said, "I've only been here a couple of days, I am wondering if you could give me directions to get to the post office?"

"Sure," said Kevin, just go straight down this street that we're on until you come to Main Street. It's two blocks away. When you get to Main, turn right and go one block. The post office will be on your right at the next intersection."

"Thanks," said the man. "In case you're interested, I'm holding meetings all this week at the First Presbyterian Church. Why don't you come tonight? I'm going to be talking about 'How to Get to Heaven'."

"You're kidding me," said Kevin, "how can you tell people how to get to heaven while you don't even know the way to the Post Office?"

Today's Comment: Back in the 1950's I had occasion one Saturday night to have dinner with a chaplain serving in a hospital. The thing that connected us in the first place was that his last name was Goldsmith. This was the first time that I had ever met a Goldsmith other than my immediate family. We compared notes for a few minutes as to our ancestry. His was Ireland, mine was England. The rest of our time together was spent discussing what we believed, where we agreed and where we disagreed.

I asked him many questions. One of my questions was this: "You're a chaplain in the hospital, what would you say to a person who felt he was dying and wanted to know how to be sure that he would go to heaven." By now we were in his office and he pulled open one desk drawer after another. He then said, "I have a book here somewhere which I would read to him." I thought to myself, the patient would die before he ever found his book.

Pray that we will always have a ready answer to tell someone how to get to heaven.

By the way, when we separated that night the chaplain turned to me and said, "The difference between what you believe and what I believe is, I believe it is my good works that will get me to heaven, but you believe it is a gift."

Today's Golden Nugget of Truth: "He who believes in the Son has everlasting life, and he who does not believe the Son shall not see life, but the wrath of God abides on him." John 3:36

Today's Philosophical Tidbit: "I wouldn't trust the best fifteen minutes I ever lived to get me into heaven." Adrian Rogers

May 19
Yield Not To Temptation

Today's Smile: I have a clipping in my files from the *Lacombe Globe*, Lacombe, Alberta published back in the 1960's. It is about Dr. Chilton Penfield who was exasperated when he couldn't find a parking place in London, England. He parked his car in a no-parking zone, with a note left on his windscreen: "I have circled this block twenty times. I have an appointment to keep. Forgive us our trespasses."

He returned to find a police ticket with a similar note, "I have circled this block for twenty years. If I don't give you a ticket, I lose my job. Lead us not into temptation."

Today's Comment: When was the last time you were tempted? Probably this week or maybe even today. Temptation is all around us. Well, the temptation is not sin, but yielding to the same is. We may run from temptation, but that doesn't end being tempted, however, it can help us to be a little stronger for the time when we face another temptation. The best ways that I know to ward off temptation is the Word of God. The more we immerse ourselves in the Word of God the stronger we will become; we will have a defence against temptation. Pray that the verses we read or memorized, God will bring to our mind in times of temptation.

Today's Golden Nugget of Truth: "No temptation has overtaken you except such as is common to man; but God is faithful, who will not allow you to be tempted beyond what you are able, but with the temptation will also make the way of escape, that you may be able to bear it." First Corinthians 10:13

Today's Philosophical Tidbit: "Every time we say yes to temptation, we make it harder to say no the next time." Jerry Bridges

May 20
Are You Ready For
The Coming Of The Lord

Today's Smile: Lucy was invited to her girl friend's university graduation dinner. She was thrilled to be invited and was seated at a table beside the most handsome young man she had ever seen. Lucy enjoyed the evening but was especially attracted to the young man Gordon, seated beside her. She was delighted when at the close of the evening Gordon asked her if he could take her out for dinner the following week. Without hesitation she responded that she would be delighted.

Friday, the night of the big date arrived, she had her hair set, chose her best evening dress was all ready waiting at 7:00pm, the time when Gordon was to pick her up. She waited, frequently looking in the mirror to make sure every hair was in place and that her make up was just right. Seven thirty came, no Gordon. Eight o'clock came, no Gordon. Eight thirty, no Gordon. Finally figuring that she had been "stood up," she changed her clothes, put on her nightgown and a housecoat, broke open a bag of potato chips, grabbed a Pepsi from the fridge, turned the television on and curled up on the couch.

At 9:00pm the doorbell rang. She went to the door and there was Gordon, dressed in his best with a bouquet of roses. He took one look at her and said, "I'm two hours late and you're still not ready!"

Today's Comment: The second coming of our Lord Jesus Christ has no time set. Not even the angels know when He is coming again. We might fix ourselves up and feel prepared today, but tomorrow slack off. The Bible teaches that we should always be prepared. If He doesn't come today, make certain that you are prepared for tomorrow. The Bible teaches us that He could come anytime.

I heard of an elderly lady who was on board a plane which was flying through severe turbulence. Everyone around her was in a panic while some were praying. The man seated next to her asked her why she was so calm and why she wasn't praying. She responded by saying, "I'm all prayed up. I have nothing to worry about." May we all be "'prayed up" and ready for His coming.

Today's Golden Nugget of Truth: "Therefore you also be ready, for the Son of Man is coming at an hour when you do not expect Him." Matthew 24:44

Today's Philosophical Tidbit: "Let us live as people who are prepared to die, and die as people who are prepared to live." James Stewart

May 21
Changing The Labels

*T*oday's Smile: Sven, a farmer, had submitted a complaint to the Minnesota state government questioning whether or not his property markers were placed in the correct spots. As he compared his property with his neighbors, things didn't line up properly. He wanted to make certain that the property lines were where they should be.

Clifford and Olaf, government surveyors working for the State of Minnesota, were assigned to check out Sven's property. Clifford and Olaf were very congenial and spent many hours surveying Sven's farm. Before they left that evening, Sven's wife fixed a sumptuous dinner for them, which included Swedish meat balls, boiled potatoes, plus other delectable dishes, topped off with rice pudding and coffee.

A few weeks later, Clifford arrived at Sven and Dagmar's place to show them the report re their property lines. "You were very kind to Olaf and me," said Clifford, "that I decided it would be best if I personally met with you and answered any questions that you may have, rather than send the report through the mail. We are afraid you will be unhappy, as the report contains some bad news.

"What's the bad news?" asked Sven.

"Well, the bad news is this; simply stated your farm is not in Minnesota, it is in Iowa."

Sven responded enthusiastically, "That's not bad news, Clifford, that's the best news that I've heard in a long time. Why just yesterday I told Dagmar that I did not think that I could stand the cold and snow of another winter in Minnesota."

Today's Comment: Moving state boundaries when the property remains the same will not change the weather. Placing a different label on a bottle will not change the contents. Putting sheep clothing on wolves doesn't change the animal. Changing the cover on a book doesn't change the story. Calling sin by a more pleasing word, making it sound "not so bad after all," does not alter the truth that it is still sin.

Too many people today are giving different meanings to what has been said. They are giving misinformation about some historical events. Some go so far as to say that it did not happen. There are those that misconstrue documents, etc. Others have misapplied scripture. Changing meanings, rearranging facts, does not alter what was originally said or done. You can misinterpret what God has said and say it isn't true, but it does not change what God has said. His Word stands forever. Pray we will always remember that God's Word is the truth, no matter what man may say or believe.

Today's Golden Nugget of Truth: "Let God be true but every man a liar." Romans 3:4

Today's Philosophical Tidbit: "The fact that nobody wants to believe something doesn't keep it from being true." Author Unknown

May 22
Encouraging One Another

T oday's Smile: Rev. W. E. Thorn relates an experience about his early years in ministry. He tells about a motherly woman who paid him a big compliment

"Following the service she took me by the hand and said, 'You are a model preacher.' Naturally, in those days, compliments did not come often so I wanted to make the most of it. On the way home I told my wife about it. She did not say much. I guess she knew better.

During the next few days I called it to her attention several times. She apparently was not as impressed as I was. Finally, she took about all she could. After a moment she had found the word 'model' in the dictionary. She looked at me and read: 'Model, a small imitation of the real thing.' That's all it took for me. Later a lady said that I was a warm preacher. I figured that one out for myself. It meant not so hot."[1]

Today's Comment: Be honest now, don't we all like to be the recipient of a compliment now and then? Criticism is far too plentiful. The best compliment I ever received for my preaching was when I was still a student in Bible College. One Sunday morning, when I was home for the summer, I was asked to preach at a little Baptist Church. This church had a student pastor from a nearby university.

He came every Sunday to preach. This one Sunday he was away and I was asked to fill in.

At the close of the service, a woman came up to me and said, "I guess you must not be very educated. I understood everything that you said." I appreciated that "back handed" compliment. I have been taught to aim my message to a junior high school age. That way the majority of your audience will comprehend what you are saying. I have been so encouraged over the years by the teens that have told me they appreciate my sermons.

Pray that we might be able to encourage someone today.

Today's Golden Nugget of Truth: "So encourage each other and build each other up, just as you are already doing." First Thessalonians 5:11 (NLT)

Today's Philosophical Tidbit: "Don't forget that a person's greatest emotional need is to feel appreciated." Author Unknown

May 23
Yield Not To Temptation

oday's Smile: Gregory, who was a plumber, received an emergency call one Saturday afternoon. He figured that it would take him two or three hours. His son, Jordan, had been kept home from school on Thursday and Friday because he wasn't feeling well. As Gregory left for the job, he said to his son Jordan, "Son, you've been home the last couple of days. I know you had planned to go swimming with your friends this afternoon, but I don't want you to leave the house while I am gone."

As he was returning home, he drove by the swimming hole where the kids usually swam and noticed his son was frolicking with the other boys. He stopped the car, walked over to the hole and said: "Jordan, I told you that I did not want you to go swimming. The cold water is not going to help your cold."

"But dad" replied Jordan, "I didn't intend to go swimming, I just came down here to watch and I fell in."

Well, Gregory began to feel sorry for his son until he noticed that he was wearing his bathing suit. "And why the bathing suit?"

"Dad, I brought along my bathing suit in case I was tempted."

Today's Comment: I came across another story which is similar. A mother walked into the kitchen and found that her 4 year old boy had climbed up on top of the counter eating cookies. When she asked what he was doing on the counter. "Mommy," he said, "I just climbed up here to smell the cookies and my tooth got caught."

Isn't it true that when we yield to temptation that we always have some excuse or reason as to why we yielded? We need to follow the advice of Paul the apostle to young Timothy. "Flee these things. . . Follow righteousness, godliness, faith, love, patience, gentleness. . . Fight the good fight of faith. Lay hold on eternal life." (First Timothy 6:11, 12). Pray that we will be prepared for the temptations that come our way. Temptation in and of itself is not sin, but yielding to the temptation is.

Today's Golden Nugget of Truth: "But put on the Lord Jesus Christ, and make no provision for the flesh, to full its lusts." Romans 13:14

Today's Philosophical Tidbit: "Temptation usually comes in through a door that has deliberately been left open." Author Unknown

May 24
That Sure Is Odd

Today's Smile: There once lived a boy whose name was Odd. It seemed odd that his parents would give him the name "Odd." As a child he was teased. In his teen years he was teased. As he grew up, people continued to make fun of his name. Even after he became a successful attorney his name was the butt of many a joke.

When he came to the place of writing out his last will and testament together with his final wishes, he wrote: "I've been the butt of jokes all my life. I'll not have people making fun of me after I'm gone." With that bit of advice he asked that his tombstone not engrave his name.

After his death and burial a tombstone was placed at his grave. His tombstone was just a large blank granite stone. As people passed by they would say, "That's odd!"

Today's Comment: The word "odd" has many meanings. We talk about having an "odd shoe," meaning there is no mate to that shoe. Maybe you have more pages than the amount indicated and you may say you have "200 odd" pages. Maybe you've had the "odd job," in other words not the regular job. We speak of the "odd moment" or two, meaning incidental moments.

There are more meanings. In reference to people, you may say, so and so is odd, or he is acting in an odd manner. Sometimes we may use the word "peculiar" in place of odd. The Bible talks about being peculiar. This does not mean that Christians are to be oddballs or crackpots ready for a psychiatrist. Some people may think that is what Christians are. When the Bible speaks of peculiar people it means a chosen generation. As a chosen people, we are special to God and have a special message to share with the world. Pray that we will give out the odd gospel tract now and then or have the odd conversation with a friend re the things of God.

Today's Golden Nugget of Truth: "But ye are a chosen generation, a royal priesthood, an holy nation, a peculiar people; that ye should show forth the praises of Him who hath called you out of darkness into His marvellous light. First Peter 2:9 (KJV)

Today's Philosophical Tidbit: "We are so afraid of being offensive that we are not effective." Vance Havner

May 25
Give A Hand

Today's Smile: During the 1980's, I served as the Senior Pastor of the Kamloops Alliance Church in Kamloops, British Columbia. One Sunday morning in the middle of my sermon, there was a power failure and the lights in the sanctuary went off. We were in darkness. Not being able to see my notes, I asked everyone to raise their hands. Within a couple of seconds, the lights came back on. I then reminded the congregation that "many hands make light work."

Today's Comment: There may well be a double meaning to the words "many hands make light work." The congregation that morning did not make the lights come back on, but we enjoyed a hearty laugh. However, the more people involved in a community project or a church ministry, the better it is, the lighter the work.

Statistics reveal that in the average church 80% of the work is done by 20% of the people. The same percentage figures indicate that 80% of the financial giving is done by 20% of the membership. Sad statistics!

It reminds me of a football game where thousands sit in the benches or bleachers and a handful are down on the field playing the game. Just think if the church had 80% of the people doing ministry and 80% involved in giving, what would that ministry accomplish for the spreading of the gospel?

Are you just a pew sitter or do you share in the ministry and in giving to the ministry? The more people that are involved in ministry the better it is for the ministry. Much more is being accomplished. Furthermore the better it is for the people. There would be less stress and burn out. Pray that many hands will become involved in the ministry and make it lighter for all involved.

Today's Golden Nugget of Truth: "Five of you shall chase a hundred, and a hundred of you shall put ten thousand to flight." Leviticus 26:8

Today's Philosophical Tidbit: "Snowflakes are frail, but if enough of them stick together they can stop traffic." Vance Havner

May 26
It's No Joke

*T*oday's Smile: It was recess at Central School and the Principal was on duty. The children were relatively well behaved. The weather was gorgeous and all the children seemed to be having fun. The Principal turned momentarily and saw Teddy making all kinds of horrible faces at a couple of the girls. She said to Teddy, "You know Teddy, when I was your age I used to make faces at the boys. One day my teacher told me that if I made too many ugly faces that my face would freeze and stay like that the rest of my life."

Teddy looked up intently at the Principal and said, "Well you can't say that you weren't warned."

Today's Comment: When we were young, there were many people that offered advice, such as the next door neighbor, teacher, parent and friend. Much of it was true and wise advice, but some of it was a spoof. A joke. You needed to know the difference.

Let me remind you that God's Word is not a mistake. There is no error, no exaggeration. God's Word is not a spoof. It is not a joke. God's Word is true! Many preachers, evangelists, missionaries, Sunday School teachers, along with many people have told us that there are consequences for disobeying His Word? No your face won't freeze and stay that way, but unless we repent we shall perish That is true! Pray that we would heed the advice of those many people, knowing consequences will yet come.

Today's Golden Nugget of Truth: "I tell you, no; but unless you repent you will all likewise perish." Luke 13:3

Today's Philosophical Tidbit: "You can't repent too soon, because you don't know how soon it may be too late." Author Unknown

May 27
Laughing At Ourselves

*T**oday's Smile:* A half dozen gals, all secretaries working for a large company and all in their forties, decided to go for dinner one Friday night. It was agreed that they would meet at the Ocean View Restaurant because the waiters were so friendly, but also quite handsome.

Ten years later, all of them in their fifties now thought it would be fun to go out for dinner again. It had been ten years since they had been together. They no longer all worked in the same office. Some of them were at different jobs. They agreed that they would meet at the Ocean View Restaurant because the selection of food was excellent.

When they were all in their sixties, the idea was put forward that they should get together again. Several had retired by now but it was ten years since they had last met together. They chose the Ocean View Restaurant because they could dine in peace and quiet and the restaurant had a beautiful view of the ocean.

Another ten years had passed. Now they were all retired and in their seventies and some of them were facing some health issues. Anyhow they agreed to meet and decided that the Ocean View Restaurant was the best place as it was wheelchair accessible and had an elevator.

Well, it seemed like only yesterday, but another ten years had passed and all of them were still around and in their eighties. It took them some time to decide on a place, but they finally agreed that they would like to get together for dinner and meet at the Ocean View Restaurant since, as best they could remember, none of them had ever been there before.

Today's Comment: Believe me I am not making fun of those in their 80's. I am one! The people that I coffee with at this age and stage of life enjoy laughing at themselves. I find it good medicine to laugh at some of our actions. Our kids and grandkids do, so why shouldn't we? I enjoy every day. It is gift from God.

However, maybe you have had some ups and downs in your journey through life. We have had some tough times in our lifetime. We all have. We could worry about them becoming depressed. I have found a couple of ways to deal with problems. There are more, but there are two that come to mind. The first one is to cast our cares on the Lord. He has told us to do that. That's number one. The second one is to enjoy a little bit of humor or laughter. I find that telling jokes, hearing jokes, laughing at jokes, and some of them being ourselves, goes a long ways in lightening our load and brightening our path.

Pray that if we're a little down today that our spirits might be lifted and maybe God would use a little humor to bring that about. He might even use this book. If we share today's joke with someone we might also brighten their day.

Today's Golden Nugget of Truth: "A merry heart makes a cheerful countenance, but by sorrow of the heart the spirit is broken." Proverbs 15:13

Today's Philosophical Tidbit: "Blessed are they who can laugh at themselves, for they shall never cease to be amused." Author Unknown

May 28
Give Clear Instructions

*T*oday's Smile: Several years ago Josh discovered, as he was preparing to go to work early one morning that the battery on his Volkswagen Beatle was dead. He was a little late, so ran into the house asking his wife to give him a push with their second car, a big old Chrysler. He told her that because the Volkswagen was an automatic transmission, she would have to get up to at least 30 mph before he could get the car started. That was fine with her. So Josh got back into his car. His wife got into the Chrysler but took off down the road. He wondered where on earth she was going.

There he sat wondering what she was doing, and getting a little impatient. She had been gone for a minute. Then it happened. He glanced up at the rear view mirror and there was the big old Chrysler, his wife at the wheel, coming towards him at about 40 mph. It suddenly dawned on him that he should have been a little more specific when he told her that she would have to get up to 30mph before the VW would start.

Today's Comment: Sometimes we think that we have given clear instructions, but somehow what we thought we said and what the hearer heard was different. In this life we often misunderstand what was said. Others misunderstood what we say. May we be clear in what we are saying. Some of you know from experience that you have to be specific with your children. With some even specific instructions written out are often not fulfilled.

My siblings have delighted in telling a story about me when I was about ten years of age. My mother sent me to Woolworths. Some of you may remember those "five and dime" stores. I read mom's note to the clerk, "one roll of white tissue paper." The clerk asked me what color I wanted. I asked her what colors she had. She listed them off. I said that I would like pink. When I returned home, Mom questioned the pink tissue paper. Fortunately, Mom was very loving and understanding and I was forgiven. Of course I told mom that I read the note to the clerk. The clerk's listening wasn't any better than my reading.

So today, let's make certain any instructions or sharing that we do is clear. Pray that any sharing of the gospel that we do will be plain and simple, easily understood.

Today's Golden Nugget of Truth: "Pray that I may proclaim it clearly, as I should." Colossians 4:4 (NIV)

Today's Philosophical Tidbit: "When the mouth stumbles, it is worse than the foot." African Proverb

May 29
A Belief That Behaves

*T*oday's Smile: A pastor was a part of a tour group that was visiting missionaries in their place of ministry. The leader of the group asked the pastor if he would be willing to greet the believers sharing a brief message with them. He agreed to do so, but was a little fearful because of the language barrier along with the fact that he would be speaking through a tour guide.

The tour guide, who had been a missionary, was very familiar with the people and sought to put the pastor at ease. "Look, I will be the one who will be interpreting for you. Why don't we practice a few times before the villagers begin to arrive? I am sure that you will not have any difficulty."

"I'll try," said the pastor, "I'm not in the habit of practicing what I preach."

Today's Comment: That is so true of many who call themselves Christians. We do not always practice what we preach. Our actions speak louder than words. A few lines from Edgar A. Guest says: "And the lecture you deliver may be very wise and true, but I'd rather get my lesson by observing what you do. For I may misunderstand you in the high advice you give, but there is no misunderstanding how you act and how you live."

Do we have a belief that behaves? Pray that we will demonstrate or practice what we preach.

Today's Golden Nugget of Truth: "But do you want to know, O foolish man, that faith without works is dead?" James 2:20

Today's Philosophical Tidbit: "Character is what you are in the dark." D. L. Moody

May 30

God Is Missing

*T*oday's Smile: A mother was having a lot of problems with her eight and ten year old sons. In talking with her neighbor friend Rita, she learned that Rita's pastor was excellent in dealing with young boys suggesting that she would contact her pastor and see if he would meet with her boys.

The pastor agreed to do so. The day came when the two boys, who were not Sunday School or church attendees went to see Rita's pastor. The pastor invited the ten year old boy to come into his office first. The eight year old was to sit in the waiting room until it was his turn.

The ten year old sat in the pastor's office. There was a brief bit of silence. The pastor then spoke to the young boy and said, "Where is God?" The boy sat motionless not knowing what he should say.

The pastor looked at the young fellow and asked again, "Where is God?" Once again the stunned boy stared at the floor and did not answer.

There was a long pause and the pastor once more asked the boy, "Where is God?" With that the boy grabbed his cap and ran out of the office and said to his brother who was still nervously sitting in the waiting room, "Quick, let's get out of here. The church has lost God and they're trying to blame us."

Today's Comment: God is missing in our nations today. He is missing in the lives of millions of people. There is a void in our country and in the lives of many and only God can fill that emptiness. Mankind is trying to fill that void with pleasure, with possessions, with power, with plenty of things that have no lasting satisfaction or purpose. God alone is the answer to the emptiness that many experience in life.

Is your life empty? Have you received the Lord Jesus Christ as your own personal Lord and Savior? Without Him, you are lost! With Him, you have One to whom you can commit every care and circumstance of your life. He is the only One that can fill that God shaped vacuum. Pray today that the void in the lives of many will be filled with Jesus.

Today's Golden Nugget of Truth: "Why do you spend money for what is not bread and your wages for what does not satisfy? Listen diligently to Me, and eat what is good, and let your soul delight itself in abundance. Incline your ear, and come to Me, hear and your soul shall live." Isaiah 55:2, 3

Today's Philosophical Tidbit: "It's a mad, bad, sad world, but God is still in control." Author Unknown

May 31
Money Is Not Everything

*T*oday's Smile: An Alaskan oil tycoon decided to go south for a long overdue vacation. He visited many of the southern US states and figured he needed to go to Texas and meet some fellow tycoons who were in the oil business. He travelled from place to place meeting up with several people who were in the oil business.

He happened on one rather multi-billionaire oil man who was having his morning coffee in the small town café. They got into a little friendly debate as to which of the two states had the most oil. The Alaskan said to the Texan, "I'll tell you something. There is so much oil in Alaska that I am sure that I could buy enough gold to build a solid gold wall, five feet high and two feet wide all the way around the Texas border."

The Texan adjusted his cowboy hat, picked a blade of grass and began to suck on it, and finally said, "I'll tell ya what, y'all go right ahead and build that wall of gold and if I like it, well, I'll buy it."

Today's Comment: Do you secretly wish that you had more money? Maybe you've been vocal about it. I've never had a lot of money. I did not become a pastor because of the money. In my first pastoral ministry in Northern Alberta I received $100.00 per month. That was my total income. I was single for the first ten months of my pastoral ministry and out of that one hundred dollars I paid my tithe, paid for my board and room, car expenses, and managed to squeeze out enough money to go visit my fiancée once every three weeks. A round trip to her home was 480 miles. I was still earning that amount of money when I married her. Thankfully my wife did not marry me for my money. That was back in 1959. We've raised three children, lived comfortably, never went hungry and always had a place to sleep.

Why did I tell you all of that? Because money is not necessary to bring you happiness or fulfillment. We have had a happy, contented marriage being blessed with three loving children and five grandsons. God has met all of our needs. We've been richly blessed. As we pray today let us thank God for the many temporal blessings which He has given to us.

Today's Golden Nugget of Truth: "Give me neither poverty nor riches, feed me with the food You prescribe for me, lest I be full and deny You, and say, 'Who is the Lord?' Or lest I be poor and steal, and profane the name of my God." Proverbs 30:8, 9

Today's Philosophical Tidbit: "Material wealth is either a window through which we see God or it is a mirror in which we see ourselves." Warren Wiersbe

June 1
Life Is Short

oday's Smile: Our children and grand-children have had the annual school photo taken. Yes, cameras were around when I attended school, but there was no such thing as an annual photo. In one grade the teacher took us outside on the school lawn and we posed for a class photo. That was the only class photo taken in all my years of elementary schooling. Unfortunately the teacher was the only one that had a copy of the same.

In another school, not mine, the children had a class photo taken. The teacher was trying to encourage each student to purchase a copy of the group photo. "Just think," she said "how nice it will be to have a class photo and when you are grown up, married, have children or maybe grandchildren, you'll be able to say to your family there is Peter. He's a lawyer. There is Susan. She is a professor at Yale.

There is Devin. He is a missionary in Africa. This photo will be a real treasure."

While the teacher was making her sales pitch a voice from the back of the class room rang out, "Yea and there's the teacher, she's dead!"

Today's Comment: Maybe you have some old school photos of your classmates. They may have just become engaged. Maybe they just had their third child. They might have been promoted in their company, or maybe they are retired. However, long ago that school photo was taken we all have to admit that life is short. We never know when our days will come to an end.

I have conducted many funerals over my years of ministry. The funeral of the youngest was for an infant that lived just a few hours, whose passing brought the father into a personal relationship with the Lord. As for the oldest, I had a funeral for one who was 103. My question is, are we prepared for that day when time for us will come to an end? Do we have family members that are unprepared for eternity? Pray that today they may sense their need of getting right with God.

Today's Golden Nugget of Truth: "Jesus answered and said to him, most assuredly, I say to you unless one is born again he cannot see the kingdom of God." John 3:3

Today's Philosophical Tidbit: "Life is short; death is sure; sin the curse; Christ the cure." Author Unknown

June 2
Church Hopping

Today's Smile: A man was travelling from one island to another in the deserted South Pacific. He ran aground on a small uninhabited island. He managed to live off of the plants and wild life which he found on the island. After several years living by himself on that island, a small ship came in view and the man waved frantically in order to get the attention of the sailors. These sailors saw the man and sailed ashore.

The stranded islander was so pleased to see his rescuers that he prepared a lavish meal for them and then gave them a tour of the small island. Having seen most of the little that there was to see, one of the sailors, pointing to three huts, asked the islander, "What are those three huts that I see on that hill?"

Pointing to the first one, the man said, "That's my house. That's where I sleep and eat."

"What's the hut next to yours?"

"That's my church. I built that so I would have a place to worship."

"Interesting," said the inquisitive sailor. "But what's the other hut next to your church?"

"Oh, that is where I used to go to church."

Today's Comment: A sad commentary on today is that there are many Christians who bounce around from church to church. If something doesn't suit them, they walk out and go to another church until something there unsettles them. I know of a city where it is estimated that about ten percent of church attendees float from one church to another. I knew a man who in the first ten years that I knew him was a member of four different churches. He had hardly joined one church when he was already dissatisfied and moved on to another. This practice is widely known as church hopping.

If you are a Christian, join a church, get involved, make it your church; resist the temptation to go "church hopping." But you say that church is full of hypocrites. That's alright. There is always room for one more. Churches aren't perfect. If you find one that is, don't join it. It might then be imperfect like all the rest.

Pray that God will guide you to the right church. When you've found it, commit yourself to its ministry. Get involved and stick with it.

Today's Golden Nugget of Truth: "Let us not neglect our church meetings, as some people do, but encourage and warn each other, especially now that the day of his coming back again is drawing near." Hebrews 10:25 (TLB)

Today's Philosophical Tidbit: "The church needs workers, not shirkers and certainly not a wrecking crew." Author Unknown

June 3
Heirs Together

*T*oday's Smile: After enjoying fifty-eight wonderful years of marriage, Larry's wife passed away, and he suffered fifteen months of extreme loneliness. It now appeared, however, that his loneliness would be coming to an end. He had proposed to the lady who came weekly to clean his suite and do shopping for him. She was much younger than Larry, but they were both deeply in love.

The day after he gave Nelly an engagement ring, he met with his two eighty year old buddies for coffee. He told them, "I'm getting married in a couple of months."

"Do we know her?" asked Ben.

"Nope!"

"Is she a good cook? asked Walter.

"Nope, she doesn't cook very well. She eats out a lot," said Larry.

"Is she a good looking gal?"

"Not really."

"Then you must be marrying her for her money," joked Ben.

"Nope, she as poor as a church mouse."

"Well," said Walter, "why in the world are you going to marry her?"

Larry replied, "She can still drive!"

Today's Comment: June continues to be the most popular month of the year for weddings. Maybe you married in June, or maybe you are one that is planning to get married in June. I trust that your marriage or your planned marriage will not be based solely on whether your fiancée can drive, or is good looking, or a good cook. Those gifts or abilities are good, but there is more. Having a deep love for each other should be the starting point. However, I want to share with you the three "R's" in marriage.

There should be: (1) Genuine Respect: Practice complimenting your spouse. Nobody receives too much genuine praise or respect. Too many are the recipients of criticism. Don't belittle your partner. Someone said it well, "Love is a decision to forgive and not keep score." (2) Good Relationships: You don't fall into a relationship. You build a relationship. Build a good one. Keep short accounts. "Do not

195

let the sun go down on your wrath." (Ephesians 4:26). (3) Guarantee Responsibilities: Do your part in the marriage. Share your duties and responsibilities. Don't leave all of the work to one partner.

The duties which you share in marriage ought not to be looked upon as working at a job, rather as one sharing with your loved one, the tasks encountered in the marriage union. In our union with God, our responsibilities are viewed as being "laborers together with God." (First Corinthians 3:9) Pray too, that our marriages will be built on Jesus Christ, the solid rock foundation.

Today's Golden Nugget of Truth: "Wives. . .husbands. . . being heirs together of the grace of life. . ." First Peter 3:1, 7

Today's Philosophical Tidbit: "When I was dating my wife, I worshipped the ground that she walked on. Now I vacuum it." Norm Morrison

June 4
The Language Of Love

*T*oday's Smile: Troy had just finished his freshmen year at university and had been home for a couple of weeks. One day he asked his mother, "May I tell you a narrative?"

The mother, not being accustomed to hearing such big words, said, "Son, what is a narrative?"

"A narrative is a tale," said Troy. That night when going to bed, Troy asked, "Mother, may I extinguish the light for you?"

"Extinguish, what does that mean?" his mother asked.

"Extinguish means to put out," he explained.

A few nights later Troy's mother was hosting a Tupperware® party at their home and Buster, the old family dog, walked into the living room where the ladies had gathered. With great dignity the hostess called her son, who was nearby in the kitchen and said, "Troy, would you please come and take the dog by the narrative and extinguish him."

Today's Comment: They say that the English language is one of the most challenging languages to learn. Many words have multiple meanings; some have the identical spelling but different pronunciations and the letters joined together have many pronunciations. Take for example the letters "ough." These are some of the words using those letters: cough, tough, through, hiccough, borough, thought and more; each has a different pronunciation. Is it any wonder that people have difficulty with our language?

In my home church, and many churches in the English speaking world we have ESL (English as a Second Language) classes and offer free lessons to those learning English as a second language. In our church we also have a weekly session devoted entirely to presenting the gospel to our ESL students. God is bringing the "mission field" right to our doorsteps these days. Pray for those that teach and that many of these foreign students and immigrants will not only learn English in our churches, but learn that Jesus Christ is the only way to life everlasting.

Today's Golden Nugget of Truth: "We loved you so much that we shared with you not only God's Good News but our own lives, too." First Thessalonians 2:8 (NLT)

Today's Philosophical Tidbit: "Any method of evangelism will work if God is in it." Leonard Ravenhill

June 5
Scripture To Prove My Point

*T*oday's Smile: Luke had just passed his driving test and asked his father when they would be able to discuss his usage of the family car. His dad proposed a plan of action. "I tell you what, son, when you bring your school grades up from a C- to a B+, when you begin to read your Bible, and when you get rid of that long hair, then we can sit down and discuss your use of the car."

Two months had gone by when Luke's Dad said, "I see that you've brought your grades up, and I am very proud of you. I noticed that you have also been reading your Bible quite regularly. However, I am a little disappointed that you have not yet got your hair cut."

Luke responded by saying, "Dad, since I have been reading my Bible, I have noticed that Moses had long hair, Samson had long hair, John the Baptist had long hair, and it is likely that Jesus had long hair."

His dad replied, looking intently into his son's eyes and said, "But did you notice in your Bible reading that Moses, Samson, John the Baptist and Jesus walked everywhere they went."

Today's Comment: How often do people use scripture to justify their actions? We can find a scripture verse any time we want to prove our point. However, that doesn't always mean that we are right. The Bible is not a book of words that we can take to twist to serve our purposes. It is God's way of communicating with us as to His plan and purpose for our life. Pray that as we read His Word that God will make His message clear to us as to what He wants us to do.

Today's Golden Nugget of Truth: "Your word is a lamp to guide my feet and a light for my path. I've promised it once, and I'll promise it again, I will obey your righteous regulations." Psalm 119:105, 106 (NLT)

Today's Philosophical Tidbit: "The Bible is alive, it speaks to me; it has feet, it runs after me; it has hands, it lays hold of me." Martin Luther

June 6
Turning Point

*T*oday's Smile: Forest Goldspink, an elderly gentleman, arrived in Paris by airplane. At the Customs, in the Charles de Gaulle airport, he was having a problem finding his passport in his carry on.

"You have been to France before, monsieur?" the customs officer asked sarcastically. Mr. Goldspink admitted that he had been to France previously. "Then you should know enough to have your passport ready."

The Englishman said, "The last time I was here, I didn't have to show any passport."

"That's impossible. You English people have always had to show your passports upon arrival in France!"

The English senior gave the Frenchman a long hard look and then he quietly explained. "Well, when I came ashore at Gold Beach, Normandy on D-Day in 1944 to help liberate your country, I couldn't find one single Frenchman to whom I could show a passport."

Today's Comment: As a young teen, I remember picking up a special edition of our daily paper off of our front veranda. *The Chatham Daily News* was an afternoon paper. That day there was a morning edition. It was D-Day! The invasion of France by the Allied forces. Tuesday, June 6th, 1944 was the turning point of World War Two.

Have you experienced a turning point in your life? All of us have experienced a turnaround in the affairs of our life. We started attending school when we were five or six years of age. We graduated from school. We secured a job or took further education. Many of us went from being single to being married; from being childless to parenthood; from being a parent to being a grandparent. We may have resigned from our work; retrained for another position; relocated to another city; eventually retiring. There are numerous turning points in our lives.

However, has there been a spiritual turning point? You may be experiencing many spiritual battles but you haven't been winning. They've been losing battles. Jesus invites you to turn around, to repent, to be born again, to have a turning point experience. If you have never experienced this turning point, pray today. Invite the Lord Jesus Christ be on the throne of your life. Ask Him to come into your life. When you do that, write the date in your Bible. If you don't have a Bible, buy one. Make today your D-Day, your Decision Day; the day when your life was turned around and wholly surrendered to God.

Today's Golden Nugget of Truth: "That if you confess with your mouth the Lord Jesus and believe in your heart that God has raised Him from the dead, you will be saved." Romans 10:9

Today's Philosophical Tidbit: "A whole new generation of Christians has come up believing that it is possible to 'accept' Christ without forsaking the world." A. W. Tozer

June 7
Caught In The Act

*T**oday's Smile:* Mary Lou was sick with a terrible cough. She heard her mother working in the kitchen. Mary Lou thought that was odd. Her mother should be getting ready for work. So she got out of bed and went to see what her mom was doing. Her mother told her that she had just remembered that she promised to bake a cake for the Ladies' Auxiliary Bake Sale so she was baking an angel food cake mix.

"Mary Lou," her mother said, "I am thankful that I remembered before it was too late. I just have time to bake it, ice it and drop it off before the sale starts." When the cake was baked her mom took it out of the oven and it fell flat. "What will I do now? She had no sooner spoken and she had a bright idea. She was able to lift the center of the cake by placing a full toilet roll in the hollow center. She then skillfully covered the whole cake with a thick layer of white icing. No one could even tell that in reality the cake was a flop. Adding sparkles and M & M's made the cake look very attractive. She then turned to Mary Lou, who was making a hot lemon drink along with taking some cough syrup and said, "Honey, I'm going to drop this cake off but I want you to get dressed and be there when the sale starts and buy back this cake. I don't want anyone to see what I've done."

Mary Lou arrived at the sale a couple of minutes late and discovered that the cake had already been sold. She phoned her mother at work. Her mom was horrified and said: "What will the ladies think of me? I will be ridiculed, ostracized and the talk of the town."

Mary Lou's mom had promised to attend a fancy bridal shower luncheon on Saturday at the home of the secretary of their Ladies' Auxiliary. She didn't want to attend. The secretary was a big snob and she had felt humiliated on more than one occasion in her presence. However, she was determined to forget about the cake and go anyway. She had no reasonable excuse to stay home. The meal was delicious. However, when her mom saw the dessert, she was about ready to faint. The hostess was the one that had purchased her cake. Mary Lou's mom started to get up and call the hostess to one side and tell her what had happened when the mayor's wife, said, "Oh, what a beautiful cake!"

"Thank you," said the hostess, "I baked it myself!"

Today's Comment: Well, I am sure that the story has continued to roll in your mind and you wondered what happened when the hostess started to cut the cake. All I can say is that sooner or later we will be caught in our tracks. We cannot sin and get away with it for long. Pray today that we will speak the truth. We will be the better for it.

Today's Golden Nugget of Truth: "Be sure your sin will find you out." Numbers 32:23

Today's Philosophical Tidbit: "One reason sin flourishes is that it is treated like a cream puff instead of a rattlesnake." Billy Sunday

June 8
Improve Your Communications

*T*oday's Smile: Ming was a Chinese freshman studying in a Canadian university. He had studied the English language before coming to Canada, but was still having problems with a number of words that were similar. One day after his summer school class he went to his professor and said, "I am having problems determining the different meanings with words that are similar. For example I don't know when to use the words further and farther, and inflammable and flammable. Also a couple of words that really baffle me are the words complete and finished. What is the difference in those two words?"

"Let me explain it this way and hopefully you will remember," said the professor. "When you marry the right woman, you are COMPLETE. When you marry the wrong girl, you are FINISHED. And when the right one catches you with the wrong one, you are COMPLETELY FINISHED!!!"

Today's Comment: As we seek to learn and know the meaning of words and how to use them, we also do well, if married, to understand our spouse. There are various reasons why marriages fail with separation or divorce as result. One reason is that a husband or wife has not fully taken the time and effort to learn to understand their spouse, or listen to them. If you are struggling in this area, seek out a pastor or counselor that will help you. There are also some good books and marriage seminars that are available that may be of help. Pray for God's help making every effort to improve your communicating with one another.

Anne Graham Lotz has written: "Don't break up what God the Creator has put together in an equal, diverse, unified companionship we call marriage. God is the God of the impossible. It does not matter how bad the condition of your marriage is. Turn it over to God, follow His directions, and He can mend the brokenness."[1]

Today's Golden Nugget of Truth: "Don't use bad language. Say only what is good and helpful to those you are talking to, and what will give them a blessing." Ephesians 4:29 (TLB)

Today's Philosophical Tidbit: "When listening breaks down, marriages break up." David Jeremiah

June 9
Where Do We Begin

Today's Smile: Len had just graduated with a degree in economics and was being interviewed for his first job. The president of the company asked the young applicant as to what he thought his starting salary should be.

Len responded and said, "I have been thinking that something in the neighbourhood of $120,000.00 a year and with a good benefits package."

The president said, "Well, what would you say if I offered you six weeks' vacation, all statutory holidays, and ten sick days per year. I would also consider giving you full medical and dental, and a company car."

Len straightened up in his chair and said, "Wow! I never dreamed of anything like that. Are you kidding me?"

The president said, "Yes, I'm kidding you, but you started it."

Today's Comment: Do some of you remember the days when we all started at the bottom of the ladder and worked up. I recall that one of my uncles started work at a bank as a delivery boy delivering papers, checks, etc from the bank where he worked to other banks in the city. He gradually worked his way up in the bank. A job offer for a major canning factory became available. Uncle Joe applied. He was hired and worked his way up in that company till the day came where he was the president of the company.

Years ago we qualified for promotions by how well we did our work. Unfortunately, we've witnessed the opposite scenario where a young person had a couple of degrees behind their name, but under their leadership, the company folded. Thank God that is not always true.

The point I want to make today is, let's not be so cock sure or over confident about our abilities. There is still a place to be willing to start a job working our way up. The same goes for the Christian life. Some new converts, particularly celebrities who come to faith in Christ, are propelled into telling their story because of who they are. That has sometimes become their downfall. Pray that our goal will be to be humble and not haughty.

Today's Golden Nugget of Truth: "The humble He guides in justice, and the humble He teaches His way." Psalm 25:9

Today's Philosophical Tidbit: "Character cannot be developed in ease and quiet. Only through experience of trial and suffering can the soul be strengthened, vision cleared, ambition inspired, and success achieved." Helen Keller

June 10
Be Careful Of Your Actions

Today's Smile: Alice worked in top management with an oil company in Houston, Texas. She was flying to Calgary, Alberta for a meeting with the directors of the Canadian branch office. She arrived at the air terminal in Houston earlier than usual, so purchased a magazine, a chocolate bar and a bag of potato chips. As she began to read, she reached down and picked up a couple of chips. The bag was between her and a business man. No sooner had she taken a couple of chips and he reached in the bag and took some chips. She took another couple of chips. He did the same. She thought what nerve of the man to be snitching some of her chips. She was afraid to say anything and this continued, each of them digging into the same bag. When they were down to the bottom of the bag, the man picked up the bag and shook the few potato chip crumbs into his mouth and then tossed the bag into the waste container.

She had a little nap and then the call came to board the airplane. Once she was airborne, and drinks were being served, she thought she would eat her chocolate bar with a coffee. She opened her purse. There in front, to her great embarrassment and consternation, was her chocolate bar and her bag of potato chips.

Today's Comment: Don't know whether you've have had that experience, but I have on more than one occasion approached a person, thinking it was someone I knew and it wasn't.

It is so easy to get mixed up if you're not careful. You may think you're approaching the right person, or eating your bag of potato chips, but you're not. The same goes for the Christian life. Satan will do everything in his power to confuse us, to mix us up, to make us think were doing right.

I heard a testimony of a young lady who came from a solid Christian home. She prepared herself, as she was about to enter university, to have an answer standing up for her faith if she was ever attacked or ridiculed for her faith. That never happened, but for a little social life, she started attending clubs on the weekend. She was taking from the wrong bag of goodies and thus began her downward slide.

Pray that we will be careful that we don't take from the wrong bag, be it the kind of friends we have, the kind of books we read, the kind of movies we watch or the kind of stories we hear.

Today's Golden Nugget of Truth: "Watch and pray, lest you enter into temptation. The spirit indeed is willing, but the flesh is weak." Matthew 26:41

Today's Philosophical Tidbit: "Sinful pleasures usually start out looking like fun." Author Unknown

June 11
Are You Related To Your Mother-In-Law

*T*oday's Smile: Jerry and Priscilla were going out for a dinner. They were nearly ready to go when Priscilla reminded Jerry to be sure to put the cat outside. As their taxi drove up and they were going out the front door, the silly cat darted back into the house. They did not want the cat to be shut in the house while they were out, so Jerry went back into the house to get the cat while Priscilla climbed into the cab. She did not want it known that the house would be empty that evening and so she lied to the cab driver and told him that her husband had gone back upstairs to say good-bye to his mother-in-law.

When Jerry finally showed up and got into the cab, he turned to his wife and said: "Sorry I took so long, but the stupid old thing was under the bed and I had to poke her with a coat hanger!"

Today's Comment: Let me begin by saying that I had the world's best mother-in-law. When my wife and I were courting, I was pastor in a small town about 250 miles north of where my wife lived. Instead of the usual day off, which pastors would take, I took three days off every three weeks to go visit Leona. She was teaching school and so I had a big chunk of the day to interact with my future mother-in-law. I cherish those moments. We had only been married nine years when she passed away at a young age.

May I encourage you to build good relationships with your mother in-law. Sarcastic jokes, one-liners are the norm when it comes to referring to mother-in-laws. If you have a mother-in-law, take time today to phone her, write a letter, or email or Skype or text her thanking her for raising a great child that is now your spouse.

If you are experiencing a fractured relationship with your mother in-law or in your family circle or in your circle of friends, pray that you will be guided to do what you can to resolve the conflict and ask God to do His work in the heart of the other person.

Today's Golden Nugget of Truth: "Let no corrupt word proceed out of your mouth, but what is good for necessary edification, that it may impart grace to the hearers." Ephesians 4:29

Today's Philosophical Tidbit: "A person with a generous, encouraging, loving, godly mother-in-law is blessed beyond measure." A. Daniel Goldsmith

June 12
Easily Distracted

*T*oday's Smile: David met the most gorgeous young lady at a school reunion. She was three years younger and so they really had not connected during their school years. He was taken by her charm and beauty and since they were separated by approximately 900 miles, he asked her if it would be alright if he wrote a letter to her. Madeline was pleased by his interest and agreed to correspond.

He wrote the first letter and told her how pleased he was that they had been introduced to each other and looking forward to being able to communicate by mail. She responded, agreeing that she too was happy that their paths had crossed. They continued to write. First it was a weekly exchange, and then twice a week and eventually they were at the point where they were exchanging letters three times a week. Madeline was really taken by his interest and had her letters addressed to the office where she was receptionist and would be able to read them during her coffee break. She always made it a priority to be at the reception desk when the letter carrier popped in and placed the mail on her desk. They had what might be called a letter courtship.

The weeks of letter writing became months and the months soon stretched out to two years. He had never ever managed to travel the distance to see her in person. After two years of exchanging letters, the day finally came when Madeline was married. She married the letter carrier.

Today's Comment: It is easy to be distracted when you see someone else more often than your sweetheart. Are we as easily distracted from focusing upon our relationship with the Lord Jesus Christ? When Moses did not come back from Mount Sinai as quickly as the children of Israel had figured he should, they turned their attention to worshipping a golden calf.

What does it take for us to turn our eyes from looking to the Lord? Temporal things can cause us to look away from that which is eternal. Pray that we might heed the words of the old hymn which says: "Turn your eyes upon Jesus, look full in His wonderful face, and the things of earth will grow strangely dim in the light of His glory and grace."

Today's Golden Nugget of Truth: "Looking unto Jesus, the author and finisher of our faith, who for the joy that was set before Him endured the cross, despising the shame, and has sat down at the right hand of the throne of God." Hebrews 12:2

Today's Philosophical Tidbit: "A decision is made with the brain. A commitment is made with the heart. Therefore, a commitment is much deeper and more binding than a decision." Nido Qubein

June 13
You're A Special Person

T oday's Smile: At the site of the construction of a new Methodist Church, the building superintendent stopped to compliment one of his bricklayers on his work. In the course of their few minutes of conversation, Kyle, the superintendent casually asked, "Vince, did I hear you telling Pat the other day that you have a brother who is a bishop?"

"That's right," answered Vince. "My brother Gabriel started out as a minister of a country church, and then to a city church, and now for the last 12 years he has been a bishop."

"Here you are a bricklayer, and your brother is a bishop," said Kyle. "It sure is a strange world. It just seems like the brains were not given out very fairly, does it?"

"No," said Vince, as he proudly slapped mortar along the line of bricks, "My poor bishop brother Gabriel could not lay bricks if his life depended on it."

Today's Comment: We are not all endowed with the same gifts and abilities. In my younger years, I recall that some of my peers were trying hard to be like someone else. I determined that when I had to give my senior class message in Bible College that I would speak about being ourselves, and not trying to be someone else. I've long since lost those notes, but that was my little message. We may not be called to be bricklayers, or pastors, or teachers, or homemakers. God has a divine blueprint for each of us.

When it comes to Christian ministry, we are members of one body, the body of Christ. We each have a different function. We are not all hands or feet or eyes or ears. Let's find out where we fit and do our work as unto the Lord. Some of us are called to work behind the scenes. Others have an upfront ministry which is more visible. Pray that whatever we do and wherever we do it, that we do it as unto the Lord. He has a perfect plan for our lives.

Today's Golden Nugget of Truth: "Just as there are many parts to our bodies, so it is with Christ's body. We are all parts of it, and it takes every one of us to make it complete, for we each have different work to do. So we belong to each other, and each needs all the others." Romans 12:4, 5 (TLB)

Today's Philosophical Tidbit: "You are special in the plan of God and the mind of God and God has a very special way for you." Adrian Rogers

June 14
Created Equal

T oday's Smile: Kenneth and Corey had been looking for work for a couple of weeks. They finally were hired by a local contractor. Since they had little experience in construction work, the boss decided to give them a little test to see how well they could figure out a matter which might have similar concerns were they on a job site. So he sent them out to the front lawn of the construction office and asked that they estimate the height of the flag pole. The two of them went to the pole and were standing at the base of the pole looking up when a middle aged woman walked by. She sensed that they had a problem, and so asked what they were doing and why the confused look on their face. "We are supposed to determine the height of this flagpole," said Kenneth, "but we don't have a ladder."

The woman took a wrench from her purse, loosened a couple of bolts and then laid the pole on the ground. She then took a tape measure from her purse, took a measurement and proudly announced to the fellows that the pole was twenty-eight feet, six inches. They thanked her, and as she walked away, Kenneth turned to Corey and said, "That's just like a woman. We want the height and she gives us the length."

Today's Comment: In many parts of the world, women are put down. They are treated as slaves with heavy demands placed upon them. When God created woman He didn't take a foot bone or a part of Adam's head, God took a rib. Why? Woman was made to be a companion, someone who came alongside, not over man or under man. Men and women were created equal, but possessing different roles and responsibilities.

So pray men and boys that you will always treat the lady and girl in your life with respect, whether she is your mother, sister, wife or daughter, don't belittle them. They are special!

Today's Golden Nugget of Truth: "So God created man in His own image; in the image of God He created him; male and female He created them." Genesis 1:27

Today's Philosophical Tidbit: "All places where women are excluded tend downward to barbarism; but the moment she is introduced, there come in with her courtesy, cleanliness, sobriety, and order." Harriet Beecher Stowe

June 15
Are You Fearful

*T*oday's Smile: Craig and Paula were married in Washington, DC spending their first night at the Watergate Hotel. It had been a fun packed wedding and soon after arriving at the hotel, they simply dropped their suitcases, and sat down on some comfortable chairs and, with a cup of coffee, reliving the excitement of the day. Craig interrupted Paula at one point and said, "I just remembered my folks telling me about this hotel. Do you realize that we are staying in the famous Watergate Hotel known for the Watergate scandal back in the 1970's which ultimately led to the resignation of President Nixon? I wonder if this place is still bugged."

He gets up out of his chair, and begins by looking behind the pictures on the wall, behind the drapes, and eventually pealing back the carpet a bit. "I found it. Sure enough this place is still bugged. Look here it is!" he exclaims. He gets his Swiss army knife, unscrews a small disc shaped plate on the floor, and throws it out the window.

The next day when they were checking out, the hotel manager asked the newlyweds how they enjoyed their night at the Watergate. "How was your room? Was it what you had expected? What about the service? Were you satisfied? Did you hear any unusual noise?"

Craig said, "Sir, why are you asking me these questions?

The hotel manager said, "Well the couple, whose room was directly under yours, complained this morning that the chandelier fell last night, missing them by only inches."

Today's Comment: There are people who are filled with various phobias, are fearful and afraid about many situations. They are afraid to eat in a restaurant. Someone may have poisoned the food. They are afraid of flying in an airplane. It might crash. Some are afraid of heights, lest they fall. The list goes on, fear of dogs, fear of germs, of attending social events, fear of thunder and lightning. Well, they may not go out into the restaurant kitchen to check or do an inspection of the airplane, but they still want to make certain everything is o.k.

You've probably heard the story of the airplane that was being tossed about on the edge of a storm. People were nervous, tense and babies were crying. A ten year old was seated by herself and was calmly reading a book. Someone asked her if she was afraid. "No," she said, "my daddy is the pilot."

God is our pilot. We need not fret and worry. Pray today that whatever situation you are facing that you will turn it over to God. His will for you will be the best. He makes no mistakes. Rest in Him!

Today's Golden Nugget of Truth: "The eternal God is your refuge, and underneath are the everlasting arms." Deuteronomy 33:27

Today's Philosophical Tidbit: "Sleep peacefully. God is awake." Author Unknown

June 16
I Want To Be My Child's Hero

T oday's Smile: Father's Day was approaching, and Arthur thought maybe he should take his son Jamie for a day of fishing. They both enjoyed being in the boat and the inquisitive lad was full of questions.

"Dad, how does this boat float?"

Arthur thought for a moment, then replied, "I don't really know, son."

Jamie came up with another question, "How do fish breathe underwater?"

Once again the father replied, "I don't really know, son."

A little later the boy asked his father, "Why is the sky blue?"

Again, the father replied, ""I don't really know, son."

Worried that he might be annoying his father, Jamie said, "Dad, do you mind me asking you all of these questions?"

Arthur quickly responded and assured him, "Of course not, son, if you don't ask questions you'll never learn anything!"

Today's Comment: Robert Orben wrote: "For Father's Day, my kids always give me a bottle of cologne called English leather. It's appropriate; to them I always smell like a wallet."

A school teacher gave a contest to her class asking them to describe what they liked best about their father. The winning entry read, "I have so much fun with my father that I wish I had known him sooner."

Some of you who are reading this are fathers or soon to be fathers. One father wrote: "If I had it to do all over again, I'd love my wife more in front of my children. I'd laugh with my children more. I'd listen more, even to the youngest child. I'd be more honest about my own weaknesses and stop pretending perfection. I would pray differently for my children. I would be more encouraging and bestow more praise. And finally, if I had it to do all over again, I would use every ordinary thing that happened in every ordinary day to point them to God." Author Unknown.

Pray that we fathers will not miss those golden moments of opportunity when we can give positive input into the lives of our children and grandchildren.

Today's Golden Nugget of Truth: "Only take heed to yourself, and diligently keep yourself, lest you forget the things your eyes have seen, and lest they depart from your heart all the days of your life. And teach them to your children and your grandchildren." Deuteronomy 4:9

Today's Philosophical Tidbit: "The values we leave our children are more important than the valuables we leave them." Author Unknown

June 17
Making A False Statement

*T**oday's Smile:** Derek was at the check out stand with a quart of milk, a head of lettuce and two 50 pound bags of dog chow. The lady behind him asked if he had a dog. Well, Derek had a dog, he had two of them. However, he thought he would joke along with her and so he responded and said to her, "No, I don't have a dog. I am on the dog chow diet, although I probably shouldn't be because I ended up in the hospital. "But," he said, "I discovered that when I awakened in the intensive care ward with several tubes attached to me that I had lost 27 pounds." Derek continued with his story. "The way the diet works is, you fill your pockets with dog food nuggets and simply eat one or two every time you feel hungry. The food is nutritionally complete and tastes rather good."

By now, all eyes at the check out stand were on Derek when the lady behind him asked if he had gotten food poisoning from the food and whether that is why he ended up in intensive care.

"No," said Derek. "The truth of the matter is that because of this diet, I've been making frequent stops at fire hydrants and one day when I stopped at one of them a car hit me."

Today's Comment: Some speakers are notorious for telling jokes in the first person. If you didn't know any better you could be inclined to believe that it actually did happen to them. How do you know when the first person bit of humor is for real, and when it is a joke? The best I can say is consider the source and the setting.

Someone else may share something with you about a good stock investment. Be warned! The truth is they are not interested in seeing you make money, but in seeing the money put into their pockets. It is a fraud.

Worse than either of the above is when someone shares what sounds like the truth and a correct interpretation of scripture, but it is not. I was visiting a hospitalized friend when one of the volunteer spiritual care workers stopped by. I stopped talking and let him talk. I was anxious to hear what he had to say to my friend. Well, he assured us that we were all going to heaven, no matter what. When I challenged him with the fact that one must personally receive Christ as Savior, his response was that God was a God of love.

True, God is a God of love, but we do not get into heaven simply because God loves us. God loved us so much that He paid the penalty for our sin, but we must reach out in faith and personally receive Him as our Savior. Then and only then do we have everlasting life and are assured of a place in heaven.

Pray that we will not be deceived by everything that we read or hear. Making false statements about eating dog food is a joke. Making false statements about investments is fraud. Making false statements about God's Word is a blatant lie.

Today's Golden Nugget of Truth: "For God so loved the world that He gave His only begotten Son, that whosoever believeth in Him should not perish, but have everlasting life." John 3:16 (KJV)

Today's Philosophical Tidbit: "God loves us the way we are, but too much to leave us that way." Leighton Ford

June 18
What Does Your Conscience Tell You

*T*oday's Smile: Father Bey, who was on the faculty of the University of Portland, told an apocryphal story of a trip that he made by train to Saint Paul, Minnesota.

"After getting on at Portland, Oregon, I made my way through the club car. A man, standing at the small bar, noticed my clerical garb and addressed me. 'Whoeryousir?' He mumbled in slurring speech common to persons who drink too many martinis. I did not decipher what he had said. Assuming he was inquiring about my destination, as so many passengers do, I replied firmly, 'Saint Paul.' His eyes grew wide, he stood taller, took hold of the bar to steady himself, and after a short silence, said, 'Didya ever get an answer back from those Corinthians'?"[1]

Today's Comment: I never wore any clerical garb that would identify me as a pastor. Consequently, I interacted over the years with people that did not know that I was a pastor, unless the conversation got around to the subject of jobs, or someone told the person that I was talking with that I was a pastor, or if I had given a gospel tract or shared the gospel. Because of this fact, that my pastorship was not known, I have had some interesting experiences.

I was invited to an AA meeting one time with a friend who had celebrated a few years of sobriety and no longer addicted to alcohol. I was introduced as "Dan." The fellow seated across from me had a different vocabulary than what I was used to but I enjoyed interacting with him. After having punctuated nearly every sentence with a curse word or profane word as he conversed with me, someone told him at the end of the meeting that the fellow seated across from him was a pastor. He didn't know whether to hide or apologize.

Somewhere in the recesses of the human conscience there is that small voice that causes one to know right from wrong. Yet, men and women persist in doing the wrong. The Bible is clear that there is coming a day when everyone will stand before the Judge of all the earth. For the child of God it will be the Judgment Seat of Christ where we will be judged for the things done in the flesh. For those who have not responded to Christ's invitation to become a part of God's "forever family," they will stand before the Great Judgement Throne. Pray for family and friends who know what is right, but persist in rejecting God.

Today's Golden Nugget of Truth: "For since the creation of the world His invisible attributes are clearly seen, being understood by the things that are made, even His eternal power and Godhead, so that they are without excuse, because, although they knew God, they did not glorify Him as God, nor were thankful, but became futile in their thoughts, and their foolish hearts were darkened." Romans 1:20, 21

Today's Philosophical Tidbit: "The tragedy of life and of the world is not that men do not know God; the tragedy is that, knowing Him, they still insist on going their own way." William Barclay.

June 19
Have You Met Any New Friends

*T**oday's Smile:* "You must be a new member here," said a golf club member to Gary as he was about to take a swing with his number one wood. Gary didn't respond as the member continued and said, "Do you know that you can't take your first shot eight feet ahead of the marker?"

Gary simply ignored this self appointed golf judge as he continued with his lecture. "Sir," he said I am telling you that you must go back to the marker. I am the chairman of the greens committee and I will have to report you to the board."

Finally, Gary looked up at this chairman of the greens committee and said, "Firstly, understand, I am not a new member. Secondly, I have been a member of this club for two years and you are the first person that has ever spoken to me. And thirdly, this is my second shot!"

Today's Comment: So Gary had been a member for two years and this was the first member to speak to him. If you moved into a new community were you welcomed by any of your neighbors? What about attending a new church? Did you walk in and out without anyone greeting you? Put it another way, did you welcome your new neighbors to your area or a visitor to church?

It is fifty years ago now, but a widow lady reminded us recently how my wife and I called on them on a Sunday afternoon. Our church was smaller in those days, but this young family attended the morning service we visited them that afternoon. They continued to come. He eventually became an elder while she got deeply involved in our music ministry.

In one of the friendliest churches that it was my privilege to pastor, Rockyview Alliance Church in Calgary, Alberta, and much larger than the church mentioned above, we introduced the Evangelism Explosion ministry. We had three person teams that called on visitors and newcomers. We smiled one night when one team came back with the report, that a young couple that they had visited that night voiced a criticism. Their criticism was that our church was "too friendly." Did you hear that? "Too friendly!"

The couple told our team, "We cannot get out of church without people greeting us." As pastor, I received that criticism as a compliment. On the other hand, one of my wife's cousins left a church after attending for one whole year. She told us that she got tired of being greeted every Sunday and asked if this was her first Sunday.

If you don't serve as a regular greeter at your church, why not reach out to a visitor or stranger and welcome them. Oh yes, don't ask them if this is their first Sunday. They might have been attending for a year. Simply tell them, "I don't think I've met you before. I am. . ."

Pray that you will do your best to be friendly to the strangers and newcomers.

Today's Golden Nugget of Truth: "If you are friendly only to your friends, how are you different from anyone else? Even the heathen do that." Matthew 5:47 (TLB)

Today's Philosophical Tidbit: "Good friends are the sisters and brothers you found outside your family." Author Unknown

Jump Start Your Day

June 20
Keep It Confidential

Today's Smile: Philip's parents had hired a tutor to teach him for his first three grades. When it came time for grade four, his parents decided that maybe he should attend the public school.

Just before the family chauffer drove the boy to his new school, his mom reminded him that he was not to go talking or sharing with anyone about how wealthy they were. He was going to be associating with many children that did not come from the same kind of home. He agreed.

The grade four teacher, wanting to learn a little about her new class of students, gave them an assignment asking them to write a composition about their family. Philip wrote the following:

"I come from a very poor family. My parents are poor. My grandparents are poor. All of my relatives are poor. The chauffeur who drove me to school is poor. The cooks are poor. The cleaning lady is poor. The man that looks after our lawn and gardens is poor. The lifeguard at our swimming pool is poor. Everybody that works for my parents is poor.

Today's Comment: When our three children were ages 8, 6, and 3, I decided on a Saturday morning that I should take our eight year old son Danny for a little walk and tell him what he would be hearing in church the next day. My resignation would be read to the congregation at the close of the service and we would be moving to Calgary, Alberta. I asked him not to tell anyone that we were moving to Calgary. I learned later that after we had arrived at church that he saw one of the ladies, fortunately an elder's wife, and said, "We're moving, but I can't tell you where."

Have you ever shared with a family member or friend and asked that they keep it to themselves, only to hear from someone later that the friend that you confided in had shared it with others? Or maybe a friend shared something with you and told you that they are not broadcasting this around only to find out that they told the same thing to several others

What does it mean when you share confidential news or receive the same? Does that not mean that it is to be kept in confidence? Pray that we will be people who can be trusted to not betray confidences.

Today's Golden Nugget of Truth: "A talebearer reveals secrets, but he who is of a faithful spirit conceals a matter." Proverbs 11:13

Today's Philosophical Tidbit: "He who carries a tale will always make a monkey out of himself." Author Unknown

June 21
You'll Never Be Humiliated

Today's Smile: I think that with the advent of the internet, we have had more laughs as family and friends pass on jokes and legends. One of those e-mail legends predates the internet dating back as far as 1940. Here's how the tale is told.

In Washington, a government survey was commissioned to study the migratory habits of birds. All kinds of species were caught and released by the Washington Biological Survey with an abbreviation on the metal strip reading "Notify Fish and Wild Life Division. Wash. Biol. Surv." One farmer wrote to the Fish and Wild Life Division and said, "I shot one of your crows last week and followed the instructions attached. I Wash.Biol.Surv (washed it, boiled it, and served it). It was awful. You should stop trying to fool the public with things like this."

Today's Comment: I have never eaten a crow, nor do I have an appetite for one. However, you've probably heard someone say, "He had to eat crow." Eating crow is a colloquialism which means that one has been humiliated or proven wrong. It is the same as saying, "He had to eat his own words." Other similar expressions are "eat dirt" or "eat your hat" or "if I am wrong I will eat my shirt."

The apostle Paul wrote several times in his epistles these words "not ashamed" and "confident." He boldly stated that he had confidence in God and what God says is true. God does not need to speak twice. We speak and sometimes make a mistake; God does not make

218

any mistakes. When God speaks it is done. When He commands it stands fast.

So let us, who are followers of God and have surrendered our lives to the will of God, rest in the assurance that we will never have to "eat crow." We may be ridiculed, criticized and ostracized by the world in which we live, but if we rightly divide the Word of God and boldly proclaim the same we will not be humiliated. The world around us may not believe us, but God will approve us.

Pray that we will stand secure in the knowledge that God approves of us, even though the world may not.

Today's Golden Nugget of Truth: "He is the Rock; His work is perfect; for all His ways are justice. A God of truth and without injustice, righteous and upright is He." Deuteronomy 32:4

Today's Philosophical Tidbit: "God writes with a pen that never blots, speaks with a tongue that never slips, and acts with a hand that never fails." Author Unknown

June 22
He Made Them Male And Female

*T*oday's Smile: Brandon's wife died so he decided to raise his only son out in the woods, away from the rest of society. Billy was just a little fellow when he and his father moved into the woods. They were far from "civilization;" they lived strictly off the land with no human contact. The son grew up never knowing what it was to see another human being, except for his own father.

One day when the son was well on into his teen years, Brandon decided to take Billy into town. Billy saw many things that he had never even imagined existed. One thing that captured his attention was to see young girls. "Dad," he asked, "what are those?"

His father, not being very fond of women, replied, "Oh, those are geese." Well after spending most of the day in town, they finally made the long journey back into the woods where they made their home. Some weeks later, Brandon decided to make another trip into town. He said to his son, Billy, "I'm going into town again and wonder if there was something that you saw on our last trip that you would like me to buy for you."

"Yes," Billy quickly replied, "get me one of those geese."

Today's Comment: God created the first man, Adam. God said it was not good for man to be alone and so he made a helper for Adam. God performed the first operation and obviously administered the first anaesthetic as he put Adam to sleep and removed a rib and made Eve, a companion for Adam. I once preached a Mother's Day sermon using a borrowed title: "From Adam's Rib To Women's Lib." Eve was taken from Adam's side. It was not a bone from the foot or from the head, but the side that they might compliment each other.

It is only natural that young men and young women are attracted to each other. That was God's plan from the beginning. If you are a young Christian person reading this today, make certain that you marry a young person who also loves God. You may not be aware of the difficult time that some couples experience after the honeymoon and into the marriage when a believer marries an unbeliever.

As a pastor, I've been aware of marital shipwrecks because young people did not allow God to be their Guide (when it came to marrying). Don't let that happen to you. If you are looking for a mate, pray that God will guide you to one that loves God and loves you.

Today's Golden Nugget of Truth: "Do not be unequally yoked together with unbelievers. For what fellowship has righteousness with lawlessness? And what communion has light with darkness?" First Corinthians 6:14

Today's Philosophical Tidbit: "Love is sharing the best years of your life with the person who made them the best years of your life!" Author Unknown

June 23
Keep Your Promise

*T*oday's Smile: An oil tycoon from Texas suddenly became ill while visiting in Oklahoma. He was rushed to the nearest hospital and the doctors that were consulted could not figure out the source of his illness.

The billionaire stated that for any doctor that could find the root cause and restore his health that he would give them whatever they desired. He asked them to search everywhere to find a doctor that would be able to help him.

A small town doctor was the one that found a cure for the billionaire. This doctor stayed by his patient for one whole week. As he was about to leave and go back to his practice a few miles north of the city, the billionaire said to him, "Doc! I am a man of my word. You name what you would like and if it is humanly possible, I'll get it for you."

"Well," said the doctor, "I love to play golf, so if I could have a matching set of golf clubs, that would be fine."

With that, the doctor left for home. The doctor did not hear from the billionaire for several months. He had almost forgotten about the Texan's promise. Then one day, he received a telephone call from him.

"Doc," he said, "I bet you probably thought that I had forgotten all about you. I have kept my promise. I have a matching set of golf clubs for you. The reason it took so long is that I could not find two of them with swimming pools that I thought were good enough. So I have found two clubs and had pools installed in both of them and they're all ready for your use."

Today's Comment: When we promise to do something for someone, do we keep our promise? It is easy to say, "We'll have you folks over for lunch sometime," but never do so. How often have we told someone, "I'll pray for you?" A fellow pastor told me one time that when he says "I'll pray for you," that he does it immediately in case he forgets later.

Let's not make promises that we know we will never be able to keep. Did we promise our child or grand child that we would take them somewhere, or buy them something and never follow through? Being on the receiving end, did someone ever promise you that they would do something for you and fail to fulfill? You remember that don't you?

Many years ago I was going through some deep waters. I broke down and shared with some fellow pastors after a gathering of pastors. One of them said, "I'll be over tomorrow to see you and pray with you." I was so encouraged by that and eagerly awaited his visit the next afternoon. He never showed up. I was already under a heavy load, and this didn't help.

Pray that we will not promise what we cannot fulfill, but keep the promise that we do make.

Today's Golden Nugget of Truth: "It is better to say nothing than to make a promise and not keep it." Ecclesiastes 5:5 (NLT)

Today's Philosophical Tidbit: "We must not promise what we ought not, lest we are called on to perform what we cannot." Abraham Lincoln

June 24
Lacking The Basic Necessities

Today's Smile: Marilla, who was in her 70's and living by herself, answered a knock on the door. It was a vacuum cleaner salesman. "Good afternoon," said the young salesman. "If you would be so kind as to give me a few minutes of your time, I will demonstrate the very latest in our new high-powered vacuum cleaner."

"I'm sorry," said Marilla as she started to shut the door. "I'm too poor to buy a vacuum cleaner. I don't have any money."

The young salesman managed to get his foot in the door and pushed it wide open. "Don't be in a rush, lady," he said. "You must see my demonstration and then you can say 'no'." As he spoke, he threw some chicken manure on her hallway carpet. "If this vacuum cleaner does not remove every trace of this manure, I promise you that I will eat every bit that is left."

Marilla, stepped back, and her frown turned into a big smile as she said, "Well, young man, I hope you have a strong stomach. Start eating. My electricity was cut off this morning."

Today's Comment: Statistics are ever changing, however, at the time of writing I learned that: "1.4 billion people in developing countries live on $1.25 a day or less."[1] "22,000 children die each day due to conditions of poverty."[2] "2.3 billion people suffer from water-borne diseases each year."[3]

Much more can be said about the world's poorest. In our western countries, we also have our poor, though they may appear rich compared to those developing countries. They are still considered poverty stricken.

Some people have been born into poverty and have a difficult time rising above that level. Some are poor because they are lazy. Some are poor because of the lifestyle that they have chosen. No matter the reason for their poverty, they are poor. They are in God's heart and in Christ's compassion. Thank God for every church and benevolent ministry, be it overseas or in our own land, that reaches out with compassion to those in need. Pray for these ministries and support them. Acquaint yourself with such agencies in your own locale.

Today's Golden Nugget of Truth: "But whoever has this world's goods, and sees his brother in need, and shuts up is heart from him, how does the love of God abide in him?" First John 3:17

Today's Philosophical Tidbit: "Beware of the Christian with the open mouth and the closed pocket book." Author Unknown

June 25
Servant Leadership

*T*oday's Smile: A young man had just graduated from university with a degree in engineering and was so excited as he contemplated his future. He caught a taxi and was just so exuberant that the taxi driver asked: "Well, you seem to be having a good day. What's so exciting in your life?"

"I just graduated yesterday from the university and I can't wait to go out into the world and see what's in store for me. I can see it all in my mind. Good paying job, a nice home, a brand new auto, vacations in Spain, the Caribbean, Alaska, a wife and kids. The sky is the limit!"

Before the taxi driver started down the road, he turned back and looked at his passenger and extending his hand to this promising young man said, "Congratulations, I graduated from the same university, class of 1981."

Today's Comment: Since my area of ministry throughout the years has been that of a pastor, my thoughts naturally turned in that direction. Many graduates from Bible Colleges and Seminary have graduated with one or two degrees behind their name. They left school prepared to turn the world upside down. Some of them did just that, but not for the better. They entered the ministry full steam and it wasn't long before they ran out of steam. Some of the most promising young men and women that I knew in my student days and pastoral years had a disastrous end to their ministry. Some no longer attend a church or show any interest in spiritual matters.

It you're a recent graduate and about to enter the Christian ministry as a pastor, don't try to turn the church around in your first year. Listen to the congregation. Listen to your Board of Elders or Deacons. Listen to the Lord.

Pray that we will be men and women with servant hearts, not superior heads.

Today's Golden Nugget of Truth: "Shepherd the flock of God which is among you, serving as overseers, not by compulsion but willingly, not for dishonest gain but eagerly; nor as being lords over those entrusted to you, but being examples to the flock." First Peter 5:2, 3

Today's Philosophical Tidbit: "One of the hardest secrets for a man to keep is his opinion of himself." Author Unknown

June 26
Marital Commitment

Today's Smile: Grady Wilson, associate evangelist with the Billy Graham Evangelistic Association tells the story about his wedding.

"Dr. (William) McCarrell had told me that my cue to kiss the bride would be: 'Let us pray.' But he didn't tell me he was going to pray three times during the ceremony! In the early part of the ceremony he had an invocation, sort of. He said, 'Let us all pray.' When he did, I leaned over and kissed Wilma prematurely.

Jimmie (Johnson), my best man, stage whispered, 'Not now, you moron.' I had to lift her veil to kiss her, and I did kiss her. Then when Dr. McCarrell spoke those words, 'With all my worldly goods, I thee endow,' Jimmie whispered again, 'There goes your shotgun and your rod and reel.' Some of the wedding party heard that and became tickled.

Finally, Dr. McCarrell came to the genuine kissing place. 'Let's bow our heads.' Precious few bowed their heads. They wanted to watch. So I kissed Wilma again. I had already kissed her at least three times - again and again and again. And then Dr. McCarrell again announced, 'Let's pray.' Can you imagine that? Everybody in that congregation thought we had a kissing disease. But we were married fair and square. Then Dr. Mc intoned, 'I now pronounce you man and wife.' This time, after our kissing bout, I hesitated. Dr. Mc nodded at us, instructing, 'You may now kiss the bride.' I lost track of the kisses."[1]

Today's Comment: Thank God today for the many happy godly marriages that we continue to see in the lives of those who have walked together for years. I'll never forget Mr. & Mrs. Tom Jones. They were the parents of my uncle Charlie, who married one of my Dad's sisters. I remember when I was a young boy seeing these two aged people walking together holding hands. They had a deep love for each other and also for the Lord.

It was Mr. Jones who knelt beside me at the altar and led me in a prayer to receive Christ as my personal Savior when I was about 8 years old. My wife and I visited these folks when we were on our honeymoon. They had just celebrated 70 years of marriage.

When it comes to the priorities in your life, being committed to your spouse is second only to your commitment to God. Third is commitment to your family. Any commitment to your job, profession or anything else in your life must be fourth on your list of priorities. Pray that we have our priorities right.

Today's Golden Nugget of Truth: "Therefore what God has joined together let not man separate." Matthew 19:6

Today's Philosophical Tidbit: "Happy marriages begin when we marry the ones we love, and they blossom when we love the ones we marry." Tom Mullen

June 27
The Secret Of A Good Marriage

Today's Smile: Morty and Violet had been married for over sixty years, when Violet became very ill. It had been a good marriage and they shared openly with one another throughout the years. They seldom argued and they were the envy of many of their peers. However, there was a shoe box which Violet kept under the bed and told Morty that he was never to open it. Now that she was ill and her future didn't look too hopeful she told Morty that he could open the box, if he wished.

Morty had complied with her wishes all through the years and never once did he open the shoe box. Well, he opened the box and in it he found three doilies and $17,000.00. "Babe, what is this all about?" he asked.

"Well sweetheart, when we were married my grandmother told me that the secret to a long happy marriage was to never argue with your husband. She went on to say that if I ever got angry with my husband I should crochet a doily."

Morty was so moved he could not keep back the tears. Three little doilies were in the box. She had only been angry with him three times in over sixty years. "Babe, you've explained the little doilies and you have made me so very happy, but where did all this money come from money?"

"Oh that sweetheart, that is what I made from selling all the other doilies!"

Today's Comment: Several years ago at the wedding reception for one of our children, my brother David and his wife sang a duet. Before they sang the duet, David, in his jokingly fun loving way said, "Helen and I have had 17 good years of marriage. Out of 22 years, that's not bad." How long have you been married? Were they all good years, or only some of them?

The secret of a good marriage is not crocheting a doily when you get angry and it is not going for a long walk. That's another story. Maybe you've heard it. The husband was told to go for a long walk whenever he felt anger towards his wife. As the story goes, the husband was in excellent health. He had had many long walks.

What are the secrets of a good marriage? There are probably many things that could be said. Here are a few: Friendship, fellowship, companionship and prayerfulness. Four other words which I feel are necessary are: Loving, trusting, communicating and laughing. You can add more to these. If some of these are lacking, try adding to your marriage and see if it makes a difference.

Pray that we who are married have all the ingredients necessary to make for a lasting marriage.

Today's Golden Nugget of Truth: "And above all things have fervent love for one another for love will cover a multitude of sins." First Peter 4:8

Today's Philosophical Tidbit: "The tragedy today is that many Christians think they are fighting flesh and blood in their marital and parenting issues, rather than realizing that Satan has an agenda to destroy their home. Whoever controls the family controls the future." Tony Evans

June 28
Make Sure You Know All The Facts

T *oday's Smile:* Stanley was looking for summer work. The only summer job that he had ever had before was helping his neighbors. Now he wanted a full time job for summer and so he went down to the student employment office and looked at different "help wanted" ads. He saw one. The place of employment was only a few blocks from his home. The ad read: "Retailer wanted for imported canaries." He got the address and went over to the small office of the wholesaler."

He was ushered into the manager's office. Stanley responded to several questions put to him by the manager, as to age experience, work ethics, and whether he would be able to work for July and August. In answer to the question re experience, Stanley said, "I haven't had a full time job before. I've helped my neighbors keep their yards clean and neat. I don't know much about canaries, but I am willing to learn.

You can talk to any of my neighbors. I know they have been happy with my work."

"Well, I am willing to give you a try at retailing," said the manager. "How would you like it if I paid you a base wage of seventy-five dollars a week and a dollar for every bird? Does that sound acceptable?"

"Yes sir. That sounds real good."

"Do you have any questions, Stanley?"

"I have one question. I assume that all of the canaries have to be re-tailed, but how did the canaries lose their tails in the first place?"

Today's Comment: This story makes me think of how often people launch into an agreement when they do not know all the facts or understand what it is they are getting into. Some have been hired on, not knowing or maybe not seeing a written job description only to find that they were expected to do more than they had thought. I've heard of others that have bought into a business partnership only to find out that their new partner was deep in debt. The money this new partner had invested didn't even pay off the debt. Others have entered into marriage, not knowing everything they should have known about their spouse.

Pray that you will fully understand what you are getting yourself into, be it a job, a relationship or some other commitment.

Today's Golden Nugget of Truth: "That you may know the certainty of those things in which you were instructed." Luke 1:4

Today's Philosophical Tidbit: "Wise people have heads like nails, which keeps them from going too far." Author Unknown

June 29
Not Afraid Of Hard Work

*T**oday's Smile:* A country boy applied for a salesman's job at a large complex in the city. It was the biggest store of its kind and had everything. The boy indicated that he had been a salesman in the country store. The owner of this city store took a liking to him and so told him that he could start the next day. "I'll come around at closing time to see how you've done," said the boss.

At closing time the boss arrived and asked, "How many sales did you make today?"

"I only sold to one customer," was the young boy's response.

"Only one?" the boss exclaimed. "Why most of my staff make twenty or thirty sales a day. How much was the sale worth?"

"It was over one hundred thousand dollars," said the young man.

"How did you manage that?" asked the flabbergasted boss.

"This man came in," replied the boy, "and I sold him a small fish hook, then a medium hook and finally a really large hook. Then I sold him a small fishing line, a medium one and a big one. I asked him where he was going fishing and he said down at the coast. I said if he was going to the coast he would probably need a boat, so I took him over to the boat department and sold him that twenty foot schooner with the twin engines. Then he said his Volkswagen beetle wouldn't be able to pull it, so I took him to the auto department and sold him a new Sport Utility Vehicle."

The boss took two steps back and asked in astonishment, "You sold all that to a guy who came in for a fish hook?"

"No," answered the young salesman, "actually, he came in to buy a bottle of cough syrup for his wife and I said to him, your weekend's shot, you may as well go fishing."

Today's Comment: Hard work usually pays off. Many people in the western world went through the depression of the 1930's. My grandparents did, my parents did. I live in a part of the country where there is a large number of people who emigrated from Russia, Ukraine, Germany and The Netherlands. Most of these people knew hard times back in their native land. Many of them lived through World War II, and some had parents and grandparents that came following World War I. Many of the millionaires in this area are immigrants or the children of immigrants. Why are they where they are financially? They were not afraid of work.

On a spiritual note, I have visited some of America's large churches, which are mega churches today because the founding pastor and succeeding pastors modelled work and motivated the members of the congregation. They knocked on doors. When they saw a need, they started a ministry to meet that need. These churches have grown because its leaders and members were men and women of passion and not afraid of hard work. But in all cases they needed the blessing of God, and the Spirit of God to sustain and motivate.

Pray that as Christians we will be fully committed to the ministry of the church and the spreading of the Gospel.

Today's Golden Nugget of Truth: "And let us not grow weary while doing good, for in due season we shall reap if we do not lose heart." Galatians 6:9

Today's Philosophical Tidbit: "You don't build a reputation on what you're going to do, but on what you've done." Author Unknown

June 30
Do I Bother You

T oday's Smile: Ravi had the nicest fruit and vegetable market. He had an abundance of local fruit, plus a lot of imported fruit and many exotic fruits. His market was a popular destination for all kinds of people. However, there was one customer that he would rather not see, but she came every Saturday. Ravi treated her with respect, though she was a very picky customer.

One Saturday morning, this woman asked for two pounds of oranges. She asked Ravi to wrap each orange in a separate piece of paper. He obliged. "And I want a pound of cherries and I want you to also wrap each one of those separately. Without showing any impatience, Ravi took each cherry and wrapped it in a piece of paper. By the check out counter was a large container of raisins. Pointing to them, she said, "I would like. . ."

By now, there were ten people in the check out line. Ravi, having spent several minutes wrapping each orange and cherry, told the woman, "Ma'am, those raisins are not for sale!"

Today's Comment: Are we guilty of pestering people? Do we monopolize their time? Do we butt in when others are talking? Do we stop to think that others have their schedule, work or other activities planned for the day? Do we show up for appointments late thereby wasting time for the other person or persons

There is a flip side to that question. Are we faced with people who continually take advantage of us, taking up our time, phoning us continually, interrupting our schedule? Do we appreciate it? The question then arises, how do we handle such?

First, God's Word teaches us that we should pray for them. (Matthew 5:43, 44). We need to put this situation into God's hands. Second, ask the Lord for wisdom. Maybe we should do nothing, or maybe we should talk to them about it. Talking may not be best for all, but it might help in some situations.

Several decades ago there was a woman who phoned our house several times a day with trivial matters, none of which were of any great importance. She simply wanted to talk. This was long before we had the telephone display showing the phone number of the caller. After weeks of numerous phone calls, we politely let her know that we had several others that needed some of our time and asked that she limit her calls to once a day.

So today let's pray that we will be considerate and understanding of others and their time and if we are experiencing such a problem that God would give us the wisdom and the strength to know how to deal with it.

Today's Golden Nugget of Truth: "So when He (Jesus) heard that he (Lazarus) was sick, He stayed two more days in the place where He was." John 11:6

Today's Philosophical Tidbit: "If Jesus was led by His Heavenly Father and did not immediately respond to every call and circumstance that came His way, then we, as children of our Heavenly Father, should not let others detour us from God's plan for our life." A. Daniel Goldsmith

July 1
We Stand On Guard For Thee

oday's Smile: Today's smile is reported to be a true story. I checked *Snopes* and *Truth or Fiction* and they have no information re the same. Whether it is true or one of those made up stories, I hope it will bring a smile. Read on. . .

The Canadian Revenue Agency returned the Tax Return to a Canadian taxpayer indicating the importance of an accurate tax return. It appears that the taxpayer answered one of the questions incorrectly.

In response to line 305 of the T1General Tax Return which deals with whether one has any dependents, the taxpayer wrote: "2.1 million illegal immigrants, 1.1 million crack heads, 4.4 unemployable scroungers, 80,000 criminals in over 85 prisons plus 650 idiots in Parliament and the entire group that call themselves Politicians."

The CRA returned his tax papers stating that the response he gave was unacceptable. The taxpayer responded, sending it back to the CRA asking, "Who did I leave out?"

Today's Comment: Many people do not like paying taxes. They grumble, they gripe. They complain about government mismanagement of our money. Let's face it. Do you realize that our taxes pay for the education of our young, the first responders, security, defence and infrastructure. How would we travel if we didn't have roads, super highways, bridges, tunnels, etc? Some of our money goes towards medical expenses and safety nets. Don't forget the enjoyment of our parks, lakes and rivers, etc. There are so many more things of which we are the recipients.

July 1st in Canada is a national holiday, *Canada Day.* Canadians are reminded of their roots. Canada became a country, *The Dominion of Canada* on July 1st, 1867. Since that time Canadians have had freedom of religion; freedom of association with whomever; freedom of the press; freedom of expression. There is much more that space does not permit.

Canada has been blessed by God and blessed others. May the prayer of all Canadians today be the words of the fourth stanza and refrain of Canada's national anthem, *O Canada.* "Ruler Supreme, Who hearest humble prayer, Hold our Dominion in Thy loving care; Help us to find, O God, in Thee a lasting rich reward, As waiting for the better day, We ever stand on guard. God keep our land, glorious and free, O Canada, We stand on guard for Thee, O Canada, We stand on guard for Thee."

Today's Golden Nugget of Truth: "And Jesus answered and said to them, 'Render to Caesar the things that are Caesar's and to God the things that are God's'." Mark 12:17

Today's Philosophical Tidbit: "Good government is a bargain at any price."

July 2
Clearly Understood

*T*oday's Smile:* I was at a hobby and craft sale recently and selling my book *Jokes Quotes & Anecdotes - Made Especially For Citizens With Seniority.* One elderly lady stopped by the table glanced at my book and then said to me, "I get my jokes from Dr. David Jeremiah." She then proceeded to tell me the latest bit of humor that he had shared.

Dr. David Jeremiah is one of my favorite radio and television preachers. He is the senior pastor of the Shadow Mountain Community Church in El Cajon, CA. His Bible teaching ministry is spiced up with some appropriate humor. He shared some years ago about a time when his wife Donna was giving their little son David a bath. Their son is a big man today, but when he was a little boy, he really wasn't little, he was big and he was chubby.

Donna Jeremiah was so overcome with love for her son David that in her sweet motherly tone said to him, "I love you, you little tub," and then gave him a big hug. Two or three nights later she said the same thing again, "I love you, you little tub."

Son David looked at his Mommy and responded by saying, "Mommy, I love you, you little toilet."[1]

Today's Comment: How well do children comprehend what adults say? I heard Taranda Greene, who was the wife of Anthony Elden (Tony) Greene share her testimony. The Greenes were well known Southern Gospel Singers. Tony passed away in September 2010. Taranda shared how a lady came up to her and her children and expressed her sympathy by saying something to the effect that she trusted that they would draw comfort from knowing that her husband and father of her two girls was in heaven. One of the girls said, "Don't you know!"

When they got home, Taranda asked her daughter why she said, "Don't you know!" Her daughter replied stating that Jesus didn't know

233

who was heaven, how could we. To prove her point she misquoted Jesus' words: "Our Father, who *are* in heaven?"

In this summer season, let us stop and pray for all camp leaders, DVBS workers, neighborhood club teachers and all those who are seeking to convey biblical truths to young children. Pray that the gospel will be clearly presented and fully understood and that many will pray to receive Christ as their personal Saviour.

Today's Golden Nugget of Truth: "That I may make it manifest, as I ought to speak." Colossians 4:4

Today's Philosophical Tidbit: "A child's life is like a piece of paper on which every passerby leaves a mark." Chinese Proverb

July 3
Have Faith In God

T oday's Smile: Three Englishmen, Robert, Richard and William, met often for a "spot of tea." A new Tea Room opened up in their area and the three of them thought that they would see what it was like. It was closer than the place where they normally met. If the tea was to their liking and the staff were friendly, they might consider going their on a regular basis.

When the waitress arrived ready to take their order, Robert ordered a cup of weak tea. Richard chimed in and said, "I'll have tea, too. I want mine as strong as you make it with a slice of lemon." When William gave his order for tea he asked that she would make sure that the cup was clean.

When the waitress returned she said, "O.K. Now which one of you asked for a clean cup?"

Today's Comment: I'm sure that you have had a few dinners, a cup of tea or a coffee in a restaurant. Have you ever asked that they serve it on a clean plate or in a clean cup? Some of you may have, but the vast majority of us were thinking of the food and the drink. We took it by faith that the dishes and cutlery would be clean. Grant it, there has been an occasion or two when there was a dirty cup or dish, but we don't usually ask that the dishes be clean. We have faith in the restaurant that they serve their food on clean plates.

We exercise faith every day. We have chairs, couches a bed, etc. I have never ever met any person who made the furniture that I sit on, but I sit on such believing that they will hold me. I have never been on an airplane where I knew the pilot, but I have flown several thousand miles. I don't know anyone that made the canned soup, that I enjoy occasionally, but I've had many a bowl of soup throughout my eight decades plus. I should take that back. I did work briefly, one summer, for a major food canning company. I met the fellow that put the pork in the pork and beans. I'm sure he only used one hog a year, because it's almost impossible to find amidst the beans. We exercise faith every day in many ways.

Do we have faith in Almighty God? He who flung the planets and stars into orbit; He who made the mountains and the seas; He who made the fowls that fly; He who made the creatures of earth; the great God and Creator, can we trust Him? Is He not greater than any issue that we face, including our problems, our decisions and our future?

Let's pray today that we will have the faith, be it ever so small, to cast ourselves on the great and powerful God. He holds the universe in the palm of His hand. Whatever you face today, trust Him! Have faith in God!

Today's Golden Nugget of Truth: "For whatever is born of God overcomes the world. And this is the victory that has overcome the world - our faith." First John 5:4

Today's Philosophical Tidbit: "Faith makes the uplook great, the outlook bright, the future glorious." Author Unknown

July 4
Freedom Of Expression

Today's Smile: When President James Garfield was a college boy, so the story goes, he was walking along the sidewalk with two live-wire companions. They met up with an aged man who had a long white beard. He was using two canes. Without thinking, but acting a little foolishly, Garfield bowed politely and said, "Good morning, Father Abraham."

Taking his cue from that, one of Garfield's friends said, "Good morning, Father Isaac." The third boy, not to be outdone, bowed and said, "Good morning, Father Jacob."

The old man glared at them over his spectacles and said, "Young men, I am neither Abraham, Isaac, nor Jacob. I am Saul, the son of Kish, I am out looking for my father's asses, and I think I have found them."

Today's Comment: Today is *Independence Day* in the United States of America. It is a country where you can tell a joke; give an exaggerated story about your friend or draw a cartoon about some high official and we can all laugh. A land that has enjoyed freedom of religion, belief, opinion, expression, assembly, demonstration, petition and association.

I remember sitting by the radio, when I was a young boy, listening to *Major Bowes Amateur Hour*. There was a commercial about four great cars, Plymouth, Dodge, Desoto and Chrysler. There was also the weekly spinning of the wheel to determine the order in which the evening's talent would perform. As the wheel was spun the words "around and around she goes and where she stops nobody knows" were intoned. What I remember best is Kate Smith's weekly rendition of *God Bless America*.

Though some of America's freedoms are under attack, God has blessed America and made it a blessing. The United States of America has blessed the world through its Christian ministries. Think of the great pastors, evangelists, missionaries, Christian Colleges, Seminaries, Christian radio and television stations, Christian books, periodicals and the many para-church organizations and benevolent ministries that have come from America. No other nation in history has done as much for the proclamation of the gospel as has the United States.

Though I was born, raised and still live in Canada, I say thanks for "the good old USA." I spent three wonderful years there, graduating in 1957 from Columbia International University, Columbia, South Carolina. I had a pastoral internship at a Conservative Baptist Church in Michigan. I met my wife in Pennsylvania.

Pray today for America's leadership. Pray that Americans will continue to have the fundamental freedoms upon which the country was built, and pray that God's people will continue to let their light shine brightly throughout the land.

Today's Golden Nugget of Truth: "Render therefore to all their due: taxes to whom taxes are due, customs to whom customs, fear to whom fear, honor to whom honor." Romans 13:7

Today's Philosophical Tidbit: "We ought to be thankful that we are living in a country where folks can say what they think without thinking." Author Unknown

July 5
The Innocence Of A Child

Today's Smile: Franklin had been away for several days and had arrived at his home in Oklahoma City, OK just before midnight. A terrible thunder storm had just hit the city moments before he walked into the house. As he entered the bedroom, he found his two girls sleeping in bed with his wife. He decided not to waken them and slept in the guest room that night.

The next morning as they were seated around the breakfast table, all happy to see one another, Franklin said to his girls that it was alright to sleep with mommy when he was away if there was a bad storm, but when he was home that he would like to sleep with mommy.

About a month later, Franklin had another business trip out of town. The airplane was a little late arriving back in Oklahoma City and consequently there were nearly a hundred people in the terminal waiting for loved ones. As Franklin entered into the waiting area, Lucy, his five year old daughter, ran to give him a hug and shouted, "Daddy, I got good news for you!"

"What's the news Honey?"

"Nobody slept with mommy while you were away!"

Today's Comment: I love the innocence of young children. It is refreshing and often the cause for much laughter. Back in the 1960's I was pastor of the Vernon Alliance Church in Vernon, BC. Behind that church, on another street was the German Church of God. As we were driving into the church parking lot, with some friends in the car with us, our son Brian said to our company, and pointing to the Church of God, "That is God's Church. This is Daddy's church."

Well it wasn't my church. Though we did not have the word *God* in our church name, it was nevertheless God's church. Oh that all churches would have God in them. I am afraid that there are some churches which have been reduced to a mere club. People get together to socialize more than worship. Thank God today for every church where God is in control and it is His church. Pray for the pastors that they will continue to "hold forth the Word of God."

Today's Philosophical Tidbit: "Holding fast the Word of life, so that I may rejoice in the day of Christ that I have not run in vain or labored in vain." Philippians 2:16

Today's Philosophical Tidbit: "The only way to know how parishioners see your church is to look at it through their eyes." Author Unknown

July 6
The Humble Shall Be Exalted

Today's Smile: Eight year old Nicholas boarded an airplane in Los Angeles bound for Milwaukee. His mom and dad were divorced and he was flying to visit his father. He was seated beside a woman who was well known in the social circles of Los Angeles. She was also an author and anticipated using her laptop on the flight to do some writing. They were barely in the air when Nicholas began to ask the woman question after question. He was non-stop with his chatter. The woman became irritated and buzzed for the flight attendant and demanded another seat in the airplane. "I have work to do," she said, "and I need to be where it is quieter. I can't be answering questions for the next three and a half hours."

After checking, the flight attendant returned and said, "There are no empty seats in economy, but I will check to see if there are any in first class." The woman thanked the attendant and quickly closed her laptop putting it in its case. The attendant returned and said that she had found one in first class. "It is our company policy to never move a person from economy to first class, but being that it is distracting, especially since you have work to do, we can make the switch to first class. So, Nicholas you get your bag under the seat and please come follow me to first class. We don't want you to be bothering this woman while she is busy with her work."

Today's Comment: All too often the complainer usually gets what he or she demands. The one who doesn't gripe does not get the attention. As it has been often said, "The squeaky wheel gets the grease," meaning of course that the person who protests or complains the loudest or longest will sooner or later attract some attention and get what they want. It is encouraging now and then to see the person who does not complain, who is simply a steady prodder and does his or her work get rewarded.

I know many people who work behind the scenes. They are not out front in the prominent positions. Their stories don't make headline news. They work in the kitchen, while others sit at the head table. They visit the shut-in or home bound person, while others are up front on stage where all see them. They work in the nursery while others sing in the choir.

Everyone is important and we don't all have the same gift or talent, but it is good when those working where the masses do not see them are occasionally thanked publicly for their work and ministry.

You may not be in a position to thank them publicly but how about sending an encouragement card or letter, or a phone call telling them that you appreciate their faithfulness. Don't forget to pray for them.

Today's Golden Nugget of Truth: "Do you want to stand out? Then step down. Be a servant. If you puff yourself up, you'll get the wind knocked out of you. But if you're content to simply be yourself, your life will count for plenty." Matthew 23:12 (MSG)

Today's Philosophical Tidbit: "Staring up to admire your own halo will often make you a 'pain in the neck'." Author Unknown

239

July 7
No Secrets In Marriage

*T*oday's Smile: Adam and Joy were on their honeymoon. Both had a problem that they had never shared with each other. Adam had smelly feet while Joy had bad breath. They had managed to disguise their problem in all of their dating and get together. Adam always soaked his feet putting after shaving lotion on them, while Joy gargled her mouth frequently during the day, also carrying a breath freshener with her at all times. All went well until they were married and spent their first night together.

Waking up their first morning their secrets would finally be known. Adam had awakened first and lay there in bed wondering how he was going to tell Joy that he had the world's smelliest feet. Joy finally awakened and her first thought was, I must tell my sweetheart about my bad breath. They were both troubled and hence there was a moment or two of silence. Joy finally blurted out, "Honey, I have something that I have to tell you."

"Yeah, I guessed it," says Adam, "you just ate my socks."

Today's Comment: If you are married, would you say that you have a good marriage? A good marriage is one where husband and wife are open with one another. A lot of marriages are like the six o'clock news, sharing only the events of the day. Others share their thoughts. That's a bit better. The most intimate relationship is when a couple can share their feelings. How are you doing?

I can do better and maybe you can, too. God ordained the first marriage and He is willing and able to help each married couple today if they will seek His help. Let's pray today that we, who are married, will do better.

Today's Golden Nugget of Truth: "Love is patient, love is kind. It does not envy, it does not boast, it is not proud. It is not rude, it is not self-seeking, it is not easily angered, it keeps no record of wrongs." First Corinthians 13:4, 5 (NIV)

Today's Philosophical Tidbit: "God created marriage. No government subcommittee envisioned it. No social organization developed it. Marriage was conceived and born in the mind of God." Max Lucado

July 8
What Were You Thinking

*T*oday's Smile: Reid flew his own plane and got tired of the long automobile trips from the airport to his country cottage which was situated on a lovely lake. So he equipped his plane with pontoons so he could land on the lake in front of his home. However, on his first trip with his newly equipped plane, he headed for the airport as he had always done. As he was going in for the landing his terrified wife yelled, "What are you doing? You are supposed to be landing on the lake."

Fortunately, he was able to swing his plane around and head for the lake. After he landed safely on the water, he heaved a big sigh of relief and turned to his wife and thanked her and said, "That's about the dumbest thing I've ever done!" Then he opened the door, stepped out of his plane, and fell directly into the lake!"

Today's Comment: We've all made some dumb moves. How many times have you said, "Why did I do that?" We weren't thinking. Our mind was somewhere else other than on the task at hand. It is easy to let our mind wander unless focused on what we should be focusing on.

When we are at the Sunday morning worship service, do we concentrate on the words of a hymn or chorus when singing the same, or are we just enjoying the melody. What about when the pastor is preaching? Are we wondering if we set the oven timer? Are we mulling over in our mind Saturday's golf game and how we could have done better? Maybe it is a date planned for later in the week.

How often has our mind drifted off somewhere else when reading the Bible or when praying? Pray that God will help us to control our mind and concentrate on the present.

Today's Golden Nugget of Truth: "Fix your minds on what is true and good and right. Think about things that are pure and lovely, and dwell on the fine, good things in others. Think about all you can praise God for and be glad about." Philippians 4:8 (TLB)

Today's Philosophical Tidbit: "Most of us are lazier in mind than in body." Author Unknown

July 9
Don't Miss Your Opportunity

T *oday's Smile:* Jimmy's mother was busy preparing lunch when she glanced out the kitchen window and saw her son "playing church" with their cat. He made the cat to sit quietly, though it appeared to have dozed off to sleep like many parishioners do. She smiled as she thought of her son maybe some day being a preacher.

A few minutes later she heard loud meowing and hissing and she went over to the open window to see that Jimmy was now baptizing the cat in a tub of water.

"Jimmy," she said, "stop that right now! The cat is afraid of water!"

Jimmy looked up at his mother and said, "But Mom he should have thought about that before he joined my church."

Today's Comment: That story reminds me of our three children who loved to play church on Sunday afternoons, as though they did not get enough that morning. We have old reel to reel tape recordings of them, singing, praying, reading scripture and a giving brief sermon. We have pictures of them, too. One picture shows one of our boys singing holding a *Cat In The Hat* book as a hymnal. Those were fun years.

Now those years are long in the past, with our two boys in their fifties and our daughter in her late forties. The Bible exhorts us to teach our children the Word of God and to train them in the way they should go. If you are a parent with young children, lead them in paths of righteousness. The years go by all too quickly and they are soon on their own, raising their families. Pray that we will not miss our teaching opportunities today.

Today's Golden Nugget of Truth: "You shall teach them to your children, speaking of them when you sit in your house, when you walk by the way, when you lie down, and when you rise up." Deuteronomy 11:19

Today's Philosophical Tidbit: "The small boy's definition of parenthood was suggesting that his mother and father were babysitters for God." Author Unknown

July 10
Are You Listening To Me

T *oday's Smile:* Glen walked into a medical clinic and the receptionist asked him what he had.

He replied by saying "Shingles."

She took his medical insurance card, verified his name and address and told him to have a seat. Ten minutes later, a nurse called him into a room, recorded his weight, his height, and his blood pressure and asked him what he had. He replied that he had "Shingles." She told him to wait and the doctor would see him soon.

When the doctor came into the room, he asked what he had. "Shingles," said Glen.

The doctor asked, "Where are the shingles?"

He responded by saying that "They're outside in the truck. Where do you want them unloaded?"

Today's Comment: How often have we been guilty of not taking the time to listen to what is being said? We jump to conclusions. We hear the first few words and assume the rest. It is interesting that over the years, I have had books, read articles and heard speakers share about being a better speaker and communicator. We took a homiletics course in Bible College about how to prepare a sermon. We had public speaking courses. How many times have you read a book or heard a speaker talk about being a good listener?

A friend told me that he was having coffee with some of his friends. They often met and there was one man, in that group, who always monopolized the conversation. One man in that group had had enough. One day he said to his talkative friend, "Would you be quiet and let someone else talk!"

Are you one that monopolizes any given conversation? Stop sometime and give the other person an opportunity to speak. You might learn something. The same may be said about our prayers.

Many times we come to God with a shopping list of requests. Pray that we will take time to listen to Him. Ponder the words of the old hymn written by William Dun Longstaff: "Take time to be holy, the world rushes on; Spend much time in secret, with Jesus alone."

Today's Golden Nugget of Truth: "He who has an ear, let him hear what the Spirit says. . ." Revelation 3:22

Today's Philosophical Tidbit: "The trouble with nearly everybody who prays is that he says *Amen* and runs away before God has a chance to reply. Listening to God is far more important than giving Him your ideas." Frank Laubach

July 11
Don't Forget To Pay Your Bill

*T*oday's Smile: The manager of the small town farm supply store became worried when he began to review the list of farmers with accounts that were long over due. To add to his dilemma these farmers were no longer actively making purchases from his store. He decided on a rather unique approach.

He sent a bill to each of them, only he doubled the amount that they owed the store. This plan produced amazing results. Customers who had let their debts go unpaid were now very upset seeing that the new bill stated that they owed so much more than they thought. One by one they made their way to the farm supply store and complained bitterly. "I am very sorry for the bill that you received," the manager told everyone. "Please accept my apologies. How would it be with you if I cut your bill in half and just charge you 50%? Would that be acceptable with you?"

Without complaining anymore, each one cheerfully paid the 50% and they were more than satisfied. So was the manager. He now received the full price of the original bill.

244

Today's Comment: Are we paying our bills on time, or have we let them lag? Over the years I have heard many disappointing stories about people who have not paid their bills for purchases made. I have known people in the construction business who have not received their pay for work done. I know of those who have borrowed money and never paid it back. There are far too many people who have not kept to their agreement.

May we not be guilty of such. I know there are those who have been caught in down turns in the economy, or by loss of job, etc. The wife of one such friend got a job to help her husband pay his debts. He was committed to paying his bills even if it took years. We as Christians should live lives that are above reproach. The world is full of people who are dishonest, cheaters, liars, you name it. As children of our Heavenly Father, pray that we will be an example to the world around us of what a true follower of Christ is really like.

Today's Golden Nugget of Truth: "That you may become blameless and harmless, children of God without fault in the midst of a crooked and perverse generation, among whom you shine as lights in the world." Philippians 2:15

Today's Philosophical Tidbit: "When wealth is lost, nothing is lost; when health is lost, something is lost; when character is lost, all is lost." Billy Graham

July 12
Concentrate On What You're Doing

*T*oday's Smile: It was a hot day and Peggy spotted an ice cream store. She chose her favorite, maple walnut. Another customer had entered as she was placing her order and she turned to see who was beside her. This customer turned to look at her at the same time. She found her eyes were glued on the most handsome man she had ever seen in her life. His eyes made her knees buckle and her mind was in a whirl. Having received her cone, she opened her purse paying with cash, then walking out of the store with her heart still pounding. Gaining her composure she suddenly realized that she did not have her cone, so she turned to go back into the store.

At the door she again came face-to-face with this handsome brute coming out. He said to her, "Are you looking for your ice-cream cone?"

Unable to utter a word she nodded yes. "Well, lady, you put it in your purse with your change."

Today's Comment: Do you have a problem concentrating? Obviously Peggy did. Do you hear what someone says to you? We can be hearing someone talk, but we are not listening. We are not concentrating on what is being said. We then excuse ourselves by saying, "I thought that you said to turn up the television," when what they said was to turn it off.

What about when we gather for worship on a Sunday morning? Stop yourself the next time you're singing a hymn or a chorus. Were you thinking about what you were singing or were you singing because you're familiar with it and you like the melody?

When the pastor preaches, are you wondering if you unplugged the iron, or about that fellow that you will meet at the office tomorrow morning and what he will say because you do not have that report ready. Are we listening?

Oh we hear him talking, but are we listening? Are we concentrating? You probably never ever put your ice cream cone in your purse, but not listening to what is being said, has its consequences. Pray that we will be better listeners.

Today's Golden Nugget of Truth: "I listen carefully to what God the Lord is saying, for He speaks peace to His faithful people." Psalm 85:8 (NLT)

Today's Philosophical Tidbit: "It is easy to hear because our ears are always open, but harder to listen, because our mind may be closed." A. Daniel Goldsmith

July 13
Have You Exhausted Your Patience

T oday's Smile: In Williamsburg, Virginia, a tour guide, who was dressed in Colonial clothing, fell and broke his wrist. He was still sitting in the hospital emergency room when a Canadian from New

Brunswick, who was passing through town, stopped by the hospital for some emergency medical attention.

The Canadian had never been to Williamsburg before and was unfamiliar with the tourist attractions. When she walked into the emergency waiting room she saw this tour guide sitting there in his Colonial uniform. She stopped, stared, looked him up and down and then asked the guide, "How many years have you been sitting here waiting?"

Today's Comment: That story reminds me of a few years ago when I had cataract surgery. The ophthalmologist, who performed the surgery, placed a shield or patch over the eye to keep me from rubbing the same. I went to his office the next morning to have it removed. There were about ten of us sitting there, each of us with one eye patched. A woman walked in, stopped, took one look at us all and asked, "What! Has there been a special at Wal-Mart®?"

Have you spent long hours sitting waiting for someone or waiting to be called into an office? Do you wait patiently? Waiting has to be the hardest thing for many people to do. We live in an age when everything has to move. It has to happen now. I remember hearing a commercial on a Detroit radio station advertising for a certain hospital. The commercial stated that if you go to their hospital emergency without getting attention within twenty minutes, your treatment is free.

I used to go to a pizza place occasionally for lunch. They placed a timer on the table and if you were not served within ten minutes, you got a coupon for a free meal next time. I ate free meals about four times in a row. They eventually stopped that practice. Guess they were losing money. At least they didn't make much money off of me.

The Lord, in His Word, exhorts us to be patient. If today you have to wait a few minutes for a person, or even wait a few seconds at a traffic light, pray that you don't lose patience.

Today's Golden Nugget of Truth: "A hot-tempered man stirs up dissention, but a patient man calms a quarrel." Proverbs 15:18 (NIV)

Today's Philosophical Tidbit: "Better to be patient on the road than a patient in the hospital." Author Unknown

July 14
He Knows Where He's Going

*T*oday's Smile: Bessie was born and raised in Windsor, Berkshire in England. During her college days she met Aleck, who was from Scotland. After graduation they married and Aleck took his bride to Banffshire in the north of Scotland. Since Aleck made frequent trips to Toronto, Bessie would often take her son Connor and spend a weekend with family in Windsor or London while Aleck was away. Her brother Terry drove a route master, commonly known as a double decker bus in London. He had suggested that the next time the two of them came to London he would take Connor with him on the bus and let him see the sights of London.

The day came and Connor went with his uncle Terry. He sat in the front seat and was enjoying his ride and all the sights of the big city. After about a half hour of sitting in that seat, his uncle suggested that he go upstairs and maybe he would be able to see things much better. So he climbed the stairs, but he came back down in a matter of seconds. His uncle asked him why he was back so soon. "Didn't you like it up there?"

"Uncle Terry," he said, "it's too dangerous up there. There's no driver!"

Today's Comment: No driver. Well, we all like to know that there is a driver behind the wheel; a pilot and co-pilot in the cockpit; an engineer and more in the locomotive. We also like to know that these people know where they are going.

One December evening my wife and I, together with some friends boarded a chartered bus for a guided tour in Vancouver seeing the Christmas lights. Our driver didn't have a schedule re the light tour. He wasn't sure where he was supposed to go. By the time we arrived at the famous Stanley Park, they were turning the lights off. That was to be the highlight, and we missed it.

We want a prime minister or president or chairperson, or leader who knows how to lead. We desire a pastor with vision and one who can give guidance in spiritual matters. We want teachers for our children who know what they are to teach. The list goes on.

There is One who knows the end from the beginning. In Sunday School we often sang *Savior like a Shepherd lead us. . .* They were only words to a fine song then. Throughout life that has been the prayer of my heart. "Lord Jesus lead me, guide me along life's path." If you are looking for guidance, if you need someone who will not lead you astray, someone who knows what's ahead, call upon the Lord Jesus Christ. Pray that He will lead you in the right direction. He is in the driver's seat. He knows the way.

Today's Golden Nugget of Truth: "I will instruct you and teach you in the way you go; I will guide you with My eye." Psalm 32:8

Today's Philosophical Tidbit: "If you have God as your co-pilot, isn't it about time you changed seats?" Author Unknown

July 15
Have You Laughed Today

*T**oday's Smile:* Before the days when Music Pastors in churches worked hard at developing a theme that complemented the sermon, there were many interesting ways in which the worship services happened. In my home church in Chatham, Ontario, the senior pastor's wife told a children's story each Sunday morning. Her stories were continued from one Sunday to the next. On one particular Sunday, she got to the place where the boy in the story, who had disobeyed his parents in going where he should not have gone, ended up in quicksand. The pastor's wife was very dramatic in her presentation and described how the boy was slowly sinking, sinking, sinking until the sand was up to his neck. "Now boys and girls, we will find out next Sunday what happened to Bobby."

A student team of musicians were present that Sunday morning and their next musical selection scheduled was a trumpet solo enti-tled, *From Sinking Sand He Lifted Me.* The congregation could not keep from laughing, and the trumpeter had to stop playing.

Today's Comment: Well, events such as this were not limited to small churches. Bev Shea, soloist with the Billy Graham Evangelistic Association for several decades, was welcomed on one occasion in a church and was invited to sing a solo. The pastor said, "We are going to dedicate Bev's solo to all the expectant mothers present this morning." Bev's solo was *He Is Able To Deliver Thee*. Bev sang the first verse while the congregation snickered and then Bev also had to stop.

You've probably had times when something happened and you choked up with laughter and could hardly control yourself. Laughter is good for you.

Norman Cousins, who was an American political journalist, author and professor was given up to die. He determined that he would not spend his last days in gloom and sadness. So he got videos of all the funny people he could find and watched them for hours. He later wrote that ten minutes of belly-laughing relieved him of pain for an hour. He eventually recovered from his illness and went back to work.

God made us to smile and laugh. Of course there are times when it is appropriate and times when we refrain from laughing. Pray that today you will enjoy God's gift of laughter.

Today's Golden Nugget of Truth: "A merry heart does good like a medicine, but a broken spirit dries the bones." Proverbs 17:22

Today's Philosophical Tidbit: "Laughter is the hand of God on the shoulder of a troubled world." Zig Ziglar

July 16
Children Are A Gift From God

T oday's Smile: Marianne was the mother of nine children, that included one set of twins and one set of triplets. They ranged in ages from two to thirteen. She took them to Central Park for the day. They played on the slides, swings, teeter totters and strolled through the park.

The time came for lunch. She had a great lunch for her brood, complete with sandwiches, cookies, pickles, chocolate bars, potato chips and cold drinks. As Marianne spread a sheet for a table cloth for their picnic lunch, one of the city police officers walked by, doing his patrol of the park. When he saw her he asked, "Are these all your children, or is this a picnic?"

"They're all mine," said Marianne, "and it's no picnic."

Today's Comment: The old nursery rhyme says, "There was an old woman who lived in a shoe, she had so many children, she didn't know what to do. . ." Susanna Wesley gave birth to 19 children, nine of which died in infancy. She once wrote to her husband John, who was away for over a year. She said, "I am a woman, but I am also the mistress of a large family. And though the superior charge of the souls contained in it lies upon you, yet in your long absence I cannot but look upon every soul you leave under my charge as a talent committed to me under a trust. I am not a man nor a minister, yet as a mother and a mistress I felt I ought to do more than I had yet done. I resolved to begin with my own children. . ."

Children are a trust given to us by God. Seek God for His wisdom in how to love them and value every day that you have with them. They grow up all too quickly and are soon out of the nest. Pray that your children will know how to fly and where to fly when they leave your nest.

Today's Golden Nugget of Truth: "Teach them (commandments) to your children. Talk about them when you are at home and when you are on the road, when you are going to bed and when you are getting up." Deuteronomy 11:19 (NLT)

Today's Golden Nugget of Truth: "One important lesson that parents must teach their children is how they will conduct themselves when they are no longer under parental control." A. Daniel Goldsmith

July 17
Maybe I'm To Blame

Today's Smile: Sarah was taking two of her granddaughters on their first train ride. They were travelling from Vancouver, BC to Calgary, AB. A vendor came through their car selling pop rocks. Neither of these girls had ever seen a pop rock before. Sarah bought a bag for each of the girls.

One of the grand-daughters quickly opened her bag and popped one into her mouth. Just then the train went into the Spiral Tunnel near

Field, BC. When they exited from the tunnel, she looked at her sister and said, "I wouldn't put one of those in your mouth if I were you."

"Why not?" asked the sister. "Well, I took a bite of one and I went blind for a few seconds."

Today's Comment: Do you sometimes play the blame game? It is so easy to blame others for the unfortunate circumstances you find yourself in life. We may blame the neighbors, our work, our associates, the boss, the church, the deacons, the pastor or any number of family members. Could it be us?

If we have so many people in our lives that are hard to get along with, should we not take a look in the mirror? We need to examine ourselves. Look into the mirror of God's Word. Maybe it is not everyone else in our lives. It might just be that our attitude needs to change. God is in the business of changing people. Pray that He will change us.

Today's Golden Nugget of Truth: "If it is possible, as much as depends on you live peaceably with all men." Romans 12:18

Today's Philosophical Tidbit: "You've told others about the problem people in your life. Have you told God? He might change those problem people, or He might change you." A. Daniel Goldsmith

July 18
How's Your Appetite

Today's Smile: Lauren had invited her new neighbor over for tea. Lauren was showing her neighbor the carpentry work that her husband had done in the den with all the new shelves and cabinets. The two ladies then got looking at some family pictures that had recently been taken. At that point, Lauren's young son, called and said, "Hey, mom, I made your tea." He had recently learned to make tea when he was camping with his dad and older brother.

Like a little gentleman, he brought the tray with two cups of tea to his mom and her neighbor. He also brought some freshly baked chocolate chip cookies that his mom had made that morning. "Sweetheart, this is quite a surprise," Lauren said to her son. "Thank you very much. Did you have any problem finding the tea strainer?"

"I couldn't find it mom, so I used the fly swatter," he replied. His mother nearly fainted as the neighbor set her tea cup back on the end table. "Oh, mom, don't worry, I didn't use the new one, I used the old one that was in the garage."

Today's Comment: How would you react? Would you continue drinking? My wife and I were sitting in a food court in a mall in Bangkok, Thailand. I had just been measured for a suit and was told to come back in one hour and they would have the jacket made, minus the sleeves. So putting in time we ordered a piece of strawberry shortcake and a cold drink. As I was putting my fork into my dessert a fair size bug crawled out my piece of cake. My wife was horrified. A waiter was walking by and saw what had happened. "Sorry about that," he said, "I'll get you another piece."

My wife said, "You're not going to eat another piece are you?" I was a little younger and a little more foolish, or senseless, but I ate the second piece. I might think twice now.

However, my mind goes to the many missionaries who are faced with such circumstances much worse. What do they do? I recently heard a missionary who was visiting with some nationals in their hut. The man sat scraping caked mud off of his feet, then without washing or wiping the knife stood up and cut some bread for the missionary. Not all missionaries, these days, face such incidents, but many do. They need our prayers. Offer a special prayer today for your missionary friends

Today's Golden Nugget of Truth: "To the weak, I became as weak, that I might win the weak. I have become all things to all men that I might by all means save some." First Corinthians 9:22

Today's Philosophical Tidbit: "I'm a fool for Christ. Whose fool are you?" Author Unknown

July 19
I Know Where You Work

Today's Smile: A man was flying in a hot air balloon and realized he was lost. He lowered the height of his balloon until he saw a man down below. He lowered the balloon a little bit more and almost touched the ground. He shouted, "Excuse me, but can you tell me where I am?"

The man below said, "Yes you're in a hot air balloon, hovering about thirty feet above this field."

"You must work in Information Technology," said the balloonist.

"I do," replied the man. ""How did you know?"

"Well," said the balloonist, "everything you have told me is technically correct, but it's of no use to anyone."

The man below responded by saying, "You must work in Management."

"I do," replied the balloonist, "but how did you know?"

"Well," said the man on the ground, "you don't know where you are, or where you're going, but you expect me to be able to help. You're in the same position you were before we met, but now it's my fault."

Today's Comment: Have you ever guessed at a person's occupation by listening to them or watching them and been right on? Occasionally we have been correct. My question today is, would someone be able to guess by our speech and actions that we are in the army of the Lord? I am not so concerned if someone guesses that I am a preacher. What I desire most is that they know for certain that I belong to God. Pray that the image of God will be reflected in our lives today.

Today's Golden Nugget of Truth: "Be imitators of God, therefore, as dearly loved children and live a life of love, just as Christ loved us and gave himself up for us as a fragrant offering and sacrifice to God." Ephesians 5:1, 2 (NIV)

Today's Philosophical Tidbit: "Those born of God will develop a likeness to their Father." Author Unknown

July 20
A Family Gathering

*T*oday's Smile: Brianna's mother died when she was only one year old and her father had remarried a year later. When Brianna was seven they moved to California. Within a few days Brianna met a girl about her age that lived across the street. The neighbor had a trampoline in the backyard and so invited Brianna to come and jump with her. It didn't take either of them long to become acquainted. Brianna's new friend was full of questions. "Where did you move from? Why did you come here to Anaheim?"

Brianna said, "We moved from Fargo, North Dakota because Daddy figured he would have lots of work out here."

"What does your Daddy do?"

"He is a magician and does lots of tricks. One of his big tricks is to saw people in half."

"Wow," said her friend, "that must be a funny trick." Her friend asked many more questions.

Before Brianna ran back home for lunch, her new friend asked if she had any brothers or sisters. "Yes," said Brianna, "I have two half brothers, and I have a little half sister."

Today's Comment: Today, more than ever before, we see many blended families. A second marriage has taken place, either because of death or divorce. I've seen blended marriages that appeared like they were made in heaven. A widow and widower coming together, bringing their family, and the children and grandchildren involved, welcoming each other with open arms.

There are also some sad second marriages where the children of one family have a hard time accepting their parent's new partner, or the new spouse may have problems with the new partner's children. Rejection is the result.

If you find yourself in such a setting, cast your burden on the Lord and draw from His strength. Things may change, they may not. Pray that the Lord will give you the grace that you need in such a relationship and move on. You can't deal with the other person's life. You can only deal with your own heart and attitude. Make sure your heart is right with God and with the new family member(s).

Today's Golden Nugget of Truth: "God sets the solitary in families. . ." Psalm 68:6

Today's Philosophical Tidbit: "The bond that links your true family is not one of blood, but of respect and joy in each other's life." Richard Bach

July 21
A Bag Of Wind Or A Windbag

T oday's Smile: At a Family Bible Conference on a hot July day, two speakers, one a Bible teacher the other a director for an overseas mission were scheduled for the evening service. The first speaker was an expository Bible teacher who appeared to be giving a Bible survey of the whole Bible. He talked, reached for the pitcher of water, pouring a glass of water and continued to talk. He talked some more, and took another glass of water. He talked another twenty minutes and took another glass of water. He finally finished, poured the remaining water into his glass and sat down.

The missionary director who oversaw the work of his mission in Africa, Asia, and Australia took to the podium. As he began his talk he said, "I have travelled the world for many years. I have seen many wonders of the world, including some of the Seven Wonders of the World. I have been on all continents and seen many different cultures. However, this is the first time that I have ever seen a windmill run by water."

Today's Comment: Do you know people who talk too much? They're easy to spot. You don't have to listen too long. They have something to say on every subject. There should be a balance between sharing in a conversation and listening to a conversation. It is so easy to spot others who talk a lot. Have we ever listened to ourselves?

I have had to smile at myself sometimes when I've been thanked for my advice and counsel. Really, I said very little, I just listened. Oh, that we might be good listeners and good talkers. That's a goal for our time of prayer. Don't do all the talking. Let the Lord speak to you, too.

Today's Golden Nugget of Truth: "So then, my beloved brethren, let every man be swift to hear, slow to speak, slow to wrath." James 1:19

Today's Philosophical Tidbit: "The only difference between 'silent' and 'listen' is the arrangement of the letters." Author Unknown

July 22
Thinking Of Marriage

*T*oday's Smile: A young couple got married and went on their honeymoon. When they got back, the bride immediately called up her mother. "Well," said her mother, "so how was the honeymoon?"

"Oh, mama," she replied, "the honeymoon was wonderful! So romantic..." Suddenly she burst out crying. "But, mama, as soon as we returned, Sam started using the most horrible language, things I'd never heard before! I mean all these awful four-letter words! You've got to take me home... please Mama!"

"Darling," her mother said, "calm down! You need to stay with your husband and work this out. Now, tell me, what could be so awful? WHAT four-letter words?"

"Please don't make me tell you, mama," wept the daughter, "I'm so embarrassed, they're just too awful! Come get me please!"

"Darling, baby, you must tell me what has you so upset. Tell your mother these horrible four-letter words!"

Sobbing, the bride said, "Oh, Mama..., he used words like: dust, wash, iron, bake, cook..."

"Darling, I'll pick you up in twenty minutes," said the mother.

Today's *Comment:* I have no idea the ages of people who hold this book in their hands, but I would say today that if you are planning to get married and are afraid of those four-letter words, you had better re-think your plans. Marriage involves dusting, washing, ironing, baking, cooking. It also means cutting the grass, cleaning out the garage, repairing the sink, taking out the garbage, shoveling snow and maybe the added joy and responsibility of raising children, being a parent and maybe even a grandparent.

Marriage brings with it joys and sorrows, happiness and sadness, ups and downs, but it is worth it all. Let me tell you that after 55 plus years of marriage to my best friend, I'd do it again. When the Lord is the foundation for our marriage, then we can say "for better for worse, for richer for poorer, in sickness and in health, to love and to cherish, till death us do part." Pray that your marriage will be the best.

Today's Golden Nugget of Truth: "For although the first woman came out of man, all men have been born from women ever since, and both men and women come from God their Creator." First Corinthians 11:12 (TLB)

Today's Philosophical Tidbit: "Marriage is an exclusive union between one man and one woman, publicly acknowledged, permanently sealed, and physically consummated." Selwyn Hughes

July 23
The Gift Of Evangelism

Today's Smile: Leighton Ford, who was an associate evangelist with the Billy Graham Evangelistic Association, was speaking at a crusade in Halifax, Nova Scotia.

"Leighton arranged for Billy to preach at the closing rally in Halifax. Billy came a day early and slipped into the back of the stadium where he noticed a man who seemed to be under conviction as Leighton preached. At the invitation Billy offered to go forward with him if he wanted to make a decision. The man didn't recognize Billy. He looked at the evangelist carefully and shook his head. 'No, thanks. I think I'll wait for the big gun tomorrow night'."[1]

Today's Comment: When I was in my early teens, my folks used to listen to *Songs In The Night"* a radio broadcast originating live from The Village Church of Western Springs, Illinois. Billy Graham was the pastor of that church. *Songs in The Night* was broadcast late Sunday nights over WCFL Chicago. George Beverley Shea was the soloist.

After listening to Billy Graham on that radio broadcast for about two years, my Dad was so excited and happy to take five of us teens to The Olympia Stadium in Detroit, March 1946, to hear Billy Graham in person. Never will I forget seeing 20,000 people fill the Olympia Stadium to hear the gospel. To see the response to his invitation to receive Christ was thrilling. I had never before seen so many people at one time listening to a preacher. That's about how many people were living in my home town.

I've followed the Graham ministry over the years and have been so grateful that he faithfully preached the simple gospel message. It was a personal thrill to attend many of the Graham meetings in Detroit in 1953, again in Chicago, Minneapolis and to be very much involved in his Calgary crusade in 1981. Thank God for the great ministry which the Billy Graham Evangelistic Association has had over the years.

It was an added blessing to hear my boyhood chum, Leighton Ford, in a crusade in Wainwright, AB and our home town of Chatham, ON.

Thank God for all of those whom God has gifted in a special way to preach the gospel to the masses. Yes, and thank God for all who tap people on the shoulder and say, "I will go with you." Sharing the good news of the gospel of Jesus Christ is not limited to the "big guns." Pray that God will use us to be sharers of the good news.

Today's Golden Nugget of Truth: "For we do not preach ourselves, but Christ Jesus the Lord, and ourselves your bondservants for Jesus' sake." Second Corinthians 4:5

Today's Philosophical Tidbit: "A church without evangelism is a contradiction in terms, just as a fire that does not burn, is a contradiction." Author Unknown

July 24
Falsifying The Truth

Today's Smile: Max and Polly had seven children ranging in ages from three to 16. They needed a bigger house and so the nine of them went together looking for another house that would meet their needs. It was not an easy task. They found suitable housing, but when the landlords saw that there were seven children, they objected. Mac and Polly, accompanied by their children, did this for several days when Max finally said to his wife, "Why don't you take the four youngest and go out to the cemetery and visit the grave sites of their grandparents."

Max took the three older ones with him. They spent most of the morning looking at different houses. About 11:30am they found a place that was just right. The landlord asked the usual question, "How many children do you have?"

Max answered with a deep sigh, "Seven, but four of them are with their dear mother in the cemetery." They got the house.

Today's Comment: Sometimes you can tell the truth but leave a false impression. True, the wife and four children were in the cemetery, but they were on top of the grass and not under it. Make certain that when you speak, you do not speak in such a way as to give a false impression. It is so easy to do when you do not want your hearer to know the real truth.

I knew a pastor, who years ago spoke at a conference and in his introduction he said, "On my way here the other day I was reading my Bible." He gave the name of the book, chapter and verse. He then proceeded to give his message based on that scripture portion. As a young preacher I thought this guy is something else. He prepared his message while travelling to this conference.

A fellow pastor told me later, "I heard him speak at another church, and he said 'on my way here I was reading my Bible,' and he named the same book, chapter and verse." Now the truth was he probably was reading that portion of scripture on his way. He was probably going over his notes and thoughts relative to sharing the same. However, the impression he left was that God gave him that message as he was on his way. Let's pray that we will tell the truth without leaving false impressions.

Today's Golden Nugget of Truth: "Truthful words stand the test of time, but lies are soon exposed." Proverbs 12:19 (NLT)

Today's Philosophical Tidbit: "The most deceptive liars are those who live on the edge of truth." Author Unknown

July 25
Media Madness

Today's Smile: Matt was sitting on his front porch enjoying a cold glass of lemonade when his elderly neighbor Mabel came out of her house checking her mail box. There was no mail so she walked back in the house. A few minutes later, she once again came out and checked her mail box. Again no mail. About five minutes had passed when she came out for the third time, looked in her mail box but this time let out a scream.

Matt called to her and asked if there was something wrong. "Yes," she said, "my son Neil said he wanted me to have a computer so I could communicate with him and my other children and grand-children, so he bought one for me. I turned it on this morning for the first time, and it says "I've got mail. I've checked the mail box three times and there is no mail."

Today's Comment: I bought my first computer when I was 55 years old. I'm not what you would call a techie, but I have learned sufficient over the years to enjoy emails, surf the web for information, type sermons, documents, and this is my second book which I have typed. It has been one modern invention, which has flooded the world and has become a useful tool.

Most of us would say that the computer is a neutral thing. Yet what frequently comes on the monitor is biased. How many have been innocently led into a pornographic site, because of a pop-up that appeared? The same goes for television and smart phones, etc.

I remember many years ago, when television was relatively new, I read about a man who had purchased a TV. As the delivery men were carrying it into the house, he noticed the slogan on the box, "This brings the world into your house." He immediately said to these men, "Take it back. I don't want the world in my house!"

Make certain that you and your family know where the "off" button is on your computer and television, yes, and smart phone.

Don't let the world's philosophy and shameful entertainment invade your home. A good guide would be to censor and put a time limit on what your family members watch. How much time do we spend on a computer, television, smart phone compared with reading and studying God's Word, the Bible? Pray that all the family will know where the "off" buttons are and know how to use them.

Today's Golden Nugget of Truth: "Do not love the world or the things in the world. If anyone loves the world, the love of the Father is not in him. For all that is in the world, the lust of the flesh, the lust of the eyes, and the pride of life, is not of the Father but is of the world." First John 2:15-16

Today's Philosophical Tidbit: "Nature forms us, sin deforms us, the penitentiary reforms us, education informs us, the world conforms us, but only Jesus transforms us." Author Unknown

July 26
Going The Second Mile

Today's Smile: Carl had served in pastoral ministries for thirty years and then was the President of his denomination for eight years. He had concluded his second term as president, retired moving to Arizona. About four months after settling in Arizona, Carl was invited to Kansas City to be the devotional speaker at the Missouri district pastors retreat. They were all very pleased to have him share with them once again from the Word of God.

In his closing remarks, and thanking them for the invitation to once again share with them, he said, "You all know where Mesa is. I want each one of you to know that if you are ever in that area to give me a call. If you are in need of a meal, a bed, or if you find yourself short on cash, please do not hesitate to phone me. It doesn't matter what day of the week or what hour of the day, even if it is the middle of the night, please give me a call, and I'll be happy to pray for you."

Today's Comment: My wife and I know what it is like to have out of town friends phone us at all hours of the day. We served for six wonderful years in British Columbia's beautiful Okanagan Valley.

It was and is a tourist's paradise. Vernon was where we made our home. It is surrounded by three beautiful lakes. The valley is the home of some of Canada's most delicious fruit: apples, peaches, pears, cherries, plums, grapes, plus berries, etc. One of those years we had company arrive at our door beginning July 6th and there was an unbroken stream of relatives and friends until August 15th.

There was not one day that we did not have either company for coffee, dinner, overnight company sleeping in our beds, or camping in our back yard. Sometimes we had two lots of company that knew us but not each other. It was tiring, but enjoyable. We were happy to be a host and hostess and welcome people into our home.

Is there someone today that you could welcome into your home, either for coffee or a meal, or maybe take them to a pleasant restaurant? Pray that God will guide you in befriending others.

Today's Golden Nugget of Truth: "Be hospitable to one another without grumbling." First Peter 4:9

Today's Philosophical Tidbit: "Even when you think you have no more to give, when a friend cries out to you, you will find the strength to help." Author Unknown

July 27
Do You Remember

Today's Smile: My wife and I attended the wedding of some good friends. I was pastor of the bride's home church, and the groom was a brother of one of my brother-in-laws. Ray was a professor of music at the Prairie Bible Institute. He was teased now and then for his forgetfulness. At the wedding, the master of ceremonies shared the following story about Ray, the groom. The story has been told about others, but it still brought a laugh.

Professor Ray was walking across the campus during summer session when he stopped to talk with one of his music students. They chatted for about five minutes. When they were about to go their separate ways, Ray asked the student, "Tell me which way was I going when we stopped to talk? Was I headed for the Music Center or for the Dining Hall?

"Professor, you were headed for the Music Center," replied the student.

"Thanks," said Professor Ray. "Then I've had my lunch!"[1]

Today's Comment: I've found that the older we get, the more prone we are to forget where we were going or what we were doing. I've sometimes walked into my study to do something and then when I get there, I forgot what it was that I was going to do. Of course, you don't have that problem. Or do you?

Do we get so busy and preoccupied during the day that we more often than not, forget God? Do we focus our thoughts and actions on our work, our studies, recreation, and whatever else fills our day and at the end of the day realize that we didn't pray today? I've found that we need to make a concentrated effort to focus our thoughts on the Lord Jesus Christ and the things of God. We don't have to confine our prayer and focus to a few moments in the morning or at evening. When you walk, drive, or sit waiting for a bus or for a person, you can focus your thoughts on God.

A few years ago while reading Psalm 119, verse 165 seemed to leap off of the page. "Seven times a day I praise You, because of Your righteous judgments." I remembered that the prophet Daniel prayed three times a day. Now I read that King David prayed seven. It would be worth a try. So I began to break my times of scripture and prayer into sections throughout the day, not seven but several. If that quiet time in the morning gets cut short at times, pray that God would help you organize your day so that you have shorter devotional times but more often.

Today's Golden Nugget of Truth: "Finally, brethren, whatever things are true, whatever things are noble, whatever things are just, whatever things are pure, whatever things are lovely, whatever things are of good report, if there is any virtue and if there is anything praiseworthy, meditate on these things." Philippians 4:8

Today's Philosophical Tidbit: "Our minds were not made to be a garbage can, but a file cabinet. Fill it with thoughts worth keeping and cherishing." A. Daniel Goldsmith

July 28
Stretching The Truth Into A Lie

*T*oday's Smile: Several guys had gone away for a weekend of fishing. They broke up in twos and went to different locations during the day. They had arranged to meet at Starbucks® at 3:00pm for a cup of coffee in order to share their experiences of the day.

One fellow told about fishing in McMillan's Creek where he caught a seventeen pound spotted sea trout! Another who had gone further down the creek told of yanking his line out of the water only to discover he had hooked a lighted lantern.

"Now wait a minute, Lyle, you may have hooked an old lantern, but I think you are stretching the truth a bit to say that it was lighted."

"Maybe I did stretch my story a little bit, but I'll tell you what, if you take ten pounds off of your trout, I'll blow out the lantern."

Today's Comment: This is not the first day that I have made comments regarding speaking the truth. We need to be reminded to always speak the truth. Many people speak the truth, but exaggerate a little which distorts the truth and makes it a lie. The apostle Paul reminded the early church many times to speak truthfully and not to be guilty of lying.

We live in such a dishonest world. Two of the sins which many commit over and over, be it in the home, the school or the work place are lying and cheating. Pray that our Christianity will be more than simply a profession void of holy living. If we have submitted our lives wholly to the Lord, then let Him control our thoughts and actions?

Today's Golden Nugget of Truth: "Do not lie to one another, since you have put off the old man with his deeds." Colossians 3:9

Today's Philosophical Tidbit: "People who do a lot of kneeling won't be doing much lying." Author Unknown

July 29
Credit Card Or Christ

T	*oday's Smile:* Every morning Karen would open her front door, walk out on to the porch shouting at the top of her voice, "Praise the Lord." She had been doing this ever since she placed her faith in the living Lord. She was so excited about her new found faith and she wanted her neighbors to know it.

Her next door neighbor was an atheist and he did not appreciate her exclamations of "Praise the Lord." Having endured it as long as he could, he thought he would counter her words. So he decided that when she shouted out "Praise the Lord" he would shout back, "There is no Lord."

One day the atheist neighbor heard Karen praying for food. Thinking it would be amusing to hear her response he purchased three big bags of groceries for her and left them on her porch. The next morning this dear lady opened her door walked out on to the porch and immediately noticed the bags of groceries. She said, "I wonder who the Lord used to answer my prayer." The neighbor was laughing and responded by saying, "It wasn't the Lord it was me."

Without missing a beat, Karen shouted out, "Praise the Lord for giving me this bountiful supply of food and making my atheist neighbor pay for it."

Today's Comment: Have you ever wished that credit cards had never been made available? Today, if we are low on cash, it is so easy simply to use that plastic money and keep on going. I think back to the early years of my pastoral ministry, before credit cards. All we had was the money that was in our pockets or checking account.

My wife and I lived in a parsonage, or manse, whatever you wish to call it. It was a house provided for us by the church. Our total cash income, our salary from the church was a whopping $240.00 each month. At one a point in our lives, we were short of cash. It was a Friday morning. I was in my study at the church. I could not study. I needed some money. I walked round and round in the sanctuary and cried out to God for some money. The burden was lifted. I had a peace

266

in my heart that God had heard my prayer and we would receive the needed cash.

I went back to my desk and my preparation for Sunday. Now I thought that the Lord would answer my request by someone sending money to us in the mail. There was mail delivery Fridays and Saturdays in those years. No check in the mail arrived at the church or at our house.

Saturday around 6:00pm, there was a knock at our door. A lady from the church was there. She thrust an envelope in my hand and said, "You guys must have been praying about this." The long and short of her story was that at noon that day, she and her husband were eating lunch in silence. The silence was broken. Both confided in each other, that the Goldsmiths had been on their minds. "Well, said the first one, I've been thinking that they need some money." The other had the same thought. "Well," said the first one, "let's give them some." In that envelope that evening was $40.00. That was better than half a week's salary.

Pray that we will be more dependent upon God. Credit cards have become a substitute for prayer.

Today's Golden Nugget of Truth: "Don't worry about anything; instead, pray about everything; tell God your needs and don't forget to thank Him for His answers." Philippians 4:6 (TLB)

Today's Philosophical Tidbit: "Make it a matter of prayer; cease to make it a matter of care." Author Unknown

July 30
Constantly Complaining

Today's Smile: Amos, a regular customer at the Club Café, was a constant complainer. There were others that were regular customers and they were always amazed at the patience with which Sally, a waitress, treated Amos. Quite often, Amos would leave his coffee sit on the table and then call Sally to complain that it was cold. She graciously took his cup refilling it with hot coffee. As she brought it back to him she would give him a big smile pinching him on the cheek saying, "There you are you old goat." One constant complaint in the summer months was about the temperature in the café.

"Sally," he called, "it's too hot in here would you turn the air conditioner on." Sally would walk to the back of the café and then return and go about her job of waiting on customers. Ten minutes later Amos called for her again, "Sally, it's too cold now. Shut that air conditioner off!" As soon as she was able, she would go to the back of the café again.

This was almost a daily ritual, and it was really quite noticeable because no other customer every complained about the heat. Finally, after hearing this conversation for about three weeks, Andrew a new bank manager in town said to Sally, "Why don't you throw that guy out!"

"Oh, he doesn't bother me," said Sally. Furthermore, "we don't even have an air conditioner."

Today's Comment: When I read that story I thought of two things worth commenting on. One, are we that patient? Do we react to people who complain without any basis for the complaint? Do we react with a smile and comply with their wishes? The little ditty comes to mind, which some men may want to revise. You've all heard it. "Patience is a virtue, possess if you can, seldom found in women, never found in man!"

The other thought that came to mind was that of complaining. Are we constant complainers? You know that there are people that always look on the negative side of things. Nothing is ever right, no matter what it is, the weather, the neighbor, work place, or the church. Some people can find fault with absolutely everything. They act like they were baptized in vinegar.

Pray that we will not be numbered among the complainers, but with those who have an abundance of patience.

Today's Golden Nugget of Truth: "Do all things without complaining and disputing. . ." Philippians 2:14

Today's Philosophical Tidbit: "The more we complain about our problems, the more problems we will have to complain about." Zig Ziglar

July 31
Leaders Make Great Targets

Today's Smile: Scott and his wife Cynthia lived in Florida and had invited some of their staff for dinner. After the dinner, he took them out the back to show them his new Olympic sized swimming pool in which he kept an alligator. He said to his staff, I would like to throw out a challenge. For anyone who would like to take the plunge and swim from this side of the pool to the other side without being attacked or destroyed, I will give you one million dollars, or my Texas ranch, or the hand of my daughter.

No sooner said and he heard a splash. There in the pool was his accountant swimming so fast that the alligator probably didn't even see him.

Scott walked over to his accountant as he quickly climbed out of the pool. "Well sir," he said, "I did not think that I would have any takers for my offers. But I will keep my promise. What would you like, one million dollars, my Texas ranch, or my daughter Samantha?"

"You're a very generous man, Scott, but I don't want any of those."

"You don't want to accept any of my offers. Well, what do you want?" asked Scott.

"I want the name of the staff member that pushed me in the pool."

Today's Comment: The first time I heard that story, it was told by one who was elected as president of his denomination. Have you ever been put into a place of leadership, or on a committee or a job and you wonder how did I get here? Who assigned this job to me? Who appointed me to this place of leadership? Maybe the expectations are more than I can fulfill.

Positions of leadership are difficult places to be in. Anyone who has been the president of a country, mayor of a city, chairman of a committee, president of a society, CEO of a business, coach of a sports team, pastor of a church or any other place of leadership know that there are those who support you but also those who oppose and find fault.

I remember a woman in one of the churches where I was pastor who was forever finding fault with one thing and another. I came up with the idea that maybe she should have a ministry of some sort within the church. She was slotted into a place of leadership. That ended her complaining. She was now in a place of leadership and could well be the recipient of other people's complaints. Do we pray for leaders as much as we criticize? Today, let us forget our fault-finding and pray for those in places of leadership.

Today's Golden Nugget of Truth: "Therefore I exhort first of all that supplications, prayers, intercessions, and giving of thanks be made for all men, for kings and all who are in authority. . ." First Timothy 2:1, 2

Today's Philosophical Tidbit: "A leader cannot lead until he knows where he is going." Author Unknown

August 1
God Doesn't Play Tricks

T *oday's Smile:* A magician was employed by a cruise ship and worked the summer season on ships that left Seattle, WA sailing to Alaska. Since there were different passengers every week the magician was able to do the same tricks again and again. There was one problem and that was the captain's parrot attended every show. After about a month the parrot knew all of the magician's tricks.

As the magician sought to perform his tricks the parrot would say, "Look that's not the same hat." "Why are all of the cards the Ace of Spades?" Or "Look, he is hiding the flowers under the table."

One sunny morning, the ship was too close to the shore, hit a rock and sank. The magician and the parrot both managed to survive by clinging to a piece of wood. They stared at each other, but not a word was said. Finally, just before sundown, the parrot said, "O.K. I give up. Where is the boat?"

Today's Comment: I'm sure you have watched a magician perform his or her tricks. It might have been a professional magician or a grandchild who had learned some tricks and wanted to entertain you. I have not been smart enough to figure out their slight of hand or whatever they might be hiding.

There are a lot of things that we cannot comprehend or understand about God, but we trust Him. "Sometimes we weep because of what He does, but we trust what He does. There are moments when we wish He would not do what He does, but we trust what He does. We sometimes cannot figure out why He does what He does, but we can trust what He does."[1] He made the world and all that is in it and He knows what is best. He knows what He is doing even when we may not.

Pray that we may fully trust the Lord. God is not playing any tricks on us.

Today's Golden Nugget of Truth: "O the depth of the riches both of the wisdom and knowledge of God! How unsearchable are his judgments, and His ways past finding out." Romans 11:33 (KJV)

Today's Philosophical Tidbit: "God is a scientist, not a magician." Albert Einstein

August 2
God Knows Our Needs

Today's Smile: Bernice asked her husband Orville if he would go to the store and get a carton of milk. Then she added, "And if they have avocados get six."

He wasn't gone long and came home with six cartons of milk. Bernice asked him "Why did you buy six cartons of milk?"

"Well," said Orville, "I bought six cartons of milk, because you said that if they had avocados to get six."

Today's Comment: Did that one go over your head? Maybe you need to read it again. This little story reminds me of a tale that my siblings delight in telling. It is about me when I was around five years of age. Mom and Dad parked in front of a Fruit Market and sent me in to buy a dozen lemons. Fred, the owner of the store, and a friend of my folks, came out to the car and asked my parents what I was supposed to be buying. They responded by saying, "one dozen lemons."

"Oh," said Fred, "Danny asked for a dozen watermelons."

Some of us have had problems shopping since we were kids. Some of us may need to make certain our wife writes out a note for us before we do the shopping.

When it comes to praying and asking God for something, He won't have to ask someone else what we said. He knows before we ask what we need. He will always meet our needs, not necessarily our wants. So let's pray that He will provide what we need today and that we will be satisfied.

Today's Golden Nugget of Truth: "Be not therefore like unto them, for Your Father knoweth what things ye have need of, before ye ask Him." Matthew 6:8 (KJV)

Today's Philosophical Tidbit: "My boss complained that I don't listen to him, at least I think that is what he said." Author Unknown

August 3
Do We Care About Others

Today's Smile: Janelle's grandmother lives by herself. One day last week, she phoned 911 for the very first time. "What is your emergency?' asked the operator.

"Fire!" responded the grandma. Once connected she began by saying, "I had a new rock garden built in the spring. I have some very expensive shrubs, and the flowers are all in bloom and. . ."

"Lady, this is the fire department. You need to be phoning a flower shop or a nursery."

"No, I don't," she said. "I want the fire department. I share a driveway with my neighbor and I don't want you to drive over my flower garden when you come to her place because her house is on fire."

Today's Comment: We've heard a lot about the *Me* generation. The Baby Boomers were dubbed the *Me* generation during the 1970's by writer Tom Wolfe. People began to focus on self, "I, me, and mine." That trend has continued with a culture of self-centeredness, self-realization and self-fulfillment, also known as the culture of narcissism. A new trend in recent years is using a smart phone and taking "a selfie," a picture of one's self. Reminds me of the little boy and his sister who were both riding a rocking horse. The boy said, "If one of us would get off, there would be more room for me."

That is so contrary to biblical teaching. The Bible exhorts us to be looking out for others, be considerate of others, put others first. We used to sing a chorus written by Bruce Metzger in 1951: "Jesus and others and you, what a wonderful way to spell joy. Jesus and others and you, in the life of each girl and each boy. 'J' is for Jesus for He has first place, 'O' is for others you meet face to face, 'Y' is for you in whatever you do, put your self third and spell JOY."[1]

True, we need to also care for ourselves and not be a door mat for everyone, but there is a tendency in today's culture to be looking after *number one* rather than reaching out and caring for others. At least that is what a lot of television commercials would lead us to believe - "You owe it to yourself," they say. Pray that we will be guided in our relationships and inter-action with others, and not be so focused on self.

Today's Golden Nugget of Truth: "Don't be selfish: don't live to make a good impression on others. Be humble, thinking of others as better than yourself." Philippians 2:3 (TLB)

Today's Philosophical Tidbit: "Christianity demands a level of caring that transcends human inclinations." Erwin Lutzer

August 4
Doers Of The Word

*T*oday's Smile: Billy Graham was extremely tired trying to be as inconspicuous as possible. He had his hat pulled down low over his eyes and he was wearing sunglasses, of all things at night. On that plane close to where he sat was a man who had too much to drink. He was disturbing everyone on the plane. Finally, thinking that it might help matters, someone said to the drunkard. "The well known radio and television preacher, Billy Graham, is seated right behind you.

"The drunkard, turned around, blearily looked Billy in the eye, and asked, 'Are you Billy? Are you the Reverend Billy? Boy put her here and shake my hand. Billy, I've been listening to you preach for years and I want to tell you this, your sermons sure have done me a whole lot of good'."[1]

Today's Comment: You can go to church every Sunday and listen to the pastor preach a sermon. You can walk out of church, go home, eat your Sunday dinner, go to work, live your week and do it all over again next Sunday. However, if you have never applied the truth of God's Word to your life, if you've never invited Christ into your life, you are not a follower of Christ. It is that simple. The Word of God must be personalized in our own lives.

I knew a man who read through the Bible every year for forty years, but never professed faith in the Lord Jesus Christ. Reading the Bible, listening to sermons, these are not sufficient. You must be born again! If you have never prayed to receive Christ as your personal Savior, do it today!

Today's Golden Nugget of Truth: "For by grace are ye saved through faith; and that not of yourselves, it is the gift of God, not of works, lest any man should boast." Ephesians 2:8, 9 (KJV)

Today's Philosophical Tidbit: "Going to church doesn't make you a Christian any more than going into a garage makes you an automobile." Billy Sunday

August 5
Look On The Bright Side

T oday's Smile: Rudolf was a well respected and famous Russian meteorologist. He had a 100% accuracy rate when it came to forecasting the weather and when he said that it was going to rain, it rained. One night, despite clear blue skies, he made the prediction on the 6:00pm news broadcast that a violent storm was approaching. It was going to cause some flooding.

When he arrived home that evening, his wife brought up the subject of his forecast of rain. You have made a big mistake, my dear. Your listeners are going to be laughing at you tomorrow. Today has been one of the nicest of the season. "How could you predict rain when the odds are against you?"

He responded by saying, "What I said is true. When I say it is going to rain, it will rain." Their arguing did not end when he entered the door, it continued around the supper table and most of the evening. Her last words to her husband after crawling in bed were that it was not going to rain.

That night, one of the worst rainstorms their city had ever seen began around 2:00am. When they got up in the morning, Rudolf's wife looked out the window and sure enough there had been a heavy downpour. The sewer drain in front of their house was plugged with leaves and debris causing the water to back up onto their front lawn. Rudolf snuck up behind her giving her a morning embrace and said, "What did I tell you? Didn't I say it was going to rain?"

"Yes, dear, you were right again, as always, but how do you speak with such confidence and authority when the sky is clear and there are absolutely no clouds anywhere? How do you do it?"

He replied, "Rudolf the Red knows rain dear!"

Today's Comment: The weather man has a lot of ears listening to him wanting to hear what tomorrow will be like. Will it be sunny or rainy? I worked at a radio station in my younger years when it was a two man job. I spun the records, operated the controls, turning on the microphones, adjusting volume, etc. while the announcer sat in another room with a window between us. One day in giving the weather, and failing to check the condition of the sky before giving his report, he came to the point where he said, "In Chatham at the present moment the sky is. . ." He leaned back in his chair and looked up and out the window behind him. Seeing a big cloud, he continued, ". . .overcast." Well, the sky was not overcast. It was a beautiful sunny summer day, but it so happened that a big cloud was all that the announcer could see.

That is like a lot of people. They always see the grey or cloudy side of things. When all around is beautiful, or satisfying, or the people are agreeable, there is always one that sees some imperfection, or is not satisfied, or is finding fault.

One pastor friend told me one time that in his church the board had redefined a unanimous vote. They agreed upon a high percentage vote but not 100% because there was always someone that would be opposed and they would never be able to pass a motion because one person controlled the meeting by disagreeing.

Do you only see clouds? Are you that disagreeable person? Do you stop progress? Do you delight in arguing all the time? Pray that God will help you to look on the sunny side.

Today's Golden Nugget of Truth: "It is honorable for a man to stop striving, since any fool can start a quarrel." Proverbs 20:3

Today's Philosophical Tidbit: "An argument is where two people are trying to get in the last word first." Author Unknown

August 6
What Is Really Important

*T*oday's Smile: Pastor Henry had promised to take his family on a picnic Saturday afternoon. However, he first had to do a little touch up and revision on his sermon for Sunday. Madison, the youngest of his four children walked into his study and asked when they would be going on the picnic. He responded by telling her it would be in a little bit. She sat on a chair in his study for a couple of minutes and then asked again, "Daddy when are we going on the picnic?"

"Not yet," said her Daddy. "Honey, I've got to concentrate for a few more minutes. Why don't you go back into the family room and wait for me. I'll come and get you and your brother and sisters as soon as I am finished."

Well, after about five minutes, the little impatient preacher's daughter opened the door and stuck her head in and asked if he still had to constipate.

Today's Comment: I remember well when my wife was expecting our third child. I thought I would help her a bit so I took Danny, our oldest to my study at the church. It was a week before his fifth birthday. I took a small table and chair from the primary department, put it in the corner of my study, gave him a coloring book and some crayons. I then said to him, "Now, son, Daddy has a lot of work to do, you just sit there quietly and do some coloring."

He started to color and after a few minutes, started talking. "Danny," I said, "Daddy has a lot of work, please do your coloring." He was quiet for few more moments and again started talking. Again

I asked him to not interrupt me while I was working. He continued to interrupt me. At that point, a still small voice within said to me, "Would you stop what you are doing and listen to your son's questions?" So, I put my pen down and asked what was on his mind.

My young son was full of questions about Jesus, and how you became a Christian. It was there in my study at the Vernon Alliance Church, Vernon, BC, that my son prayed to receive Christ as his personal Savior. If you ask Danny (I should add that he is in his fifties and no longer "Danny." It is now "Dan.") today when he invited the Lord Jesus Christ into his life, he will tell you it was there in my study, Saturday, August 6th, 1966. I should add that when we came home and he announced to his mother that he had invited Christ into his life, that my wife told him that August 6th was the anniversary date of her salvation. Her mother led her to the Lord when she was 8 years old.

Pray that you will be sensitive to those who may want to ask a question when you are busy.

Today's Nugget of Truth: "But Jesus said, Let the little children come to Me, and do not forbid them for of such is the kingdom of heaven." Matthew 19:14

Today's Philosophical Tidbit: "Human interruptions may be divine appointments." A. Daniel Goldsmith

August 7
It's Time To Pray

Today's Smile: Pastor Ian was a pastor of a small country church in Montana. He had been called away on short notice. His mother, who lived in Missouri, had suffered a stroke and it did not look like she would survive. In the rush to get away on Friday morning, he was unable to get a supply pastor and so asked one of his deacons to take the service.

Martin, the deacon, was a very successful rancher. Being a slow reader, he usually shared extemporaneously. Just before he was about to share his message, the head usher handed him a note. Lucy White had phoned the church during the service asking if the pastor would pray for her husband. The usher had scribbled her request on the back of a bulletin. The request read: "Ivan White, having gone to sea, his wife desires the prayers of the congregation for his safety."

When Deacon Martin read the request, this is how it sounded: "Ivan White, having gone to see his wife, desires the prayers of the congregation for his safety."

Today's Comment: As those who have received the Lord Jesus Christ as our personal Savior, we are privileged and blessed to be able to commune with our God through prayer. Whether it is asking for safety in travel, wisdom in making a decision, guidance in our day's activities, having to meet with someone, yes, maybe our spouse, we are encouraged to bring everything to God in prayer.

Joseph M. Scriven wrote the words to that old familiar hymn: "What a friend we have in Jesus, all our sins and griefs to bear! What a privilege to carry, everything to God in prayer. . ." There is nothing that is too big or too little to share with God. Yet, all too often we try working out our problems, or involving ourselves in some activity without having first talked with God.

Before we start tackling a situation or trying to solve a problem, let's take it to God in prayer.

Today's Golden Nugget of Truth: "Praying always with all prayer and supplication in the Spirit. . ." Ephesians 6:18

Today's Philosophical Tidbit: "Every faithful prayer is heard the moment it is prayed, but God chooses to answer in His own way and in His own time." David Wilkerson

August 8
Amen Brother, Amen Sister

*T*oday's Smile: A man had been lost and walked on the hot prairies for two days. He came to the home of a country pastor. Tired and weak, he crawled up to the house and collapsed on the doorstep. The pastor took him in and nursed him back to health. Feeling better the next day, the man asked the pastor for directions to the nearest town. The pastor gave him the directions and offered to lend him one of his horses. The pastor told him that he would be going into town later that day telling him where to leave the horse. "However, there is a special thing about this horse," said the pastor. "You have to say 'Thank God' to make it go and 'Amen' to make it stop."

Anxious to get to town, the man thanked the pastor and got on the horse. He said, "Thank God" and sure enough, the horse started walking. A bit later he said louder, "Thank God, thank God," and the horse started trotting. Feeling really brave, the man said, "Thank God! Thank God! THANK GOD!" and the horse was soon up to a full run!

About then he realized he was heading straight for a river and yelled "Whoa!" But the horse didn't even slow down. The river was coming up very quickly and he did everything he could to make the horse stop. "Whoa, stop, hold it!" Finally he remembered "AMEN!!!"

The horse stopped a mere four feet from the river's bank, almost throwing him into the river. The man, panting and heart racing, wiped the sweat from his face and leaned back in the saddle. "Oh!" he said, gasping for air, "Thank God."

Today's Comment: The Bible exhorts us to be thankful in all things. However, the word 'amen' means "So be it!" It is a word of confirmation. However, there are times when it is said without much thought, or at an inappropriate time.

I recall hearing a radio broadcast from a church in Detroit, Michigan. The pastor was preaching with much fervor and enthusiasm while people were encouraging the pastor with their "amens, praise the Lord, and hallelujahs." It was July 4th weekend and in his sermon he said, "This weekend it is expected that about 400 people will die on our highways." With that some responded with an "amen." Did they really mean "So be it?"

When you say "amen" you are agreeing with what is being said. When you say "amen" whether audibly or in your spirit, it is your prayer that you are agreeing with the pastor.

Today's Golden Nugget of Truth: "And all the people said, Amen, and praised the Lord." First Chronicles 16:36 (KJV)

Today's Philosophical Tidbit: "Remember, life is not a privilege; it's a gift." Author Unknown

August 9
Are You Communicating

*T*oday's Smile: Three fellows in South Carolina were digging for archeological artifacts. At ten feet, they found copper wire. "Y'all know what this means," said one of them. "This means our great grandparents were using telecommunications a hundred years ago."

When that discovery hit the news media, two brothers in Wyoming decided to see what they could find. They dug down fifteen feet and found copper wire. "Hey, this is better than the find in South Carolina," said the older brother, "the settlers here in Wyoming had telecommunications one hundred and fifty years ago."

As the news continued to spread, a couple of Minnesotans decided to see what they could find. They dug ten feet and found nothing. They dug fifteen feet and still found nothing. They continued to dig and at twenty feet, they still found nothing. "Hey Sven," shouted Ole, "Ya know vat dis means?"

"No, vat does it mean?" asked Sven.

"It means," explained Ole excitedly, "dat two hundred years ago, before Minnesota was even a state, the settlers here ver already vireless!"

Today's Comment: Wireless communication has been here a long long time. Read the Bible. Abraham prayed, Joseph, Daniel, Elijah, Jonah, Peter, Paul and a long list of other Bible characters all prayed. Prayer is a wireless connection with our Heavenly Father.

So before radio, television, remote controls, cordless phones, laptops, smart phones etc. there was a wireless connection. God created it and He did so that we might communicate with Him.

As I was putting these thoughts together today, I thought of my early years at home. I used to wake up school day mornings to the *Nation's Family Prayer Period* broadcasting live from the Cadle Tabernacle in Indianapolis, Indiana on Cincinnati, Ohio's 50,000 watt clear channel radio station, WLW. The words of the theme song of that broadcast, where Dr. Howard Cadle and later Dr. B. R. Lakin were pastors, were: "Ere you left your room this morning, did you think to pray? In the name of Christ our Savior did you sue for loving favor, as a shield today?" Then the refrain: "Oh, how praying rests the weary! Prayer will change the night to day; so when life seems dark and dreary, don't forget to pray." What a thrill for me when, in my forties, we had the joy of having Dr. B. R. Lakin in our home for dinner.

As children of God we have a wireless connection with God. There is no charge, no monthly fees, no batteries and no shut down for repairs. It is 24/7 forever. Avail yourself today of this connection that was made possible through the sacrifice of the Lord Jesus Christ. It is called prayer!

Today's Golden Nugget of Truth: "The Lord is near to all who call upon Him, to all who call upon Him in truth." Psalm 145:18

Today's Philosophical Tidbit: "Prayer is an open line to heaven. There is no distance to prayer." Author Unknown

August 10
God Is The Great Fixer

Today's Smile: Patsy received a call that her daughter was ill. She stopped by the pharmacy to get medication. When she went back to her car she realized that she had locked the keys inside the car. She found an old coat hanger nearby, but did not know how to use it. She bowed her head and prayed to God for help. Within a couple of minutes a fellow on a beat up old motorcycle parked alongside of her. When he saw her standing there looking somewhat bewildered, he asked if there was a problem.

"Yes," she said. "My daughter is sick and I just bought this medicine for her and I find that I locked my keys in my car. Do you know how to use this coat hanger?" He took the coat hanger and within seconds he had unlocked her car door. Patsy gave the man a big hug and through her tears expressed how grateful she was for his help. "You're a very nice man, and I deeply appreciate your help," she said.

"Lady, I am not a very nice man. I was just released from prison two days ago. I've been serving time for car theft."

With that, Patsy gave him another hug and looking skyward said, "Oh thank You, thank You God, You not only sent help to me immediately, but You sent a professional!"

Today's Comment: When my daughter was still single and in her early twenties, she went for a ride in her car and drove along the shores of a nearby lake. She stopped the car and got out for a few moments. When she went back to the car she discovered that she had locked the keys in her car. She looked around for a coat hanger but could find none. She walked up the lakeshore road and came to a little old house. When she knocked on the door, a most undesirable looking fellow answered. She told him her problem and he promptly joined her walking back to the car. He didn't use any coat hanger. He had a pocket full of keys and managed to unlock her car. She was grateful for the help, but she would never know how close she was to falling into the hands of the wrong kind of person. Another professional!

Thank God that some of those car thieves, drug dealers, rapists and murderers have made a change in their life. God specializes in changing lives. As a Bible College student, I sat on the bed of an inmate listening to his story how he had received Christ in the State penitentiary. I was so impressed by the sweet spirit of this man and his glowing testimony. On the way back to the college campus, I was riding with the State's head chaplain. I asked why my new friend was serving time in prison. His response was, "He was a murderer. He killed a couple who owned a small grocery store."

God is at work in our prisons. Pray today for Prison Fellowship and the many other ministries and personnel who faithfully visit those who are incarcerated and thank the Lord that many respond to the invitation to receive Christ, continuing to live changed lives.

Today's Golden Nugget of Truth: "I will give you a new heart and put a new spirit in you: I will remove from you your heart of stone and give you a heart of flesh. And I will put my Spirit in you and move you to follow my decrees and be careful to keep my laws..." Ezekiel 36:26, 27 (NIV)

Today's Philosophical Tidbit: "No one is so good that he can save himself; no one is so bad that God cannot save him." Author Unknown

August 11
A Functioning Faith

*T*oday's Smile: A man was stopped by the police around 2:00am and was asked why he was speeding and furthermore where he was going at this time of the morning. The man replied, "I'm on my way to a lecture about alcohol abuse and the effects that it has on the human body. I will also be addressed on the matter of smoking and the problem of staying out late."

The officer responded by saying, "Really? Who is giving that lecture at this time in the morning?

The man replied, "My wife will be the lecturer."

Today's Comment: Is our life style what it should be? How would we feel if our private life was revealed for all the church to see? Are we deserving of a lecture? If we are a follower of Christ, as we claim to be, are we walking in our Lord and Savior's footsteps? The Word of God exhorts us to be different from the world. We are told that we need to separate ourselves from the ways of the world. Our life style, our actions, our words, our interests should be different.

True we will be like them in many ways. We may go to the same school, travel the same bus, and work in the same office. We may attend the same sports games, perform the same domestic tasks, shop at the same store. We are like the world in many respects, but our desires and purposes should be different. Pray today that we will live so that we will not need to be lectured for our waywardness.

Today's Golden Nugget of Truth: "As He who called you is holy, you also be holy in all your conduct." First Peter 1:15

Today's Philosophical Tidbit: "Our mannerisms must match our message to be effective." Author Unknown

August 12
What's The Purpose Of The Game

*T*oday's Smile: Clyde was playing center field in his first game with a minor league. After two errors back to back, the hot headed manger stormed out on to the field, grabbed Clyde's glove and told him to go sit down. "I will show you how to play center field!"

The first ball was a high fly which fell to the ground because the manager was blinded by the sun and lost sight of it. The second hit headed between first and second base. The manager ran full speed towards right field with his eye on the ball and collided head on with the right fielder. The third batter hit a line drive and the ball hit the manager between the eyes and knocked him to the ground.

As he was being carried out on a stretcher, he passed by the dug out and the center fielder and he hollered at him saying, "Boy, you've got that center field so messed up that nobody can play there."

Today's Comment: There is all too often the tendency to blame others. True sportsmanship does not play the blame game. True sportsmen realize that it is a game and a time of competition, but it is much more than that. This needs to be instilled in the minds of young beginners. Playing sports is a time of learning and improving skills, striving towards a winning goal, doing better than before, but also a time of fun.

True sportsmanship was no more evident than at the 2014 Winter Olympics in Sochi, Russia, when Canada's cross country coach Justin Wadsworth gave a ski to Russia's Anton Gafarov. Anton fell with a broken ski during the men's semi final of the cross country sprint, and Justin gave him a ski so that he could finish the race. We need more sports people like Justin. Oh yes, and true sportsmanship knows how to lose gracefully.

As Christians, we are all in a game, the game of life. Our goal is Godliness. Pray that we will run the race with our eye on the Goal and that we will help others along the way, enabling them to finish well.

Today's Golden Nugget of Truth: "And everyone who competes for the prize is temperate in all things. Now they do it to obtain a perishable crown, but we for an imperishable crown." First Corinthians 9:25

Today's Philosophical Tidbit: "True sportsmanship is knowing that you need your opponent because without him or her, there is no game." Author Unknown

August 13
Maybe You Shouldn't Tell It

Today's Smile: A young ventriloquist traveled to small towns and villages where a ventriloquist was seldom, if ever seen. He is telling his usual jokes with the support of his dummy. A woman in the fifth row stands up on her chair and shouts out, "I've heard enough of your denigrating jokes. What makes you think that you can stereotype us like you're doing? What does our physical appearance or ethnicity have to do with our worth as human beings? Its guys like you that keep people like me from being respected at work and in our community, because you continue to perpetuate discrimination all in the name of humor."

The young ventriloquist begins to offer an apology, but the woman interrupts and says to the young man, "I'm not talking to you, sir. I'm talking to that little jerk that is sitting on your knee."

Today's Comment: I love humor and good clean jokes. However, I learned a lesson when it comes to telling ethnic jokes. On June 30th, 1987 Canada introduced a shiny new 11-sided coin. It was a one dollar coin, a cost-saving measure, replacing the one dollar paper bill. Soon after it came out, I was paying my bill at a restaurant and commented on the new coin. I said to the clerk, "Do you know that they are recalling these coins in (naming a particular place)?" He looked surprised and questioned the reason. I said, "Because they are breaking their fingernails trying to get the chocolate out." He laughed.

The lady just ahead of me was very upset and turned to me and said, "You got to be kidding!"

I looked back at the clerk as she left the restaurant and he said, "I believe that is where she was from." Right there and then, I thought that I need to think twice before telling jokes that would be hurtful.

A few years ago, I read that "A genuinely good joke is worth a whole lot, but it should be subjected to this test: When some woman blushes with embarrassment; when some heart carries away an ache; when something sacred is made to appear common; when a man's weakness provides the cause for laughter; when profanity is required to make it funny; when a child is brought to tears; when not everyone can join in the laughter; IT'S A POOR JOKE, DON'T TELL IT!"

Pray that we will enjoy a sense of humor, but pray that we will be discreet in what we share.

Today's Golden Nugget of Truth: "Let the words of my mouth and the meditation of my heart be acceptable in Your sight, O Lord, my strength and my Redeemer." Psalm 19:14

Today's Philosophical Tidbit: "Be sure your brain is in gear before engaging your mouth." Author Unknown

August 14
Be Sure You Dress Properly

Today's Smile: Jeremy was studying at the school of medicine at the University of New Mexico in Albuquerque, New Mexico. During his summer vacations, in order to make some of the money that he needed for his schooling, he held two jobs. During the day he worked as a butcher. In the evenings, he worked as an orderly at a hospital. With both of these jobs, he wore a white coat.

One evening, he was asked to wheel a patient on a stretcher into the surgery ward. The woman patient took one look at Jeremy and let out the most unearthly scream. "Oh, no," she wailed, "it's my butcher!"

Today's Comment: When I was actively serving as a pastor, I dressed on Sundays and my work week days in the manner in which I thought a pastor should dress. I met with hurting people. I had lunch with business men. I visited in the hospital. I did not want to look like I had just walked in from the barn or off of the beach.

One day, on my day off, I slipped into the office, dressed very casually, wearing blue jeans and a well worn shirt, and one of the ladies of the church walked into the church office and saw me in this attire. She stopped, stared and spoke with a surprised expression on her face, "Pastor, I have never, in all my days seen you dressed that way!" Well, she was not criticizing, just laughing. I didn't look like her pastor.

When it comes to our Christian life-style and manner of dress, how do we look? I don't mean our clothing, our outward appearance, but what about the inward dress. Do we appear differently?

The apostle Paul writes to the church in Colosse and reminds them that since receiving Christ as their personal Lord and Saviour that there are things that they must put off. There are things they should put on. Put off uncleanness, evil desire, covetousness, anger, malice, filthy language, etc. Don't wear these any more. Put on tender mercies, kindness, humility, patience, etc.

It was unfortunate that the butcher and orderly were dressed very similarly. Pray that as Christians that our inward dress will be different from that of non-Christians.

Today's Golden Nugget of Truth: "Therefore gird up the loins of your mind, be sober, and rest your hope fully upon the grace that is to be brought to you at the revelation of Jesus Christ; as obedient children not conforming yourselves to the former lusts, as in your ignorance; but as He who called you is holy, you also be holy in all your conduct, because it is written, 'Be holy, for I am holy'." First Peter 1:13-15

Today's Philosophical Tidbit: "Remember, your true character is revealed by what is on the inside." Author Unknown

August 15
Together Still

*T*oday's Smile: A woman in her forties was about to be married but she was a bit nervous about her honeymoon. Some of her lady friends in the church wanted to encourage her and so they decided to send a telegram to her with an encouraging verse of scripture. (Remember telegrams?) The verse that they chose was I John 4:18 "There is no fear in love, but perfect love casts out all fear." That was a good choice. Words were limited in the telegram and so they agreed to simply have printed "I John 4:18."

In transmitting the telegram, the operator wrote John 4:18, omitting, by mistake, the "I" which stood for the word "First." If you look up John 4:18, as the nervous bride to be did, it reads, "The fact is, you have had five husbands, and the man you now have is not your husband. What you have just said is true."

Today's Comment: I want to ask the married folk who are reading this today, "Were you a bit nervous before you got married?" I wasn't nervous. I was very relaxed on the day of our wedding. I had very little to do the morning of my wedding. I spent my last single night at the home of some friends of my bride.

It was a small town, so the day of the wedding I walked down town around noon for something to do. As I was walking back to the home, I passed the church and guests were already arriving at the church for "my" wedding and I had to get cleaned up and dressed. Suddenly I realized that I needed to get a move on.

Well, I couldn't have asked for a better lady to share life with. I honor her today. She is a godly woman and has been a trooper. She is a wonderful mother to our children and grandchildren. I've said many times that she has been the real *Assistant Pastor*. We never became rich in this ministry, but all of our needs have been met. Leona is my companion and at this stage of life we cherish every day as a gift from God. Today is our wedding anniversary, married August 15, 1959.

If you are married or about to be married, I trust you will have as blessed and joyous a marriage as we have had. As you pray today, commit and submit your marriage to the King of kings and to the Lord of lords.

Today's Golden Nugget of Truth: "In the same way, you husbands must give honor to your wives. Treat your wife with understanding as you live together. She may be weaker than you are, but she is your equal partner in God's gift of new life. Treat her as you should so your prayers will not be hindered." First Peter 3:7 (NLT)

Today's Philosophical Tidbit: "We've grown to be one soul, two parts; our lives so intertwined that when some passion stirs your heart, I feel the quake in mine." Gloria Gaither

August 16
We Need Each Other

*T**oday's Smile:* Harold, Henry and Homer were triplets. Their mother had given each one of them a dime and told them to go down to the little country store, the only one in their village, and buy a treat for themselves. Harold asked the clerk for ten cents worth of jellybeans. Since the jellybeans were on a high shelf, Mrs. Smith, the clerk, got the step ladder from the store room, got ten cents worth of jellybeans and gave them to Harold. She returned the ladder to the store room. There upon she asked Henry what he would like; he wanted ten cents worth of jellybeans. So she went getting the ladder again and once again took out ten cents worth of jellybeans giving them to Henry.

This time before returning the ladder she turned to Homer and asked if he wanted ten cents worth of jellybeans. "No thank you Mrs. Smith!" he replied. So she returned the ladder to the storeroom and came back to wait on Homer.

"Well, Homer, what can I get for you?"

"I'd like five cents worth of jellybeans!" he replied.

Today's Comment: In our second year of marriage my wife and I moved to a small hamlet in central Alberta where I became pastor of two small churches. We lived in a hamlet consisting of 65 people. There was a country store in that hamlet which became a gathering place. People stopped to chat with neighbors and farmers who came for supplies. It had a homey atmosphere.

We don't have too many country stores anymore. Today 80% of Americans and Canadians live in cities. There are people all around and yet millions don't know the interaction and good times that were to be had in the country store. Millions and millions of people are lonely. The first thing that God said was "It is not good that man should be alone. . ." Genesis 2:18. We need friends. We need fellowship. We need one another.

Have you reached out to lonely people close by? Or are you one of the lonely, like the a little boy who was afraid to sleep alone. His mother sought to comfort him by saying that God was with him. His response was, "Yea, but I want someone with skin on." Pray that we will come alongside the lonely befriend them, also pointing them to One greater than ourselves who wants to be their friend forever.

Today's Golden Nugget of Truth. "And the Lord, He is the One who goes before you. He will be with you. He will not leave you nor forsake you; do not fear nor be dismayed." Deuteronomy 31:8

Today's Philosophical Tidbit: "Snuggle in God's arms. When you are hurting, when you feel lonely, left out, let Him cradle you, comfort you, reassure you of His all-sufficient power and love." Kay Arthur

August 17
Get The Facts Straight

oday's Smile: Bradley lived in a small town on the west coast of Washington State. He had built up an independent hardware store that had about everything one needed. At his store you didn't have to buy a package of screws, or washers, etc. If you needed two screws, you could buy two screws. If you needed one hinge, you could buy one hinge.

Dylan was a young high school graduate and had been hired by Bradley. He caught on quickly and Bradley was very satisfied with this young fellow's work. He always had a warm smile interacting well with the customers. One day, Bradley saw Dylan greeting a tourist, who had come from the east and was touring the west coast. As Bradley approached, he heard Dylan say, "No sir, we haven't had any for about three weeks, and it doesn't look like we will be getting any soon."

Bradley was a little upset with this comment. As the customer walked towards the exit, Bradley caught up to him and said, "Sorry sir, we will have some soon. In fact, we placed an order for it on Monday of this week. Would you like to be put on a list and we can call you when it comes in?"

Well the tourist, with a puzzled look on his face, left the store, declining the store owner's offer. Bradley then went over to Dylan and said, "Never ever tell a customer we don't have something. If they ask for something that we don't have, simply tell them that we have ordered it and it's on its way. What was it that the man asked about?"

"Well, sir he said he understood that we get a lot of rain in Washington State and he asked if we had any in the last week."

Today's Comment: Butting in when you don't have all the facts makes me think of those who have never studied the Bible and yet speak with authority (whose authority) spouting off that there is no God. They don't have all the facts. They make a judgment call by what they see. They haven't read God's Word.

I've read letters to the editor and remarks written by people who adamantly spout off that there is no God and that Christians are simply disillusioned and use God and the church as a crutch. Ernest Hemingway, an American author and journalist not only denied the existence of God but looked upon organized religion as a menace to our happiness. He said, "All thinking men are atheists." Look at his life, four marriages and a suicidal ending.

Some *thinking men*, to use Hemmingway's words, have set out to prove that God did not exist. They did a thorough investigation and many who did such a study came to faith in Christ. They discovered that their beliefs were wrong. C. S. Lewis and Lee Strobel are two among many who have written about their journey from atheism to the assurance of salvation.

Let's not be guilty of butting in when we don't have all the facts. If you are reading this book and you like to disprove the reality of God and the authenticity of His Word, pray that God would open your mind to the truth that there is indeed a God and someday you will have to stand before Him. Do a study of the Bible, get the facts, the truth, you may well see what many others have, that there is one God existing in three persons, Father, Son and Holy Spirit.

Pray that God would open your mind to the truth that there is indeed a God and someday you will have to stand before Him.

Today's Golden Nugget of Truth: "For all those things My hand has made, and all those things exist, says the Lord. But on this one will I look: On him who is poor and of a contrite spirit, and who trembles at My word." Isaiah 66:2

Today's Philosophical Tidbit: "In this I rejoice, I know the One and only God, the Creator and sustainer of life, and this God knows me." A. Daniel Goldsmith

August 18
New Life

oday's Smile: Bradley had recently met Kayla and they had dated for a couple of months. He had a brief appointment in Lancaster County and asked Kayla if she would like to accompany him for the day. His appointment would only take about an hour and they could spend most of the day taking in the tourist attractions. She agreed.

They set off early Saturday morning. He was finished with his appointment a little before noon. They grabbed a quick bite to eat and then, since they were in Amish country, he asked if she would like to go for a horse and buggy ride. She was excited about that, so Bradley rented a horse and buggy and the two of them set off down one of the country roads.

They were enjoying their time together when suddenly the horse dropped dead. As they sat wondering what they should do, Bradley said, "I think before we do anything else, this would be a good time for a kiss."

"Why a kiss?" she asked.

"A kiss will give us that nice tingly feeling. It will breathe new life into us."

"Then why don't you kiss the horse and breathe new life into it, and we can continue our ride."

Today's Comment: Do you have that lifeless feeling? Dragging physically? Feeling like you are in need of a shot in the arm? Emotionally and spiritually drained?

We tend to seek help in times like these often with medication. Some may have suggested that you need to get away. Give yourself a break. If it is a physical matter, these remedies may well be the solution. However, if it is a spiritual vacuum that you are experiencing, no medication or any number of other things will fix the problem. What we need is a fresh touch from God.

God can brighten your day, lift your spirits and infuse you with new life, enabling you to continue on.

My paternal grandmother's favorite hymn was Breathe on Me, Breath of God. The first and last stanza's read: "Breathe on me breath of God, Fill me with life anew, That I may love what Thou dost love, And do what Thou wouldst do. Breathe on me breath of God, So shall I never die, But live with Thee the perfect life, Of Thine eternity."

Pray that you will know what it is to walk in newness of life.

Today's Golden Nugget of Truth: "Therefore we were buried with Him through baptism into death, that just as Christ was raised from the dead by the glory of the Father, even so we also should walk in newness of life." Romans 6:4

Today's Philosophical Tidbit: "When we begin to see life the way God sees it, we see that life has an ever flowing spiritual undercurrent. All of life flows from that spiritual dimension. Everything we do in the physical, mental, or emotional realm has a spiritual component to it." Charles Stanley

August 19
Helping Hands

*T**oday's Smile:* Eleven year old Jose had never traveled very far from his home in Cancun, Mexico, but he had always dreamed of going to the United States, especially did he dream of going to New York City and to Yankee Stadium. He wanted to see the New York Yankees play baseball. Well, his dream finally came true. One of his uncles, Edmundo, had emigrated to the United States three years earlier and had invited his nephew Jose to spend a couple of weeks with him.

One afternoon, soon after arriving at his uncle's place, he ventured out on his own to Yankee Stadium. He didn't have any money and was unable to purchase a ticket but a ticket seller was so moved by his story that he told Jose to wait a few moments and he would find a place for him.

Well, you should have heard Jose describe his adventure when he got back to his uncle's place. "Uncle Edmundo, I didn't have any money for a ticket, but a nice man found me a place. He led me to a perch near the American flag. And you know uncle, those Amigo's are so nice. Before the game they all stood and looked up at me and sang, *Jose can you see. . ."*

Today's Comment: Today's smile brought two things to my mind. One of them was the *Make-A-Wish Foundation* which plans and pays for an outing, maybe a trip to Disneyland, or any number of other events for children with life threatening medical conditions.

The other thing that I thought of was an illustration which I have used in a sermon. It was about a barefooted ten year old boy peering through the window of a New York City shoe store. He was shivering with cold when a lady asked him, "My little fellow, why are you looking so earnestly in that window?"

"I was asking God to give me a pair of shoes," was his reply. The kind lady took him by the hand and into the store and asked the clerk to get a half dozen pairs of socks for the boy. She then asked the clerk if he would give her a basin of warm water, soap and a towel. Removing her gloves, she knelt down and washed his little feet and dried them with the towel. When the clerk brought the socks to her, she asked if he would fit the boy with a pair of shoes. As she was paying for the socks and shoes the young boy grabbed her hand and thanked her and then asked, "Are you God's wife?"

God's wife is not all that bad a description for the Bible tells us that the Lord Jesus Christ is the Bridegroom, and we who have personally received the Lord Jesus Christ as our Saviour are His Bride. Pray that we will live and act like we belong to Him.

Today's Golden Nugget of Truth: "Beloved, let us love one another, for love is of God; and everyone who loves is born of God and knows God. He who does not love does not know God, for God is love." First John 4:7, 8

Today's Philosophical Tidbit: "The sanctifying work of the Spirit makes possible that for which we were created in the first place - to be a physical and visible expression of the moral character of God." Charles Price

August 20
Have I Made Myself Clear

*T*oday's Smile: Although the Dobson family had recently moved into a new neighborhood, their son Lou had made a good many new friends, ten of whom were invited to his birthday party. When the happy day arrived and he opened his presents, his folks were amazed to see that eight guests had presented him with a sweater.

Later as his mom was talking with the next door neighbor boy's mother and was sharing how that Lou had received so many sweaters, the neighbor said coolly, "Well, after all, you were the one who wrote on the invitation what you wanted me to buy."

For a few minutes Lou's mother was stunned into silence and then realized what had happened. Since the party was being held in the basement, which is always cool, she had written on each invitation: "Please have your child bring a sweater."

Today's Comment: Many years ago we invited some friends for dinner. They declined feeling that it would be too much work for my wife, since we had a young family and a busy schedule. So we asked if they would come for coffee. They agreed to that.

At six o'clock when my wife was on her hands and knees scrubbing the kitchen floor, there was a knock at the door. Who should it be but the folks that declined our dinner invitation? Since no dinner was prepared for guests we invited them in and I said that I would go buy a bucket of fried chicken. "No," they said, "we'll come back later." They left and came back for coffee at 8:00pm.

A few incidents like that over the years always remind me to be sure that I have been clearly understood. More than mixing up the details regarding a birthday party, a dinner or meeting with someone, pray that we will be clear in our presentation of the gospel and no one will misunderstand us.

Today's Golden Nugget of Truth: "Pray that every time I open my mouth I'll be able to make Christ plain as day to them." Colossians 4:4 (MSG)

Today's Philosophical Tidbit: "Silence never makes any blunders." Author Unknown

August 21
Taste My Words Before I Speak

oday's Smile: Dale was working in a small corner grocery store. He was fairly new at the job and wasn't particularly relating well to the customers. The owner of the store was very cordial and accommodating being a real people person. His customers loved to deal with him because they always got exactly what they wanted. Dale was far from being like his boss.

One morning a lady walked into the store and said to Dale that she only wanted to buy half a cabbage. A whole cabbage was too much for her. This irritated Dale, so he picked up a cabbage and walked out into the back room and approached the manager by saying, "Some idiot wants half a cabbage." As he said that he caught sight of the lady who had followed him into the back room. Without missing a beat, he added, "And this lady would like the other half."

Today's Comment: It is not always that easy to transition your way out of what could be a very demeaning or embarrassing situation. Many years ago we had a boarder. One day my wife and I were downstairs in the family room, near her room. She was not at home at the time, or so we thought. As we were about to make some comment about her, one of us referred to her as "What's her face!" To our surprise, she had entered the room behind us and said, "What's her face is here and my name is Miriam."

Pray that we will not speak rudely or despairingly of others, but to speak kindly and graciously.

Today's Golden Nugget of Truth: "Let your speech always be with grace, seasoned with salt. . ." Colossians 4:6

Today's Philosophical Tidbit: "Please God, make my words today sweet and tender, for tomorrow I may have to eat them." Author Unknown

August 22
I Will Make You Fishers Of Men

Today's Smile: Chad had been fishing all day, but did not get as much as a strike. His wife used to complain that the time he spent fishing was a waste of time. In order to let her know that it was not time wasted, he stopped at a fish market on his way home. He said to the clerk, "Just stand over there and throw me four of your largest trout and I will catch them."

"Throw them? What for?" asked the stunned clerk.

"Well," said Chad, "my wife thinks fishing is a waste of time. I don't want to lie to her, but if you throw them to me, I can truthfully tell her that I caught them."

Today's Comment: We've all heard the fishermen's stories about the one that got away and how big it was. Then there are times when one fishes and catches nothing. Several years ago, three of us fellows went salmon fishing one afternoon in the Strait of Juan de Fuca, just off the coast of Victoria, BC. We caught nothing. Guess our wives figured we wouldn't because when we docked, the three wives and children had already fixed a barbecue supper for us.

Jesus told us to be "fishers of men." Sometimes when we go fishing, seeking to share the gospel with others, we manage to catch one. Those are times of rejoicing when a sinner prays to receive Christ as Saviour. Then there are those times when we are just as diligent about sharing with others, but they are not interested.

Fishing that afternoon off the coast of Victoria did not stop me from fishing again. So if you have shared your faith with another and there was little interest on their part, don't give up. Pray and cast your line again. There are lot of *fish* in the world that need to be pulled in to Christ.

Today's Golden Nugget of Truth: "Then He said to them, Follow Me, and I will make you fishers of men." Matthew 4:19

Today's Philosophical Tidbit: "Fishers of men cast their nets in faith and draw them in with love." Author Unknown

August 23
Telephone To Glory

*T*oday's Smile: Jessica's husband Norm surprised her on her birthday with a smart phone. Norm wanted to be able to keep in touch more often since she now had a part time job at a ladies dress shop so they were not always home at the same time. He explained all the features as to how to phone him, and how to receive incoming calls. He also showed her other features such as checking weather forecasts, which she loved to do on the television.

Anyhow, it was her first day with her new phone. She had some errands to run before going to work in the afternoon. Her phone rang, it was Norm. "Hi, honey," he said, "how's your morning been?"

"Oh, I have been busy doing a little shopping and buying some things for Scot before he leaves for college."

"Has Scot or Sandy phoned you yet?"

"No, dear, you are the very first person to phone me. But how did you know that I was in the mall? Did Scot tell you that you could reach me here?"

Today's Comment: We have become so used to being able to communicate with family and friends from wherever we are to wherever they are. We recently were on a trip to the Maritime Provinces on Canada's east coast. My wife and I were able to talk to our three children, who live in Alberta and British Columbia. It didn't matter if they were in their home or in a mall or at work, we connected. What's more, it didn't cost one cent extra. It was part of the plan.

As I said earlier in this book, we have a line of communication to our Heavenly Father. We can be in college, at home with the family, at work, in church, anywhere, and we are able to instantly make contact. His line is never busy. We never have to leave a voice mail waiting for a call back. Our gracious Lord has His ear tuned to hear our voice at anytime, day or night. We can be happy or sad, and He will always listen to us. He hears and He answers our prayers. A call to Him is also free. He paid the price with the sacrifice of His precious Son, our Savior the Lord Jesus Christ. Don't forget to pray and call Him today? He is waiting to hear from you.

Today's Golden Nugget of Truth: "Because He has inclined His ear to me, therefore I will call upon Him as long as I live." Psalm 116:2

Today's Philosophical Tidbit: "Heaven is full of answers to prayers for which no one ever bothered to ask." Billy Graham

August 24
Who's To Blame

*T*oday's *Smile:* Sue finally solved that age old problem as to the reason why she was gaining so much weight. It was not the bacon and eggs every morning, or the chocolate bar or the bag of potato chips as a mid afternoon snack. It was not the hamburger and chocolate milk shake that she consumed quite frequently when out with her lady friends. It was none of these. It had nothing to do with over eating. Sue discovered that it was the shampoo that she used to wash her hair.

One morning, as she was showering and setting the bottle of shampoo on the shower rack, she noticed for the first time the words on the label, "For extra volume and body." No wonder she was gaining so much weight. It was the shampoo that she used when showering.

So, Sue got rid of that shampoo and is now using a dish soap when she showers. That label says: "Dissolves fat that is otherwise difficult to remove."

Today's Comment: It is quite easy to blame things or people for our problems in life. It is often neither of these. We are to blame. We need to take responsibility for what has happened. It was our decision to do what we did that caused such a response or reaction.

The blame game started in the Garden of Eden. Adam blamed Eve and Eve blamed the serpent. Someone has added to that and said that the serpent didn't have a leg to stand on.

Let us own up to the fact that maybe, just maybe we are the problem. We are not the cause for all of our problems, but perhaps some of them could have been avoided if we had made a better choice.

Pray that we will strive to be blameless in all of our dealings.

Today's Golden Nugget of Truth: "Each of us must bear some faults and burdens of his own. For none of us is perfect!" Galatians 6:5 (TLB)

Today's Philosophical Tidbit: "No one is a failure until they blame somebody else." Author Unknown

August 25
Extreme Makeover

*T*oday's Smile: Grant received a parrot as a gift. The parrot had a terrible vocabulary. Every word out of the bird's mouth was rude, obnoxious and laced with profanity. Grant tried to teach the bird to "clean up" its speech by consistently saying only polite words.

One day Grant yelled at the parrot. The parrot yelled back. Grant shook the parrot and the parrot got very angry. In desperation he grabbed the bird throwing it into the freezer. The parrot squawked, kicked, screamed and scratched. Suddenly that behavior stopped. All was quiet for a minute. Fearing that he had hurt the parrot, Grant opened the door to the freezer. The parrot calmly stepped out onto Grant's outstretched arm and said, "I believe I may have offended you with my rude language and actions. I am sincerely remorseful for my inappropriate transgressions. I fully intend to do everything I can to correct my rude and unforgivable behavior."

Grant was stunned by what the parrot said. As he was about to ask the parrot what had made such a dramatic change, the bird spoke up, very softly, "May I ask what the turkey did?"

Today's Comment: Parrots may have problems, but so do people. Profanity, addictions, temper, lying, stealing, cheating, immorality, the list goes on. What a joy to see a radical change in the lives of people, sometimes overnight.

When I was in my teen years, I heard Dr. P. W. Philpott preach at Blue Water Bible and Missionary Conference, a summer family camp, a half hour's drive from my home. Dr. Philpott was born and raised in my home area. It was enjoyable to hear this famous preacher tell tales about his growing up years. He related how he used to ride on a horse drawn wagon being driven by Rev. Josiah Henson, the character about which the book *Uncle Tom's Cabin* was written. In his youth, Philpott skated on the river that flowed past the conference center.

One of the many stories which he told was about a fellow he called "Joe." In his younger years, Philpott worked as a blacksmith. Joe also worked in the same shop. Everyone working in that shop heard that Joe had "gotten religion" the night before. All eyes were on Joe, as he was notorious for his foul speech.

The morning after becoming a Christian, Joe hit his finger with a hammer. Out of his mouth came a volume of cursing and profanity. Everyone turned to look. Dr. Philpott says what happened next made a lasting impression on him. Joe took off his cap, knelt down at the anvil praying silently. He stood, put his cap back on, continuing with his work. Never again did Philpott nor any of his co-workers hear bad words from Joe's mouth. A radical change, yes an overnight change.

Dr. Philpott later had a radical change in his life. He gave his life to the Lord. He became a Salvation Army officer, took over a struggling church in Hamilton, ON, and in 1922 assumed the pastorate of the famed Moody Memorial Church in Chicago, IL. It was during his leadership there that the present day Moody Church building was erected.

God is in the business of extreme makeovers. Pray that many today will be radically changed by the transforming power of God.

Today's Golden Nugget of Truth: "And I thank Christ Jesus our Lord who has enabled me, because He counted me faithful, putting me into the ministry, although I was formerly a blasphemer, a persecutor, and an insolent man; but I obtained mercy because I did it ignorantly in unbelief." First Timothy 1:13

Today's Philosophical Tidbit: "Your worst days are never so bad that you are beyond the reach of God's grace, and your best days are never so good that you are beyond the need of God's grace." Jerry Bridges Read Appendix "B"

August 26
Figures Don't Lie, But Liars Figure

Today's Smile: A South Dakota farmer passed away. When the three sons read his Last Will and Testament they found that it

301

was fairly easy to settle his estate. However, he had several mules and this posed a bit of a problem. In his will it stated that the oldest son was to receive half of the mules, the second son was to receive one third of the mules and the youngest son was to receive one-ninth of the mules. That was acceptable to the three sons but there was a problem for which the lawyer didn't have a solution. Their dad had left seventeen mules and how could they divide them into one half, one third and one ninth. It couldn't be done.

They phoned over to their uncle Landon who lived on the farm next to their Dad's. Uncle Landon used to teach mathematics in his younger years and they figured that he could help them solve the problem. He hitched up one of his mules and road over to meet with his nephews. "I'll tell you what I will do boys," said the uncle, "I will add my mule into the mix and make it eighteen mules instead of seventeen." He then began to do the math.

"Taylor," he said, "since you were to receive half of the mules, you get nine of them." That left nine mules. He gave Blake, the second son, six of the mules, which was one third. "Dalton, your dad willed one ninth of the mules to you, which is two." The uncle then added up nine, six and two which came to seventeen. With the problem solved he hitched up his mule and rode home.

Today's Comment: Starting with my grade ten mathematics high school teacher, I have heard a few math puzzles over the years for which there were no solutions, but a trick answer was always given. The answer sounded correct but really wasn't.

Life is often like that. There are a lot of issues that one cannot solve. Someone may come up with a solution which sounds reasonable, but it is still not right. Products do not work as advertised. Promises made by politicians are not fulfilled. Entertainment billed as being the greatest show ever ends up being a big disappointment. There are also many religions that are working hard to make converts but what they offer still leaves emptiness. Jesus Christ alone will give lasting peace, joy, hope and fill the void which is in the heart of every person.

If your life is empty and you're seeking fulfillment in all the wrong places, breathe a prayer to God Almighty. He will solve your problem, but not by trickery.

Today's Golden Nugget of Truth: "Let no one deceive you with empty words. . ." Ephesians 5:6

Today's Philosophical Tidbit: "O what a tangled web we weave when first we practice to deceive." Walter Scott

August 27
Are We Cheerful Givers

*T*oday's Smile: Many years ago two young university students, both having received Christ as their Savior, made a promise to each other that they would both give ten percent of their income to the Lord's work and be accountable to each other. That was fine. Their income was small and it seemed to be no problem to give a tithe at the time.

One of those boys became a business man. When the business man made his first ten thousand dollars in a year, he gave one thousand. When he earned one hundred thousand, he gave ten thousand. One year he made one million dollars and wrote a check for one hundred thousand. Eventually, as his business grew he earned for himself six million dollars in one single year. That year he found it extremely hard to part with six hundred thousand dollars.

He decided to go see his old boyhood chum, who was a pastor in the next state. During their visit, the business man told his pastor friend the purpose for his visit. He reminded him of the promise that they had made to each other regarding giving ten percent to the Lord's work. "We've both kept our promise over the years," said the business man, "but I'm at the point now where I cannot give the ten percent anymore. I cannot afford to write a check for six hundred thousand dollars and I've come to ask if we can break our covenant that we made when we were in our teen years."

His pastor friend got down on his knees there in the office and prayed silently for some time. Finally, the businessman asked, "What are you doing? Are you praying that God will let me out of the covenant to tithe?"

"No," said the pastor. "I am praying for God to reduce your income back to the level where one thousand dollars will be your tithe!"

Today's Comment: David Church quotes a CNN article about tithing. "The churches of the U.S. last year received about $4 billion in donations. If the 112 million Americans who claim a religious affiliation had given one tenth, the traditional tithe, of their personal income to churches, that total could have topped $25 billion. It takes money to advance the Kingdom of God in this world yet, according to this article, the average Christian in America gives only $35.71 to God's work each year. And we wonder why America is straying so far from God."[1]

As a child my parents taught me to give one tenth of what I earned to the Lord's work. We in turn taught our children to do the same. I recall, some years ago, being seated next to one of my grandsons, who was nine at the time. He had just been given one hundred dollars. He showed me a handful of change, ten dollars worth, and whispered as the offering bag was approaching, "Mommy has been teaching us to give ten percent." As the bag was passed to him, he dropped in ten dollars worth of coins.

Pray that we might teach by example that giving to God should be our first priority.

Today's Golden Nugget of Truth: "Will a man rob God? Yet you have robbed me! But you say, in what way have we robbed You? In tithes and offerings." Malachi 3:8

Today's Philosophical Tidbit: "I have held many things in my hands, and I have lost them all; but whatever I have placed in God's hands that I still possess." Corrie Ten Boom

August 28
Too Good To Be True

T oday's Smile: A drifter had returned to his boyhood town and was being treated to lunch by an old classmate who was a mechanic in the small town. To their surprise along came a gal that they had both gone to school with some twenty-five years earlier. In a brief conversation with her they learned that she was having a difficult time selling her old car. It had 279,000 miles on it and nobody was interested in it, even though the body was in excellent shape. Well the drifter pointed to his mechanic friend and said, "He can roll back the odometer for you."

"I know it is illegal," said the mechanic, "but I'm sure it will sell. Come see me Friday morning at 7:30am." She went to his garage and he altered her odometer as promised.

About a month later the mechanic saw this woman again. He asked her if she had managed to sell her car after he had adjusted it. "No," she replied, "but I want to thank you for rolling back the odometer. I have decided to keep it since it only has 60,000 miles on it."

Today's Comment: Too many people are deceived these days because they read something or heard something and they believed it to be the truth. I have received emails from friends and the emails have some startling statements which are not true. They are either about the government, or some food that you shouldn't eat, about some tragedy and money is needed, or some wild story about a well known individual. The list goes on. When you tell your friends that it is false, some find it hard to believe that you are right and the story is wrong. They received it from a trusted friend and their friend should know.

There are millions that are deceived by false teachers. True, they may use the Bible, but they are leading people astray. I remember a friend of some years ago who heard an enthusiastic preacher stating things that were entirely the opposite of what the scripture taught. She believed him. Why? Because he was a preacher and it sounded right. There are many in the world today that are compromising the truths of God's Word to suit their liking and proclaiming it as the truth. It sounds good, but it is false. Pray that you will not be misled by false teachers. Search the scriptures for yourself. Get another opinion.

Today's Golden Nugget of Truth: "These were more fair-minded than those in Thessalonica, in that they received the word with all readiness, and searched the Scriptures daily to find out whether these things were so." Acts 17:11

Today's Philosophical Tidbit: "A text taken out of context becomes a pretext." Author Unknown

August 29
The Power Of A Smile

*T*uday's *Smile:* The children were all in bed, while Charlie and Ruth were sitting in the family room enjoying a hot chocolate before calling it a day. They were reminiscing on how quickly the years had slipped by since they first met. They were still young, but they had been married fourteen years. They had been fourteen wonderful years. They had had their sorrows, but also their joys and a lot of fun times with their three children.

Charlie had a great sense of humor and was always coming up with some crazy story. He was also a great tease. On this particular night, he said to Ruth, "Sweetheart how is it that God would ever make a woman like you so beautiful and so stupid at the same time?"

Ruth also was not lacking when it came to a little fun and laughter. "Well, honey, let me explain it to you. God made me beautiful so you would marry me, and stupid so I would marry you."

Today's Comment: I had about two thirds of this book written when a friend gave me a daily devotional book entitled: *Daily Inspiration From The Lion's Den.*[1] The devotionals and comments come out of the experiences and testimonies of believers in what we call "the persecuted church." As I began reading that book on a daily basis, I wondered whether I should continue to write this book. Should we be laughing when there is so much suffering?

We have been told that humor is good for us. Smiles, jokes, humorous happenings help us through our days. Dr. Adrian Rogers writes: "Your sense of humor is a gift from God. Research studies have shown that laughter, along with a well-rounded sense of humor, is one of the sure signs of intelligence. It is also known to produce endorphins in your body that generate feelings of well being."[2] So I kept writing.

If you know someone that needs to smile or laugh today, pray that you might be able to give them a smile, lifting their spirits.

Today's Golden Nugget of Truth: "Be glad in the Lord and rejoice, you righteous; and shout for joy, all you upright in heart." Psalm 32:11

Today's Philosophical Tidbit: "God must have meant for us to laugh, or else He would not have made so many mules, parrots, monkeys and human beings." Abraham Lincoln

August 30
Is Our Faith Private Or Public

*T*oday's Smile: Trisha was spending the weekend with her grand-mother when she turned to her at lunch on Saturday and asked, "Nana, how old are you?"

"Sweetheart," said her nana, "young girls don't ask their grand-parents for their age."

"Awe Nana, I won't tell anyone," she replied. No more was said. However, after lunch Trisha was nowhere to be seen. A half hour had passed and her grandmother started going through the house looking for her. Finally, she found her, sitting on the floor in the grandmother's bedroom.

When the little girl looked up and saw her grandmother, she quickly said, "I know how old you are, Nana. You're 69."

"How did you find that out?" asked the grandmother.

"I found your driver's license and it says what year you were born and I figured it out. You're 69. And I know something else, too. You made an 'F' in sex."

Today's Comment: We hear and read so much these days about privacy laws. I sometimes think that it is carried to extremes, but for generations there have been unwritten privacy laws in families. There are still elderly people that do not want to share their age, and many other personal details.

For a more current incident, I have had blood work done every month for several years. I got to know the lab technicians on a first name basis. One day my wife had to go to the clinic for blood work.

A day or so later, I was there for my monthly check-up and I had the same lab technician that had done my wife's blood tests. So I said to her, "I understand you met my wife the other day."

She looked at me and with a smirk on her face, put her finger to her mouth, indicating silence and said, "Privacy laws." She would not confirm with me that she had dealt with my wife.

Those privacy laws seemed to have been in effect in the lives of many Christians for years and years. We talk about everything else with our neighbors and fellow employees, etc., but how many of them know that we are born again Christians? Do we keep that to ourselves? Someone made the statement that too many Christians function like secret service agents. Pray that God will help us to do better in sharing our faith.

Today's Golden Nugget of Truth: "Let the redeemed of the Lord say so, Whom He has redeemed from the hand of the enemy." Psalm 107:2

Today's Philosophical Tidbit: "We are to be channels of God's truth, not reservoirs." Author Unknown

August 31
What If

*T*oday's Smile: Colby spent most of one Saturday seeking acceptance in a firefighter's school. He had to write a two hour exam. He had to pass a grueling physical exam, doing as many push-ups as possible in two minutes; hauling a 200 pound dummy up a ladder and down again; dragging 100 feet of hose filled with water, etc., doing it three times in 20 minutes. He also had a thirty minute interview.

A question put to him in the interview was, "What would you do if you arrived at the scene of a fire, an empty warehouse, and you could not get the hose to unwind and come off of the truck?"

"I would radio for another truck," said Colby.

"What if the two way radio wouldn't work?"

"I'd use my cell phone."

"What if you were out of cell range?""

"I would run to the nearest pay phone."

"What if that phone was vandalized?"

"I guess I would run a couple of blocks and get my Uncle Roger."

That question stumped the interviewer. "Why would you go get your uncle?"

"Uncle Roger has never seen a fire as big as he is going to see."

Today's Comment: Throughout the years we've often been asked hypothetical questions. What if we make all these arrangements and. . .? What if we buy these tickets for the trip and. . .? What if the children don't want to. . .? What if? What if? What if?

There are other "what if" questions that we should face. What if we live all our life for pleasure and satisfying our flesh? What if we are trusting in our good works to get us to heaven? What if we never respond to the gospel invitation and receive Christ as our personal Savior???? What if?

These questions are far more important and need to be answered. What if we die tonight and we are not prepared to meet God? What then? If you do not have an answer, or are unprepared, pray right now and turn your life over to God. Let Him be the Lord of your life. See Appendix "A"

Today's Golden Nugget of Truth: "And as it is appointed for men to die once, but after this the judgment." Hebrews 9:27

Today's Philosophical Tidbit: "If you're headed in the wrong direction, God allows U-turns." Author Unknown

September 1
The Simplicity Of The Gospel

*T*oday's Smile: Canadian Evangelist Barry Moore, founder and president of Barry Moore Ministries shared with me a story about two of his team members who attended a Sunday morning service in an American black church. The service was lengthy and highly charged with dedication and sincerity. When the guest speaker, elderly, knowledgeable and respected, stood to preach he remarked that he was expected to be finished at twelve o'clock. It was then five minutes to the noon hour.

Standing graciously at the pulpit, the elderly visiting pastor said he would be finished at 12 o'clock. He then proceeded to preach as follows:

My first point is - Salvation is GOOD when you is young.

My second point - Salvation is BETTER when you is old.

My third point - Salvation is BEST when you is DEAD.

He then reverently pronounced the benediction at thirty seconds to twelve.

"That was the best sermon on salvation that I ever heard," said one of Barry's associates.

Today's Comment: There were five black churches in the small city of Chatham, Ontario where I was born and raised. It was a joy and delight to attend a couple of those churches on occasion. Our dear brothers and sisters have great enthusiasm and a unique way of conveying truths, and a very expressive way of worshipping.

A friend told me about attending a funeral for a young man who had stood outside of one of those Chatham churches waving his finger at the church and cursing the same. Soon after that incident the young man went swimming one day, diving into the river hitting a submerged park bench and dying a few hours later.

When the pastor rose to preach the funeral message for this young man he chose as his text First Samuel 20:3 "As the Lord liveth, and as thy soul liveth, there is but a step between me and death." The pastor then began his sermon and said, "There is but a step between me and death." He repeated it, "There is but a step between me and death." For the third time he said, "There is but a step between me and death." He then had the audience repeat it with him a couple of times. That was the extent of his sermon.

Though I was not present at that service, that sermon has stuck in my mind for sixty plus years. Need I remind us all, that there is "but a step between me and death." One breath away. "Salvation is GOOD when you is young. It is BETTER when you is old, but let me say again, it is BEST when you is DEAD." Are you looking forward to that which is still ahead? It is the best! Pray that you will be ready and not miss out on the joys and glories of that eternal home.

Today's Golden Nugget of Truth: "But now they desire a better, that is, a heavenly country, Therefore God is not ashamed to be called their God, for He has prepared a city for them." Hebrews 11:16

Today's Philosophical Tidbit: "Give the future prayerful consideration; that's where you will spend the rest of your life." Author Unknown

September 2
I Don't Know About Tomorrow

*T*oday's Smile: Dalton's wife was constantly begging him to let her go horseback riding with him. He always had a "no" for her. He reminded her of her heart condition and told her that she was not strong enough. One day when he was working at the store, she decided she would ride a horse by herself. Even though she had no lessons or prior experience, she mounted the horse unassisted. The horse immediately sprung into action galloping at a steady and rhythmic pace.

She began to slip from the saddle. In terror, she grabbed for the horse's mane, but could not get a firm grip. She tried to throw her arms around the horse's neck, but she continued to slide. The horse galloped along, seemingly oblivious to its slipping rider. Finally, giving up her frail grip she attempted to leap away from the horse and throw herself to safety. Unfortunately, her foot got entangled in the stirrup. She was now at the mercy of the horse's pounding hooves as her head struck against the ground again and again. She was mere moments away from unconsciousness and began to cry. Eldon, the Wal-Mart® greeter heard her, walking over to her, he unplugged the horse.

Today's Comment: We may never know, on planet earth, how many times that we came near to a tragic accident that may have taken our life. Fifty plus years ago, I was pastor of three small churches. Driving home from a prayer meeting one night, seeking to amuse myself as I travelled the 35 miles, I had my left foot on the dimmer switch, which was on the floor of that Volkswagen Beetle. I was curious to see how quickly I could flick to the high beams after an oncoming car had passed.

With one such flick of the dimmer switch, I suddenly saw a cow standing in the middle of my lane. Fortunately, at that moment there were no oncoming cars and I had just enough space between the cow and me to swerve and miss it. It wasn't until I arrived home and shared my experience with my wife that I realized how close I came to what may have been my last day on earth. There have been several other "close calls" of which I am aware. How many are there that I have been unaware of?

None of us know what a day will bring or what the next moment will bring. Dr. V. Raymond Edman, long term president and then chancellor of Wheaton College, Wheaton, IL, was preaching in chapel. His chapel message topic was *The Prestence of the King*.

These were his opening words: "This will be the first time in more than ten months that I have attempted to speak in public. But I want you to consider with me the invitation to visit the King." He was ten and a half minutes into that message when he had a heart attack and was ushered into the presence of that King!

Pray that we will live today, speak, act and think as those who are ready to meet the King of kings. None of us know when we will be ushered into the presence of the King.

Today's Golden Nugget of Truth: "You will show me the path of life; in Your presence is fullness of joy; at your right hand are pleasures for evermore." Psalm 16:11

Today's Philosophical Tidbit: "I don't know about tomorrow, I just live from day to day." Ira Stanphill

September 3
Together Still

*T**oday's Smile:* Leroy and Grace had been dating for some time. Leroy invited her to spend the long weekend with him, his parents and his siblings at the cabin on the lake. Grace was very impressed with his family noting how loving and caring they were with one another. She was especially taken with Leroy's dad. "Your

Dad is so thoughtful," she said. "I noticed how every morning he took a cup of coffee to your Mom while she was still in bed."

Some weeks later, getting close to their wedding day, Grace once again told her fiancé how much she loved his family feeling so accepted by them. She reminded him how much she admired his Dad with his acts of love and especially the coffee which he took to his wife every morning. "Tell me," asked Grace, "does this little ritual run in the family?"

"It certainly does," replied Leroy. "I take after my Mom."

Today's Comment: I have seldom taken a cup of coffee to my wife while she was still in bed. I have one good reason why I don't. My wife does not like eating or drinking in bed. I have to agree with her. Both of us would rather get up, sit in an easy chair or at the table enjoying food and drink. I think that eating and drinking in bed is the most awkward and uncomfortable way in which to do either. However, I do often make breakfast. It is usually oatmeal porridge and sometimes with raisins and nuts, a heaping spoonful of brown sugar along with a little milk and cream.

Let me ask the husbands today, are you still courting your wife? How long has it been since you held the car door open for your wife? What about a rose, or a meal out? Maybe even a drive to get an ice cream cone. Maybe shock her by picking up a towel to dry the dishes someday. A young husband was helping his wife with the dishes, but all the while complaining. "This is not a man's job," he said to his wife."

"Oh yes, it is!" she replied, as she quoted from Second Kings 21:13, "I will wipe Jerusalem as a man wipes a dish, wiping it and turning it upside down!"

Pray that we husbands will still court our wives. With the Lord in our lives, marriage is the most sacred and satisfying relationship.

Today's Golden Nugget of Truth: "Husbands love your wives, just as Christ also loved the church and gave Himself for it." Ephesians 5:25

Today's Philosophical Tidbit: "In marriage, each partner is to be an encourager rather than a critic, a forgiver rather than a collector of hurts, an enabler rather than a reformer."
H. Norman Wright

September 4
Travelling Too Fast

*T*oday's Smile: A man well into his sixties was speeding in a speed zone where the maximum speed limit was 30 mph. A police officer stopped the driver. "Do you realize that you were travelling 47 mph?" the officer asked. "Not only that," said the officer, "but I see that your tires are nearly bald, and your brake lights do not work. Let's have your driver's license. . . How do you pronounce this name?"

"Valpestilchinic Grimawisenchuk," replied the man.

"Well," said the officer. "I'll let you go this time, but I don't want to stop you again."

Today's Comment: Have you ever received a speeding ticket? What about a warning? Was your name too hard to pronounce? Back in the 1970's, I was stopped by a police officer and issued a ticket for speeding in a school zone. I was on a road I seldom travelled totally unaware that I was in the school zone. As the officer handed me the ticket, I said to him, "This sure shatters my record. I've been driving for twenty-seven years and this is my first ticket."

"Sorry," he said.

About two minutes later, I once again saw the flashing lights behind me. I said to my friend who was a passenger, "What did I do this time?" I was stopped by the same officer.

"Tell me," he said, "were you telling me the truth? Is this your first speeding ticket?" I assured him that I had told him the truth. "Let me have it back. Drive carefully!"

Wow, my first speeding ticket and he took it back. It doesn't always happen that way. Pray that we will drive like we've never had a ticket and don't want one.

Today's Golden Nugget of Truth: "Remind them to be subject to rulers and authorities, to obey, to be ready for every good work." Titus 3:1

Today's Philosophical Tidbit: "Have you ever noticed that in traffic the man who is in front of you is sightseeing, while the man behind you is in a hurry?" Author Unknown

September 5
God Wants To Use You

Today's Smile: I've heard a couple of stories about two different blind individuals who challenged the famous golf legend, Arnold Palmer, to a golf game. Since the individuals that challenged Palmer to a game have different names and different story lines, I'm really not sure whether the stories are for real or fictitious. At any rate, they're good stories.

This blind individual said to Arnold Palmer, "Arnold, I can beat you at golf, I know I can. Being blind is not a handicap, I am sure that I can beat you. In fact I will give you a $1,000.00 a hole if you play with me.

Arnold replied and said, "You know that I respect you and all your accomplishments. You've overcome a lot of obstacles despite your blindness, but you can't beat me at golf. I would be stealing your money." However, the man would not give up. He was persistent and finally Arnold was a bit irritated and said, "OK, you're on. I'll accept your offer and I will beat you any time, any where, you just name it!"

"OK. How about meeting me tonight and we will play nine holes at midnight?"

Today's Comment: I stand in awe when I see and hear testimonies of people with a disability yet being persistent, living full and productive lives. In spite of their disability, many are totally committed to the Lord Jesus Christ and sharing the gospel.

Let me name three. David Ring, a Christian evangelist and motivational speaker who has cerebral palsy. Since 1973, David has challenged millions of people with his signature message, "I have cerebral palsy. What's your problem?"

Joni Eareckson Tada became a quadriplegic as the result of a diving accident when in her teens. Joni has blessed and challenged many through her books, songs, art, radio and television programs plus her many speaking engagements.

Thirdly, there is Nick Vujicic who was born with without arms and without legs. Nick has traveled the world, sharing his story. Nick says, "If God can use a man without arms and legs to be His hands and feet, then He will certainly use any willing heart!"

Pray that we, who are not limited with physical disabilities, would be as enthusiastic in sharing and helping others find the Lord as those mentioned above.

Today's Golden Nugget of Truth: "They have wholly followed the Lord." Numbers 32:12

Today's Philosophical Tidbit: "We can't always give thanks for everything, but we can always give thanks in everything." Ruth Bell Graham

September 6
Does Jesus Live In You

*T*oday's Smile: Four year old Nancy went with her mother to see the family doctor. As Dr. Williams took his otoscope and looked in her ears he asked Nancy, "Do you think I'll find Big Bird in here?" Nancy was silent. He then took a tongue depressor and looked down her throat and asked, "Do you think I'll find the Cookie Monster down there?" Again Nancy was silent. Finally, he put a stethoscope to her chest. As he quietly listened to her heartbeat, he asked, "Do you think I'll hear Barney in there?"

"Oh, no!" replied Nancy, "Jesus is in my heart. Barney's on my underpants."

Today's Comment: I like the story of the little boy who was about to have heart surgery. The surgeon explained to the parents and to the boy that he would be opening up the little fellow's heart. "You'll find Jesus there," the boy interrupted.

The surgeon looked up annoyed, "I'll cut your heart open," he continued, "to see how much damage has been done."

"But when you open up my heart, you'll find Jesus in there," said the boy. This conversation went on and every time the surgeon said something about the heart, the boy would interrupt and say, "You'll find Jesus there. He lives there."

The surgeon went to his office after the surgery and recording his notes from the surgery, ". . .damaged aorta, damaged pulmonary vein, widespread muscle degeneration. No hope for transplant, no hope for cure. . . prognosis, death within one year." He stopped recording, "Why?" he asked aloud. "Why did You do this? You've put him here. You've put him in this pain. You've cursed him to an early death. Why?"

The Lord answered, "The boy, My lamb, was not meant for your flock for long, for he is a part of My flock, and will forever be. In My flock, he will feel no pain, and will be comforted as you cannot imagine. His parents will one day join him here, so they will know peace, and My flock will continue to grow." The conversation continued between the surgeon and the Savior. The surgeon's heart was broken. He prayed. He surrendered to the Lord.

He then met with the little fellow and his parents. As he sat beside the bed, he wept. "Did you cut open my heart?" asked the boy.

"Yes," said the surgeon.

"What did you find?" asked the boy.

"I found Jesus there," said the surgeon.

Does Jesus live in your heart? If not, pray and invite Him in today.

Today's Golden Nugget of Truth: "But as many as received Him, to them He gave the right to become children of God, even to those who believe in His name." John 1:12

Today's Philosophical Tidbit: "The difference between heart belief and head belief is the difference between salvation and damnation." Gypsy Smith

September 7
Have Limitations But Contented

*T**oday's Smile:* Wayne and Brett were walking their dogs when they came to a new restaurant. Wayne said, "Let's go in and see what this new restaurant is like and get a bite to eat."

"We can't go in there," said Brett, "look at that sign in the window. It says NO PETS ALLOWED!"

"Ah don't worry about that sign," said Wayne. He put on his sunglasses and walked up to the door. As he tried to go into the restaurant, he was stopped at the door by the host.

"Sorry, sir," said the host, "no pets are allowed in this restaurant."

"Can't you see that I am blind and this is my seeing-eye dog?"

"But it's a Doberman Pincher. What blind person uses a Doberman Pincher as a seeing eye dog?" demanded the host.

"Oh," said Wayne, "you must not have heard it on the news, but they are now using Doberman Pinchers, and they do a great job."

Well, Wayne was permitted to go into the restaurant and Brett followed with his dog. "Don't tell me," said the host that a Chihuahua is the latest type of seeing-eye dog."

Brett responded in an angry voice, "You mean they gave me a Chihuahua?"

Today's Comment: I had a senior couple in the Lethbridge Alliance Church who used to joke with me that if I saw them sitting in the audience and the husband was to the left of the wife then they were on speaking terms, but if the husband was to the right of the wife, they weren't speaking. He said, "I'm blind in one eye and the wife is deaf in one ear. So if I don't want to see her and she doesn't want to hear me, you'll know by the way we are seated."

My heart goes out to those who are hard of hearing and have poor vision. It is amazing that many of these folks have adjusted well and are accepting of their condition. Fanny Crosby is a prime example of one who had a fulfilling ministry in spite of her blindness. Fanny was one of the most prolific hymnists in history, writing over 8,000 hymns and gospel songs in her ninety-five years. *To God Be The Glory, Blessed Assurance, Pass Me Not Oh Gentle Savior,* and *Praise Him, Praise Him,* are some of her familiar ones.

Pray that God will continue to use these kinds of folks to challenge the rest of us to be all that God wants us to be.

Today's Golden Nugget of Truth: "My grace is sufficient for you, for My strength is made perfect in weakness." Second Corinthians 12:9

Today's Philosophical Tidbit: "True contentment is the power of getting out of any situation all that there is in it." G. K. Chesterton

September 8
Can't Take It With You

*T*oday's Smile: Tiffany was walking slowly through the appliance department and spotted a nice upright home freezer. As she stood looking at the same, a friendly salesman came along and shared with her some of the features of this freezer: frost free, fast freeze, a big drawer which could hold a turkey, a door alarm which sounded if you didn't shut the door tightly, and more. "It sounds like a great deal," she said, "but at the moment we just can't afford to purchase it."

"Lady," said the salesman, "with this freezer you will save enough on your food bills to pay for it."

"I know what you're talking about," she replied, "but we're paying for our washing machine with the money saved at the Laundromat. We're paying for our car with the taxi money that we are saving. We're paying for our house with the rent money that we're saving. I'm sorry, but we just can't afford to save any more!"

Today's Comment: In Canada we have what is called the "Family Allowance." The parent, usually the mother, receives a check once a month with income according to the number of children under 18. More than one salesperson has told us that we could purchase their product with our family allowance check.

Well, we never did manage to save very much by spending more and more. We learned that spending money we lose, especially if we spend it on that which is consumed or perishes. If we don't spend it all, than we leave it all behind and still lose. Like the billionaire that died, where upon the question was asked how much he left behind. The answer was simply, "He left it all!" However, what we give to God's work and ministry produces eternal dividends. That is one sure and safe place to save money.

Pray that we will be good managers of our money and send some of it on ahead of us.

Today's Golden Nugget of Truth: "Do not lay up for yourselves treasures on earth, where moth and rust destroy and where thieves break in and steal; but lay up for yourselves treasures in heaven, where neither moth nor rust destroys and where thieves do not break in

and steal. For where your treasure is, there your heart will be also."
Matthew 6:19-21

Today's Philosophical Tidbit: "The money you spend will end. The money you gave you saved." A. Daniel Goldsmith

September 9
Don't Forget To Leave A Tip

oday's Smile: Many years ago when Quinton was a teenager, he took off for the west coast, riding in a Pullman car and sleeping in an upper berth. Train travel was the in thing in those days. This was Quinton's first trip in a Pullman and his trip was three days and three nights. Quinton saw people giving Chuck, the porter, a tip when they got to their destination. So he asked Chuck, "What is the average tip?"

Chuck responded by saying, "The average tip is $5.00." So on Monday afternoon when Quinton had finally arrived at Portland, Oregon he put a five dollar bill in Chuck's hand and thanked him for his good care. Chuck looked at the five dollar bill. Looked at the front, with the president's picture on it, turned it over and looked at the back. He then reached out and shook hands with Quinton and said, "Young man, you are the first person to ever give me the average!"

Today's Comment: Do you despise paying tips? You get your hair done and you leave the barber or hairdresser a tip. You have a meal in the restaurant, you leave a tip. You spend a night or two in a hotel and you give the porter a tip. On and on it goes. Giving a tip is a part of our western culture, like it or not.

As a Christian are we a good testimony by our tips or are we cheapish? When I was a pastor in Calgary, Alberta, in preparation for a sermon re being a good testimony in the community, I phoned a nearby restaurant that was always full Sunday noon with church goers. I asked the manager about the Sunday noon tips. He told me that because the tips received by his staff Sunday noon were so poor that he had a hard time getting his staff to work that shift.

We've heard a lot in recent years about *lifestyle* evangelism. Some of the best witnessing or sharing is when people see how you

320

live. You then have an open door to share with them verbally. Pray that we will be a good witness, even it does hurt our pocket book.

Today's Golden Nugget of Truth: "Let your light so shine before men, that they may see your good works and glorify your Father in heaven." Matthew 5:16

Today's Philosophical Tidbit: "I would not give much for your religion unless it can be seen. Lamps do not talk, but they do shine." Author Unknown

September 10
Standing Strong In The Storm

*T**oday's Smile:* It was the beginning of the school year. A professor at the local university, who was an atheist, began his year by asking who in his freshmen class was a Christian. One lone young man raised his hand to indicate that he was a follower of Christ. The professor then said to this young man, "So you believe in miracles." I suppose you believe that myth about God parting the waters of the Red Sea to let Moses and the children of Israel walk across."

"Yes sir," responded the student.

"Well, let me tell you, young man, God did not part any Red Sea. The children of Israel, if in fact they did exist, waded across the Red Sea in water that was no deeper than six inches."

"Praise the Lord!" said the young man.

"What do you mean Praise the Lord?" the professor retorted, "That was not a miracle."

"Oh yes it was," said the student. "If what you say is true sir then that is an even greater miracle, for that would mean that God drowned Pharaoh's army in six inches of water!"

Today's Comment: Young people today who are attending a secular university need our prayers. It seems that a professor in a university can tear Christianity to shreds without any recourse. The young Christian can be criticized and made the butt of sarcastic remarks, but what is done? Usually nothing.

When I was a teenager I played a baritone horn in The Salvation Army band. After many an early Sunday morning street meeting, the band would march back to the Citadel (church) and we usually passed the house where my grade nine home room high school teacher lived. Monday mornings, he would tell the class that he saw me tooting my horn often taking the occasion to pick on me and tease me.

Let's pray for our young people, whether elementary, high, or at the college and university level, it takes a strong faith to withstand the verbal onslaughts regarding our faith. Don't forget to pray for our Christian schools, elementary, high school, college and universities.

Today's Golden Nugget of Truth: "Watch, stand fast in the faith, be brave, be strong." Second Corinthians 16:13

Today's Philosophical Tidbit: "One person with conviction is worth more than one hundred with only an interest." Zig Ziglar

September 11
Rescue The Perishing

oday's Smile: One Sunday morning, after Pastor Alvin had finished greeting all of the parishioners as they left the church building, he noticed that Dennis White was waiting for him, staring at the large plaque in the lobby. Dennis was the pastor's new neighbor who had been coming to church with the pastor for about six Sundays. He was the only son of a single mom who worked at a fast food restaurant Sunday mornings.

While the pastor had been greeting people, Dennis spotted this plaque listing several names; each one had a small USA flag mounted beside the name. When Pastor Alvin walked over to Dennis ready to take him home, the young boy asked, pointing to the plaque, "Pastor, what is this?"

The pastor replied, "Well, Dennis, that is a memorial to all the young men and women that died in the service."

Dennis stood motionless, staring up at this plaque for another few seconds. Turning to the pastor, with a puzzled look on his face and in a trembling voice asked, "Which service pastor, the morning service or the evening service?"

Today's Comment: Do you belong to a church where people are dying in the services? I don't mean physical death, but dying from starvation of the Word of God.

If you're in a dying church, maybe you are the one that can breathe life into that gathering. Has God put you there for a reason? The easiest thing to do would be to leave finding another church. Before you take that action, see if there isn't something that you can do. Start a prayer meeting. Pray for the pastor, the deacons, and the teachers. Pray that God would do a new thing in your place of worship and maybe it will begin with you. If you do not see a change, then by all means find a Bible believing church where you will be fed spiritually.

Today's Golden Nugget of Truth: "Who knows whether you have come to the kingdom for such a time as this?" Esther 4:14

Today's Philosophical Tidbit: "The most powerful weapon on earth is the human soul set on fire for God." Author Unknown

September 12
Is There A Correct Posture For Prayer

Today's Smile: Three pastors were in restaurant having lunch. The Baptist pastor shared that he was reading a new book about prayer. He said, "The author strongly recommends that one should pray standing or walking as there is less of a tendency to fall asleep."

The Pentecostal pastor disagreed. He said, "I do my best praying on my knees with my hands lifted toward heaven."

The third pastor said, "I have prayed standing up and I prayed for years in a kneeling position, but the most effective position for me is lying prostrate, face down on the floor."

In the booth next to them was an electrician who was by himself but heard the pastors' conversation. He spoke up and said, "Let me tell you pastors that the best praying that I ever did was hanging upside down on a power pole."

Today's Comment: What is the right posture when it comes to praying? The most common throughout the years has been that of kneeling. Over the years I have witnessed many ways in which people offer prayer to God. In addition to kneeling, there is sitting, bowing, lying prostrate on the floor, standing, looking heavenward with eyes open, walking, leaping and uplifted hands.

There are times when I can't sleep that I lie in bed praying. I have prayed with many people and others have prayed with me using the telephone. A friend of mine prays regularly with a missionary friend by means of Skype. My wife and I have prayed many times while travelling in a car. I remember the first time I heard a car driver pray. I was ten years old. I figured that this lady had her eyes shut while she was driving and that she had to be super spiritual. I thought a prayer could/should not be uttered unless the eyes were closed.

Well, it is not the bodily posture that is important when we pray, rather the posture of our heart. It is not our outward action, but our inward attitude. Wherever you are as you read this, you can breathe a prayer. You may be sick in bed, sitting in your easy chair, seated around the breakfast table, reclining at some vacation spot or flying in an airplane, pray!

Today's Golden Nugget of Truth: "Continue earnestly in prayer, being vigilant in it with thanksgiving." Colossians 4:2

Today's Philosophical Tidbit: "To be a Christian without prayer is no more possible than to be alive without breathing." Martin Luther

September 13
A Wonderful Helper

Today's Smile: An elderly man who lived alone in Ireland wanted to spade his garden so that he could plant his potatoes. It was too hard a job for him. His only son, who would have helped him, was in Long Kesh Prison. So the elderly man wrote a letter to his son and mentioned his predicament.

Immediately, the son telephoned his Dad and said, "Dad, don't dig up that garden. That's where I buried my guns!"

At 4:00am the next morning, a dozen soldiers showed up and dug the entire garden without finding any guns.

Confused, the old man wrote another note to his son telling him what had happened, and asking him what to do next.

His son's reply was: "Now plant your potatoes, Dad. It's the best I could do at this time."

Today's Comment: That is a different way of being helped. It is not one that I recommend.

Reading that smile caused me to reflect on many of the wonderful helpers that God has brought into my life and who assisted me in a time of need.

In my early years it was my parents, grandparents, other family members, friends and teachers. In my pastoral years there were hundreds and more that volunteered their services in the church; many who gave a word of encouragement. In my retirement years there have been neighbors who have lent a hand with some chores, plus our children and grandchildren.

Do we see some around us that need a little help? Is there a young person, a single mom, an invalid, a senior, or others? Maybe the need is for a handyman, visit the lonely, serve in the church nursery, offer a ride, provide a meal, etc. Pray that we will be willing to step into that spot that is in need of a helper.

Today's Golden Nugget of Truth: "Do not withhold good from those to whom it is due, when it is in the power of your hand to do so." Proverbs 3:27

Today's Philosophical Tidbit: "We are not primarily put on this earth to see through one another, but to see one another through." Peter DeVries

September 14
It's Hard To Be Humble

Today's Smile: A young man left his home in Texas and moved up to Canada, settling in the foothills of the Canadian Rockies in Southern Alberta. He managed to purchase his own ranch and did very well for himself. Having been gone for about six years, his mother and father finally made their first visit north. The son took his father on a tour of his ranch.

As they drove on one of the roads on the son's ranch, suddenly a jack rabbit hopped out in front of them. The son stopped the truck to let the rabbit pass. The father asked, "What was that?"

"Dad," said the son, "that was a jack rabbit. You know what a jack rabbit is."

"Yes son, but you must remember that we grow them a lot bigger back home in Texas. I didn't recognize it."

They continued on their tour when they came upon a couple of buffalo roaming on the range. The son once again stopped the truck as they watched them. The father was a little perplexed. "What are those?"

"Dad," said the son, "those are buffalo. Are you telling me that you didn't recognize buffalo? There are quite a few of them here."

"Yea, they do look a bit familiar. I guess it's just because back home in Texas we grow them much bigger. It must be that your winters are so much colder here in Alberta than back home that these creatures don't grow to be as big as those back home."

The son was a little perturbed at his Dad and all of his bragging about Texas. He loved his home back in Texas, but he also loved his ranch in Alberta. The son said nothing. They drove along in silence. Finally, they came to a spot in the ranch where there was a slough on each side of the road. There crossing the road was a large snapping turtle slowly making its way across the road. "Now, tell me son, what on earth is that creature?"

Without missing a beat, the son said, "Dad, that is a wood tick!"

Today's Comment: We live today in a culture filled with braggarts and self-centered individuals. People are lovers of self more than lovers of God. Much attention is spent on self advancement, appearance, approval and much more. People love themselves so much that they have no time for their neighbors or God. The commercials of today contribute greatly to the self culture. How often have we heard phrases like "You owe it to yourself." "Treat yourself." "Pamper yourself." "You will be really happy or contented with this new car, or your future home in this neighborhood."

When people acquire all of the things to make them satisfied, many tend to look down on others. We sometimes refer to them as the "upper crust." They live in an "elite section" of the city. It is hard to be humble. It is difficult to relate to many others. Country singer and song writer Mac Davis wrote the song, "Oh, Lord, it's hard to be humble when you're perfect in every way. . ."

We are to be humble not braggarts. We are to look at others as better than ourselves. We are to take the lowly seat, not the high one. Pray that as children of God we will be humble not haughty.

Today's Golden Nugget of Truth: "A man's pride will bring him low, but the humble in spirit will retain honor." Proverbs 29:23

Today's Philosophical Tidbit: "Satan's number one weapon is pride. God's number one defense is humility." Larry Burkett

September 15
Where Will You Spend Eternity

*T*oday's Smile: Werner used to make it a daily ritual to read the obituaries in the morning newspaper. Some of Werner's friends thought that they would play a trick on him. So they convinced the editor of the paper to go along with their plan. They paid for Werner's obituary to be printed.

As per usual, Werner was sitting at the breakfast table reading the morning newspaper. Once again, as was his habit, he read the obituary column. There to his surprise was his obituary, Werner Brown. He could not contain himself and quickly called his friend Eric. "Eric," he said, "Have you read this morning's paper?"

"Not yet," said Eric.

"Well, turn to section C and page 10 and look at the obituaries." Eric opened the paper and read, and there to his surprise was Werner Brown's obituary.

"Werner, is that really you I'm talking with?"

"Yes, it's me," said Werner.

"I'd like to know where are you calling from, Werner?"

Today's Comment: We may smile, but don't let your family or friends question as to where you have gone when you pass on from this life. Make certain that you know where you are going, that you know in whom you are trusting. Make sure that your loved ones and friends know that you are a child of God. May they not have to ask, where you're calling from?

There have been some sad funerals that I have participated in where the family or friends have expressed that they were not sure as to whether the deceased was prepared to meet God.

If you're not sure where you will spend eternity, pray today that God will open your eyes to see that He alone is the Way to life everlasting.

Today's Golden Nugget of Truth: "For I know whom I have believed and am persuaded that He is able to keep what I have committed to Him until that Day." Second Timothy 1:12

Today's Philosophical Tidbit: "Keep the faith, but not to yourself." Author Unknown

September 16
Sipping Saints

Today's Smile: The pastor, in his conclusion to a sermon on temperance said with great emphasis, "If I had all the beer in the world, I'd take it and pour it into the river." With even greater emphasis he said, "And if I had all the wine in the world, I'd take it and pour it into the river." Finally, shaking his fist in the air, he said, "And if I had all the whiskey in the world, I'd take it and pour it into the river." With that he sat down.

The music director stood, and very cautiously and with a smile on his face said, "I chose this closing hymn before I knew what the pastor's closing remarks would be. Please take your hymnals and turn to number 491, *Shall We Gather At The River.*"

Do you know someone that is struggling with an alcoholic addiction? Pray for them that they might find God to be the One to deliver them.

Today's Comment: Thank God for all the passionate preachers who speak with conviction. Would that God's people would stay away from alcohol. Unfortunately, that is not the case. What was once considered a *no-no* for Christians has become a more acceptable indulgence. Too many well meaning Christians sipped a little then a little more and even more until they lost control, lost their respect, their job, and eventually even their family. Pray that we will remember that our body is the temple of the Holy Spirit.

Today's Golden Nugget of Truth: "Do not look on the wine when it is red, when it sparkles in the cup, when it swirls around smoothly, at the last it bites like a serpent, and stings like a viper, your eyes will see strange things, and your heart will utter perverse things." Proverbs 23:31-33

Today's Philosophical Tidbit: "If you pour whiskey on your lawn, it will come up half cut." Fred Fleck

September 17
What's Your Name

Today's Smile: Logan was hired to work as a clerk in a large department store. He was assigned to work in the men's clothing department. On his first day, when he reported for work, he met the clothing department manager for the first time. Before the store opened, the manager called him aside and asked, "What is your name?"

Logan replied by saying that his name was Logan. The clothing department manager said, "We don't call anyone in this department by their first name, especially when dealing with our customers. We get a lot of politicians, executives and bank managers that buy clothing here. Calling people by their first name breeds familiarity. We want to keep our cliental coming. They buy expensive clothes. So we prefer to show due respect and we address them as Mister or Doctor and their last name, and they also call us by our last name."

"That's fine," said Logan.

"Good," said the manager, "now what is your last name?"

"Darling, Logan Darling!"

The manager said, "O.K. Logan I want you to unpack this box of sport jackets. . ."

Today's Comment: I was new in town and was to have my first funeral at one of the funeral homes. I was introduced to the manager. His last name was Graves. I wanted to say something but having just met the man I decided that I should be silent. He had probably been the brunt of too many jokes. However, one of his staff spoke up and said, "That's a pretty good name for an undertaker, isn't it?"

On another occasion, we were visiting my parents and they took us to a Child Evangelism Banquet. They introduced some of their friends to us who were seated across the table from us and my mother said, "I want you to meet Mr. & Mrs. Donald Duck."

Well Mr. Duck was quick to respond, saving us from embarrassment, and said, "This is something for a duck to be eating turkey."

I don't know what your name is, but more than your given names and surname is the name that you make by the kind of life you live. What kind of name do you have in the community, in the church, in your family circle? Let's pray that we will be known as kind, gracious, patient, understanding and an encourager. That is the name that counts.

Today's Golden Nugget of Truth: "A good name is to be chosen rather than great riches, loving favor rather than silver and gold." Proverbs 22:1

Today's Philosophical Tidbit: "A good name is doing what is right when no one is looking." A. Daniel Goldsmith

September 18
Have You Got Your Ticket

Today's Smile: Oscar and Patricia had planned on rewarding themselves with a month's long cruise from Los Angeles to Australia. They were going to celebrate Patricia's retirement, having worked thirty years for a Credit Union. Now that they were both retired, they had the time and the money.

Patricia, as usual, had done all of the packing. When they arrived at the pier where they were to board the cruise ship, Oscar counted off one by one all the baggage that Patricia had packed. "While you were doing all of your packing, why didn't you bring the piano, too?" he said.

"Oh come, on," said Patricia, "is that the kind of talk I am going to have to put up with for the next month?"

"No, I really wish that you had brought the piano," he said with a disappointed expression, "I left the tickets on top of it."

Today's Comment: Have you started out on a trip and forgot your tickets? It's easier, for most air travelers, now that we don't need tickets. Our name is in their computer. However, what about a ticket to a game or concert or a banquet? What's worse is leaving behind your wallet or purse. There are many things, be it a driver's license, passport, credit card, etc that we need as we travel. You know the slogan, *Don't leave home without it*! The message was that you will not feel safe or secure and enjoy your day unless you have that credit card.

Need I remind you that there is another ticket that we need to be sure that we have. It is the ticket to heaven. Jesus Christ paid for that ticket. He offers it freely. Be sure to reach out and receive it. Pray for family and friends that have not yet received their ticket to heaven.

Today's Golden Nugget of Truth: "Therefore you also be ready, for the Son of Man is coming at an hour when you do not expect." Matthew 24:44

Today's Philosophical Tidbit: "When God gets ready for you, you better be ready for Him." J. D. Sumner

September 19
Where Did We Come From

*T*oday's Smile: Five year old Sophia was playing with her Barbie dolls in the family room. When her mother walked into the room, Sophia turned and asked, "Mommy, where do people come from?"

Her mother sat down on the floor with her little girl and told her how God made Adam and then Eve and they had children and those children had children and on an on. "That's where we came from, Sophia!"

That night was her Daddy's turn to tuck her in bed. As he knelt down to give her a good night's kiss, Sophia said, "Daddy, do you know where people came from?"

"Yep," he responded, "we came from monkeys." Well, now she was confused. After he turned out the light, she lay there thinking. Mommy told me that God made our first parents and now Daddy tells me that we came from monkeys. The next morning when she was having breakfast with her Mommy, she told her that Daddy had said that people came from monkeys.

"Well," with a grin on her face, her mother exclaimed, "I was talking about my side of the family."

Today's Comment: Some fathers may act like a monkey sometimes. My son Brian is a great one for entertaining his boys and our entire family with his antics. He has us all laughing, especially his little act of swinging his arms and chattering away, sort of monkey-ish.

I trust that you are not in doubt as to where you came from. God created our first parents. God made us in His image, but sin entered into the world and that image was destroyed. We are now in the image of man, Adam. We were born into this world as sinners, but since God yearned so much for that fellowship with Him to be restored, He made provision in the sacrifice of His Son, to pay the penalty for our sin and redeem us. He does not force us to turn back to Him, but invites us to turn in repentance and faith. He will live His life in and through us. I trust that you've done that. If not, why not pray today and invite Him into your life?

Today's Golden Nugget of Truth: "The first man was of the earth made of dust; the second Man is the Lord from heaven. As was the man of dust, so also are those who are made of dust; and as is the heavenly Man, so also are those who are heavenly." First Corinthians 15:47, 48

Today's Philosophical Tidbit: "God stepped from behind the curtain of nowhere and stood upon the platform of nothing and spoke a world into existence." Author Unknown

September 20
Rearing The Restless

*T**oday's Smile:* Children's church was cancelled and so Billy had to sit with his grandma for the entire worship service. He was fairly attentive for the congregational singing and the choir selections, but when the pastor started to preach he was very fidgety and misbehaving. He played with the pew Bible; threw the hymn book on the floor; walked along the pew; tore up church envelopes. Grandma was not used to looking after him in church. This went on for about ten minutes. She physically tried to make him sit still. Finally she leaned over and whispered in his ear. He immediately straightened up and did not make a move for the rest of the service.

After the service the young mother seated behind them asked, "I am curious. What did you say that made your grandson behave?"

"I told him that if he continued to misbehave that he might make the pastor lose his place and he would have to start his sermon again."

Today's Comment: My parents were both involved in the music ministry in The Salvation Army during my childhood. Since there was no nursery or children's church, I sat beside my father in the cornet section of the band. Mom was in the songsters (choir). My brother recalls also sitting beside Dad. The band master had a five cent piece on the chair for him, which was an incentive for him to sit still.

In one of my early pastoral ministries, the mid week prayer service was held in a home. One young couple brought their little fellow with them every week. Everyone knelt and everyone took their turn praying. One night after everyone had prayed the first person started to pray again for the second time. This little fellow had been quiet during the prayer time, but that was too much for him and he exclaimed, "Awe more prayer!"

If the church that you attend does not have a children's church, you may have to be creative in getting your child or grandchild to sit quietly. Try practicing at home. Have the child sit still while reading to them or having them listen to music. Above all pray that God will give you wisdom. No two children are the same.

Today's Golden Nugget of Truth: "Correct thy son, and he shall give thee rest; yea, he shall give delight unto thy soul." Proverbs 29:17 (KJV)

Today's Philosophical Tidbit: "Rearing children is like holding a wet bar of soap; too firm a grasp and it shoots from your hand; too loose a grasp and it slides away; a gentle but firm grasp keeps it in your control." Author Unknown

September 21
A Date With The Lord

Today's Smile: Jake was a hunter. Every hunting season his wife would ask him if she could go hunting with him. The answer was always "no!' Finally, he agreed to take her hunting with him. He gave her very specific instructions as to what to do and what not to do. When they arrived at a popular hunting area, he pointed east and told her to go in that direction and he would go in the opposite direction. He told her that when she shot a deer, he would hear the shot and she was to stand guard by her deer and he would come and help her take it away.

The unexpected happened. He heard a bang! He quickly retraced his steps and went to where his wife was. He arrived at a bit of a clearing and saw his wife in the distance with an old cowboy leaning up against a tree and his wife had her rifle up against his chest. When he got closer he heard the cowboy saying, "Alright lady, alright, you can have your deer, but let me get my saddle off of him first."

Today's Comment: I have a son-in-law and three grandsons who are avid hunters. My daughter has gone with her husband on more than one occasion. I read her Facebook two days before their wedding anniversary and this is what she said: "Yay! Our 23rd anniversary weekend. I'm sitting here thinking a perfect date for my hubby would be going hunting. . . I actually do love going with him hunting in the back woods just as much as a fancy night out. It's all fun to me." On one occasion when he went by himself, she had two pictures to show him when he came home. Two deer had come within 100 feet of their house. He hadn't seen any on his hunt.

Many couples, with many years of marriage behind them, still love to have a date night each week. It may not be hunting deer, but you can make a date to go some place with your "dear," even if it is just a coffee! Keep nourishing that relationship. Keep your marriage alive and well!

Another date that we have is that six days a week we have a date in our living room where we take time to read God's Word and have prayer together. Pray that we will not miss that date.

Today's Golden Nugget of Truth: "May God who gives patience, steadiness, and encouragement help you to live in complete harmony with each other, each with the attitude of Christ toward the other." Romans 15:5

Today's Philosophical Tidbit: "The family that prays together stays together." Patrick Peyton

September 22
Make Every Word Count

*T**oday's Smile:* The Sunday morning worship service had begun, but Pastor Bob, the senior pastor, was no where to be seen. As the choir was singing, the pastor made his appearance. He had about the largest band-aid ever made on his left cheek.

When it was time for him to deliver his sermon, he began by apologizing. He told the congregation that he was deeply sorry for being late, but that the radio alarm clock did not sound off as the electricity in his area of the city was off. He had to resort to using an old straight razor. He then proceeded to tell them that while he was shaving his face he was thinking about his sermon and cut himself. He then launched into his lengthy sermon.

At the close of the service one of the parishioners handed him a note. Pastor Bob looked at it after all the parishioners had left. It stated: "Next Sunday when you are shaving, think about your face and cut your sermon."

Today's Comment: During my years as a Bible College student, I was given several opportunities to try my hand at preaching. I am forever grateful for a country pastor who invited me several times during those school years, along with my home church pastor. One of those early sermons had seventeen points. On another occasion, I preached for 55 minutes with very few notes. Since those early days, I've tried my best to make every word count but not have so many As I've aged I have taken more notes to the pulpit thereby I have shortened my time for speaking.

Some pastors do tend to speak longer than they should. I heard about a little boy that was taken to church one Sunday morning by his grandmother. It was the first time he had ever heard a pastor preach. The pastor droned on and on, or so it seemed to the little fellow. The little fellow finally turned to his grandmother and asked, "Is it dark outside yet?"

It has been said that it is alright to have a train of thought if you have a terminal. Pray today for pastors that they will be Spirit filled men of the Word who know how to begin a sermon and when to end it. Pray that they will feed their flock with food that can easily be digested and contribute towards spiritual growth.

Today's Golden Nugget of Truth: "And my speech and my preaching were not with persuasive words of human wisdom, but in the demonstration of the Spirit and of power that your faith should not be in the wisdom of men but in the power of God." First Corinthians 2:4, 5

Today's Philosophical Tidbit: "Don't use a gallon of words to express a spoonful of thought." Author Unknown

September 23
Love Your Neighbor

*T**oday's Smile:* Graham and Ashley bought an older house which they intended to remodel. While eating breakfast their first morning, they noticed the neighbor hanging the wash on a clothes line. Ashley said: "That laundry is not very clean. She sure doesn't know how to wash very well." Graham looked on, but remained silent.

The next wash day, Ashley said the same thing again. She continued to make this remark every time the neighbor hung out her wash. About one month later, Ashley was surprised to see a nice clean wash hanging on the line. She turned to Graham and said, "Look, she has finally learned how to properly wash clothes. I wonder who taught her."

Graham turned to his wife and said, "Honey, I got up early this morning and cleaned our windows."

Today's Comment: What we see when we look at others and their actions depends on what we look through. If we look at others from a critical view point, we will see many faults. If we look at others from a jealous standpoint, we will be covetous. However, if we look at others through a loving point of view, we won't see their faults. It all depends upon our perspective.

Alfred Lord Tennyson's grandfather gave him 10 shillings for writing a eulogy about his grandmother. When his grandfather gave him the money, he looked into the face of young Alfred and said, "There, that is the first money you ever earned with your poetry, and take my word for it, it will be the last." His grandfather was wrong. Most of us have studied Tennyson's poetry in school. *Crossing the Bar* and *The Charge of the Light Brigade* are a couple of examples.

Let's pray that before we pass judgment on a neighbor that we make certain that our windows are clean. We will probably see things differently.

Today's Golden Nugget of Truth: "For all the law is fulfilled in one word, even in this: You shall love your neighbor as yourself." Galatians 5:14

Today's Philosophical Tidbit: "When you throw mud at your neighbor, you lose ground." Author Unknown

September 24
Full Of Hot Air

*T*oday's Smile: Russ, Jackson and Joe were classmates. They often met up with each other and walked the last couple of blocks to school. Russ began one day by bragging about his father and how fast he was. "He's fast," said Russ, "he's the fastest runner that I know. He can shoot an arrow, and run so fast he can get to the target before the arrow."

"You think that's fast," said Jackson. "My dad loves to hunt. He is an expert at shooting moose. He can run so fast that he can shoot his gun and be standing beside the moose before the bullet arrives."

Well, Joe said, "You guys don't know anything about speed and running. Why my father works for the government. He is a civil servant. His work day ends at 4:00pm and he can be home sitting in the living room reading the afternoon paper by 3:30pm."

Today's Comment: There are many braggarts in this world of ours. Some brag a little, some a lot. They are so obnoxious and forever telling others what they have accomplished. They crave to be first, to be number one, to be the fastest, greatest, smartest, etc. The Bible calls that pride. The Pharisees of Jesus' day wanted to be seen as having it all together, looking like God. They wanted to be seen as being very pious, when in reality the opposite was true.

What kind of life are we living? Do we have a tendency to brag or boast a lot? If people really knew us would they see a proud heart or a humble spirit? Pray today that we have the spirit of humility, the spirit of Christ. These are the people that are most like God.

Today's Golden Nugget of Truth: "Though the Lord is great, He cares for the humble, but He keeps His distances from the proud." Psalm 138:6 (MSG)

Today's Philosophical Tidbit: "There has never been a person with an inflated ego who wasn't full of hot air." Author Unknown

September 25
Any Excuse For A Drink

*T*oday's Smile: It's that time of year again when the young folks are all back in the school classroom. Do you remember all those experiments in the science class?

In one such science class the elementary school teacher in a Christian school was seeking to teach her class about the evils that awaited them if they should consume alcohol. What better place to teach this then in a science lab.

So the teacher had a glass of clear water and a glass of alcohol. She placed a couple of worms in each of the two glasses. The worms in the water wiggled around. The worms in the glass of alcohol soon died. She then asked the class if they could see the lesson in her experiment.

Sean raised his hand and said, "The experiment teaches us that if you have worms, you should drink whisky."

Today's Comment: Seems like a lot of people will grab on to any excuse for a drink. Drinking alcohol has been shown to be a frequent factor in accidental injury in the home, on the roads, in workplaces and during leisure-time activities. It is also the cause for many falls, collisions, fires, drowning, damaging marital and many other inter-personal relationships.

It seems that many people do not know how to have a party without having alcohol. While many are just taking their first drink, many others are trying to break the habit. In my home church, Sevenoaks Alliance Church, a former alcoholic and his wife began an *Addiction Recovery Ministry*, meeting weekly. In the first four years of its ministry, 600 different people attended one or more meetings. Several have placed their faith in the Lord Jesus Christ and are now living changed lives.

The Lord is all powerful and if given opportunity can cure drinking habits. He is also powerful in that He can keep one from taking that first drink. If drinking alcohol is your problem, or taking drugs, give God the opportunity to help you. Pray today for the many people that are trying to break with their addictions. Pray that they let Christ be their Helper.

Today's Golden Nugget of Truth: "Wine is a mocker, strong drink is a brawler, and whoever is led astray by it is not wise." Proverbs 20:1

Today's Philosophical Tidbit: "The devil gives you the champagne at night, but you get the real pain in the morning." Oscar Van Impe

September 26
Keep On Praying

Today's Smile: Barry, who was a news correspondent and was visiting in Israel, had been told about a very elderly Jewish man who had been going to the Western Wall to pray twice a day for many years. The news man spotted the man at the Wall.

He watched as this elderly man slowly turned to leave, using a cane he came walking very slowly towards Barry. "Pardon me, sir, but I am Barry Dulles. I am a news correspondent visiting here in Israel for a few days. I was told about your faithful praying all these years. I would like to ask you a couple of questions. Would that be O.K?"

"Yes," said the man. "What do you want to know?"

"First, what is your name?"

"I am Asher Feinberg." He said.

"Asher, how many years have you been coming to the Western Wall to pray?"

"I am 80 years old," said Asher, "and I have been coming here since I was 20. Sixty years, every day!"

"That's wonderful," said Barry. "What do you pray for?"

"I've been praying that all politicians would tell us the truth and put our interests ahead of theirs. I've been praying that governments and families might learn to live within their means and not spend more than they have. I've been praying that all of our children and grandchildren would grow up to love their neighbors and be good citizens. I've been praying for all the wars to cease. I've been praying for peace."

"That's mighty big prayer request," said Barry. "How do you feel after all these many years?"

"I feel like I have been talking to a wall!"

Today's Comment: If you pray regularly, do you sometimes feel like you're talking to a wall? I should use an expression I've heard some people say, "I don't feel like my prayers have gone past the ceiling." There are times when we feel for sure that God has heard our prayer. There are other times when we begin to wonder whether we've been heard.

May I encourage you? Don't give up. I've known of people who have prayed for years for the salvation of a loved one. I read where one pastor said that he prayed for the salvation of his father for 45 years. The father finally repented of his sin and invited Christ into his life. Some did not see their prayers answered, but they were answered after the pray-er had died. Let's not give up. Let's keep on praying!

Today's Golden Nugget of Truth: "Pray without ceasing." First Thessalonians 5:17

Today's Philosophical Tidbit: "When it comes to prayer, don't hang up, hang on." Author Unknown

September 27
A Willing Worker

*T*oday's Smile: A guest lecturer was speaking at a business men's luncheon. He gave several pointers in saving time and dealing with staff. However he added, "Don't try these techniques at home."

"Why not?" asked someone from the back of the dining room.

"Well," said the lecturer, "I tried them a few years ago. I had watched my wife's routine of making breakfast. I had wondered why she made so many trips from the refrigerator, to the table, to the cupboard, to the stove, often just carrying one item at a time. I suggested that she should try carrying more than one thing at a time and save time and energy."

A man sitting at a table close to the speaker then asked, "Did it save time?"

"Yes," said the speaker. "Whereas it used to take my wife fourteen minutes to get breakfast ready, now I do it in twenty-one."

Today's Comment: In my last pastoral ministry at Sevenoaks Alliance Church in Abbotsford, BC, I was the pastor of pastoral care and senior adults. I spoke to the Senior Pastor stating that we had about 100 young couples in the church and no pastor was assigned to work with them. He said, "Why don't you do something." Well, it was not my area of ministry but I planned a big event for them and things took off from there.

I heard a pastor of one of America's large churches say that a lady said to him one day, "We ought to have a ladies ministry." He encouraged her to start one. A man told the pastor that they should have a cassette ministry with the pastor's sermons. Again the pastor encouraged him to start one. The pastor said that most of the ministries in the church, where he was senior pastor, were the result of a member making a suggestion and in many cases spearheading the same.

Do you see a need or a potential ministry for your church? Pray about it and then talk to your pastor. You may have some ideas that the leadership has never thought about.

Today's Golden Nugget of Truth: "So we ourselves should support them so that we can be their partners as they teach the truth." Third John 1:8 (NLT)

Today's Philosophical Tidbit: "Have your tools ready and God will find you work." Author Unknown

September 28
What's In A Name

Today's Smile: The story has been circulating for years about a young woman who became a nurse in a hospital. At one point in her career she worked in the Intensive Care Unit, but she was no longer permitted to answer the telephone. As the story goes her last name was Picabo, pronounced Peek-A-Boo. When the phone used to ring, she would greet the caller by saying "Picabo, (Peek-A Boo) I.C.U.

Today's Comment: Do you have a name that is an embarrassment? When I was in Bible College there was a student there whose last name was Bagg. In sharing one time, he told us that we needed to meet his sister "Meta." Meta Bagg! Don't know that that was the truth, but it brought a laugh. Well, I trust that you're not embarrassed by your name.

The main thing is that we are not an embarrassment when we wear the name Christian. I heard about some Christians having a meal in a restaurant. One of them ripped the waitress up and down and complained about his food, asking her to take it back to the kitchen and get him another one. After she left, one of his friends looked him in the eye and said, "I dare you to share your faith with her when she returns!" That's not only an embarrassment to the name Christian but also a disgrace. Pray that today we will exalt the name of Christ.

Today's Golden Nugget of Truth: "But the fruit of the Spirit is love, joy, peace, longsuffering, kindness, goodness, faithfulness, gentleness, self-control." Galatians 5:22, 23

Today's Philosophical Tidbit: "Does your life shed light or cast a shadow?" Author Unknown

September 29
Love For The Brethren

*T**oday's Smile:* The First Baptist Church and the First Methodist Church were at a main intersection but on opposite sides of the street. Many of the Baptists were finding it difficult to find a parking place Sunday mornings as several of the Methodists parked in the Baptist parking lot since their service started earlier than the Baptists.

The Baptists could have towed the Methodist's cars away, or they could have started patrolling their parking lot early Sunday morning, or they could have written a letter to the offending church asking them to park somewhere else. Being good Baptists, not wanting to offend them, and then too the Baptists had relatives in the Methodist church, they came up with a far better approach. One Sunday morning they stuck a bumper sticker on every car in the Baptist parking lot, Baptists and Methodists alike. With no exception every car got a bumper sticker which read, "I'm proud to be a Baptist!" That solved the problem.

Today's Comment: Well, there have been denominational differences for years. I think the best thing I can say today is to quote what I put in my book *Jokes Quotes & Anecdotes - Made Especially For Citizens with Seniority.* The author is anonymous. The article is entitled *The Wooden Leg.*

"A Free Methodist was working in a gold mine and was involved in an accident They took him to a Catholic Hospital and a Pentecostal surgeon amputated his leg. A Presbyterian woman felt sorry for him so she put an ad in the Mennonite Herald advertising for a wooden leg. A Christian & Missionary Alliance woman read the Presbyterian woman's ad in the Mennonite Herald about the Free Methodist in the Catholic Hospital whose leg had been amputated by a Pentecostal surgeon.

Her husband had been a Baptist but he was dead now, and he had had a wooden leg which he had left behind. So she called The Salvation Army and they sent a Captain to the Christian & Missionary Alliance woman's house to pick up the Baptist leg. He promptly took it to the express office giving it to the Lutheran express office operator who took it up to the Catholic Hospital handing it to the Christian Reformed nurse who strapped the Baptist leg on the Free Methodist and made A UNITED BRETHREN OUT OF HIM." Author Unknown

Pray that we will have a sincere love for our brothers and sisters in Christ.

Today's Golden Nugget of Truth: "Respect everyone, and love your Christian brothers and sisters. Fear God, and respect the king." First Peter 2:17 (NLT)

Today's Philosophical Tidbit: "Christians may not see eye-to-eye, but they can still walk arm-in-arm." Author Unknown

September 30
Giving To The Lord

Today's Smile: A minister wondered how he would be able to get the congregation to give some extra money to take care of several needed repairs to the church. When he arrived at church on Sunday morning, he discovered that the regular organist was sick and had arranged for a substitute. He was rushing around doing last minute things in preparation for the service and so quickly handed an order of service to the substitute and said, "I did not get time to choose a hymn to be sung following my announcement re the needed finances. Would you please choose an appropriate song?"

When the time for the announcements came, he addressed the congregation and said, "Beloved, we have had a problem with a leaking roof; the furnace is in need of repairs; there are some lose tiles and there are a few other things that need tending to. The board of deacons has met and we are asking that many of you would consider giving some extra money in this next month to care for these repairs. I am asking today that if you can make a pledge for at least $100.00 if you would please stand."

At that point, the substitute organist started to play *The Star Spangled Banner.*

Today's Comment: Unfortunately some pastors and evangelists have resorted to trickery or deceptive ways and means to solicit a greater response from people when it comes to giving. When we give gifts is it because we were tricked into the same? I believe that for the most part that we give gifts, be it birthday, anniversary, Christmas or any other special time because we are expressing our love for that person or persons. Maybe some give because they feel compelled to do so, but giving should be from a heart of love. The same goes for giving to your church or any other Christian or benevolent ministry.

I was in a church service on one occasion in the state of Washington when, I was reaching for my wallet and preparing to give when the pastor of that church began by asking, "How many will give $50.00? Let me see you wave your bill." Then he lowered it to twenty, then ten and five, and one. I put my wallet back into my pocket and decided that I was not interested in giving to be seen. Pray that our giving will be from the heart.

Today's Golden Nugget of Truth: "So let each one give as he purposes in his heart, not grudgingly or of necessity, for God loves a cheerful giver." Second Corinthians 9:7

Today's Philosophical Tidbit: "Don't give from the top of your purse, but from the bottom of your heart." Author Unknown

October 1
Your Pastor Needs You

*T*oday's Smile: Back in the early 1970's I was what has been dubbed, a *solo* pastor. It was before the days when I had an associate pastor or a youth pastor. Consequently, I did the entire pastoral visitation. One day I visited a four year old boy who was hospitalized. Normally, I would take a booklet or some reading material to hospital patients. What could I give this young boy? I decided that I would purchase a little rubber ball as a gift for him.

Later that day his mother went to visit him and he showed her the ball that I had given to him. "Where did you get that," his mother asked.

"My uncle gave it to me," he said.

"Your uncle! Which uncle? Uncle Mark? Uncle Tom? Uncle Curtis?"

He responded to each of his mother's inquiries by saying, "No!" Finally, he said, "You know, that uncle that stands up at the front of the church and hollers."

Today's Comment: Pastor Appreciation Month is usually celebrated in the month of October, but is sometimes held in another month, if more convenient for the church. It is a time, when in a special way, the pastor(s) are remembered and thanked for their spiritual leadership. However, we would do well to show our appreciation throughout the whole year and not just in October.

Pastors are human. They get discouraged. They have health issues. They have to balance their budget. They experience family issues just like everyone else. They spend time studying the Word of

346

God, visiting the sick, counselling couples desiring marriage, comforting the bereaved, leading the congregation, proclaiming (maybe hollering) the Word of God, plus a multitude of other matters. So be sure to pray for your pastors today, and consider sending a note of encouragement to one or more of them.

Today's Golden Nugget of Truth: "Let the elders who rule well be counted worthy of double honor, especially those who labor in the word and doctrine." First Timothy 5:17

Today's Philosophical Tidbit: "A moment or two spent encouraging your pastor when there are rough waters in the church will mean more to him than an hour spent praising him when all is smooth sailing." A. Daniel Goldsmith

October 2
Seeing The Potential In Our Youth

*T**oday's Smile:* Albert Runge was given some employment at the Toccoa Falls Christian High School in Toccoa Falls, Georgia. He was a city boy but was assigned work on the school farm. I quote from his biography: "He took me to the school's farm in his red Ford and left me in the barnyard in the care of a farm boy. The atmosphere smelled foul and my shoes were ruined in the cow muck. The first live cow I ever saw up close looked ferocious and dangerous to me. I asked the boy who was supposed to help me, 'What am I supposed to do here?'

'Y'all supposed to milk the cows.'

'How do I milk a cow?' I inquired.

'Y'all pump the cow's tail.' He seemed sincerely helpful. He put a milk pail under the right place, handed me the tail of the cow and instructed me on how to pump the tail to get the most milk from the cow.

I said, 'But I am not getting anything.'

'Well, you have to pull harder,' he retorted. But still no milk came, and the cow seemed annoyed.

Just then the head farmer came in and asked me, 'Young man, what are you doing?"

'I'm milking the cow.' He told me that I was a menace to myself and sent me back to Kelly Barnes with a note telling him the story. Kelly almost fell to the floor, laughing and crying all at the same time."[1]

Today's Comment: In my last pastoral ministry, I was one of eight staff pastors. For a period of time the senior pastor, my boss, was Rev. Albert Runge. Al was born into a Jewish home in Brooklyn, NY. While in his teen years, he came to know the Lord Jesus Christ as his personal Saviour. He was desirous of serving the Lord, but was from a poor home and not the smartest student. After his first month at Toccoa Falls he was out of money and the school was out of scholarships. The principal was led of God to find student employment for Al. The farm was his first job at the school. It was also his last farm job.

Do you know young people that struggle financially and have little or no encouragement from home? Al's home church in Brooklyn, which gave him sufficient funds for his first month, plus the staff at the school both saw potential in young Al and were not disobedient to the voice of the Lord.

Al lives about a ten minute walk from my place. We are together often for prayer, coffee and fellowship. Reflecting on Al's life and ministry, he went on to earn high marks and a couple of degrees in his studies in college and seminary. He has been pastor of four thriving churches, has had a radio ministry and is an author. Why? Because some men and women saw potential in the heart of this young man and helped him.

Pray that if God should prompt you to encourage some student today that you will not hesitate to encourage one in whatever way you are able.

Today's Golden Nugget of Truth: "A generous man will prosper; he who refreshes others will himself be refreshed." Proverbs 11:25 (NIV)

Today's Philosophical Tidbit: "Many people go far in life because someone else thought they could." Author Unknown.

October 3
Questionable Behavior

*T*oday's Smile: This is the only time in this book, that I've continued a story from the previous day. When Al failed the dairy farm job, which we shared yesterday, he was taken to the kitchen. Let me continue quoting from his book.

"Off we went again in his red Ford. This time he took me to the kitchen and left me in the care of two hefty cooks. They had 150 live chickens to be prepared for dinner. They took me outside along with the live chickens to a tree stump. . . They handed me an axe and explained how to grab a live chicken by its neck, place it on the stump and chop off its head. . .

"I had never killed anything before. I nervously took the first chicken by the neck and placed its head on the stump. The chicken looked up at me pitifully as if to say, 'Please, mister, don't hurt me.' I thought, 'It's either you or my job.' I chopped off its head, but to my surprise it didn't die. The headless chicken kept kicking and jerking. I threw it down and yelled at it, 'In the name of the Lord, come out of that chicken.' The cooks heard me and came running to see what the commotion was all about. When I explained, they broke out into hysterical laughter. They supervised as I killed all the rest of the chickens. The more chickens I killed, the easier it became." [1]

Today's Comment: When I was still a young pastor serving in a new pastorate, I received a phone call from a lady asking me to come to their home and cast the demon out of her husband. I had never had a call like that before. What should I do? I contacted one of the elders and asked if he would go with me. When we arrived at the house, the husband welcomed us in. We sat and visited with the husband and wife, talked about his problems and shared some scriptures. There was no opposition to the suggestion that we pray. We all knelt to pray. The elder prayed, the wife prayed, the husband prayed, and I prayed. The elder agreed with me that this husband had some emotional issues, but he was certainly not demon possessed.

John MacArthur says: "There is no clear example in the Bible where a demon ever inhabited or invaded a true believer. Never in the New Testament epistles are believers warned about the possibility of being inhabited by demons. Neither do we see anyone rebuking, binding, or casting demons out of a true believer... Christ and the apostles were the only ones who cast out demons, and in every instance the demon-possessed people were unbelievers."[2]

Pray for those whom you may know whose attitudes and actions no longer resemble that of a Spirit filled follower of Christ.

Today's Golden Nugget of Truth: "Let us fix our eyes on Jesus, the author and perfecter of our faith. . ." Hebrews 12:2 (NIV)

Today's Philosophical Tidbit: "When the Holy Spirit inhabits a person, no demon can set up house as a squatter." John MacArthur

October 4
Eat To Live Or Live To Eat

*T*oday's Smile: I thought that I should include at least one recipe in this book. Since it is nearing the Canadian Thanksgiving, I am giving you a tip on cooking a turkey. Americans and others need to file this recipe away for your Thanksgiving turkey dinner.

The secret ingredient is using uncooked popcorn as a stuffing ingredient. This is excellent for any who have a problem determining when the turkey is thoroughly cooked. Follow the steps below. The recipe is for a turkey 8 to 10 pounds. If the turkey is larger, adjust the measurements accordingly.

> ½ cup melted butter
> 1 cup stuffing
> 1 cup popcorn

Preheat oven to 350 degrees. Brush turkey well with the melted butter, salt and pepper.

Fill cavity with stuffing and popcorn. Place in baking pan making sure the neck end goes into the oven first.

After about 4 hours listen for the popping sounds. When the turkey's butt blows the oven door open and the bird flies across the room. . . . you know for sure that the turkey is done and ready to eat!

Today's Comment: Recipes, cook books, cooking shows, etc are in abundance. Why? There are probably two basic reasons: (1) Eating is necessary for our survival and most of us eat three times each day. (2) We love eating. It's easy to swallow tasty food and drink. We love it so much that when you come home hungry you might ask your mother or your wife, "What's for dinner?" If you are alone you are probably wondering as you head for home, "What shall I prepare for dinner?"

We seldom have a group gathering anymore, without food and drink. Either they are full course meals or lunches, snacks or possibly only coffee. It appears family gatherings, business meetings, church gatherings, etc. are not complete anymore without eating and drinking.

In our world today there are millions upon millions that go to bed hungry. They are starving for food. There are others who, because of medical problems, have no sense of taste or appetite. Do we, who have an abundance of food and are able to enjoy the same, have control of how much we eat? We may be careful in that which we watch, which we read, which we hear, or even what we say, but when it comes to eating, many lack self-control.

Controlling our appetite may well be *food* for thought and something we need to ponder today. Pray that our eating and drinking will bring honor and glory to our Heavenly Father.

Today's Golden Nugget of Truth: "You know the old saying, 'First you eat to live, and then you live to eat'? Well, it may be true that the body is only a temporary thing, but that's no excuse for stuffing your body with food, or indulging it with sex. Since the Master honors you with a body, honor Him with your body!" First Corinthians 6:13 (MSG)

Today's Philosophical Tidbit: "If you're such a glutton that you demand breakfast in bed, go sleep in the kitchen." Author Unknown

October 5
Factual Or Fictional

Today's Smile: A motivational speaker was invited to speak to a group of pastors at their annual retreat. He began his speech by saying, "The most relaxing and restful years of my entire life were in the arms of a lady who was not my wife."

The pastors were shocked. The speaker then continued by saying, "That lady was my mother." The pastors all burst into a hilarious laughter.

Returning to his pulpit, one of the pastors decided that the joke had gone over so well at the retreat that he would tell it in his Sunday morning sermon. He was not as outgoing as the motivational speaker, and not accustomed to telling jokes in his sermon, but thought it was worth a try.

He shyly began his sermon by saying, "The greatest years of my life were spent in the arms of another lady, and that lady was not my wife." Like the pastors at the retreat, the congregation was shocked. He stood silent for about ten or twelve seconds trying to recall the rest of the joke. Finally he blurted out, "and I can't remember who she was."

Today's Comment: Have you ever started to tell a joke and forgot the punch line? Most of us have. Hearing a joke without the punch line we usually end up laughing at the joke teller. That's not bad, but hearing half a story and passing it on can prove disastrous.

Years ago an outstanding Christian psychologist, whom I knew personally, was chatting with some friends after a session at a conference. He told his friends that his wife had left him. A passerby, heard him say, "My wife has left me." What the passerby did not hear was that she had gone away for a few days to visit some friends. In no time at all a story spread across the country that the wife of this outstanding Christian had left him.

A story circulated several years ago about a well known marriage counselor who had left his wife. A pastor friend of mine did not believe that and phoned the counselor's office to determine whether it was true. The marriage counselor's secretary said, "At the moment, he and his wife are out conducting a marriage enrichment seminar." Certainly there were no grounds for the rumor.

Pray that we will not be guilty of sharing incomplete information that could be damaging to others.

Today's Golden Nugget of Truth: "First check the facts to see if the rumor is true." Deuteronomy 13:14 (TLB)

Today's Philosophical Tidbit: "Gossip is a breeze stirred up by a windbag." Author Unknown

October 6
Believing Prayer

T *oday's Smile:* The story is told about a small town where a new tavern was being built near to a local church. In response to this building project, the church called special prayer meetings, praying that the tavern would not become a reality.

One week before the grand opening of the tavern, lightning struck burning the tavern to the ground. After the fire, the church folks started talking around town about the power of prayer. In short order, the tavern owner sued the church on the grounds that the church was "ultimately responsible for the demise of his building, either through direct or indirect actions or means." The members of the church vehemently denied any responsibility or any connection to the fact that the church had been destroyed.

As the case made its way into the court system, the judge looked over the complaint by the tavern owner and response by the church commenting that he did not know how he should decide on this case. He said, "It appears from the information that has been given to me that the tavern owner is the one who really believes in prayer, and the congregation does not."

Today's Comment: Do we believe in prayer? The early church prayed for the apostle Peter who was imprisoned (Acts 12:5-19). An angel of the Lord delivered Peter out of prison. After Peter was out of prison, and the angel had left him, he went to the house of Mary, the mother of John whose surname was John. Several people had gathered together to pray for Peter. When Peter was finally allowed to come in, people who had been praying for him apparently were filled with disbelief.

Have there been times when we prayed and God answered, but we were so surprised when God answered? Instead of asking if we believe in prayer maybe I should have asked whether we expect an answer. Too many prayers are simply a ritual and lack fervency and expectancy. In our praying, let's pray expectantly.

Today's Golden Nugget of Truth: "Therefore I will look to the Lord; I will wait for the God of my salvation; My God will hear me." Micah 7:7

Today's Philosophical Tidbit: "When you attend a special prayer meeting to pray for rain, take an umbrella with you." Author Unknown

October 7
Are You A Worrywart

*T**oday's Smile:* Brian was five years old and had been attending kindergarten for about a month. His mother was a worry-wart and was so concerned when he started to school that she walked with him every morning. One day he asked his mother if he could walk by himself like the big boys. She agreed, but had another plan.

She asked her neighbor Shirley Goodnest whether she would mind following Brian at a distance and keeping an eye on him. Shirley didn't mind as she usually went for a morning walk with her pre-schooler Marcy. So Brian started walking by himself. The third day he met up with a friend and the two of them walked to school every day thereafter. After a couple of weeks, Brian's friend Jacob asked, "Have you seen that lady that seems to follow us every morning?"

"Yes," said Brian. That's our neighbor Mrs. Goodnest and her daughter Marcy."

"Why do you think she is following us?" asked Jacob.

"My mommy worries about me all the time. Every night before I go to bed she makes me say Psalm 23 in my prayers. That Psalm says, 'Shirley Goodnest and Marcy shall follow me all the days of my life.' So I guess I am going to have to get used to it."

Today's Comment: Are you a worrier? It has been stated that a high percentage of our worries never come to pass. So if you are preparing yourself for tomorrow by worrying today, you are simply robbing today of the joy which you could be experiencing. If you're like me, most of your worries occur when you can't sleep at night. Your mind tends to go over all of the things that might happen. So what good comes of it all? Nothing! What I worried about didn't come to pass. The only thing that really happened was that I lost sleep. Pray that we will give all of our worries, be they large or small, to the Lord and leave them with Him.

Today's Golden Nugget of Truth: "Casting all your care upon Him, for He cares for you." First Peter 5:7

Today's Philosophical Tidbit: "Worry doesn't take the sorrow out of tomorrow it takes the strength out of today." Adrian Rogers

October 8
Why Are Some Smart People Stupid

*T*oday's Smile: An organization whose members have an IQ of 140 or higher were holding a convention in San Francisco. Some of the members had lunch together one noon. While seated, waiting for their lunch to be served, they noticed that the salt shaker contained pepper and the pepper shaker was full of salt. One of them asked, "How can we swap the contents of the bottles without any spilling, using only the implements at hand? This was clearly a job for these intelligent patrons.

They debated amongst themselves, presenting several ideas. Finally they agreed on a brilliant solution which involved a napkin, a straw and an empty saucer. They called the waitress over to dazzle her with their great solution.

"Ma'am," they said, "we couldn't help but notice that the pepper shaker contains salt and the salt shaker..."

"Oh," the waitress interrupted, "I'm sorry about that. I see that I put the caps on the wrong bottles." So she unscrewed the caps of both and switched them.

Today's Comment: There are many *intelligent* people in this world who circumvent the simple truths in the Bible and are forever trying to find an answer or solution for their questioning mind.

How many of the world's *smart* people are trying to figure out where man came from? What about the universe, the planets and stars? They spend billions trying to give an explanation as to the origin of our universe. There are those that deny the fact that Noah built an ark and that there was a flood. They ridicule the Exodus account of Moses leading the Children of Israel across the Red Sea followed by Pharaoh's army drowning in that sea.

Doesn't common sense tell us that there had to be a master planner behind all that we see in our world? There is nothing in our world owned by man that came into existence without a designer and some workers. Why would you want to believe that this great universe came into existence on its own?

Though there are many who do not agree with the findings, there are several websites about the discovery of Noah's ark[1] and several bodies and wheels, etc in the Red Sea which they figure is that of Pharaoh's army that drowned.[2] I recall as a young teen reading an account in the Reader's Digest about the discovery of the ark.

Whether or not these findings are the ark and the remains of Pharaoh's army, I don't need them to prove to me that God is real and His Word is true. Many intelligent men and women have been blinded by Satan, lest they should see and believe. (Second Corinthians 4:3, 4)

Pray that their minds and hearts might be opened to see and believe that the one true God is the creator of this world and holds it together in the palm of His hand. We are accountable to Him.

Today's Golden Nugget of Truth: "According to some people, there are a great many gods, both in heaven and on earth. But we know that there is only one God, the Father, who created all things and made us to be His own; and one Lord Jesus Christ, who made everything and gives us life." First Corinthians 8:5, 6 (TLB)

Today's Philosophical Tidbit: "What can be more foolish than to think that all this rare fabric of heaven and earth could come by chance, when all the skill of science is not able to make an oyster?" Jeremy Taylor

October 9
An Unhealthy Lifestyle

*T*oday's Smile: A woman who was walking down a quiet residential street, noticed a little old man rocking in a chair on his porch. She called out to him as she passed. "Hello there! I couldn't help but notice how happy you look. What's your secret for a long happy life?"

"I smoke three packs of cigarettes a day," he replied. "I also drink a case of whiskey a week, eat nothing but fast food, and never exercise."

"Wow!" The woman was amazed. "How old are you?" she asked.

"Twenty-nine," he replied.

Today's Comment: This was sent to me as a joke. There was a faint smile on my face when I first read this, but that smile did not last long. I debated whether to include it in this book; I have, not so much to make you smile, but rather if you are a younger person, to do some serious thinking.

When I was about 14 or 15 years of age, a group of us as young people were taken one fall evening to Michigan Avenue in the city of Detroit. What I saw was a big contrast to the quiet street where I lived which was only about an hour's drive away. There I saw a man sleeping in the gutter; others were staggering on the sidewalk. They were dirty, wearing shabby clothes with a spirit of hopelessness evident. A few minutes later I was standing in front of a tavern. As I looked through the window I saw a sad dejected woman, the only person in there, sipping a mug of beer.

Where we stood, listening to The Salvation Army preaching the gospel at a street meeting, I counted 13 bars and taverns in that one city block. It made a life long impression on me. The scene that I witnessed that night, which was in the 1940's, has remained with me all through the years.

For the child of God our body is the temple of the Holy Spirit. Let's pray that God will help us to keep away from those impurities which wreck the body and ruin the soul.

Today's Golden Nugget of Truth: "Do not mix with winebibbers. . . For the drunkard and the glutton will come to poverty." Proverbs 23:20, 21

Philosophical Tidbit: "A bar to heaven, a door to hell, whoever named it, named it well." Author Unknown

October 10
Are You Out Of Step

*T**oday's Smile:* Victor was a drill sergeant and had his soldiers out on a march. He noticed one of his young recruits was out of step. Not wanting to be too harsh on the soldier, knowing he had been on a sick leave for a few days and knowing this was his first day back, the sergeant drew alongside of his soldier and said, "Mac, do you know that all of the rest of this platoon is out of step except for you."

"I didn't hear what you said, sarge."

Raising his voice the sergeant said, "I said the rest of this platoon is out of step except for you!"

"Thanks for the compliment, sarge!"

"No, I want to know what you think is the solution?" responded the sergeant.

"You're in charge, sarge. If I were you I'd tell them to smarten up."

Today's Comment: As a Christian, do you sometimes feel like you're out of step with the world? You feel all alone. Everyone else is going another direction, marching to another drummer. You may find yourself in a workplace, a college campus or in a community and you are the only follower of Christ. Their entertainment, goals, the things they spend their money and their free time on are different than yours. Unfortunately many Christians who find themselves in that situation change step and blend in with the world. They find it too hard to go it alone, to be different.

When it comes to being out of step or in step, we see two kinds of professing believers today. There are those that have taken the doctrine of separation to extremes becoming isolationists. Then there are those who want to fellowship with any and all, no matter what they believe. There is a balance between these two extremes.

We are to love the people of the world, the sinful, how else will they be reached with the truth of the gospel? But we are to be separated from the sins of the world. We are not to be partakers of their sins. So pray that you may be out of step indulging in the pleasures of sin, but be in step with the people of God.

Today's Golden Nugget of Truth: 'Therefore come out from among them and be separate, says the Lord, do not touch what is unclean, and I will receive you. I will be a Father to you, and you shall be My sons and daughters, says the Lord Almighty." Second Corinthians 6:17, 18

Today's Philosophical Tidbit: "The hardest thing in the world is to keep balanced." L. E. Maxwell

October 11
They Lived Happily Ever After

*T*oday's Smile: Four year old Monica loved nursery school, especially the story time. Every day she would come home all excited to tell her mommy about the story that the teacher had shared that morning.

The day that the teacher shared the story about Snow White and Prince Charming, Monica could not contain herself. The moment she walked in the door, her tongue was in gear. "Mommy, the teacher told us about Snow White. Her mommy died and her new mommy didn't like her. Her new mommy wanted a man to kill her, but he didn't kill her and she lived with some dwarfs. When the bad queen heard that she was living with those dwarfs, she went to see her and put a hat on Snow White's head and choked her, but the dwarfs undid the hat and she lived. And then the bad queen came again and gave her a bad apple. This time she really died."

"That is such a sad story, Monica."

"But there is more, mommy. A prince came along and saw that the dwarfs put her in a box; I think it was a glass box. He looked at her and loved her and begged to take her with him. The dwarfs let him. He kissed her and she spit out the apple and lived again. And you know what happened next?"

"They lived happily ever after," replied her mother.

"No!" Monica said with a frown on her face, "they got married!"

Today's Comment: Many years ago I gave marriage counselling to a young couple. The morning of the wedding, the bride to be, phoned me up saying that she was confused not knowing whether to get married or not. I quickly arranged to meet with her before she went for her hair appointment. I suggested that she delay her wedding if she was uncertain. "Yes, but people are coming and we have booked the restaurant," she said.

I told her that was not important. "I'll go to the church and tell them the wedding has been postponed and that they will still be able to meet at the restaurant for the meal."

She sat there confused and finally said, "No, we will get married." That was a Saturday. Tuesday she was knocking at my door and said that she made a mistake. The marriage ended soon after that and the couple divorced.

A wedding ceremony does not make a marriage. There must be a deep abiding love and commitment to each other for a marriage to work and be "happy ever after." Marriage is not to be "entered into lightly."

There will be surprises in marriage. There will be things that you never discussed or thought about. However, with the promise that you're going to make it work, pray that God will be the Head of your house and draw upon His strength. Marriage should be a triangle affair; God, husband and wife. With God in your marriage you are on the road to a happy and lasting marriage.

Today's Golden Nugget of Truth: "Love does not demand its own way. It is not irritable or touchy. . ." First Corinthians 13:5 (TLB)

Today's Philosophical Tidbit: "A good marriage requires the decision to be married for good." Author Unknown

October 12
Know What They're Talking About

*T**oday's Smile:* Benny went shopping with his sister and saw a big display of thermoses. There was a variety of colors and sizes. He picked up a shiny silver colored thermos. As he did so, the clerk told him that it was a good one and that many kids bought them to take along with their school lunch. "It keeps hot things hot and cold things cold," she said. He liked that idea, and so he pulled out a pocket full of change and bought one. He couldn't wait to take it to school the next day.

He arrived early the next morning and was showing his grade two teacher. Excitedly, he told her that it keeps hot things hot and cold things cold. "That sounds great, Benny," she said. "What do you have in it today?"

"I've got some hot chocolate and a popsicle!"

Today's Comment: Words standing alone do not convey a great deal of meaning. If we said the word "door" or "pencil" or "airplane" we would know what it is, but it doesn't say anything about it. So we put words together and make a statement. Even then they may be confusing, as in today's smile: "Keeps hot things hot and cold things cold." They have to be interpreted or understood in the light of the context.

How about those crazy headlines that we often see. Don't know the newspapers but here are two such headlines: *Federal Agents Raid Gun Shop And Find Weapons.* Another one: *Bugs Flying Around With Wings Are Flying Bugs.* Once you read the article you understand what the editor is writing about.

So when it comes to understanding God's Word, we need to consider the context. Words and phrases taken out of context can give a wrong meaning. Many false cults use biblical quotes lifting them out of context and making them mean something that they do not mean. Pray that you do not misunderstand the truths which God desires that you know.

Today's Golden Nugget of Truth: "Study to show thyself approved unto God, a workman that needeth not to be ashamed, rightly dividing the word of truth." Second Timothy 2:15 (KJV)

Today's Philosophical Tidbit: "Writers seldom write the things they think. They simply write the things they think other folks think they think." Elbert Green Hubbard

October 13
Who Is Criticizing

T oday's Smile: The wife of a hard-to-please husband was determined to satisfy him for just one day. "Darling", she asked, "what would you like for breakfast this morning?" He growled, "Coffee, toast, grits, sausages, and two eggs - one scrambled and one fried."

She soon had the food on the table and waited for a word of praise. After a quick glance at his plate, he exclaimed, "Well, if you didn't scramble the wrong egg!"

Today's Comment: Some people are never happy no matter what we do, no matter what we say, no matter what lengths we go to in order to satisfy them.

Does it hurt when people criticize us? Does it make us depressed? Do we continue to think about the inappropriate criticism? You may be the exception, but most of us have received our criticism, especially if we are in any place of leadership. Constructive criticism has its place, but much criticism leveled at us is uncalled for. It is not constructive, it is downright hurtful.

Let's cast the negative criticism upon the Lord and move on. Let's not be controlled by one whose only goal is to hurt us. Our goal should be to please God. If we are confident that we are doing God's will and that the criticism was not constructive in any way, then let the critics criticize and the complainers complain. May our goal be to please God.

Today's Golden Nugget of Truth: "For what credit is it if, when you are beaten for your faults, you take it patiently? But when you do good and suffer, if you take it patiently, this is commendable before God." First Peter 2:20

Today's Philosophical Tidbit: "Don't mind criticism. If it is untrue, disregard it; if unfair, keep from irritation; if it is ignorant, smile; if it is justified it is not criticism, learn from it." Author Unknown

October 14
Stick To Your Diet

*T*oday's Smile: A lot of food had been consumed by the McDonald family in Charlottetown, PEI. It was the Canadian Thanksgiving weekend. The morning after the big feast of turkey and all the trimmings, James figured for sure that he had put on about four or five pounds over the weekend. Since his wife was busy in the kitchen preparing breakfast, he figured he could quietly slip into the bathroom. He wasn't quiet enough though because she heard him and headed in his direction hoping to plant a good morning kiss on his cheek.

What did she see? James was standing on the bathroom scale weighing himself and sucking in his stomach. She thought to herself, "He thinks that he will weigh less by sucking in his stomach." His dear wife teasingly said to her husband, "That's not going to help you."

James replied, "Oh yes it will. It's the only way I can see the scale."

Today's Comment: Is there anything wrong with getting together with family and friends and eating? Absolutely not! Thanksgiving is a time when many families are together, eating, having fun and enjoying the opportunity of being together.

The Canadian Thanksgiving is the second Monday in October. Quite a few Canadians eat more than they should. Turkey and all the trimmings! It's hard not to have second helpings. However, that's not limited to only Canadians.

Jesus was fully God and fully man, the God-Man. As a man on this earth, He lived a full life. He walked and talked and worked. He got together with family and friends. He socialized and ate and drank, yet without sin. He probably controlled His appetite. As humans, we sometimes lose control of our appetite. Don't let that get you down. Just enjoy those times with family, giving thanks for family, but also giving thanks for belonging to the family of God.

So if we stepped on the scale this morning and didn't like what we saw, we have today and our tomorrows. Thank God that we have another chance to do better. Pray that it might be so.

Today's Golden Nugget of Truth: "Whether therefore ye eat or drink, or whatsoever ye do, do all to the glory of God." First Corinthians 10:31 (KJV)

Today's Philosophical Tidbit: "Overweight is something that easily snacks up on you." Author Unknown

October 15
A Hidden Agenda

*T*oday's Smile: Ned took his grandfather to the barbershop. His grandfather had very little hair not having been to a barber for some time. However, he thought that since a big celebration was being planned for his 60th wedding anniversary that he should look his best.

When the grandfather inquired about the senior price, the barber told him that the going senior rate was $15.00, but said he, "Since it's your wedding anniversary I'll knock off ten dollars and just charge you five."

"Well, thanks for your kindness," said Ned's grandfather. When the barber was finished cutting his hair, grandfather handed the barber a twenty dollar bill. The barber gave him $5.00 in change. "I thought you said you were only going to charge me $5.00. You've charged me the full price of fifteen."

The barber responded by saying, "No, I only charged you five dollars for the haircut, but ten dollars for finder's fee."

Today's Comment: Hidden fees! We've been told to read the fine print when making a large purchase. How often have we heard about politicians having hidden agendas? So many people and services have other plans or prices that are not evident at first.

Are we guilty of hidden secrets? Are there habits or things in our life, present or past that have not been revealed? If the truth were known, would we be ashamed? There are so many professing Christians who appear to be in fellowship with God and talk the talk, but suddenly we hear that they have fallen, they had a secret sinful life, but managed to hide it. They are not really walking the walk. Pray that we will have a clean record, being what we profess to be. The secret sins, if not confessed to God now and forsaken, will someday be revealed.

Today's Golden Nugget of Truth: "For I want you to understand what really matters, so that you may live pure and blameless lives until the day of Christ's return. May you always be filled with the fruit of your salvation, the righteous character produced in your life by Jesus Christ, for this will bring much glory and praise to God." Philippians 1:10, 11 (NLT)

Today's Philosophical Tidbit: "Purity of heart is blooming the same colors in the middle of the wilderness when no one sees you." Matthew Henry

October 16
Your Lies Will Catch Up With You

T oday's Smile: Timothy desperately wanted some days off, but he knew that his boss would not grant such. He tried to think what he could contrive that would cause the boss to send him home. He had the bright idea that if he acted a bit crazy that maybe the boss would send him home. So he managed to hang upside down from the ceiling by locking his feet around the water pipe. As he hung there he began to make some strange noises. His secretary, Melinda, asked him what he was doing.

"I'm pretending to be a light bulb so that the boss might think that my mind is in overload."

Well, it worked. A few seconds later Timothy's boss walked into his office and asked, "What on earth is wrong with you?"

"'I'm a light bulb," said Timothy.

The boss responded by saying, "I think that you are definitely under stress. Why don't you take the rest of the week off and see if a little bit of rest at home will help you."

With that, Timothy got down, thanked his boss and walked out of the office. Melinda started to follow him out when the boss asked, "And where do you think you are going?"

She replied and said, "I'm going home, too. I can't work in the dark!"

Today's Comment: This story makes me think of hearing and reading about people who have deliberately lied by phoning into their place of employment, stating that they were sick. They were not sick, but had things they wanted to do that day and used some of their sick days. I read that one out of every eight people who seek to claim benefits for being sick are really not sick. Among excuses which I read about were benefit claims for such absurd conditions such as acne and blisters.

I had a friend who was a private investigator. He told me many stories about his investigative and detective work. One such was a man who claimed back injuries and was unable to work. The employer was suspicious and hired my friend to follow him. He found the man, out on the golf course enjoying a round of golf.

God keeps the books and I trust that we are honest when it comes to claiming sick leave. Some day we will stand before the Judge of all the earth. As a child of God it will be the Judgment Seat of Christ. Pray that you will be numbered among the believers and that you will hear Him say, "Well done good and faithful servant."

Today's Golden Nugget of Truth: "The man of integrity walks securely, but he who takes crooked paths will be found out." Proverbs 10:9 (NIV)

Today's Philosophical Tidbit: "A lie is like a snowball. The longer it is rolled on the ground the larger it becomes." Martin Luther

October 17
Pride And Arrogance

*T*oday's Smile: Three long time friends who had climbed the ladder of success had chartered a plane to go moose hunting in Alaska. A young scout accompanied the three men, serving as their guide. The plane had barely taken off from Anchorage when there was engine trouble. The pilot, who was wearing a parachute, turned to the four passengers and told them, "We're about to crash, grab a parachute and jump."

The four fellows discovered that there were only three parachutes instead of four. One of them quickly grabbed a parachute and said,

"You know I am a cardiologist and my patients need me." With that he jumped.

The second parachute was picked up by a man who said, "I am one of the smartest men in the United States. My work has to do with exploration and my country needs me." He jumped.

That left the scout and an older man, who was a friend of the other two, but he was retired and had several health issues. He turned to the young scout and said, "Sonny, I am old and most of my life is behind me, you take this last parachute and jump."

"Sir," said the young scout, "there are two parachutes left. The smartest man in the United States just grabbed my back pack."

Today's Comment: Probably most of us have someone in our life that wants us to know how important they are. They spare no words in letting you know how many degrees they've earned and all of their accomplishments. They have met so many important people in life wanting you to know that too.

The Bible exhorts us to be humble, not proud. To be servants, not lords. To take the lowly place, not the high. In the flyleaf of one of my Bibles I have written the words of an anonymous writer: "The desire of my heart is so to live, that people will say as I pass, not what a wonderful Christian he is, but a wonderful Christ that he has." Pray that that would ever be our goal.

Today's Golden Nugget of Truth: "God resists the proud, but gives grace to the humble." James 4:6

Today's Philosophical Tidbit: "Heap big smoke, no fire. Him talk a lot, him not so hot." Eldred Hubbard

October 18
Beauty On The Inside

*T*oday's Smile: Tiny boarded an airplane in Bellingham, WA and was going to Fresno, CA to visit his daughter, who had just moved there. Tiny, that was his nickname, weighed 365 pounds. Once he was seated on the airplane, he asked a flight attendant for a seat belt extension. After they were airborne and the attendants were serving drinks, he asked the flight attendant, who handed him his coffee, when it was that the airline started putting a physical description of the passengers on their luggage. He said, "I think it is very rude to describe one's physical appearance on the luggage. I know I am overweight, but I don't think the airline needs to say so on my luggage."

"I'm sorry," said the attendant, but we do not put a tag on your luggage with any personal description or information."

"You most certainly do," said Tiny. "When I checked in the gal who took my luggage put a tag on my bag which said FAT."

The attendant broke out in laughter. "Sir," she said, "this plane is flying to Fresno, CA and FAT is the abbreviation for the Fresno Air Terminal!"

Today's Comment: Many years ago, Paul Harvey told a story about a woman who was overweight and blamed her weight problem on the city street traffic. This woman would go to bed at night, but the traffic outside of her bedroom would keep her awake. So, rather than toss and turn in bed she would get out of bed and prepare something to eat, thus causing her, she said, to be overweight.

The point I want to make today has nothing to do with weight problems. What needs to be said is, "Don't be making fun of people who may be overweight or just skin and bones. Don't be calling them names or bullying them. We are all precious in God's sight. He loves us all, big or little, large or small, fat or thin. God looks at the heart of man, the inward beauty, whereas man is more preoccupied with outward beauty.

To illustrate what a priority our appearance has become, look at these statistics. Statistics for the USA state that, "Cosmetic plastic surgery procedures were performed on 14.6 million people in 2012."[1] "Eight billion dollars is spent annually on cosmetics."[2] Compare that with "11.4 billion dollars spent on all Christian foreign missions for one year."[3] Cosmetics amount to more than two thirds of what is spent on foreign missions.

Let's pray that our priorities will be right when it comes to spiritual beauty and physical beauty.

Today's Golden Nugget of Truth: "Do not let your adornment be merely outward, arranging the hair, wearing gold, or putting on fine apparel, rather let it be the hidden person of the heart, with the incorruptible beauty of a gentle and quiet spirit, which is very precious in the sight of God." First Peter 3:3, 4.

Today's Philosophical Tidbit: "If last night's sleep was our beauty sleep, why did we waste time looking in the mirror this morning?" A. Daniel Goldsmith

October 19
Untapped Wisdom

*T*oday's Smile: One of the famous scientists in the United Kingdom devoted a lot of his time to speaking at various colleges, universities and gatherings of scientists. One night he said to Simon, his chauffer, "Simon, you have been driving me around this country for close to ten years. I'm a so tired tonight, I don't think that I could stand up before that crowd of students and give my speech and field any questions. Why don't we stop somewhere along this route and change clothes. I'll drive, and you give my speech."

Well, they arrived at the dinner. Simon gave a wonderful presentation of Einstein's quantum theory of light. He then opened it up for questions and did extremely well, answering a variety of questions. One question came from a pompous professor who asked an extremely esoteric question about antimatter formation, digressing now and then to let everyone present know that he was no fool. Without wasting one second, Simon stared at the professor and said, "Sir, the answer to that question is so simple that I will let my chauffer, who is sitting at the back, answer it for you."

Today's Comment: There are numerous people in lesser positions that have much wisdom, but are seldom asked for their opinion or advice, or if given it is rejected. Some of the smartest people I know are back benchers; they are in the office downstairs in the basement. They sit in the pew. They are not in the top spots. Do we listen to them?

I have a nephew who worked for a company and his job was to travel extensively gathering information along with presenting ideas to the executives. One of his innovative ideas was turned down. When a competitor came forth with a product similar to that which he had proposed, the top brass at his company began to scramble. They requested that report which they had rejected. The problem was, the competitor had gained the market and they had missed out. They had been too late, not willing to examine his proposal.

Pray that we will be open to hear the opinions of others. They may have some good ideas that we never ever thought about.

Today's Golden Nugget of Truth: "Fools think their own way is right, but the wise listen to others." Proverbs 12:15 (NLT)

Today's Philosophical Tidbit: "Those who want to learn, listen. Those who know it all, interrupt." Author Unknown

October 20
Detox Your Thoughts

*T*oday's Smile: Isaiah and Clark were good friends, but Isaiah was an optimist and Clark was a pessimist. There were many things upon which they could never agree. One day Isaiah decided that he would try to get Clark to be a little more optimistic. So he decided to take him on a day's hunting trip.

Isaiah had a boat and always took his dog along with him when they went hunting. They sailed out to the middle of the lake. Within no time at all Isaiah, the optimist shot a duck. It fell on the water and Isaiah's dog, upon command, jumped out of the boat to retrieve the duck. To Clark's surprise, the dog walked on water, picked up the bird and walked back.

Isaiah looked at his pessimistic hunting companion and asked, "What do you think of that?"

Clark simply replied in his pessimistic manner, "Your dog can't swim, can he?"

Today's Comment: There are some people who always look on the dark side of everything. No matter what you do or what you say, they never see any good in anything. Researchers have stated that optimists enjoy better health, and live longer lives. Optimists look at the successes in life, whereas pessimists dwell on the failures. Optimists welcome input and feedback, but pessimists don't.

Today, if you are the pessimistic type, try for one day to look on the bright side. Then try it another day and yet another. As a child of God, the best medicine that I know for pessimism is to look to the Lord. Read His Word. Cry out to Him for help. Pray that God will help you to look beyond your problems and pessimistic views. With God in your life, the future is always bright.

Today's Golden Nugget of Truth: "For I know the thoughts that I think toward you, says the Lord, thoughts of peace and not of evil, to give you a future and a hope." Jeremiah 29:11

Today's Philosophical Tidbit: "The future is as bright as the promises of God." William Carey

October 21
A Servant Or A Spectator

T oday's Smile: Joel took his grandmother to a football game. She knew absolutely nothing about football, but since it was his 19th birthday, she thought she would go and see what she could learn. Joel did a little explaining about the game before it started, but she was so taken up with the big bag of popcorn that she didn't grasp too much of what he was saying. Once the game started he was cheering his team, and grandma just sat and watched and ate popcorn.

When Joel took her home, Gramps, who had been watching the news on television, shut it off and said, "O K Babe, tell me all that you learned tonight."

"Well," she said, it was a weird sort of game. Every once in awhile they would form a little circle and I guess they were praying that they wouldn't get hurt because they were forever falling. When they started to play one of the players bent over. The first time he did this, I thought it was to tie his shoes. Anyhow, he threw the ball between his legs and the guy that caught it didn't seem to know where to go. He started in one direction and then changed his mind.

It was an interesting evening. I ate three hot dogs, a bag of popcorn and drank two Pepsi's, but I really felt sorry for those guys on the grass. They were running and stopping and I don't know why they were chasing one another for twenty-five cents. I counted 22 people on that grass, getting all the exercise, and 30 or 40 thousand sitting yelling 'get that quarter back'."

Today's Comment: Football is a lot like many churches. There are a lot of pew-sitters. They come Sunday after Sunday, stand, sing, sit, watch, listen and then go home. There are a few people who are up on the platform who sing and speak. Between Sundays there are a few who teach clubs, and lead Bible studies, and attend prayer meetings, and practices, but very few in contrast to the many at a Sunday morning service.

Research has shown over the years that only 20% of any given congregation is involved in the ministry of the church. The other 80% are simply spectators. These spectators do not pay for what they are getting. Statistics reveal that 20% of the parishioners pay 80% of the offering, while 80% pay the remaining 20%. Where do we fit? Pray that the percentage will increase where more will share in the giving and ministry.

Today's Golden Nugget of Truth: "As each one has received a gift, minister it to one another, as good stewards of the manifold grace of God." First Peter 4:10

Today's Philosophical Tidbit: "Alone we can do so little; together we can do so much." Helen Keller

October 22
Fault Finding

T oday's Smile: Ray arrived at the office a moment or two late. He seemed rather hyper and his secretary asked, "What happened to you?"

"I tell you, you should have seen that women that was passing me on the freeway this morning. She was a hazard to the traffic. As she was passing me, I glanced to my left and there she was driving a Jaguar going at least 80 mph. She had her face up next to her rear view mirror putting on her mascara. The next thing I knew she was moving over into my lane. I hit the brakes in order to avoid a collision and in so doing, I dropped my shaver into my coffee which

I was balancing on my left knee and it spilled all over my laptop which I had on my right knee."

Today's Comment: I had my left turn signal on ready to make a left turn. The oncoming car had its left turn signal on. What stopped me from turning was that he was coming at a good speed and I questioned whether he was indeed going to turn left. He didn't. He just kept going straight ahead. He was talking on his cell phone.
It's easy to see the faults in others, whatever they may be. Do we have any faults? Are we also guilty of the same? We may not be shaving, or putting on mascara, or talking on a cell phone while driving, but are there other questionable things that we do, all the while pointing an accusing finger at others? Let's pray that the Lord will show us what our bad habits and activities are before we start finding fault or pointing a finger and another.

Today's Golden Nugget of Truth: "And why do you look at the speck in your brother's eye, but do not consider the plank in your own eye?" Matthew 7:3

Today's Philosophical Tidbit: "When looking for faults use a mirror, not a telescope." Author Unknown

October 23
Standing Strong

*T*oday's Smile: Kendra had an appointment with a counselor at her church. She had previous visits with the counselor and in each case had found the help that she needed. This time was different. She shared with her counselor that her husband said that "If you continue to see that counselor at that church I will beat the tar out of you."

"Well," said the counselor, "I think you need to keep focusing on those matters that we have dealt with previously, continue to have faith, trusting the Lord to work in your husband's heart."

"I have been doing that, and I continue to call out to the Lord, but. . ."

"But. . . what is it my child? Is there something more that you wanted to share?"

"But. . . Yes, there is, but I don't want to tell you."

"Please feel free to share with me. That's why I'm here; to listen to you offering some help and advice. Don't hesitate."

Reluctantly, she confessed, "My husband. . . my husband said that if I don't quit coming to you, sharing my problems, he will beat the tar out of you too."

"In that case," said her counselor, "I would think that it would be best for you to get another counselor. They have a counseling ministry in the church across the road."

Today's Comment: Some of us, when confronted with opposition may be inclined to run. Get someone else to do it. We don't like opposition.

Today there are millions around the world that are experiencing opposition for their faith in Jesus Christ. It is a daily occurrence. Most of them have no place to run. *Daily Inspiration From The Lion's Den,* is a daily devotional book, written by Paul Estabrooks, with stories about brothers and sisters in what we call "The Persecuted Church." One story, which demonstrates the commitment of these dear believers, is about a Chinese medical doctor whom he referred to as "Aunty Esther."[1]

In an attempt to get her to renounce her faith, she was beaten and tormented. She responded, "I can't deny Jesus. I love Jesus!" Eventually, she was banished to the basement of the hospital where for eleven years she scrubbed floors and cleaned toilets. Her meager salary of 50 dollars per month was cut to 15 dollars, out of which she had to buy the cleaning supplies and her food. She said, "My hospital had the cleanest floors and cleanest toilets in all of China." Through it all she practiced the presence of God all the while singing as she toiled.

Hospital staff questioned her throughout those years as to the source of her joy. She responded, "When you have Jesus in your heart, it doesn't matter what job you do or what position you have. It only matters that you love Him and are faithful and loyal to Him."

After the revolution ended, she was reinstated and even given her old job back along with back pay for all that she had been deprived of. God was sufficient for all that she faced and she stood strong in face of the storm. Pray that we will stand strong in the time of storms.

Today's Golden Nugget of Truth: "Blessed is the man who trusts in the Lord, and whose hope is the Lord." Jeremiah 17:7

Today's Philosophical Tidbit: "No Christian has ever been known to recant on his deathbed." C. M. Ward

October 24
The Joy Of The Lord

*T*oday's Smile: Leslie was the town drunk. He went to his brother-in-law's funeral in Brooklyn. There at that service he heard the gospel clearly presented. He was so convicted that later that day, while staying with his sister, he began to ask questions about what he had heard. She shared with him as best she could, but asked him if he would like to go to church with her the next day, being Sunday. Once again the gospel was clearly presented, and Leslie responded to the invitation to receive Christ as his personal Savior. He went to see her pastor a day or two later and was introduced to some good follow-up material.

Later that week he went back to his hometown in Vermont. He had never been to any of the churches in his hometown before. He had spent most of his time in the taverns. So he went to the church that was closest to him. The preacher gave a good message. Leslie began to say "Amen, Hallelujah, Praise the Lord." He was so enthusiastic about his new found faith, having heard people in his sister's church using these exuberant expressions.

The parishioners near him began to arch their eyebrows. After about a dozen or so of his words of praise, an usher, tapped him on the shoulder and asked him what his problem was. "I just got religion," said Leslie.

"Well, you didn't get it here," responded the usher.

Today's Comment: Would a newcomer into our community see any difference between us and our unbelieving neighbors? Does our Christianity show? I heard about a man who loved to party and drink his booze. He enjoyed the companionship of one of the village pastors. He said of this pastor, "He drinks along with us, smokes a big fat cigar, and enjoys a shady joke with us, but," said he, "there is

375

another pastor a couple of blocks away that is different. I've never heard him swear or use profanity. He's never been seen in a bar or tavern. He is a perfect gentleman. I've been thinking that if I should be on my death bed, I'd like that pastor to tell me how to get to heaven and to pray with me."

Two pastors, but one's religion showed. Pray that Christ may be seen in us today.

Today's Golden Nugget of Truth: "Make a joyful shout to the Lord, all you lands." Psalm 100:1

Today's Philosophical Tidbit: "You can tell a man's character if you know what makes him glad, what makes him sad, and what makes him mad." Author Unknown

October 25
Love Is Not Rude

*T*oday's Smile: The neighbor's daughter was fairly talkative at home, but quite shy when with strangers. The day came for the little girl's dental appointment. As she sat in the big dental chair, she appeared very tense. Dr. Brown did his best to try to relieve her of some of her tension. He usually found that if he could engage his little patients in a conversation before he started working on their teeth it would help them forget about some of their fears.

So he began by asking her whether she had any brothers or sisters. There was no response. Next he asked her if she had gone away during the summer. No response. Since he knew the little girl's grandparents, he asked if she had seen her Nana and Papa in the last week. She still was tense and did not answer any of his questions.

So he asked, "How old are you?" She held up four fingers. Well that was the first response that he had. Thinking maybe he was on to something, he then asked, "How old is that?"

With that, she looked him straight in the eye and said, "Can't you count? I'm four!"

Today's Comment: As I think back to my childhood and upbringing, the first thing that comes to mind is that my parents, my relatives, my teachers, etc. did not speak harshly to me. They were not rude. I was never told I didn't amount to anything, or that I ought to be ashamed of myself. I was treated kindly. I was loved, I was appreciated, I was complimented. Such examples of kindness were demonstrated to me in my early years.

Another thought that comes to mind is, I was raised in a pre television era. I didn't sit by the hour in front of the tube watching shows with misbehaved children and impatient parents shouting at each other, bad mouthing one another. I was exposed to a lot of good examples.

So how do parents cope today in a different world than what I knew? My heart goes out to you parents. You may not be able to control other people and how they act, but you can still set an example by the way you act and talk. If you are rude, your children will imitate you ending up being rude, yes to doctors, dentists, teachers, and others they meet.

Pray that God will help you to lay out some guidelines for children when it comes to television and all of the electronic games that children play. Too many of these gadgets are filled with examples of disrespect and rudeness.

Today's Golden Nugget of Truth: "Train up a child in the way he should go, and when he is old he will not depart from it." Proverbs 22:6

Today's Philosophical Tidbit: "The best way to teach character is to have it around the house." Author Unknown

October 26
Something For Nothing

*T**oday's Smile:* Hazel had been a widow for about three months. She was finding it extremely lonely, especially in the evenings. A friend suggested that she should get herself a pet. So she took that advice and browsed through a pet store. Finally, after looking at cats, dogs, snakes, canaries, etc, she decided to purchase a parrot.

The clerk told her that the parrot that she purchased was a great talker and would keep her company. At the end of the first week, she went back to the store and complained that the parrot hadn't said one word. "Oh," said the manager, "didn't Betty tell you that you should have purchased a swing when you bought the bird?"

So a swing was purchased. Another week passed and the parrot still didn't speak. Hazel went back again, this time she purchased a ladder, and then the next week she purchased a mirror. Each time the manager told her that if she added these features to the cage that the parrot would talk. After all those purchases and wasted time, she stormed back into the pet shop.

"I bought your parrot, which you said was the most talkative parrot in the store. I bought a cage, a swing, a ladder and a mirror, all of these things that you said would help. I just want to tell you Mr. Manager that the parrot died."

"Died! I can't believe that," said the pet store manager. "Did it ever say anything?"

"Yes! Just before it died, as it lay there breathing its last, it said with a very weak voice, 'Don't they have any food at that store'?"
Today's Comment: The Lord Jesus Christ tells us in His Word that He is the Bread of Life. He is the One that can meet the inner cravings and desires of our life. We may substitute what He offers by adding other things. We might think that good works, church attendance, giving to the poor and all these things and more will help us, but Jesus is the only One. He is the answer to our deepest longings. Let us feed on Him, and His Word. Cry out to Him in prayer. He will satisfy your spiritual hunger, not only helping you to talk, but putting a song in your spirit. He freely offers to satisfy our hunger and thirst.

Today's Golden Nugget of Truth: "Ho! Everyone who thirsts, come to the waters; and you who have no money, come, buy and eat, yes, come buy wine and milk without money and without price." Isaiah 55:1

Today's Philosophical Tidbit: "Read it (the Bible) to be wise, believe it to be safe, and practise it to be holy. It contains light to direct you, food to support you, and comfort to cheer you." Author Unknown

October 27
We're All Getting Older

Today's Smile: Angela had been deeply involved in the community and in the church. She served as secretary on the chamber of commerce for her small town, and also as president of ladies ministry at her church. She taught piano lessons in her home, and had written several novels. She was a busy lady! However, her body was beginning to deteriorate. She had developed heart problems, had colon cancer, walked with the aid of a walker, and had much pain from her arthritis.

She managed to get an appointment at a medical clinic. She was examined for all of these ailments. The time came for her to sit down and listen to the doctor as he shared the results from all of the tests. After he shared with her the results, Angela looked him in the eye and asked, "Doctor, can you cure me?"

He responded by saying, "As we age, so do our bodies. Weakening of the heart and some of these other ailments are bound to happen." He continued and said, "A doctor is not a miracle man. We can't make an older woman grow younger."

"Who wants to be younger?" asked Angela, "all I want is to grow older!"

Today's Comment: Well, no matter what age we are at, we're all growing older. Some people have been so indoctrinated that God will heal them of any and all diseases that when He does not answer the way they expect, they become bitter and angry with God. The following article is long, but I trust that it will put the matter of illness in its right perspective

"There are in the human body 9 major systems, skeletal, muscular, nervous, circulatory, urinary, digestive, endocrine, and reproductive. All of which are subject to disease, disorders, malfunctions and failures. The human skeleton contains 206 bones, all of which can be cracked or broken or disjointed. We have 500 muscles large enough to be seen by the naked eye, muscles that can be strained or sprained or sore. Bones and muscles are held together by membranes and ligaments, cartilage and tendons, that can be damaged, torn, displaced, bruised or destroyed.

"Outside we have arms, legs, feet, hands, but these can be arthritic or weary or sore or broken or amputated. We have eyes that can fail; ears that can grow deaf; mouths if they are cut can become diseased. A normal person has 32 teeth, all of which can be abscessed, decayed, broken or knocked out. The human body is covered by about 20 feet of skin. Skin that can itch, can be cut, scratched, bit, frost bit, or full of gangrene.

"Inside we have lungs, heart, kidney, pancreas, stomach. These can malfunction, be damaged, become cancerous. We have about 25 feet of intestines, which can become inflamed, perforated, irritated, ulcerous or malignant. We have about 6 quarts of blood that can be too thick or too thin, clotted, anemic, too much sugar or too little, have too many or too few red or white corpuscles.

"We are subject to bleeding, constipation, convulsions, cough, cramps, diarrhea, dizziness, fever, headache, boils, indigestion, inflammation, infection, jaundice, nausea, neuralgia, shock, vomiting, tumors or attacked by allergies, bacteria and fungi, and viruses and parasites and hives. There are several hundred diseases known to man. And we can catch them all. We would love to sing like the angels in praise to God, and be in the sanctuary choir, but our voices crack and squeak.

"We'd like to pray more, but we fall asleep in weariness. We'd like to serve more, but we have less and less energy the older we grow. We do not mean to be irritable, but our nerves are frayed. We want to be full of joy, but we are full of pain. We want to be on the mountain tops of spiritual victory, but our legs give out and we fall. Is it any wonder that Paul described this body as a TENT?"[1]

Today's Golden Nugget of Truth: "Therefore we do not lose heart. Even though our outward man is perishing, yet the inward man is being renewed day by day." Second Corinthians 4:16

Today's Philosophical Tidbit: "I have cancer, but cancer doesn't have me." Roger Bennett

October 28
There Is No Other Way

Today's Smile: An engineer, a psychiatrist, and a seminary professor were moose hunting in Norway. The temperature plunged quickly and a blizzard engulfed them. They had just passed an isolated cabin a few minutes prior and decided to go back, to see if they would be welcomed in from the cold.

They knocked, but there was no answer. They tried the door handle and found that the door was unlocked. It was a simple place, two rooms and a minimum of furniture. What intrigued them was a pot-bellied wood stove, made of cast-iron and suspended in midair by wires which were attached to the ceiling.

"Fascinating," said the psychiatrist. "It is obvious that this cabin owner, isolated from humanity, has elevated this stove so that he can curl up under it and vicariously experience a return to the womb."

"Nonsense," replied the engineer. "The man is practicing the laws of thermodynamics. By elevating his stove, he has discovered a way to distribute heat more evenly throughout the cabin."

"With all due respect," interrupted the theologian, "I'm sure that hanging his stove from the ceiling has religious meaning. Fire lifted up has been a religious symbol for centuries."

The three of them debated the point for over an hour without resolving the issue, when the owner returned to his cabin and found these three hunters. He was not surprised. It happened often that hunters would need a place from the cold and so he purposely left his place unlocked. As their host served them some coffee and refreshments, the three hunters asked him why he had hung his heavy pot-bellied stove from the ceiling.

"That's very simple," said the man, "I had plenty of wire and not very much stove pipe."

Today's Comment: The more people you have around you, the more differing opinions you have re a problem or a solution. There are also many opinions and beliefs about God. Some deny His existence; others have placed their faith in Him. Some say "if your good works outweigh your bad, that you will make it to heaven." Others, believing what the Bible teaches will say that it is not good works that God is looking for, but faith in His Son's death and resurrection on their behalf.

Though many people welcome all beliefs as being valid, the Bible states very clearly that there is only one way to be assured of everlasting life, and that is in the Lord Jesus Christ. Do you trust in your good deeds or have you received Jesus Christ as your personal Saviour? If you have never prayed to receive Christ, today is as good as any. Pray while there is still time.

Today's Golden Nugget of Truth: "Nor is there salvation in any other, for there is no other name (Jesus Christ) under heaven given among men by which we must be saved." Acts 4:12

Today's Philosophical Tidbit: "You're not saved by works, but you're saved by the grace of God, and it is faith that brings that grace into your heart and into your life." Adrian Rogers

October 29
Break The Will Not The Spirit

Today's Smile: Zachary, who was in grade two, had taken the scissors and cut off the ponytail of the little girl who sat in front of him. The principal phoned Zachary's home hoping to talk with either his mother or father. When the phone rang at his home, there was this soft voice, barely above a whisper that answered. Zachary's four year old brother had answered the phone. "Who is this?" the principal asked.

"It is Teddy."

"Is your father there?" asked the principal.

"He's busy," said Teddy.

"Is your mother there?"

"She's busy."

"Is there another adult there that I could talk to?" inquired the principal.

"The police."

"Teddy, may I talk with a police officer?"

"They're busy."

"Is there anyone else there?"

"The firemen"

"Please let me talk with a firefighter."

"They're busy."

"What is everyone so busy about?" asked the principal.

"They're looking for me," giggled little Teddy.

Today's Comment: Does that generate any memories of your childhood? Maybe that wasn't you when you were that age, but maybe, just maybe your children or grandchildren have pulled some inappropriate pranks. How did you react?

Dr. James Dobson is one that I admire for his practical and spiritual approach to raising children. The thought that has always been uppermost in my mind when it comes to training children is "break the will, but not the spirit." Dr. Dobson's comments: "The spirit is brittle and must be treated gently. The will is made of steel. It is one of the few intellectual components that arrives full strength at the moment of birth."[1]

A few more gleanings from Dr. Dobson: "You should not blame yourself for the temperament with which your child was born. . . You simply have to be tougher than he is, but do it without being angry and oppressive. . . Don't panic, even during the storms of adolescence. . . Don't let your child stray too far from you emotionally. . . Most importantly, I urge you to hold your children before the Lord in fervent prayer day by day by day. Begin every morning with a prayer for wisdom and guidance."[2]

Today's Golden Nugget of Truth: "Chasten your son while there is hope, and do not set your heart on his destruction." Proverbs 19:18

Today's Philosophical Tidbit: "Praise your children openly, reprove them secretly." W. Cecil

October 30
I'm The King Of The Castle

T oday's Smile: A young man, in his late twenties, had just been made the CEO of a large commercial real estate firm. He was treated to a brand new office, beautifully furnished, with the most exquisite décor, and the latest in all the modern technology, etc. It was day one. He arrived in his office and had barely become familiar with his spacious office, when a fellow walked into the waiting area.

The CEO saw him coming, and since his office door was still wide open, he quickly picked up the telephone and talked about the multi-million dollar sale that he had made, which he felt had helped him with his promotion. He went into great detail as to what he expected to do in his first 100 days in office. He finished his call, hung up the phone, and then, knowing that the fellow in the waiting room had heard his conversation, invited the man into his office. "What can I do for you," he inquired of the man.

"I have come to hook up your telephone."

Today's Comment: Human nature wants to impress other people and make them think how great, how talented and how smart we are when if the truth were known, we are nothing and nobody. A friend told us years ago about a professor at his Bible College who always sought to impress others. This professor was the chapel speaker one morning. He had been sitting on the platform, poised to plunge into his devotional. When it was time for him to speak, he literally leaped to the podium, and with raised hand began by saying, "The tie is scored!" While the students snickered, he retracted his words, and spoke less enthusiastically saying, "The score is tied."

Do we want people to look at us as someone really important? Be careful. Sooner or later we may be exposed for who we really are. Pray that we will walk humbly with our God. L. E. Maxwell used to say, "The way up is down."

Today's Golden Nugget of Truth: "And whoever exalts himself will be abased, and he who humbles himself will be exalted." Matthew 23:12

Today's Philosophical Tidbit: "None are so empty as those who are full of themselves." Benjamin Whichcote

October 31
God Loves You I'm Trying

oday's Smile: Travis and his wife were snowbirds and on their way to Florida for the winter. Travis got tired and so his wife took her turn at driving. She had driven for about an hour when she got pulled over by a North Carolina State Highway Patrol officer. "Ma'am, did you know that you were speeding?"

Travis's wife was extremely hard of hearing and turning to her husband asked, "What did he say?"

Raising his voice he replied, "He said you were speeding!"

The officer then asked, "May I see your license?" Again she asked her husband what the officer said.

"He wants to see your license!" he said.

After she handed the officer her license, the officer remarked, "I see that you are from Wheeling, West Virginia. I began my career in Wheeling before coming here to North Carolina." He chuckled a bit and continued, "I also dated the world's most cantankerous woman, there in Wheeling."

Once more turning to her husband she asked, "What did he say?"

Travis yelled back, "He says he thinks he knows you!"

Today's Comment: Any cantankerous people in your life? There must be at least one in your neighborhood, your school, your workplace, your church, and there is nearly always one on a board or committee. Oh yes, they are often found in families. How do we handle such people?

Guess that all depends on your personality. Many people argue with them. That usually makes things worse. Sometimes it is easiest to simply ignore them. The Bible exhorts us to pray for such people. It also says to love them.

It has been said that Dr. Robert Schuller was in an automobile accident. When he got out of his car and came face to face with the driver of the other car, the man spoke with Dr. Robert H. Schuller punctuating his speech with a good deal of foul and abusive language. Dr. Schuller looked the man in the eye and said, "Mister, God loves you and I'm trying!"

I am determined not to let an angry cantankerous person control my life. God is in control. I want to be like the little girl that said, "When the devil knocks on my door, I ask Jesus to answer it." Pray before you are quick to respond to an angry person. Let Christ speak through you.

Today's Golden Nugget of Truth: "But I say to you who hear; Love your enemies, do good to those who hate you, bless those who curse you, and pray for those who spitefully use you." Luke 6:27

Today's Philosophical Tidbit: "An angry man is seldom reasonable, and a reasonable man is seldom angry." Author Unknown.

November 1
Losers Can Become Winners

oday's Smile: Heather, who lived in New Hampshire, was applying for a job in a Florida lemon grove. The fellow who was interviewing her wondered about her qualifications. So he said to her, "I have to ask you this question: Have you had any experience in picking lemons?"

"Well, as a matter of fact, I have," replied Heather. "I've been divorced four times, owned three Edsels, bet several times on a losing horse, voted for the wrong president, invested money in a bank that failed, and bought property that lost more than half of its original value."

Today's Comment: Do you sometimes feel like you're a loser? No matter what you do, it turns out contrary to what you had hoped for. We've probably all had that feeling at times. I only ever invested money in stocks on three occasions. The first time was in 1970. I sold the only savings that I had, which was $500.00 worth of bonds. I invested it with a trustworthy friend who promised around 20% interest. Things went bad for him and he lost it all. His wife went back to work and between the two of them they were committed to paying back every investor their principal. The money was returned to me in full some six years later.

The second time I invested money I watched it grow to almost double and then watched it go down. When it got back to my original investment, I sold my shares. The third time I invested money in stocks, it ceased to be traded. So, I guess in a small way I've learned what it is to be a loser, at least with investments.

How should we react? Well, let me tell you what I did. Worrying over what happened didn't help any. So I simply told the Lord that all of that money was His in the first place and as a steward or manager of what He owns, I made some wrong moves. I apologized for being such a poor manager, and moved on.

We can dwell on past failures, bemoaning what we did wrong. It will not help us today. I know where my gifts and abilities are. Obviously it is not investing money in stocks. Pray that yesterday's mistakes will not rob you of today's joys.

Today's Golden Nugget of Truth: "Forgetting those things which are behind and reaching forward to those things which are ahead." Philippians 3:13

Today's Philosophical Tidbit: "The brightest future will always be based on a forgotten past. You can't go on well in life until you let go of your past failures and heartaches." Author Unknown

November 2
Words Won't Hurt You

*T**oday's Smile:* Four fellows, who were students at a small town Christian college, were enjoying a coffee together. They got talking about a fellow student who was given bad press in the student paper because he was caught smoking on campus. They wondered whether they should go as a foursome and talk with the editor. One of the fellows said that he was glad that the editor did not know about him. He shared that he was having a problem in that he was drinking a little alcohol and knew that if that was printed in the student paper that he would immediately be expelled.

"Well," said one of the others, "since you were so honest in sharing with us, "I need some prayer, too. My big problem is gambling. Being the class treasurer, I borrowed some money from the social fund for our class and bought lottery tickets. I owe a lot of money which I need to pay back to that fund before my sin is exposed."

A third student said, "I guess I need to share with you fellows, too. You've both been very open and honest. I'll be praying for you and would ask that you would pray for me that I get things right with God. I have been looking at pornographic websites."

The fourth student was extremely quiet. Silence reigned for two or three minutes. Finally, one of the guys spoke and said, "Brother, you've been silent all while we have been sharing. Is there something that you want us to pray about?"

"Well," he said, "I really don't know how to share my besetting sin."

"It's alright brother, your secret is safe with us."

"It's this way, he said, "you see, I am an incurable gossip, and I can't wait to get back to the campus."

Today's Comment: Throughout history there has been a tendency to classify sins. Murder, rape, stealing, fraud, espionage and many more crimes are viewed as horrible. Those guilty of such sins all have their day in court and handed the appropriate sentence.

Gossip is also a grievous sin, but when have you heard of a person appearing before a judge or jury and being handed a fine or jail sentence for gossiping? Yet the sin of gossip has caused endless heart aches, broken friendships, divorce, depression, resignations and sometimes even suicide.

Do you remember the little ditty that said: "Sticks and stones may break your bones, but words can never hurt you?" Tell that to a child who is always being told, "You'll never amount to anything," or "Why can't you behave like your sister?" Tell a woman who is 125 pounds overweight that she is ugly. Scream at your teenager that brings home a poor report card. Those words hurt the child, the woman, the teen. Words do hurt. Gossip which can be so hurtful and harmful is also a sin, which should be abhorred by Christians.

Be careful that you are not like some who would never gossip, but they share a juicy bit of gossip as a prayer request. Before you share what could be classified as gossip, stop. Pray that you will keep a lid on your thoughts and a lock on your tongue.

Today's Golden Nugget of Truth: "Besides, they are likely to be lazy and spend their time gossiping around from house to house, getting into other people's business." First Timothy 5:13 (TLB)

Today's Philosophical Tidbit: "The difference between a buzzard and a gossiper is that the bird waits until its prey is dead before it tears it apart." Author Unknown

November 3
The Debt Has Been Paid

*T**oday's Smile:* Ken and Harley were next door neighbors and had lived side by side for over 12 years. They were like brothers. They went fishing together, played golf together and along with their families they attended the same church. They always were the first to help each other in a time of need.

It was the fall season and Ken wanted to clean the leaves out of the eaves troughs and asked Harley whether he could borrow his ladder. "I'm sorry," said Harley, "but I loaned it to my son."

Recalling the words of his grandfather, Ken said, "My Grandpa used to tell us that we should never loan anything to our children because we will never get it back."

"Come to think of it," said Harley, "this is not even my ladder. It's my Dad's."

Today's Comment: I was taught that I should never borrow anything that I could not afford to replace if I broke the same. Borrowing has become an epidemic. Sisters borrow clothes from their sisters. Teens borrow the car from their parents. People of all ages borrow money from siblings and friends. We borrow money from the bank to purchase a house. Governments borrow from the next generations, and it would appear that those debts will never be repaid. "Seventy percent of college students carry credit cards and half of them have two or more cards."[1] I read that the average 21 year old has five credit cards, and over 40% of all U.S. families spend more each year than they earn.

Some wonder if they will ever get out of debt. However, there is a debt that has already been paid for us, the debt of sin. Too many are trying to pay off that debt by their good works. You cannot work off that debt. That debt requires a ransom, and none of us are capable of supplying a ransom. The Lord Jesus Christ became that ransom. He is both God and man, and He alone met the qualifications.

Let's pray that we will never fail to thank Him today for the supreme sacrifice of giving His life to pay the debt of our sin.

Today's Golden Nugget of Truth: "For there is one God and one Mediator between God and men, the Man Christ Jesus, who gave Himself a ransom for all. . ." First Timothy 2:5, 6

Today's Philosophical Tidbit: "One might better try to sail the Atlantic in a paper boat then try to get to heaven by good works." Charles Spurgeon

November 4
Do Not Judge

Today's Smile: Myron was a postal clerk at the local post office. He was used to irate customers and so he learned to respond in the calmest way that he could, hoping to diffuse some of the anger which customers vented. One day a woman came storming in and began complaining about their letter carrier. "What's the problem?" Myron asked, being as polite as possible.

"What's the problem? I'll tell you the problem," she said. "I went shopping this morning and when I came home I found this card saying that the letter carrier tried to deliver a package but no one was home. I want you to know that my husband was in all morning. He was waiting for the letter carrier. He never heard a thing!"

"I'm so sorry," said Myron. "I know your letter carrier very well and know that he would have rung the door bell, and if there was no response he would have knocked on the door. I'll talk to him about it."

"Good," she said, "and I hope it doesn't happen again. My husband has been waiting for this parcel for three weeks."

"What was it?" asked Myron.

"It's my husband's new hearing aids."

Today's Comment: It is so easy to blame someone else, when really we are the problem, we are the guilty one. The blame game is played all too often. I may think that it is not my fault, it is his fault; it is her fault.

An elder who resigned abruptly later asked to meet with the board to apologize for his behavior. He told the elders, "I wouldn't have done what I did if you had not forced me into it." That was not an apology.

I was taught many years ago that if there is an issue between you and another, even if you feel you're ninety-five percent right, take the step forward to initiate restitution. Pray that your goal in life will be to have a clear record, to be blameless.

Today's Golden Nugget of Truth: "Wherefore, beloved, seeing that ye look for such things, be diligent that ye may be found of Him in peace, without spot and blameless." Second Peter 3:14 (KJV)

Today's Philosophical Tidbit: "Character in a saint means the disposition of Jesus Christ persistently manifested." Oswald Chambers

November 5
Sweeter Than The Day Before

Today's Smile: Stewart wanted to do something special for his wife's 50th birthday. So, he rented a banquet room at a family restaurant and without his wife's knowledge invited their three children their spouses, grandchildren, other family members along with a few close friends. This was going to be one big surprise for Emily, his wife. Stewart had spared nothing when it came to paying for a fabulous meal and dessert.

Following the meal he had managed to put together a short program. Their two children gave a tribute to their mom, the three little grand-children sang a song for their grand-mother. One of her brothers gave a history of her growing up years telling what a mischievous little girl that she had been. The time came for opening gifts.

Stewart was so excited with his gift that he had purchased. He never was one much for shopping, but he had found a little gift shop that had a variety of music boxes. So he picked out one that sang "Happy Birthday" only he didn't like the color of the box. It was a bright orange. He asked if they had a music box that was grey, as it would compliment the rose colored walls of their bedroom. Well, the clerk quickly produced a grey music box, much to the delight of Stewart. However, he failed to listen to the tune it played.

When Emily opened her gift containing the music box and lifted the lid it immediately began to play, "The Old Grey Mare, She Ain't What She Used To Be."

Today's Comment: Well, none of us are what we used to be. Whether we are 30, 60 or 90 we change with each passing year. I recently compiled a class letter for my 1953 graduating class from Bible College. Some of my classmates sent photos. I would not have recognized a few of them if all I had was their photo. Sixty plus years has brought about many changes. We are not what we used to be.

As a child of God, we have received the gift of everlasting life. We are promised a new body that will never ever waste away or deteriorate. We won't need doctors, nurses, medicine, hospitals, etc; none of those will be needed in heaven. Oh what a joy awaits us. Your pain may be more than you can bear, but keep looking to Jesus. Pray that we will keep sweet as we walk through this earthly pilgrimage, knowing that He walks with us and in due time we will be welcomed into a place of everlasting joy.

Today's Golden Nugget of Truth: "Beloved, now we are children of God; and it has not yet been revealed what we shall be, but we know that when He is revealed, we shall be like Him, for we shall see Him as He is." First John 3:2, 3

Today's Philosophical Tidbit: "Many school class reunions today resemble a geriatric convention." A. Daniel Goldsmith

November 6
Searching For Satisfaction

Today's Smile: It was fall, and three new professors had begun teaching at a community college in Alberta. One had come from Eastern Canada, one from the United Kingdom and one from eastern Pennsylvania. Many of the men students at the college who had been raised on the Canadian Prairies, had learned to hunt wildlife at an early age. These three new professors all had to admit that they had never ever hunted wild life or game. They figured that they should try it once so that they could relate to some of their students.

They purchased the necessary gear, checked out library books about hunting big game, purchased the necessary licenses setting off one Saturday on their first hunting trip, that is their first without one or two of their students. When they saw the first set of tracks, the Math professor bent over and sniffed. "That's moose," he said, and off he went in pursuit of his moose.

That left two professors. They walked on a little further. Soon they saw more tracks in the snow. The science professor bent down and sniffed, "I think that is deer," he said, and off he went in pursuit of his animal. The remaining professor walked on by himself. He saw tracks that he had never seen in any of the hunting books that he had read. He got real low to the ground and sniffed and sniffed. He was having a little difficulty trying to detect what it might be, when suddenly a train came roaring down the tracks and ran over him.

Today's Comment: In an attempt to be accepted and relate to their peers, many are inclined to go sniffing around, trying this entertainment, mixing with that crowd, experimenting with this drug, watching that show and reading these magazines. The sniffing is endless. They are trying desperately to find happiness and fulfillment. For some they *sniffed* too long and met up with disaster. They got hooked on what they were doing, be it pornography, sex, drink, drugs or degrading entertainment.

You can sniff where you want, and do what you desire, but are you satisfied? May I ask that if you are one that is sniffing out different venues or interacting with different people or philosophies or religion for satisfaction, have you looked to Jesus? There is a God shaped vacuum in the life of every individual. If you try to fill that vacuum with anything other than Jesus, you'll never be satisfied.

Jesus will forgive your sin, and give you peace, joy, hope, complete satisfaction, fulfillment and everlasting life. But you must surrender your life to Him. He's only a prayer away.

Today's Golden Nugget of Truth: "You will show me the path of life; in Your right hand are pleasures forevermore." Psalm 16:11

Today's Philosophical Tidbit: "We have a right to believe whatever we want, but not everything we believe is right." Ravi Zacharias

November 7
Lost And Found

*T*oday's Smile: The story is told about a recent federal election in Canada. One of the Returning Officers in charge of a polling station was in a hurry to finalize things after the closing of the polls. She had everything in order knowing she had done a good job. The instruction manual said to place anything left on the table in the box provided and return to the election head office. It had been a long day, over 13 hours for her. So without thinking, she placed her cell phone and some of her lunch that remained, in the box.

She could not find her cell phone the following morning. She went to the election office to see if it had been found. One of the officers at the election head office took another officer with him and together the three of them went to the storeroom. Upon opening her box, there was her cell phone. "Oh, thank you, thank you," she said and she started to leave.

The officer called to her and said, "Lady would you also like your purse?"

Today's Comment: Losing things, forgetting where you placed things, do you have that problem? Of course you do, we all have mislaid things before today. Losing material things can be very discouraging, losing friends is disappointing, losing money can be disheartening. None of us rejoice when we lose things.

The Bible talks about losing one's soul. Some live their lives, going through the motions of the everyday activities, whether education, employment or entertainment. When life has ended, what remains is put in a box and into the ground. Is that the extent of your life?

The Lord Jesus Christ invites us to look to Him, the Lamb of God, the One who offered His life in payment for our sin. Thank God that when one prays and surrenders ones life to the Savior of the world, their lives are no longer lost, they are found, they are saved, they are secure for all eternity.

Today's Golden Nugget of Truth: "For what will it profit a man if he gains the whole world, and loses his own soul?" Mark 8:36

Today's Philosophical Tidbit: "Have you ever noticed that when you find a lost item, the last place that you looked is where you always find it." A. Daniel Goldsmith

November 8
The Humility Of Love

Today's Smile: The story is told about Kansas Senator Bob Dole and his wife Elizabeth. A magazine had written an article about the Senator and his wife's marriage. Along with the article was a photo of Senator Bob helping his wife make their bed. As the story goes, Dole received a letter from an irate male reader who complained telling the Senator that he should never be seen in a photo making a bed.

Bob Dole wrote back to the man and said, "You don't know the half of it. The only reason that Elizabeth was helping me was because the photographer was there taking her picture."

Today's Comment: If you are married, did you sit down in your first year deciding what chores you would do or what chores your spouse would do? We didn't. It just happened. I guess it was modeled at home. So when I got married, I took out the garbage; I cut the grass; I shovelled the snow. My wife has been a 'stay at home' mother most of our married years. She did the washing, ironing, cleaning house and cooking. I should also add that she was very much involved in the ministry of the church and regularly accompanied me in visitation. When I retired, it seemed natural that I should pick up a dish towel to dry the dishes plus doing the vacuuming. We never discussed it, it just happened. It was modeled for me when my father retired.

If your wife, men, has a job outside of the home, then comes home and does the cooking, cleaning, etc., that's like a second shift for her. May I encourage you husbands to pitch in where you can and help lighten her load.

Jesus was a good example. He sometimes did those tasks that no one else wanted to do: washing feet, fixing breakfast, helping children, and serving lepers. Pray that we will be willing to do small menial tasks. That's indicative of a big heart.

Today's Golden Nugget of Truth: "For I (Jesus) have given you an example, that you should do as I have done to you." John 13:15

Today's Philosophical Tidbit: "God is not so much concerned with your ability as with your availability." Author Unknown

November 9
Keeping Calm In The Storm

Today's Smile: Alan and his son were flying to Churchill, Manitoba, the polar bear capital of the world to do a story about the bears for a tourist magazine. As they were descending into Churchill, the airplane suddenly accelerated and began to climb. The plane then circled the airport a couple of times. Dwight, Alan's son, was getting quite nervous. He had not been on a plane as often as his dad. The passenger beside him sat reading a magazine and did not seem to be the least bit anxious.

Dwight spoke to his seat mate and said, "I wonder why the plane didn't land."

His seat mate said calmly, "I think that the pilot was checking the runway to see if the snow had been plowed."

"It looks plowed to me," said Dwight.

"No," said his seat mate, not even bothering to look out the window, "It's hasn't been cleared for the last three days."

"How can you tell? It sure looks clear."

"I know for a fact that it is not been cleared off, said the man, "I am the guy that keeps it clear and I've been in Winnipeg for the last couple of days."

Today's Comment: When you find yourself in a frightening experience, can you sit calmly and keep reading? You probably have heard the old story about the airplane that was experiencing some turbulence. Lightening lit up the darkening sky. There were ominous peals of thunder. The plane was like a cork tossed about on the ocean. No meals were served and everyone was told to stay put. Most passengers appeared upset, some were clinging tightly to their spouse or child, some were praying. All looked worried. A little girl sat very relaxed and seemingly not the least bit scared. A lady next to her asked her why she didn't seem worried. The little girl responded by saying, "My daddy is the pilot and he is taking me home."

Are you facing some dreadful decisions, a health concern or some upsetting news? Take these matters to the Lord in prayer and rest in His everlasting arms. He is the Pilot. He is still in control.

Today's Golden Nugget of Truth: "The eternal God is your refuge, and underneath are the everlasting arms. . ." Deuteronomy 33:27

Today's Philosophical Tidbit: "The beginning of anxiety is the end of faith, and the beginning of true faith is the end of anxiety." George Mueller

November 10
Servant Leadership

Today's Smile: Jordan had just been promoted to the position of Vice President of the small company where he was employed. He was extremely proud of this position. He bragged about it so much that his wife had had enough. She could take it no longer. "Listen, dear, this vice president title means no more than the title on your office door. I wish you would quit talking about it so much. Why they even have a vice president of peas down at that new supermarket."

"Really?" he replied. He wasn't so sure that she was telling him the truth and thought she had just made up the idea. So Jordan decided he would phone and find out whether it was really so.

He phoned and when the receptionist answered he asked to speak to the Vice President of peas. "You certainly may. Do you want the vice president of the canned peas or the frozen?"

Today's Comment: Promotions, degrees, titles seemingly elevate people way above the rest of us. Some become unapproachable. Their head swells so much it is a wonder they can walk through the door. For those who have received a promotion, they need to be congratulated. For those who have received a degree or multiple degrees, they earned it. For those who have had a title bestowed on them, they deserve it. All such persons are still human like the rest of mankind. We all have to wash our face, brush our teeth, put on our clothes and tie our shoes.

Christ is equal with God the Father. Christ is God. He was in heaven, but He condescended, He came down to our level becoming the God-Man that He might relate to us on our level and die for us. He humbled Himself. He became the Savior. He became a Servant. Pray that with all the accolades and promotions that any of us may receive, we keep our feet on the ground remembering that we are to be servants of our God.

Today's Golden Nugget of Truth: "But Jesus called them to Himself and said, 'You know that the rulers of the Gentiles lord it over them, and those who are great exercise authority over them. Yet it shall not be so among you, but whoever desires to become great among you, let him be your servant'." Matthew 20:25, 26

Today's Philosophical Tidbit: "Genuine New Testament Christianity doesn't hang out at headquarters; it gets into the trenches with the wounded and weary." Author Unknown

November 11
He Died For Me

Today's Smile: The Boeing 747 was filling up and the last few passengers were placing their luggage in the overhead compartments when suddenly, without any warning a five year old boy old started to throw a wild temper tantrum. His mother tried as best she could to calm him down, but the five year old continued to kick and scream and embarrass his red-faced mother.

The last passenger that was walking up the aisle was a smart looking U.S. Marine. The flustered mother caught his attention and pointed to her out of control son. The Marine leaned down and pointing to his chest, whispered something in the little fellow's ear. Immediately, the boy straightened up, stopped his kicking and screaming, let his mother fasten his seat belt and grabbed her hand. The passengers broke out in a spontaneous applause.

After the Marine had made his way to his seat, one of the flight attendants said to him, "Excuse me, sir," she asked quietly, "but may I ask what are the magic words that you used to calm down that little boy?"

The Marine smiled serenely and confided in her saying, "I showed him my pilot's wings, service stars, and battle ribbons, and explained that they entitled me to throw one passenger out of the plane door on any flight that I choose, and I was just about to make my selection for this flight."

Today's Comment: Today, November 11, is a day which is called in some places *Armistice Day*, or *Remembrance Day*, or *Veterans Day*. It is a day when we remember and pay tribute to those who fought for our freedoms and for many who died in the fighting. We, in the western world, owe a debt of gratitude to the armed forces.

As a young boy, growing up in Chatham, Ontario, I was very much aware that we were in a war, World War II. A Basic Training Camp was located in the city. There were uniformed soldiers on our streets, in our stores, in our churches and in our homes. Some of those later died in battle.

There is One who is greater than any of those soldiers. He did not wear a uniform nor was He respected and thanked like our soldiers were. He was despised and rejected. He was put to death by wicked men. His death was for our freedom, not just for a few years or for our life time, but for all eternity. The Lord Jesus Christ died that we might live, that we might have eternal life. Remember Him today! As we pray today, let us thank our Lord and Savior for His supreme sacrifice and also thank the thousands and thousands of service personnel who fought and died for our earthly freedom.

Today's Golden Nugget of Truth: "For scarcely for a righteous man will one die, yet perhaps for a good man someone would even dare to die. But God demonstrates His own love toward us, in that while we were still sinners, Christ died for us." Romans 5:6, 7

Today's Philosophical Tidbit: "The tragedy of war is that it uses man's best to do man's worst." Author Unknown

November 12
Self-Centered Or God-Centered

*T*oday's Smile: Calvin and Kathleen's neighbor popped into their place one evening and told them about her church's home Bible study group that she was in. She said, "I've really been enjoying that study group, until last night."

"What happened last night," asked Calvin.

"At last night's Bible study we discussed the fact that we should have someone or some small group to which we are accountable. Some of the folks present began to share a little about their besetting sin and requested prayer. It was a good evening, that is until I mustered up the courage to share my problem.

I requested prayer and shared how every morning before I went to work I spent about a half hour looking in the mirror. I wanted to make certain every hair was in place and that all my make up was just right. After all that I would just gaze at my reflection. So I confessed what I called my 'sin of vanity.' One woman in that group is a pain. Unfortunately she speaks most times before her brain is in gear. Before anyone could pray for me, she blurted out, 'Sister, that's not the sin of vanity, that's the sin of imagination'."

Today's Comment: Be it vanity or imagination, there are people that figure they have the *looks*. They gloat over their belief that there are not many people that are as beautiful or as handsome as they are. Why, if magazine editors only knew them, they would be on the cover of those magazines by the check out counter.

Then there are people who think they have the brains. They have more knowledge than their little head can hold and consequently are forever spilling it out on everyone else. They have all the answers. There are those who think that they have accomplished far more than the rest of us and start talking about themselves the moment they enter a room, telling us all what they have done. Their head is so big they have a hard time scratching it. Oh yes, and then there are those that are proud of their humility.

A self-centered life! That may be the way of the world, but it is not becoming to a child of God. Pray that our lives will not be self-centered but God-centered.

Today's Golden Nugget of Truth: "But he who glories, let him glory in the Lord." Second Corinthians 10:17

Today's Philosophical Tidbit: "Most of the trouble in the world is caused by people wanting to be important." T. S. Eliot

November 13
Readin' And Writin'

*T*oday's Smile: Keith was hired on as the new head librarian at the city library. He decided that instead of checking out the children's books by writing the names of the borrowers on the book cards, that he would have the children write their own names. He would then tell them that they were signing a *contract* ensuring that they would return the books on time.

The first customer of the day was a grade two student, who was surprised to see a new librarian. He shoved three books across the desk and gave his name to the librarian. Keith, the new librarian, pushed the books back and asked the young boy to sign the cards. The boy took his time printing his name on each book card and then, with a disgusting look, gave them back to the librarian, and said scornfully, "The other librarian that we had could write."

Today's Comment: As I sat pondering on something that I would write for *Today's Comment*, I wondered, "Have I ever thanked God that I learned to write? Have I ever thanked God that I learned to read?" I know that I have thanked God for His written Word, the Bible, but I could not think of a time when I specifically thanked God that I learned to read and write. Today, Lord, I say thank you.

I just turned around and looked at a book case behind me, full of books. I can go in the other room and see a book case in the hall, full of books. I can go in the store room and see shelves that I have built that hold more books. I can open any one of them and read what's printed. I can write, or type, as I am doing at this moment and convey my thoughts. We still have our "love letters" written before we were married. Writing is a way in which we convey our thoughts, our happenings, and our love. I have a fat file folder with encouragement notes and cards received throughout the years of my pastoral ministry.

We are blessed that not only can we communicate verbally we can put it on paper. We can read it again and again. We can pass it on to others. If you have never thanked God that you learned to read or write, do so today.

Today's Golden Nugget of Truth: "For everything that was written in the past was written to teach us, so that through endurance and the encouragement of the Scriptures we might have hope." Romans 15:4 (NIV)

Today's Philosophical Tidbit: "When I receive a note that says, 'You've made my day!' Then I can say, 'You've made my day'!" Author Unknown

November 14
It's Lonely At The Top

T oday's Smile: A noted psychiatrist was a guest speaker at an academic function in Washington, DC where several university professors, state governors, senators and CEO's were in attendance. After the psychiatrist had finished his presentation, he opened it up for questions. One of the politicians asked the psychiatrist, "Would you mind telling me, Doctor, how you detect a mental deficiency in somebody who appears completely normal?"

"That is fairly easy," he replied. "You ask a simple question which anyone should answer without any trouble. If the person hesitates in giving an answer, than you know that there is some mental deficiency there."

"What kind of question would you ask?" asked the politician.

"Well, you might ask the obvious, like this. 'Captain Cook made three trips around the world and died during one of those trips. Which trip was it'?"

The politician thought for a moment, and then with a nervous laugh said to the guest speaker, "You wouldn't happen to have another example would you? I must confess that I don't know much about history."

Today's Comment: If you have been reading this book for a couple of weeks or months or since January 1ˢᵗ, you will know that most of *Today's Smiles* are anecdotes or incidents about people. I think that we smile at jokes about people because we can sometimes identify with the same. As I said in the *Introduction* none of these *smiles* are meant to downgrade any one person or occupation. They are simply there to make us smile.

There is an abundance of *Talk Shows* that criticize people and I think the number one group of people receiving criticism today is our politicians. If you have ever been a politician, pastor, professor, etc. you likely have received your fill of criticism. I heard our mayor say recently that it does not matter what the council decides, they are right and wrong on every issue. Some agree and some disagree with decisions made. Maybe today would be a good day to turn our criticism into a compliment.

I know of a gentleman who was a director of a Christian organization. He asked for a brief meeting with Canada's Prime Minister. When he was ushered into the PM's office, the PM asked how he could help. This dear brother responded with words to this effect, "I didn't come, Mr. Prime Minister, with any big request, I just came to have prayer with you."

We may never be in a president, prime minister, or any other leader's office, but we can pray for them. You may wish to write a brief note and tell them that you are praying for them. Being a leader makes one an easy target. It is also a lonely spot to be in.

Today's Golden Nugget of Truth: "Therefore I exhort first of all that supplications, prayers, intercessions, and giving of thanks be made for all men, for kings and all who are in authority, that we may lead a quiet and peaceable life in all godliness and reverence." First Timothy 2:1, 2

Today's Philosophical Tidbit: "Politics is more dangerous than war, for in war you are only killed once." Winston Churchill

November 15
Introducing The Savior

*T**oday's Smile:* "Being Billy Graham's brother-in-law has its special responsibilities and also its lighter side. Leighton (Ford) has been introduced as Billy's mother-in-law, as his son-in-law, and once as his sister-in-law! The grandest fun came unexpectedly from a distinguished pastor and educator who was presenting Leighton to students in a college chapel.

'We are happy to have Leighton Ford as our speaker this morning,' he began. 'Perhaps some of you don't know that Leighton is married to Billy Graham's brother.' The crowd tittered and this venerable gentleman, nonplused by the reaction, was so thrown off his usually impeccable stride that he concluded, 'That makes Leighton Billy Graham's son-in-law.'

"Now the audience was beginning to double over with laughter. The speaker, startled and not realizing what he had said, plunged on to total disaster: 'So. . . now I present to you, Leighton Ford's brother-in-law, Billy Graham'!"[1]

Today's Comment: I once introduced a guest speaker for the church's anniversary weekend, by saying, "This pastor needs no introduction, only a conclusion." He was a friend with a great sense of humor, so I got away with it.

My question is how well do we do in introducing our family or friends? Are we proud and happy to introduce them? A person introducing a speaker sometimes says, "It gives me great pleasure to introduce. . ."

Are we as pleased and honored to introduce our Savior to others, or are we ashamed. Some people are so embarrassed to give God thanks for their food in a restaurant that to disguise their action, they've been known to rub their eyes or scratch their eyebrows while in prayer.

Pray that God will give us opportunities to present Christ to others, and when the opportunity is there, do so without embarrassment.

Today's Golden Nugget of Truth: "For I am not ashamed of the gospel of Christ: for it is the power of God unto salvation to every one that believeth; to the Jew first, and also to the Greek." Romans 1:16 (KJV)

Today's Philosophical Tidbit: "To avoid the risk of losing their religion, a lot of people don't take it to work with them." Author Unknown

November 16
Coping With Criticism

*T*oday's Smile: Canon Glover was guest speaker at Trinity Anglican Church. Ellis had grown up with the Canon and so invited their Anglican priest and the visiting Canon for a late Sunday dinner. Brianna, Ellis' daughter, had broken her leg earlier that week and so his wife stayed home with their daughter. Ellis helped his wife with the preparation of the evening meal and as he did so he reported on the morning service to her.

When everyone had arrived and were in the midst of eating their dinner, Brianna surprised everyone by saying that, "You must have been pretty brave to be at church this morning?"

"Why do you ask that?" inquired the Canon.

"I heard Dad tell Mom earlier that there was a canon in the pulpit this morning and that the choir murdered the anthem while the organist drowned everybody!"

Today's Comment: If we were the recipient of criticism, how would we deal with it? I read about Sir Winston Churchill, a man who exemplified integrity and respect in the face of opposition. During his last year in office, he attended an official ceremony. A row or two behind him were two men, and one of them began talking softly to the other. "That's Winston Churchill. They say he is getting senile. They say he should step aside and leave the running of the nation to more dynamic and capable men."

When the ceremony was over, Churchill turned to the men and said, "Gentlemen, they also say Churchill is deaf!"

One public official had embroidered and placed on the wall of his office these words: "To avoid criticism: Do nothing, say nothing, be nothing." That is impossible to do, unless of course you are a hermit living in the vast northern wilderness all by yourself. It is good to learn from any criticism directed at you.

James Kennedy, founding pastor of Coral Ridge Presbyterian Church, Fort Lauderdale, Florida, said: "Benefit from your critics. Let your critics be the unpaid watchers after your soul, the beneficiaries of your career. Let them help you along the way."[1]

Abraham Lincoln is a good example of that. When a young lady told him that he was an abominable boor, ill-mannered and illiterate, he took it to heart and worked diligently to become one of the most literate men who ever lived, a man whose wit and kindliness is legend. Pray that you will not let your critics crush you.

Today's Golden Nugget of Truth: "When they hurled their insults at Him, He did not retaliate; when He suffered, He made no threats. Instead, He entrusted Himself to Him who judges justly." First Peter 2:23 (NIV)

Today's Philosophical Tidbit: "When life gives you lemons, make lemonade." Author Unknown

November 17
Listen Carefully
To What Is Being Said

oday's Smile: A professor, one of his students, and one of the custodians from the local Community College went deer hunting. They had only been out about an hour when a huge buck crossed right in front of them. All three were ready at the trigger so it sounded like one shot. The buck fell to the ground. As they were approaching the animal, they realized that they had a big problem. Which one of the three of them actually shot the deer?

As they were trying to figure out their problem, a game warden appeared, checking for hunting licenses. They all produced their license. As they chatted, he learned who they were and the problem they were experiencing. This wasn't the first time that the warden had to deal with this kind of problem. It didn't take him long. "Well," said the warden, addressing the student, "It was you!"

"How did you come to the conclusion that it was my student's shot?" asked the professor.

"That was easy," said the game warden, "It went in one ear and out the other."

Today's Comment: How often has your wife or maybe your mother asked the question as to whether you were listening? Oh yes, we heard her talking, but we were not listening. The same goes for listening to the preacher. When you sit in that pew, you hear him talking, but are you listening?

We should take this a step further asking ourselves if we are listening to God? How long has it been since God has spoken to you and you heard what He said? A follow-up question would be, when you have listened and really heard what He said, did you do or say what He asked? Pray that when God speaks to you today that you are listening.

Today's Golden Nugget of Truth: "Moreover He said to me: Son of man, receive into your heart all My words that I speak to you, and hear with your ears." Ezekiel 3:10

Today's Philosophical Tidbit: "An open ear is the only believable sign of an open heart." David Augsburger

November 18
Make Restitution

*T*oday's Smile: Presley, the plumber, lived on a small acreage on the edge of town. He had a little hobby farm with a couple of cows, about 50 chickens and a few turkeys. He usually sold about ten turkeys before Thanksgiving but also another ten or so before Christmas. He enjoyed the fun of farming when his regular work day was finished, plus the added income more than paid for his taxes.

He was installing new faucets for a neighbor who lived about a quarter of a mile down the road. In the course of their conversation, the customer told Presley that he had stolen a turkey. He began to realize that it was wrong so in order to appease his conscience, he asked Presley if he would like it.

"No thanks," said Presley. "If your conscience is bothering you, I would think that the best thing would be to ask the person from whom you stole the turkey to accept it back."

"I offered it to the owner, but his response was 'no thanks'."

"Well, if the owner won't take it back, then I suppose you can keep it."

When Presley was checking on his feathered creatures that evening he noticed that one of his turkeys was missing.

Today's Comment: In 1950 I was returning to Bible College for my sophomore year. Three of us fellows set out from Detroit in an old Model A Ford to make the 2,200 mile trip west. We didn't make many miles in a day, 35 mph being our average speed, up to 45mph whenever we were going downhill. The first day, Don, the owner of the car told my buddy Neil and me that he had to make a detour and go to Alpena, Michigan. Going through Alpena, rather than straight north to the Straits of Mackinac was about an extra 90 miles. Why the detour? Well, Don had lived in Alpena as a young boy and had stolen some small article from the dime store, as they were known, probably a Woolworth or Kresge store. He drove out of his way to go to that store and give them fifty cents for the five or ten cent article which he had taken, ten or fifteen years earlier.

If you have stolen an article, lied, cheated, or whatever, make it right. Go back to the person or whoever and settle the account. Better to bear the shame and have a clear conscience, than continue to hide the sin and be tormented. Pray that we will be prompt in any confession or restitution that we need to make.

Today's Golden Nugget of Truth: "If we confess our sins, He is faithful and just to forgive us our sins and to cleanse us from all unrighteousness." First John 1:9

Today's Philosophical Tidbit: "Every confession of sin is a fresh installment of the consciousness of God, a barrier against the further commission of sin." Author Unknown

November 19
Scared Silly

Today's Smile: The Manchester Evening Times, Manchester, England, printed a story some years ago about a passenger in a taxi heading for Salford Station. The passenger leaned over to ask the driver a question and gently tapped him on the shoulder to get his attention. The cab driver screamed, lost control of the cab, nearly hit a bus, drove up over the curb and stopped just inches from a large plate glass window.

For a few moments everything was silent in the cab. Then, the shaking driver said, "Are you OK? I'm so sorry, but you scared the daylights out of me."

The badly shaken passenger apologized to the driver and said, "I didn't realize that a mere tap on the shoulder would startle someone so badly."

The driver replied, "No, no, I'm the one who is sorry. It's entirely my fault. Today is my very first day driving a cab. I've been driving a hearse for 25 years."

Today's Comment: I'm sure that you've all been frightened, or as the expressions go, "scared silly, scared out of your wits, scared the daylights out of you," and many more. Have you ever been at the place where you thought you were about to die. Were you scared? I don't remember the source, but I read about a comedian who was in an auto accident. A friend arrived at the scene of the accident. His dying comedian friend kept saying, "Don't let me die, don't let me die, I'm not ready to die." He died!

Thomas Payne the leading atheistic writer in the day of the early American colonies said as he was dying, "Stay with me, for God's sake; I cannot bear to be left alone. O Lord, help me! O God, what have I done to suffer so much? What will become of me hereafter? I would give worlds if I had them, that *The Age of Reason* had never been published. O Lord, help me! Christ, help me! . . .No, don't leave; stay with me! Send even a child to stay with me; for I am on the edge of Hell here alone. If ever the Devil had an agent, I have been that one."[1]

By contrast, as Evangelist Dwight L. Moody of the 19th century was dying. He awakened from sleep and said: "Earth recedes. Heaven opens before me. If this is death, it is sweet! There is no valley here. God is calling me, and I must go!" Moody's son said, "Father, you are dreaming." "No, I am not dreaming. . . This is my triumph, this is my coronation day! It is glorious!"[2]

As a child of God we can be assured that when the day comes that we leave this earth, Jesus will give us peace, comfort, and joy like we've never known. What's more, we will not be alone. Pray that you have that blessed assurance and you are ready for your final day.

Today's Golden Nugget of Truth: "Yea, though I walk through the valley of the shadow of death, I will fear no evil, for You are with me. . ." Psalm 23:4

Today's Philosophical Tidbit: "The greatness of our fears shows us the littleness of our faith." Author Unknown

November 20
Was It Just A Coincidence

Today's Smile: Pat was a junior at the university and desperately wanted to go home for Thanksgiving and surprise his family. However, he was flat broke, so decided to hitchhike. Hitch hiking isn't always the safest mode of travel anymore, but Pat prayed about it. When he left the campus, the weather was pleasant. He got a ride for about 30 miles, but that was with a farmer. He was dropped off out on the highway, a few miles from town. Not only was it beginning to get dark, but it also started raining.

He was soaked to the skin, when suddenly out of the darkness a car was coming slowly and stopped right opposite him. Without thinking, he opened the door and got into the back seat. He realized that the car was slowly moving again, but there was no driver. Through the darkness, he noticed that the car was headed for a curve in the road. He was frightened and began to pray. Just then a hand appeared through the open driver's window and turned the wheel so that it rounded the curve nicely. It happened a second time, and every time that there was a curve, or it looked like it was headed for the ditch, this same hand appeared.

After enduring this ride for two or three miles, the car once again stopped in the darkness of night. Pat knew this was his time. He jumped out of the car and began to run as fast as he could. Within about five minutes, he came to a country service station with a restaurant. There he shared his frightening experience as he sipped on hot chocolate.

About ten minutes later, a couple of fellows, also soaking wet and cold, came into the restaurant for a hot drink and to dry off a bit. They looked for a table, and in so doing spotted Pat. "Look Wyatt," said one of them, "there's that dummy that got into our car when we were pushing it."

Today's Comment: How often have we seen God intervene in answer to our prayer, and sometimes at the last moment? I was talking with a person by telephone. They shared a problem that they were facing. I prayed and asked God to do a miracle. Within three minutes of ending that call, my phone rang. A friend stated that he had been thinking about this person that I had been praying with and wondered if there was a problem or need and whether he could help. He did.

Some people would like to call me a dummy. They say that it was just a coincidence. Call me a dummy, say it was coincidental. I know that God answered that prayer. God's answer may not always be yes. It might be "no" or it might be "wait," but that should not stop us from praying. When you pray, seeing God answer, is not coincidental, it is providential.

Today's Golden Nugget of Truth: "Pray without ceasing." First Thessalonians 5:17 (KJV)

Today's Philosophical Tidbit: "A coincidence is an event in which a sovereign God chooses to remain anonymous." Author Unknown

November 21
God Is Not In A Rut

*T*oday's Smile: A young couple got married. When the wife prepared to bake a ham to celebrate their first Thanksgiving, she carefully cut off each end before placing it in the pan.

Her husband asked her why she did that and she replied, "I don't know, it's what my mother always did. But I can ask her."

She called Mom, who responded, "I always saw your Grandma do it, so I did the same."

They decided to check further, so the young woman called Grandma, who explained, "It was the only way I could get it to fit into my pan."

Today's Comment: Traditions! Traditions! Are we in a rut? How often do we do something because it has just always been done that way? We don't know why we do what we do, but we saw someone else do it, or maybe we have been told this is the way it should be done.

God loves variety. He is not in a rut. Look at creation. When it comes to plants consider the tiny duckweed or the mighty redwood. Take as another example the amoeba and the blue whale. What about the variety of color, of climate? Humanity has its variety. Revelation speaks of "every tribe and tongue and people and nation" (Rev. 5:9)." There are different races and different languages. The list goes on.

Do we like variety? Of course we do. We have a variety of foods, clothes, houses, cars, educational programs, jobs, etc. What about our music in church? We have the contemporary, the blended the traditional, the liturgical and more. Some pastors preach topical sermons and some are textual, or preach through one Bible book at a time. When it comes to sharing the gospel, there is mass evangelism or person to person. There are small groups but also large groups. There is radio, television, internet, and the printed page. There are schools and clinics, a multitude of different ministries. Add to this the great variety of church buildings in which we assemble weekly. God delights in it all. He is a God of variety. So don't think that your way of worship or evangelism or your way of doing things is the only way. Pray that we will see that God uses all sizes, shapes, colors, ministries, etc to accomplish His purpose.

Today's Golden Nugget of Truth: "Then God saw everything that He had made, and indeed it was very good. . ." Genesis 1:31

Today's Philosophical Tidbit: "A rut is a grave with both ends knocked out." L.E. Maxwell

November 22
Obey The Law

*T**oday's Smile:* Alf and Gordon had so much fun last year hunting elk in the Yukon that they went back again. They had a pilot fly them to a remote part of that territory. When the pilot returned to pick them up, they greeted him with their success story. Between the two of them they had killed six elk.

They started to load their gear and their six elk into the plane. The pilot stopped them. "You can only load four of those. This airplane will be overweight with six elk. I'm sorry, but you will have to leave two of them here."

Alf and Gordon were furious and said, "We came up here to the Yukon last year. The pilot, that we had then, let us load more than four. We had six elk last year and the airplane was the same make and model as this one." The pilot finally consented to let them load their six elk, on the basis of their experience the year before.

About ten minutes after taking off the plane began to sputter and lose altitude. The pilot did his best to keep the plane airborne, but within about 90 seconds, they crash landed. Once they managed to exit the downed plane, Gordon turned to Alf and asked, "Do you know where we are? Do you recognize this area?"

"Yes, I do," said Alf. "I think we are about a half mile away from where we crash landed last year."

Today's Comment: Rules or laws are made to be kept and obeyed. Grant it you may be familiar with some ridiculous laws, but most laws are there for a reason. There are laws that if obeyed are good for our health, our happiness, our prosperity, our protection, etc.

Breaking those laws may result in injustice, inconvenience, injuries, etc. It pays in the long run to obey the laws. If some laws are outrageous, there are ways and means whereby we can deal with them

There are laws that are not man-made. There are laws written into our universe by our Creator. To name but one, you dare not defy the law of gravity, unless you are equipped with anti-gravity equipment. More important than all laws and guidelines is the Law of God. The Word of God. The Bible. That must be obeyed! There are consequences if disobeyed. Pray that we will be obedient and follow the commands of the Lord as recorded in the Bible, the Word of God.

Today's Golden Nugget of Truth: "If they obey and serve Him, they shall spend their days in prosperity, and their years in pleasures. But if they do not obey and serve Him, they shall perish. . ." Job 36:11, 12

Today's Philosophical Tidbit: "If you are going the wrong way on God's one way street, stop, look, and listen, God is shouting at you to turn around before you have a tragic ending." A. Daniel Goldsmith

November 23
Falsifying The Facts

oday's Smile: It was the day before Thanksgiving and the butcher was just locking up the shop when a man pounded on the door. "Please let me in," said the man, "I forgot to buy a turkey and my wife will kill me if I go home without one."

"O. K," said the butcher. "Let me see what's left." He went into the freezer and discovered that there was only one scrawny turkey left. He took it out to show the man.

"That one's too skinny. What else have you got?" said the man. The butcher took the bird back into the freezer and waited a few seconds then took the same turkey back out to the customer.

"That one doesn't look any better either," said the man. "You had better give both of them to me."

Today's Comment: Dishonesty is everywhere: from the students in the elementary schools, to our elected government representatives.

Cheating on an exam? Failing to declare all income received for work done? Overstating the value of an item when claiming insurance for stolen or damaged goods? Filing a dishonest tax report? Altering the company's financial books and pocketing the money?

I read about a staff meeting in which the phone rang in the staff room. The newest employee answered the phone. "It's for you, boss!"

The boss replied, "Tell him I not here."

The new staff member handed the phone to his boss and said, "Here, you tell him!" His boss was furious. The new man later told his boss, "If I had lied to the caller, what makes you think that I will always tell you the truth?" That young man earned the respect of his boss and became his most trusted co-worker.

Pray that we will be honest in all of our dealings.

Today's Golden Nugget of Truth: "These six things the Lord hates, Yes, seven are an abomination to Him: a proud look, a lying tongue, hands that shed innocent blood, a heart that devises wicked plans, feet that are swift in running to evil, a false witness who speaks lies, among brethren." Proverbs 6:16-19

Today's Philosophical Tidbit: "Who lies for you will lie against you." Bosnian Proverb

November 24
Hope In A Heartless World

Today's Smile: It has been a challenge to find 366 clean jokes or humorous stories. The jokes have come from many sources, one of which was from some of my old sermon notes. I found this one today in a sermon that I preached several years ago.

A hungry old man, almost to the point of collapsing, was wandering the streets hoping he would find someone who would give him some money for a meal. He spotted a sign which said, *Inn Of Saint George And The Dragon*. He thought that with the name of a saint, perhaps someone would take pity on him. He was too embarrassed to go in the front door, so he walked around to the kitchen and knocked on the door. He asked the woman who opened the door, "Please ma'am, would you be able to give me a few scraps of food. I am famished."

She was in no mood to help this poor fellow. "A scrap of food?" she growled. "For a foul-smelling beggar? No way. Get lost!"

He crossed over the road and was about to head down the street when he glanced back at the Inn and saw the sign again, *Inn Of Saint George And The Dragon*. He decided to go back. He knocked again on the kitchen door. "Now what do you want?" the woman asked angrily.

"Ma'am," thinking that maybe this woman must be the dragon, "I am wondering if Saint George is in, if I could speak with him this time?"

Today's Comment: Have you ever met up with people that you would describe as dragon-like? That is a name in the Bible which is used to describe the devil. "He laid hold of the dragon, that serpent of old, who is the Devil and Satan. . ." Revelation 20:2.

Our news media is filled with troubling stories from every corner of the globe. "Beatings, physical torture, confinement, isolation, rape, severe punishment, imprisonment, slavery, discrimination in education and employment, and even death are just a few examples of the persecution they (Christians) experience on a daily basis."[1] Our western culture no longer fears the Lord. Biblical standards are being replaced with doctrines of demons. What are we to do?

Once again, I found an answer in one of my old sermons. I did not note the source accept to say that it was in a monthly letter received from Billy Graham. This is what Mr. Graham said: "To many people, the world seems to be out of control, but those of us who are trusting Jesus Christ know that God is controlling the ultimate outcome. We are to be faithful to Him no matter what may happen in the future."

Pray that we will not lose hope when we see what is happening in our world. What we are witnessing today was predicted. See Mark 13:7. It is not a matter of *if* but *when*. Pray that we will remain faithful to God, trusting in Him. Pray also for those suffering saints, our brothers and sisters in Christ, who are being persecuted for righteousness sake.

Today's Golden Nugget of Truth: "Blessed are you when they revile and persecute you, and say all kinds of evil against you falsely for My sake. Rejoice and be exceedingly glad, for great is your reward in heaven, for so they persecuted the prophets who were before you." Matthew 5:11, 12

Today's Philosophical Tidbit: "Fellowship with God means warfare with the world." Charles E. Fuller

November 25
How Can I Say Thanks

*T**oday's Smile:* Wanda's grandparents received a pumpkin pie as a Thanksgiving gift from their next door neighbor. As nice as the gesture was, it was obvious from the first bite that the pie tasted horrible. It was so inedible that Wanda's grandparents put it in the garbage.

The grandparents were always so appreciative of what others did for them in their reclining years that they wondered how they could graciously and tactfully thank their neighbors. The grand-mother was clever with words and so she wrote a brief thank you note which read: "Thank you so very much for the pumpkin pie. It was so thoughtful of you folks to treat us this way. We want to assure you that a pie like that doesn't last very long in our house!"

Today's Comment: I'm sure that you have had a similar experience. How did you respond when you really didn't like what was given to you? My wife and I were once the recipients of a pigeon, feathers and all, shot by one of our parishioners. I had never eaten pigeon, and the sight of the bird didn't help my stomach. What was I to do? Well, I left it in the trunk of the car for a few days and then threw it in the garbage. Fortunately, the man never asked how I enjoyed it. Thankfully, I've never been given another pigeon, although I've been told since that it is a delicacy for some people.

More important than how we respond to the gift of a pigeon, a sweater, a DVD or whatever else we may have received is how we respond to God's gift, the gift of eternal life. Are we grateful? So many people have turned their backs on God. They will not listen. They are turned off without knowing or listening to what God is offering to them. I printed a little tract, *How To Get To Heaven From British Columbia*. People have thanked me for it. Thus far, at the time of writing, only one person has refused to take it from me. To read it see Appendix "B"

Pray that when you seek to share about God's gift of salvation that God will prepare hungry hearts and open hands, people who will gladly receive what you say or what you share.

Today's Golden Nugget of Truth: "Enter into His gates with thanksgiving, and into His courts with praise. Be thankful to Him, and bless His name." Psalm 100:4

Today's Philosophical Tidbit: "Even though we can't have all we want, we ought to be thankful we don't get what we deserve." Author Unknown

November 26
Facing Problems

oday's Smile: Jesse and Lila had moved from Mississippi and bought a home from two elderly sisters in Buffalo, New York. Three of their four children were living in that area so they wanted to be nearer to their children and grandchildren. When they purchased the house in August, they were a little concerned about facing a winter. They had heard that the storms that blow in off of Lake Erie can be mighty fierce. Anyhow, they figured if those two elderly sisters had survived, having lived in that house for thirty years, then surely they could make it.

Their first winter in Buffalo caught them off guard. Winter came earlier than expected and they woke up one morning to find that the walls were covered with frost and there was a blast of cold air coming in under the exterior doors, plus about a foot of snow outside. Being unable to reach the sisters, Jesse phoned their younger brother, who lived in the area, asking him how his elderly sisters had managed to keep warm in the winter. His conversation with the brother was rather brief.

"What did he say?" asked Lila.

He said, "They have gone to Florida every winter for the last thirty years."

Today's Comment: We all face problems. How do we handle them? Many people deal with the problem head on. They do their best to rectify or repair whatever they are facing. If they run into more problems they seek out some help, either as advice or physical help. Others are inclined to walk away from the problem, doing nothing. They let it rot or ruin, fester or fail. They simply do nothing. They buy another part instead of repairing. They divorce and get another spouse instead of resolving their differences.

If Thomas Edison had walked away from his first one or two attempts at making a light bulb, we may still be in the dark. Are you facing a problem? Have you tried to fix it? Get some help if you need it. Have you prayed about it? I've found that praying when faced with a problem oft times will bring a quicker solution than any other approach.

Problems? Take them to the Lord in prayer. "The Savior can solve every problem, the tangles of life can undo; there is nothing too hard for Jesus, there is nothing that He cannot do."[1]

Today's Golden Nugget of Truth: "The Lord also will be a refuge for the oppressed, a refuge in times of trouble. And those who know Your name will put their trust in You; for You, Lord, have not forsaken those who seek You." Psalm 9:9, 10.

Today's Philosophical Tidbit: "We may ask why, when we look at things around us; but we should ask why not, when we look to God; He will help us." A. Daniel Goldsmith

November 27
Are You Wounded?

*T*oday's Smile: A woman, pending a divorce, was meeting with a judge. The judge asked, "What are the grounds for your divorce?"

She replied, "I have four acres with a three bedroom bungalow right beside a small stream."

"No," he said. "What I meant was, what is the foundation of this case?"

"The foundation is cement," she responded.

"I mean," he continued, "What about your relations? What are they like?"

"Oh, I have an uncle and aunt that live here in the city, and also my husband's parents. They're all very loving and caring."

"Do you have a real grudge?" the judge asked.

"No," she replied, "We have a two-car carport."

The judge, realizing that he wasn't getting anywhere with this woman, asked, "Is there any infidelity in your marriage?"

"Yes," she replied. "Both of my children, my daughter and my son have hi-fidelity stereo sets. We don't like their kind of music but the answer to your question is 'yes'."

"Ma'am, does your husband ever beat you up?"

"He goes to work early, so he beats me up Monday through Friday, but on the weekend I beat him up."

Finally, in frustration, the judge asked, "Lady, why, may I ask are you asking for a divorce?"

"Oh, I don't want a divorce," she replied. "I've never ever wanted a divorce. I promised when I married him, 'till death do us part.' My husband is the one that wants the divorce. He says that he is unable to communicate with me!"

Today's Comment: No one wins in a divorce. The children hurt, the family relations are divided, many friends vanish, and the couple ends up angry and confused. Divorced people need to be the recipients of some tender loving care. They need help, and especially if one or both are willing to accept help. Some churches have a wonderful support team and a caring ministry that reaches out to these broken ones. Unfortunately, there are a few churches that immediately ostracize the divorcees totally shunning and ignoring the couple.

If you are divorced try to find a church that will welcome you and offer help. You may be severely wounded, but you can be healed. There is life after divorce!

Pray today for divorcees within your circle of friends. One spouse may have been the cause for the divorce or both may be equally guilty of such separation. Whatever the reason, they are hurting. They need your prayers and maybe your help.

Today's Golden Nugget of Truth: "The Lord upholds all who fall and raises up all who are bowed down." Psalm 145:14

Today's Philosophical Tidbit: "The church is the only army that shoots its own wounded soldiers." Charles Swindoll

November 28
A Sensitive Spirit

*T*oday's Smile: Ronald bought a ticket for an evening of music presented by the city symphony orchestra and featuring Strauss waltzes. Ron went early. He had a ticket for a seat with a good unobstructed view. He was there long before most people. As the evening concert goers began arriving, they found him stretched out on three theatre seats enjoying a good sleep. They didn't disturb him, not until three people with tickets matching those three seats arrived and wanted to be seated. An usher asked him to move. "We need those three seats. Will you please move?" Ronald grunted at him and didn't move. Soon the usher had the manager there. The manager demanded that he please move. Once again, he mumbled something and made hand gestures which they took to mean, go away.

In a few short moments, the manager returned with a security officer. The officer asked that he move immediately or he would remove him from the theatre. "You're occupying three seats and these three people here have tickets for these seats. Let me see your ticket."

"It's in. . . my. . . back pocket," said Ronald. The officer reached in and retrieved the ticket and showed it to the manager.

"Oh my goodness," said the manager, "this ticket is for the first row in the balcony. This guy has fallen from the balcony."

"Yea," groaned Ronald, "tha's where I was. I was. . . in the. . . bal. . . cony!"

Today's Comment: There are people all around us who are hurting and in need of help. Do we simply pass them by? Many years ago my wife and I were struggling with a big decision. Two *prayer warriors* in our church contacted us. Neither one had conversed with the other; neither did they have any idea what we were facing. They both felt a heavy burden to pray for us. They both contacted us and we were able to share with them what we had been going through thanking them for their prayers. Similarly, it is very rewarding to know when we have sensed a burden for others when they, too, were walking a difficult path.

My question is, how many times have we missed an opportunity to come alongside of another and pray with them or help them? Pray that we will walk close to our God so that we will be sensitive to the needs of others and be able to lift up the fallen, encourage the oppressed and bring healing to the wounded.

Today's Golden Nugget of Truth: "For I was hungry and you gave Me food; I was thirsty and you gave Me drink' I was a stranger and you took Me in; I was naked and you clothed Me, I was sick and you visited Me; I was in prison and you came to Me." Matthew 25:35, 36

Today's Philosophical Tidbit: "Sometimes all a person needs is a hand to hold and a heart to understand." Author Unknown

November 29
Messed Up The Plans

*T*oday's Smile: Carter and Hugh loved to go hunting. They lived in the state of Maine but decided to explore some woods that were totally new to them. This was their first venture into the area of Cape Breton Island. As they were walking through the woods they came upon a huge hole in the ground. "Wow," said Carter, "that's some hole. I can't even see the bottom of it."

Hugh said, "Why don't we throw something down there and listen carefully and see how long it takes to hit bottom."

"Great idea! Hey, look here is an old automobile transmission," said Carter, "give me a hand and we'll throw this thing in." So the two of them picked up the transmission carried it over to the edge of the hole and on the count of three heaved it into the hole. As they were standing listening, looking over the edge, they suddenly heard a rustling behind them. As they turned around to look, they saw a goat come crashing headlong through the underbrush. It ran up to the hole and without stopping a second, jumped in headfirst. While they were standing wondering what that was all about, a farmer appeared, "You fellers didn't happen to see a goat around here anywhere, did you?"

"Funny that you should ask," said Carter. "We were standing here a couple minutes ago looking into this hole when a goat came running out of the bushes. It must have been running a hundred miles an hour."

"Naw, impossible. He was chained to an old transmission."

Today's Comment: Did you ever do something and later you found out that you had messed up someone's plans? I recall, as a young fellow, working at a family summer Christian camp. The founder and director's daughter was getting married in the main camp auditorium. Being that it was a summer camp, the auditorium was plain and simple and the floor was unpainted cement. At the front was a roll of white plastic.

As the guests were filling up the auditorium, one of them came to me and said, "That roll of plastic should have been unrolled." I wanted to be helpful, so I offered to unroll it. I walked to the front and taking hold of the plastic started to unroll the same, backing up in the center aisle all the way to the back of the auditorium. As soon as I stood up, I was bombarded by some of those in charge of the wedding. "Danny, who told you to do that? That plastic was to be unrolled just before the bride walked down the aisle." I don't remember what I did after that, but I didn't want to face the bride and her family.

God has a wonderful plan for our life. We can so easily do things our way and neglect to ask Him first what He would have us do. Pray that we will seek God first, lest we mess up His plan for us.

Today's Golden Nugget of Truth: "A man's heart plans his way, but the Lord directs his steps." Proverbs 16:9

Today's Philosophical Tidbit: "One of the most common errors is to mistake our wish for God's will." Author Unknown

November 30
Laughter Is The Best Medicine

T oday's Smile: A flight, scheduled to go from Denver to Houston, Texas was canceled. One loan agent was re-booking a long line of disgruntled travelers. One angry passenger pushed his way to the front of the line. He slapped his ticket down on the counter and said, "I must be on this flight and it must be first class."

The weary worn agent replied, "I'm sorry sir. I'll be pleased to help you, but these folks were ahead of you and I need to try rebooking their flights first. I'll get you on a flight, but please be patient.

The passenger was not impressed. Shouting at the agent so that all the passengers who were in line could hear, "Do you have any idea who I am?"

Without any hesitation, the agent smiled, picked up the public address microphone. "May I have your attention please?" she began, her voice bellowing throughout the terminal, "We have a passenger here who does not know who he is. If anyone can help him find his identity, please come to gate B-42."

Today's Comment: One can only assume that there were no longer any disgruntled passengers waiting to be re-scheduled to another flight. They had to be having a good laugh.

I recently read that scientific studies have shown that laughter is a miracle medicine. I read much more than I can place in today's comment, about how good laughter is for you. Here are a few brief statements regarding laughter.

Some articles have stated that laughter prolongs your life. The Bible testifies to that. Proverbs 14:30 says: "A relaxed attitude lengthens a man's life." Other writers have said that it makes you feel better. It gives you a positive outlook. It serves as a shock absorber to the stress that we face. Several articles stated that laughing 100 times in a day is as good as a 15 minute workout on an exercise machine.

President Abraham Lincoln was once asked how he coped with all of the stresses of the Civil War. He replied, "If it hadn't been for laughter, I could not have made it."

If you are not one given to laughter, maybe today, find one thing, read one thing, talk to one person that might make you laugh and lift your spirit a bit. It has been said that "a spoonful of honey will attract more flies than a gallon of vinegar."

So may God help us to sweeten up today, wear a smile and enjoy laughing and try to make someone else laugh. We may attract more non-Christians than when we display a sour looking face.

Pray that we might brighten someone's pathway today with a little bit of humor.

Today's Golden Nugget of Truth: "Always be full of joy in the Lord: I say it again, rejoice!" Philippians 4:4 (TLB)

Today's Philosophical Tidbit: "Allow laughter to flood your home and its echoes will last a lifetime." Ken Davis

December 1
Your Last Love Letter

*T**oday's Smile:*** The three sons of a dying man were with him a few days before he passed away. The father said that he had $150,000.00 cash in a safe and wanted each of them to throw $50,000.00 into his casket before it was closed.

The youngest son threw in his $50,000.00. The middle son threw in $30,000.00 and kept $20,000.00 for himself. The oldest son was one that never used cash. He retrieved his brothers' $80,000.00 that they had thrown in the casket putting that cash in his pocket. He then wrote a check for $130,000.00, his fifty thousand plus the total of his two brothers' cash. He then threw the check into the casket.

Today's Comment: Throwing cash into a casket doesn't work. You cannot take anything with you when you die. You leave all earthly and temporal things behind, including your cash, investments, property, etc. However, there are a couple of things that you can do with your money. Firstly, you can send some of it on ahead. You do this by giving today to Christian ministries such as your church, missions, Christian schools, Christian radio and television ministries, benevolent ministries, etc. Secondly, you can leave what remains at death to family members and to Christian ministries. These details need to be spelled out in a will. Do you have a will? Do you know that "60% of Americans die without a signed will,"[1] and "56% of Canadians"[2] do the same.

I heard a pastor friend preach a sermon entitled *Love's Last Love Letter.* The text was from Luke 15 and the story of the prodigal son. The sermon emphasis was on the father. The pastor pointed out how the father demonstrated his love to his wayward son with open arms, welcoming him home, and throwing a lavish feast.

In his sermon, the pastor told of people who did not want to leave any inheritance to a child that had walked out of their lives. Why should they remember this child in their will? Their child had absolutely nothing to do with them for years. "Here," the pastor said, "was an opportunity to demonstrate their love for their child even as Christ demonstrated his love for us. We too may have ignored our Heavenly Father for years, yet He treats us equitably as all of His other children. Why would we not treat our children equitably? This could well be a parent's *Last Love Letter.*"

Who knows but what a gesture of love like that might be a turning point in a child's life? After all it is only money. Is money more important than the soul of a child?" Leaving a gift may change a child's direction. Pray that God's will be fulfilled in your Last Will & Testament.

Today's Golden Nugget of Truth: "Naked I came from my mother's womb, and naked shall I return there." Job 1:21

Today's Philosophical Tidbit: "Christians state glibly that they love the whole world, while they permit themselves animosities within their immediate world." Calvin Miller

December 2
Obeying The Law

*T*oday's Smile: Geneva was stopped by a police officer for running a red light. Trying to avoid paying the fine, she opted to go to court and plead her case. When she appeared before the judge she begged him to let her go free. "I know," she said, "I ran the light, but I am a school teacher at a rural school and I had to be there early as it was my day to unlock the school. It was a cold rainy day and the students would be drenched unless I got there early."

"So," said the judge, "you're a school teacher. I have only been serving this court for three years and I have been waiting to have a teacher stand before me. You are the first teacher, since I came here, to appear regarding a traffic violation. See that desk over there in the corner; there is paper in the top right drawer, and also a pen. I want you to sit at that desk and with some of that paper and pen and I want you to write 'I promise never to drive through a red light again.' That will be your fine. And oh, I want you to write it out 500 times, after which you may leave the courtroom."

Today's Comment: Do some of you remember writing out lines as a form of punishment? I don't know if there are many schools, today, that would offer that as some sort of punishment. Penalties and punishments today have softened from what they were, be it in the home, school, at work or in our society and law courts. Though they may have changed, human nature tells us that there ought to be some sort of consequence following an offence or breaking of a rule or law.

I've said it more than once in this book, but there is a penalty for breaking God's law. Many people laugh at God's law, His Word. They think that we can outsmart God and He really will let us go free, after all we didn't rob a bank or murder anyone. God's law, His commands, are to be obeyed. If we violate His laws, there are consequences.

Are you tempting God? Are you trying His patience? Are you thinking He will wink at you and say, "You did your best? Come on in." Let us hear what God says and not some fellow human beings. Do you have family or friends that think that God is just a big *grand-daddy* in the sky that will let us all into heaven? Pray that they might come to see and know God for who He really is. He will keep His word which clearly spells out consequences for failing to obey it.

Today's Golden Nugget of Truth: Not all who sound religious are really godly people. They may refer to Me as Lord, but still won't get to heaven. For the decisive question is whether they obey my Father in heaven." Matthew 7:21 (TLB)

Today's Philosophical Tidbit: "Obedience cost a lot; disobedience costs even more." Author Unknown

December 3
The Devil's Language

T oday's Smile: Natalie was a grade nine student. One of her friends had been given an extra day pass for skiing and she phoned Natalie to see if she wanted to skip school and go skiing with her. Natalie jumped at the idea. As soon as her mom had left for work, she phoned the school office and said: "I am calling to report that Natalie Smithers is unable to attend school today because she has the flu."

"I'm sorry to hear that," said the principal's secretary. "I'll note her absence. May I ask who is calling?"

Natalie replied, "This is my mother."

Today's Comment: A sad commentary on the day in which we live is how many people think that it is acceptable to tell a lie. I read article which listed five steps that you should take when calling in sick. It talked about hinting the day before you call in that you're not feeling well and act a little weary and not real healthy your first day back. These are lies and they are in top jobs in our country, not just a school girl wanting to skip school. A news item stated that "Too many government employees have forgotten the meaning of an honest day's work for an honest day's pay."

I've said it more than once in this book that we need to be honest in our dealings. Lying is of the devil and it began in the Garden of Eden when the serpent lied to Eve. The Bible has many verses that speak about lying and its consequences. As Christians we are followers of Christ who said of Himself, "I am the way the truth and the life." (John 14:6). As followers of God, pray that we will be truth-tellers and have the mark of integrity in all that we do.

Today's Golden Nugget of Truth: "A false witness shall not go unpunished, and he who speaks lies shall perish." Proverbs 19:9

Today's Philosophical Tidbit: "When we tell a lie, we speak the devil's language." Author Unknown

December 4
The Nations Scattered

*T**oday's Smile:* Moshe and Shimon were both born and raised in Brooklyn, NY and were on their first visit to Mexico. They were seated in a Mexican restaurant waiting for their meal to be served. Moshe said to Shimon, "I wonder if there are many of our people in this part of the world."

Shimon said, "Why don't we ask the waiter when he brings our tortillas." So when their waiter returned, Shimon asked, "Do you have Mexican Jews?"

"I don't know senor. I ask cook." He was back at their table in less than a minute and said, "No senor, cook say no Mexican jus."

"Are you absolutely sure about that?" responded Moshe.

"I check again, senor," and goes back into the kitchen.

When the waiter had gone back to the kitchen, Moshe said, "I find it hard to believe that there no Jews here in Mexico. They are all over the world."

Once again the waiter came to their table and said, "Senor, head cook, Manuel, and two other cook say we don't have Mexican jus. We never have. All we have is orange jus, grape jus, prune jus, tomato jus and apple jus, but no Mexican jus!"

Today's Comment: The English, German, Russian, Japanese, Chinese, Ukrainians and many other nationalities have spread throughout the world. No longer are they confined to one country. The world has become a global family. "Fifty percent of Toronto's population is foreign born."[1] "Amsterdam is the most multicultural city in the world with 176 different languages spoken."[2]

Following His resurrection, the Lord Jesus Christ told His disciples, to "Go into all the world and preach the gospel." (Mark 16:15). Thank God for the thousands of missionaries that have gone into the various countries of the world to share the gospel.

Today, we are seeing the world come to our doorstep. We are able to share the good news in our western world with many people who have come from countries that are closed to the gospel and will not permit missionaries to enter and share. Pray that we will take every opportunity to proclaim the gospel to the multicultural community that lives next door in our country.

Today' Golden Nugget of Truth: "Declare His glory among the nations, His wonders among all peoples." Psalm 96:3

Today's Philosophical Tidbit: "We've drifted away from being fishers of men to being keepers of the aquarium." Paul Harvey

December 5
Don't Give Up

Today's Smile: Some years ago, I read a story about a fellow named R. D. Jones. The article about Mr. Jones had to do with a typographical error in the classified section of a small-town newspaper and the subsequent disastrous attempts to correct it. Things went from bad to worse. In Monday's paper the following ad appeared: "FOR SALE: R. D. Jones has one sewing machine for sale. Phone 948-0707 after 7pm and ask for Mrs. Kelly who lives with him cheap."

Tuesday's paper contained this correction. "NOTICE: We regret having erred in R. D. Jones' ad yesterday. It should have read: One sewing machine for sale. Cheap. Phone 948-0707 and ask for Mrs. Kelly who lives with him after 7pm."

Wednesday's paper contained yet another correction: "NOTICE: R. D. Jones has informed us that he has received several annoying telephone calls because of the error we made in his classified ad yesterday. His ad stands corrected as follows: FOR SALE: R. D. Jones has one sewing machine for sale. Cheap. Phone 948-0707 after 7pm and ask for Mrs. Kelly who loves with him."

Thursday's paper: "NOTICE: I, R. D. Jones, have NO sewing machine for sale. I SMASHED IT. Don't call 948-0707 as the telephone has been disconnected. I have not been carrying on with Mrs. Kelly. Until yesterday she was my housekeeper, but she quit."

Today's Comment: Have you ever had one of those days feeling that everything was against you and no matter how hard you tried, you just couldn't seem to do things right? You may have come to the point where you figured, what's the use. Why don't I just call it quits?

May I encourage you, don't give up. Don't be a quitter. There are discouragements in the Christian life. That is true. There are all kinds of disappointments as we walk our earthly pilgrimage. Some people disappoint us. They let us down. Someone may have done something that you thought was totally out of character. They profess to be a Christian and look what they have done. Don't let that deter you. Don't let other people's sins keep you from following God. We can find what we need to keep going and be recharged or renewed by God's Word, by prayer and by the indwelling Spirit of God.

Warren Wiersbe is credited with writing these words. "When the child of God looks into the Word of God and sees the Son of God, she/he is changed by the Spirit of God into the image of God for the glory of God." Pray that God will give us what it takes to keep going.

Today's Golden Nugget of Truth: "No temptation has overtaken you except such as is common to man; but God is faithful, who will not allow you to be tempted beyond what you are able, but with the temptation will also make the way of escape, that you may be able to bear it." First Corinthians 10:13

Today's Philosophical Tidbit: "Discouragement is actually faith in the devil." Author Unknown

December 6
Imitation Of The Real

Today's Smile: B. J. fell in love with an opera singer. He first laid eyes on her when she was on stage singing, and B. J. was in the third balcony looking at her through a pair of binoculars. He loved her voice convincing himself that he could live with her. He was so infatuated with her, that he hardly noticed that she was considerably much older than he was. Nor did he care that she walked with a limp. So after a whirlwind romance and wedding, they set off on an exotic honeymoon.

After settling into their hotel for their first night, his chin dropped as she pulled off her wig, ripped off her false eyelashes, yanked out her dentures, took off her glasses that hid her hearing aids, and unstrapped her artificial leg. Stunned and horrified, he gasped, "For goodness sake, sweetheart, sing, sing, SING!"

Today's Comment: Today is a day of substitutes. Probably the first thing that I ever remember as being a substitute was what my parents drank during World War Two. They called it "coffee sub." It tasted a little bit like coffee, but it wasn't. It was roasted grain. It is still in our grocery stores for those who can't handle caffeine. There are all kinds of substitutes or imitations.

Sweeteners for sugar. Imitation leather for the genuine. Imitation flowers and Christmas trees. Imitation brick siding for your house. Imitation diamonds.

Unfortunately, too many people are embracing substitutes when it comes to how we approach God. There are many counterfeit similarities to what the Bible teaches, but they are false. They mislead, deceiving masses of people. All religions are not the same. Satan is the master deceiver. He is a liar. What he proposes, in various forms, is not the truth. Be certain that what you believe is indeed the truth and pray that none of your loved ones will fall prey to that which appears real but is in actual fact, heresy.

Today's Golden Nugget of Truth: "But I fear, lest somehow, as the serpent deceived Eve by his craftiness, so your minds may be corrupted from the simplicity that is in Christ." Second Corinthians 11:3

Today's Philosophical Tidbit: If any person, group, or church tries to tell you that Jesus was not God, that He was only a man, then they are false teachers concerning Christianity. Author Unknown

December 7
Do You Understand

Today's Smile: Rev. Brown was well known for his expository preaching. He always had a wealth of material, good illustrations and a sprinkling of humor. He had retired a couple of years ago, but was in demand as a substitute for various churches. First Community Church had looked forward to his coming for one Sunday, filling in for their pastor. On this particular occasion he had very little to say. As he was concluding his rather brief sermon, he apologetically explained that just before he left his house to come to the church, that his dog had somehow managed to get hold of his sermon notes and destroyed most of them.

Rev. Brown went to the door of the church to greet the parishioners as they left. Several of them told him how much they appreciated his sermons in the past and were sorry that he was so brief. One of the parishioners had a different comment. He whispered to the guest preacher and said, "If that dog of yours ever has any puppies, I will pay any price to give one to our pastor."

Today's Comment: If a pastor or maybe a Sunday School teacher, or care group leader, or anyone seeking to share the teachings found in the Bible is reading this, let me share a simple plan that I followed over the years. Say what you need to in a simple way. Present your talk in a way that your listeners can understand. I was told early in my ministry that if you are preaching a sermon, make it simple enough that a junior high student can comprehend.

Following my retirement, I had a couple of interim senior pastoral ministries. In one church, where I served, my daughter and son-in law and their three sons were members of that church. The grandsons were young; the oldest one was only ten. Every Sunday I gave them each a dollar if they filled in the blanks in the sermon outline, which was in the bulletin. I was amazed at how well they had listened and wrote out the answers. I figured that if they could understand, so could parents and grandparents.

Pray that your presentation will be simple enough that a child can understand. If they understand what you're saying, you may well contribute to their spiritual life. And oh yes, keep your notes away from a dog, lest they destroy the same.

Today's Golden Nugget of Truth: "As newborn babes, desire the pure milk of the Word; that you may grow thereby." First Peter 2:2

Today's Philosophical Tidbit: "People who speak volumes usually end up on the shelf." Author Unknown

December 8
Awaiting A New Body

Today's Smile: Since Howie's wife Evelyn was sick with the flu, it fell his lot to do the grocery shopping. So he sat down with her, writing out, as his wife dictated, the list of groceries needed.

As he walked up one aisle and down the other, he slowly began to fill the grocery cart with the various items, each time checking them off of his list. The last item on his list simply said "baby food." As he stood before all of the little containers of baby food, he was mumbling, "What shall I get him? I suppose some fruit, meat, and a few vegetables although I know he doesn't like vegetables."

At the check-out counter, the friendly clerk chatted away with Bill making no comment about any of his purchases that is until she saw 24 containers of baby food. "Look's like you're expecting the grandchildren for a visit."

"Grandchildren! No not this weekend. They're all grown and some of them are out working. That baby food is for me!"

Today's Comment: Some older people buy as much baby food as some of the young parents. Why? They cannot chew as well as they once did. King Solomon was very descriptive when writing about our aging bodies. In Ecclesiastes 12 he talks about our teeth: "When the grinders cease because they are few." He mentions the arms: "In the day when the keepers of the house tremble." The knees and shoulders grow weaker: "And the strong men bow down." "And those that look through the windows grow dim; when the doors are shut in the streets, and the sound of grinding is low," talking about the eyes and ears. There is much more in that chapter. He concludes his thoughts about aging by saying in verse seven: "Then the dust will return to the earth as it was, and the spirit will return to God who gave it."

As I look back over more than eight decades, I have to say that they all went too quickly. It seems but a few years ago that I remember riding home from the store with a brand new tricycle that my parents bought for me. I was five years old. Now I sometimes wonder how many more years will it be before I hang up my car keys for the last time and start riding another tricycle or scooter.

I don't know what stage of life you are at. You may be young, and you don't even think about old age. You may be raising a family and concentrate more on your children's future. Or, like me, you may be in that age bracket that they refer to as *the elderly*.

Whatever age we are, there is an eternity ahead of all of us, and we all approach it sooner than we think. Don't spend every day worrying about your aging body. Yes, pray that you will take care of your body as best you can, but remember it will eventually perish. However, God will some day in the future give a new body to all those who have personally received Him as their Savior.

Today's Golden Nugget of Truth: "The days of our lives are seventy years; and if by reason of strength they are eighty years, yet their boast is only labor and sorrow; for it is soon cut off, and we fly away." Psalm 90:10

Today's Philosophical Tidbit: "I've reached that snapdragon stage in life. Part of me has snapped and the rest of me is draggin." Author Unknown

December 9
Little Mistake, Big Impact

Today's Smile: Rick and Stephanie Armstrong had been having a hectic schedule in the days leading up to Christmas. They both held full time jobs. Their children were involved in sports and a couple of them took music lessons, which meant driving them to the same. All four of their children were involved in the Sunday School Christmas program, which meant extra time for practices. Plus they were trying to squeeze in some time for Christmas shopping.

"Let's get our Christmas cards printed this year," Stephanie said. Well, that was fine with Rick. So one day as Stephanie left the office where she worked, she quickly ran across the road to a print shop and told them she would like a simple card printed.

"I'll have them for you in a couple of days," said Pete the printer. "I'll address them and mail them for you for a few extra dollars."

Pete the printer had them all in the mail within two days, as he had promised. Within a week or ten days, Rick and Stephanie were receiving cards from some of their friends, signed, The Modest Morrisons, The Clever Clarks, The Successful Smiths, The Jolly Jones, The Beautiful Browns and more. "What is all this about?" asked Rick.

Stephanie looked at one of the cards which Pete the printer had done for them. To her horror she discovered that Pete had made a typographical error and had printed "Merry Christmas from the *Rich* Armstrongs."

Today's Comment: A letter, a word, a glance, a tone of voice, all little things but each can convey the wrong message. A new youth pastor was hired in our church and the congregation showered them with food. They wanted to thank the congregation and so the next week, in the church bulletin, the youth pastor and his wife had submitted the words, "We want to thank you for the pantry shower last Sunday night." What appeared was, "Thank you for the *panty* shower. . ." Fortunately, that error was caught in time and another 1,500 bulletins were printed on Saturday, replacing the ones with the error.

Just little things, one misspelled word, a glance, and many more little things can cause confusion, or inflict pain. Pray that God will help us to be careful in the little details and little things in our life. Little things matter.

Today's Golden Nugget of Truth: ". . .this one thing I do, forgetting those things which are behind and reaching forward to those things which are ahead." Philippians 3:13

Today's Philosophical Tidbit: "There are no mistakes, only lessons." Author Unknown

December 10
Need Help With Your Children

*T**oday's Smile:* Vanna was beside herself. She had three young children and to put it bluntly, they were driving her crazy. She shared with her neighbor Sophie that she was worn to a frazzle. She had difficulty finding time during the day when she could take a break of any kind.

Sophie told her, "What you need to do is get your playpen out of the garage and use it again. This can separate you from your kids and then maybe you can get some free time. So Vanna brought the playpen into the house. Sophie phoned a few days later to see how things were going.

"They are wonderful!" said Vanna. "I can't believe the difference. I get a chocolate bar, a glass of iced tea and a good book and get into the playpen and the kids don't bother me for hours."

Today's Comment: Are you raising children or as a grandparent do you have a significant input into the lives of your grandchildren? How is it going? Are you going nuts, or have you sought out the advice and help of someone who has been there and done that?

We don't have to avoid the disciplining of children, but we may need some counsel along with advice for the best way of dealing with tough situations. However, that in itself is not sufficient. We also need to take these children by name to our Heavenly Father casting this burden upon Him. He cares. Pray, asking for His advice and guidance to handle these tough times, after all He is our Father.

Today's Golden Nugget of Truth: "The rod and reproof give wisdom, but a child left to himself brings shame to his mother." Proverbs 29:15

Today's Philosophical Tidbit: "A pat on the back develops character, if administered young enough, often enough, and low enough." Author Unknown

December 11
A Reason For Living

Today's Smile: The principal at Madison's elementary school had sent home a note with Madison asking her to bring her birth certificate to school the next day as there was a discrepancy in their records and they needed proof of her birth. Her mother told her to be extremely careful with the certificate. It was a valuable document and she must not lose it.

However, the inevitable happened and she lost the birth certificate. She was found sitting on the steps of the school crying when the janitor came along and inquired as to her problem. Through her tears she sobbed, "I lost my excuse for being born."

Today's Comment: Most of us have a birth certificate and it states when and where we were born, even though we do not remember our entry into this world. You really do not need a certificate to prove that you were born. You're alive. Neither, do you need a certificate to prove that you are born again. However, my question is, "Have you been born again?" "Do you have eternal life?"

We're approaching the Christmas season when we celebrate the coming to earth of the Son of God. The Lord Jesus Christ came into this world to be our Savior. He offers eternal life to all who will receive His gift. If you have never responded to His invitation receiving His gift, do so today. Pray to Him, confessing that you are a sinner, inviting Him into your life as your personal Lord and Savior. You will experience a joy and a peace that the world does not give; a reason for living. Yes, Jesus is indeed the reason for the Christmas season.

Today's Golden Nugget of Truth: "Do not marvel that I said to you, you must be born again." John 3:7

Today's Philosophical Tidbit: "If you were only born once, you will die twice, but if you were born twice, you will only die once." Author Unknown

December 12
A Place Where There's No Fear

Today's Smile: The wife of a federal district court judge decided to go to a thrift store and see what they had in ties. She had bought a new sport's jacket for her husband and had difficulty finding a matching tie which she liked. She was not accustomed to shopping at a Thrift Store, and was amazed at the selection of men's ties which she found. She actually found a couple which she thought went well with his new jacket and bought both of them. One was mostly brown with green stripes. The other one was a solid green.

He had spent days preparing for a complicated cocaine conspiracy case and he decided that he needed a break and so decided to take his wife for dinner. As he was preparing to go out for the evening, the judge decided to wear his new jacket and the solid green tie. As he was tying a knot he noticed that there was a small round disk sewn into the design of the tie. Not knowing what it was, he decided to wear the other tie which his wife had purchased at the Thrift Store.

The next morning he took the first tie to an FBI agent. The agent was also somewhat suspicious and wondered if it might be a *bug* planted by the conspiracy defendants. The agent sent the tie to the FBI headquarters in Washington, DC for analysis. A couple of days later, the FBI agent phoned him and informed him about the report from Washington. The agent said, "They're not sure where the disk came from, but they informed him that when you press the disk, it plays *Jingle Bells*."

Today's Comment: With pressure cooker bombs, unattended backpacks, buttons and gadgets in strange places, we may tend to be more suspicious of such things than our parents or grandparents would have been. The world in which we are living is controlled by the *prince of darkness* - Satan. He is the destroyer. He is out to wound, to kill and to destroy. His days, though, are limited.

Would you like to live where there is love instead of hatred? Peace instead of unrest? Safety instead of danger and insecurity? Trust instead of fear? A place is being prepared. It is called "heaven." However, it is not being prepared for everyone. It is a place which God is preparing for those who love Him, for those who have received His Son, the Lord Jesus Christ as their personal Savior. Pray for this Christmas season that many will respond to God's invitation. Today is the day of salvation.

Today's Golden Nugget of Truth: "Right now God is ready to welcome you. Today He is ready to save you." Second Corinthians 6:2 (TLB)

Today's Philosophical Tidbit: "If you are interested in the *Hereafter*, remember the *Here* determines the *After*." Author Unknown

December 13
Christmas Giving

Today's Smile: A dear old grandmother found Christmas shopping and buying gifts for her family just a little too much. So she decided one year that she would send each of her children and grandchildren a Christmas card with a check enclosed. They could buy whatever they wanted.

She carefully wrote out a card with a personal note for all thirty one of her family members, enclosing a check in each Christmas greeting card. In each card she wrote, "Buy your own Christmas present." She dutifully mailed them and was pleased with her decision. She did not have to face the crowds in the malls. She could quietly sit by the fire knowing that everyone would be so pleased.

All the children and grandchildren received their Christmas cards. Each card had a personal greeting from Grandma plus the words, "Buy your own present." However, she forgot to put the checks in with the cards. She found them two days after Christmas.

Today's Comment: For many years, my parents sent checks as Christmas gifts to my wife and me including our children and our grandchildren. Approximately 2,500 miles separated us and the postage to send a parcel was getting more costly each year. We looked forward to receiving those checks. We could buy our own present.

After my mother passed away, my father continued with the practice. The last Christmas that he was on planet earth, he said that he didn't have the energy to send Christmas cards and write out checks for all of his children, grandchildren and great grandchildren, so he asked me if instead of the usual checks to all of his family whether it would be alright with us if his Christmas checks would be made out to four Christian radio ministries that he and Mom had supported over the years. Then he suggested that we also send the money that we would spend on him as a Christmas gift to a ministry of our choice. We thought it was a great idea. So Dad sent four checks to me and I wrote letters to each of these ministries that my parents had supported, enclosing the checks.

What a wonderful memory of my Dad and his last Christmas before going home. Maybe you might consider doing the same this Christmas. Pray that you might know the mind of the Lord in this matter.

Today's Golden Nugget of Truth: ". . .remember the words of the Lord Jesus, how He said, It is more blessed to give than to receive." Acts 20:35 (KJV)

Today's Philosophical Tidbit: "If you love Jesus, give! Anyone can honk." Author Unknown

December 14
Book Never Opened

*T*oday's Smile: A few days before Christmas vacation a note was tacked on the university bulletin board in the main lobby. It read: "Brand new book entitled 'Introduction To Psychology' has never been used. Asking price $15.00. Must sell! Contact Andy, Room C-405."

The next day a note had been tacked beside it which asked, "Are you sure that it has never been used? Signed, a prospective buyer."

Later that day, with different hand writing a few words were added to the prospective buyer's note. It said "POSITIVE! IT WAS NEVER OPENED ONCE, I graded Andy's exam." Signed Bert Granger, Professor of Psychology.

Today's Comment: Some of you reading this may have just finished, or will finish your fall session in college or university. How did you do? Attending a school of higher education is a privilege. I realize that it is far more costly today than back in my days of higher education in the 1950's. Don't waste your time and money, or your parent's money by leaving your books closed or simply not applying yourself to your studies.

The same holds true for all of us when it comes to the Word of God. Is our Bible a closed book? How long has it been since we opened the Bible and studied its contents and applied its truths to our life? Open it today and pray that God will speak to you through its holy pages.

Today's Golden Nugget of Truth: "Study to show thyself approved unto God, a workman that needeth not to be ashamed, rightly dividing the word of truth." Second Timothy 2:15 (KJV)

Today's Philosophical Tidbit: "A book which is never opened is but an accumulation of paper." Author Unknown

December 15
Did You Mean To Throw It Away

*T*oday's Smile: Since Adrian's father was deceased and had been an only child, Adrian was asked by his grandfather if he would serve as his executor when he passed away.

Eventually his grandfather died and Adrian faced the task of sorting, discarding, selling, etc. When all of these matters were in the past, he decided to take a trip east and visit his sister. During his visit he learned that his brother-in-law had a new hobby, collecting old and rare books.

"Oh, I wished that I had known that," said Adrian. "Grandpa didn't have a lot of stuff. It was fairly easy cleaning out his apartment, but he had a ton of old books. I took most of them to a used book store, but some of them were worthless. There was one book that was really old, but it was so marked up I don't think anyone would have bought it. It was printed by a guy named Guten something. I can't remember his full name."

"Not Gutenberg?" gasped his brother-in-law.

"Yea, that was the name, Gutenberg."

"Adrian! You have probably thrown away one of the earliest books ever printed. I read in a magazine regarding old books that a copy of one of Gutenberg's books recently sold for several million dollars."

"Well, Grandpa's wouldn't have been worth very much. Some guy by the name of Martin Luther had scribbled all over it. You could hardly read the print on some pages because of all the notes and underlining."

Today's Comment: Have you ever given items away, or thrown them out and then later wished that you had not done so? Over the years, I accumulated a lot of books. As I approached retirement I began to get rid of some of my books. I've sold some at used book sales. I've given many others away. Then the day came when I asked myself "Why did I get rid of that book and that one?" I remember on one occasion going to the Christian book store, paying around thirty dollars for a book that I had once owned but had disposed of it.

Of greater significance is when we discard the teachings of scripture, the biblical standards that we were taught and some of those activities which we did in earlier years. Over the years I have talked with parents and pastors who have shared about their children or other individuals who have turned their back on God throwing out everything that they had learned in their childhood or teen years.

I recall a pastor telling me that in his small town church, most of the young people and young married couples move away in search of employment. He shared with me how many of them no longer attended a church or demonstrated a faith and love for God.

Pray today for that son or daughter, grandchild, or friend who has thrown away their faith and belief. Pray that they might come back to their routes, to the fundamentals of the faith.

Today's Golden Nugget of Truth: "But when he came to himself, he said. . . I will arise and go to my father and will say to him, 'Father, I have sinned against heaven and before you." Luke 15:17, 18

Today's Philosophical Tidbit: "God, like the father of the prodigal, runs to us with open arms to welcome us home." Author Unknown

December 16
The Dating Game

T oday's Smile: It was Sunday morning and Harry was off to church. He pulled out of his driveway in his 2-seater convertible, with the roof closed because of a typical Brisbane rain. As he turned off of Venetia Street on to Chuter Street he saw three bedraggled figures huddling under one umbrella. There was 81 year old Mrs. Kelly. She was very independent and insisted on getting to church by herself, despite her arthritis which was always worse on rainy days. Beside her was Dr. Williams, who was Harry's doctor. He had recently diagnosed an aneurism in Harry, which was taken care of immediately, sparing what might have been Harry's early death. He owed his life to Dr. Williams. The third person, next to Doc Williams was Emily. Emily had started attending the same church six months earlier and Harry had not had the courage to ask her for a date.

Since he only had two seats in his convertible, he had but a few seconds to decide what he should do. Who should he offer a ride to? He came up with what he thought was a brilliant idea. He pulled to the side of the road, handed his keys to Dr. Williams, helped Mrs. Kelly into the passenger seat and modestly waved them good-bye. He then huddled close to Emily under the umbrella and the two of them walked to church.

Today's Comment: I have a story similar to Harry's. I was a candidate at a mission headquarters in Pennsylvania located on a farm of over 300 acres. Candidates are those individuals considering serving in missions. Each one spends several weeks studying, working and interacting with the mission directors. At the end of their candidacy the candidate or the mission directors decide whether they are fitted for such a ministry.

The candidates were housed in different homes on that farm. There were three candidates there, two young ladies and myself. After the Tuesday night prayer meeting the two young ladies started to walk to their respective homes. One house was about a quarter of a mile away and the other about a half mile. I offered to give them a ride as it was threatening to rain. One of them said, "No thanks, we can walk."

I was not deterred by her response, but rather motivated. I had my eye on the other girl. I went and got my car, which was close by, pulled up alongside of them and told them to hop in. My old 1951 Plymouth had a front seat that seated three people comfortably. Much to my delight the girl who had said "No" held the door open so the other girl could sit beside me. That was perfect. The one seated next to me was the one that I was interested in and she was staying at the home that was the most distant. I took her home last.

She was looking after a young family. The mother was in the hospital. Since rain was about to fall, I helped her take the washing in off of the clothesline. She was so appreciative. There was something about her that I had learned to like within those first four days since she had arrived. The next Saturday we had our first date at the Pittsburg Zoo. The rest is history. I married her 13 months later.

Why did I tell you that? Because I had prayed about the girl that I would some day marry. May I encourage any younger person reading this today, or for that fact any person of whatever age, pray for the Lord's guidance when it comes to marriage. As the old wedding vow says, "It is not to be entered into lightly. . ." The two biggest decisions that I ever made in my life were: My decision to ask the Lord Jesus Christ to be my personal Savior; my decision to ask Leona to be my wife. Both decisions were the right ones. Pray that you make right decisions.

Today's Golden Nugget of Truth: "Your ears shall hear a word behind you, saying, this is the way, walk in it, whenever you turn to the right hand or whenever you turn to the left." Isaiah 30:21

Today's Philosophical Tidbit: "God always gives the best to those who leave the choice with Him." Author Unknown

December 17
Loving The Unlovable

oday's Smile: The town mayor was exhausted. It had been a hard week. One of the water mains in the down town area had frozen. His secretary was in a car accident. He received a number of phone calls complaining about the nativity display on town property. Since there were several other pressing matters, he decided to go home early on Friday afternoon.

He no sooner sat down in his recliner, when he noticed the president of the Ladies Auxiliary walking towards their front door. She was one of the most talkative people in town and he was not about to sit and listen to her jabber away for the next hour or so. He told his wife that he was going to go upstairs, staying there until she left.

An hour had passed, so he tiptoed to the stair landing and listened. There was not a sound. He was satisfied so started down the stairs. About halfway down he called loudly to his wife, "Well, honey it sounds like you finally got rid of that old bore." He barely had the words out of his mouth when he heard the woman's voice and knew for sure that she had heard his voice.

Fortunately, the mayor had a smart wife. "Yes, dear, she left over an hour ago, but Mrs. Flowlot has come in the meantime. I'm sure you would like to greet her."

Today's Comment: Are there any *Flowlots* in your life that you consider a bore? You don't look forward to spending time with them. What about your job? Do you do what you do simply for the pay check? What about attending a church service, or reading a Bible passage? Are these boring?

I believe a lot has to do with our attitude. There have been events, people and jobs that I did not relish attending, seeing, or doing. When these were in the past, I could sometimes say, "I was thankful that I went; pleased that we met; happy that I did the work.

Pray that God will give us a positive attitude when we are faced with any of the above, things that might otherwise cause us to have a negative attitude.

Today's Golden Nugget of Truth: "With all lowliness and gentleness, with longsuffering, bearing with one another in love, endeavoring to keep the unity of the Spirit in the bond of peace." Ephesians 4:2

Today's Philosophical Tidbit: "I have seen more cheerful faces on iodine bottles than on some Christians." Vance Havner

December 18
A Volunteer For Jesus

*T**oday's Smile:* The road was icy and Todd slid off into the ditch. He was only a few yards from a farmer's house. He told the farmer about his predicament. The farmer said rather than taking time to warm up the tractor he would take Buddy, his horse. Once he had Buddy hooked up to Todd's car, he yelled, "Pull Tango, pull!" Buddy didn't move an inch. Then he shouted, "Pull Misty, pull." Buddy didn't budge. Now he was saying, "Pull Dusty. Pull Dusty." There was still no movement from Buddy. Finally, he calls out, "Buddy, pull. Buddy pull." Slowly the horse dragged the car out of the ditch.

As Todd was thanking this farmer for his help, giving him a ten dollar bill, he said, "I am a little curious. Why did you call out the names of four horses? Why didn't you call out 'Buddy' the first time?"

"Well," said the farmer, "Buddy is blind and if he thought he was the only one pulling, he wouldn't even try."

Today's Comment: Do you wait until someone else volunteers for a job or ministry before you offer to help? Have you ever been the first one to raise your hand or sign a paper indicating that you would be willing to help? Why is it that many of us wait until someone else steps forward and offers before we volunteer?

According to the dictionary, a volunteer is a person who freely offers to take part in an enterprise or undertake a task. It has been a long time since I've heard the hymn sung in any church which is entitled, *A Volunteer For Jesus*. It is still in some hymnals. Let me share a stanza with you in case you've forgotten or maybe never sung it.

"A call for loyal soldiers comes to one and all; soldiers for the conflict, will you heed the call? Will you answer quickly, with a ready cheer; will you be enlisted as a volunteer?" Then the chorus: "A volunteer for Jesus, a soldier true! Others have enlisted, why not you? Jesus is the Captain, we will never fear; will you be enlisted as a volunteer?"

I need say no more, except to ask, "Will you be enlisted as a volunteer?" Pray that God will move upon your heart next time there is a call for help and it is an area in which you could serve. Don't be the last one to sign up either!

Today's Golden Nugget of Truth: "If you preach, just preach God's Message, nothing else; if you help, just help, don't take over; if you teach, stick to your teaching; if you give encouraging guidance, be careful that you don't get bossy; if you're put in charge, don't manipulate; if you're called to give aid to people in distress, keep your eyes open and be quick to respond; if you work with the disadvantaged, don't let yourself get irritated with them or depressed by them. Keep a smile on your face." Romans 12:6-8 (MSG)

Today's Philosophical Tidbit: "If you are a Christian, your life is not your own. Rather than dying, however, God asks you to live for Him as a living sacrifice. Every day, you are to offer your life to Him for His service." Henry T. Blackaby

December 19
Traits Of Good Character

Today's Smile: Wes was the owner manager of an insurance company. He had a very loyal and efficient receptionist. One afternoon, she became quite ill at work and so, Wes drove her to her home. Since his wife tended to get jealous quite easily, he decided that he would not bother to tell his wife about his taking receptionist home.

Wes and his wife Amy had made reservations for dinner that night at their favourite restaurant. On the way to the restaurant, Wes noticed a high-heel shoe was partly hidden under the passenger seat. Trying to keep from telling his wife that he drove Velma home, he waited until his wife was looking out the passenger side window. He quickly reached down, picked up the shoe and threw it out his window. He felt very relieved until they pulled into the parking lot at the restaurant. When he parked the car, he noticed that his wife was twisting and turning and looking down at the floor.

"Sweetheart," she asked, "have your seen my other shoe anywhere?"

Today's Comment: It may be old fashioned to some, but I have made it a practice never to have a lady passenger without my wife knowing the same. Those times have been very few. The best policy is to stay away from any appearance of evil or give fuel for gossip.

As a younger pastor, I would occasionally visit an older lady, old enough to be my mother. I can't do that any more, because all of the old ladies are about my age. Some of the younger set may not understand what I'm talking about, but I have never taken my secretary out for lunch unless my wife was with me, or I was in the company of others. These are preventive steps and I intend to keep it that way. I think it is pretty good advice. That's all I have to say for today, except to say, make it your prayer today that God will guide you in your relationships with the opposite sex.

Today's Golden Nugget of Truth: "Abstain from all appearance of evil." First Thessalonians 5:22 (KJV)

Today's Philosophical Tidbit: "Reputation is precious, but character is priceless." Author Unknown

December 20
It Is Your Choice

Today's Smile: Veronica was an attractive, young 19 year old lady. She had just finished her first semester at Bible College and was home for the Christmas vacation. She was glad to be home for a couple of weeks. Her parents had left the Christmas tree for her to decorate. She also had the fun of doing some shopping. After looking at several different types of tinsel, she finally decided which one she would purchase. She sauntered up to the counter where a friendly young man was manning that section. "How much is this gold tinsel garland?" she asked.

The handsome young clerk, pointing to the mistletoe above the counter said, "We have a special today. One kiss per yard!"

"Wow, that's terrific," responded Veronica. "I'll buy 12 yards."

Anticipation and expectation was written all over the young man's face. The young man measured out the tinsel, wrapped up the garland, and gave it to Veronica. As she received the parcel from the young man, she called an older man, who was a few feet behind her and who had been looking at some other items and said, "My grandpa, here, will be paying the bill."

Today's Comment: There are times when other people do things for us, whether making a purchase or setting up a date. I met Leona, who is now my wife, in July 1958. We met at a mission candidate school. There was a missionary couple there, Sam and Edna, who were home on furlough, as it was then called. We became very close friends and did many things together.

Early in my time of interest in Leona, having had about one date, Sam came after dinner one evening to where I was staying, picked up the phone and called Leona. "This is Dan," he said. "I'm wondering whether you would be free to go for a little ride?" Leona responded that she would like that. Sam hung up the phone and then turned to me and said, "Now go pick her up. I just made a date for you!"

Someone else may make a date for you, but there is one date that others cannot do for you. You must do it yourself. Your loved ones, close friends or others cannot receive Christ for you. You must make that decision. You must invite Him into your life. You must make Him the Lord of your life. No one else can do it for you. So don't be counting on your parents, because they are Christians, or your wife or anyone else. You and you alone choose or reject the Lord. I have stated it many times throughout this year, but today, if you are reading this book having never received Christ as your personal Savior, do so now. He is only a prayer away.

Today's Golden Nugget of Truth: "And if it seems evil to you to serve the Lord, choose for yourselves this day whom you will serve. . ." Joshua 24:15

Today's Philosophical Tidbit: "It is choice not chance that determines your eternal destiny." Author Unknown

December 21
Take Time To Be Holy

*T*oday's Smile: A distraught university student stood weeping beside her car. "Do you need some help?" Fred asked her.

"In a few minutes, I have my last class before the Christmas break and I can't unlock the car door. I've had this car for several years and I know that I should have replaced the battery in the remote door control," she said. Do you think that convenience store in the next block would sell batteries for this?"

Fred sized up the situation and then asked if he could look at the remote for a moment. She handed the remote to him together with the keys. Fred took the keys and manually unlocked the car door. Handing the keys back to her he said, "I would suggest that you drive to the convenience store and see if they sell these batteries. It is an uphill walk and the roads are a little slippery."

Today's Comment: We live in an age when the mindset is, I want it now. Give it to me right away. We have instant foods, instant communication, instant replays of our favourite sport, you name it, it seems like everything is "fast." Do some of you remember when we had to get up walking eight or ten feet to change the channel or volume on the television? What about waiting for the letter carrier and the letter that brought a reply to your letter of two weeks ago?

Now, with email and text messaging, you have a reply in minutes or even seconds. With a remote we can turn the ceiling fan on while still in bed. We can dim the lights. We can unlock gates, we can lock cars. We're so used to everything happening now that we don't realize that there still is an alternative way that may take longer, but still accomplish the same thing.

It is easy to transfer that thinking of everything instant, or operating it from a distance to our spiritual walk with God. Our walk with God is a process. As it took time to learn to eat on our own, to walk, to acquire knowledge, so it takes time in our spiritual walk. We are exhorted in the Bible to *wait* on the Lord, to spend time in secret.

If you are a new Christian, don't expect to have all the answers in a few weeks. I've been a Christian for close to seventy-five years and I am still growing in my relationship with God and have much more to learn. Pray that we will grow in our spiritual walk. Growing is not instantaneous. It takes time.

Today's Golden Nugget of Truth: "Be still in the presence of the Lord, and wait patiently for Him to act." Psalm 37:7 (NLT)

Today's Philosophical Tidbit: "The trouble is that I'm in a hurry, but God isn't." Phillip Brooks

December 22
Honest Before God

*T*oday's Smile: The Walker family had gathered to celebrate their Christmas a few days before Christmas. Hunter, a seven year-old boy, was asked to say thanks for the Christmas dinner. The family members bowed their heads in expectation. Hunter began his prayer, thanking God for his Mommy, Daddy, brothers, sister, Grandma,

Grandpa, and all his aunts and uncles. Then he began to thank God for the food.

He gave thanks for the turkey, the stuffing, the mashed potatoes, gravy, the Christmas pudding, the cranberry sauce, and the apple pie and ice cream. Then he paused, and everyone waited ... and waited. After a long silence, little Hunter looked up at his father and said, "If I thank God for the brussels sprouts will God know that I'm lying?"

Today's Comment: It would be good if all those who are prone to telling lies were as concerned as little Hunter and realized that God knows when we speak the truth or a falsehood. It has been said that "most Christians are habitual liars." Now some of you immediately reacted to that last sentence. Read on.

Stop for a moment and think of some recent hymns or choruses which you have sung in church. You may have sung *O Come All Ye Faithful* in the last week or so. Do you adore Christ the Lord? *Jesus Is All The World To Me*. Is He? One of Keith Green's contemporary choruses, which conveys a similar thought is: *Oh Lord, you're beautiful, Your face is all I see*. What about the old missionary hymn, *I'll Go Where You Want Me To Go Dear Lord?* Do we really mean that? Maybe the Lord hasn't spoken to us about going to Africa or South America to be a missionary, but what about our neighbor next door, or that one we work with day after day?

What about that old hymn written back in the 19th century by William R. Featherston, *My Jesus, I Love Thee?* William, of Montreal, Quebec, wrote it following his conversion to Christ at the age of 16. Do we love Jesus as William says in that first stanza, "For Thee all the follies of sin I resign. . ." or "If ever I loved Thee, my Jesus, 'tis now?" Pray that we might have a deep and abiding love for Jesus and a conscience like the little fellow who asked, "Will God know that I'm lying?"

Today's Golden Nugget of Truth: "Lying lips are an abomination to the Lord, but those who deal truthfully are His delight." Proverbs 12:22

Today's Philosophical Tidbit: "There are people who exaggerate so much that they can't tell the truth without lying." H. W. Shaw

December 23
More Than Enough

*T*oday's Smile: Jack and Michelle were celebrating their first Christmas together and invited Michelle's parents and her family for dinner. Knowing how gullible Michelle was, her Mom decided to play a trick on her daughter. Michelle had just placed the turkey in the oven where upon her mother asked Michelle surreptitiously if she would go to the corner store and purchase a couple of tomatoes plus a cucumber for the salad that she was making. The store was only a five minute walk from the house so Michelle went to get the ingredients for her mother's salad.

As soon as Michelle had left for the store, her mother quickly took the turkey out of the oven, removed the stuffing, stuffed a Cornish hen and inserted it into the turkey, and re-stuffed the turkey. She then placed the birds back in the oven.

When it was time for dinner, Michelle took the turkey out of the oven and proceeded to remove the stuffing. When the spoon hit something rather solid, she reached in and pulled out the Cornish hen.

With a look of total shock on her face, Michelle's mom exclaimed, "Michelle, you've cooked a pregnant bird!"

It took the family two hours to convince Michelle that turkeys lay eggs!

Today's Comment: I have relatives in Texas. I learned that they've had a meat specialty called *turducken*. It is a turkey stuffed with a duck and the duck is stuffed with a chicken. It is no longer limited to the southern USA. We can buy it here in British Columbia, Canada.

When we sit down to eat that Christmas dinner, too many of us will probably say, "I'm stuffed." You may not be eating turducken, but you will likely have had more than enough. There are many millions who are homeless, hungry and hurting. Our church gym is filled on Christmas Day with many from our city without family, without friends and without food who partake of a Christmas dinner. My wife and I have participated in this meal, *A Place To Call Home*, serving as a host and hostess.

453

One Christmas there was a fellow seated at our table who asked me, before the meal, if this was the kind of meal where you could go back for a second helping. I assured him it was and that he could eat as much as he wanted. I don't know where he put it all, but he had three heaping platefuls of potatoes, turkey, veggies, etc, finishing off with four desserts.

Enjoy your Christmas dinner but be sure to offer a prayer of thanksgiving for the abundance of food set before you.

Today's Golden Nugget of Truth: "I know that there is nothing better for men than to be happy, and do good while they live. That everyone may eat and drink, and find satisfaction in all his toil; this is the gift of God." Ecclesiastes 3:12, 13 (NIV)

Today's Philosophical Tidbit: "The trouble with square meals is that they make you round."

December 24
Ask For Directions

*T*oday's Smile: There is a story that is told every Christmas season about the Alaska Department of Fish and Game. As the story goes, male and female reindeer both grow antlers in the summer. The male reindeer drop their antlers at the beginning of winter, usually late November to mid December. Female reindeer retain their antlers until after they give birth in the spring.

On the basis of these statements, the traditional fictitious Christmas story depicting Santa's reindeer pulling his sleigh were not male reindeer, like Rudolf, Blitzen, etc. They had to be female because they still had their antlers.

That should have been a foregone conclusion. Why? Because they were able to find their way around, and if needed, would have asked for help. Males would have needed directions and would certainly not have asked for the same, an attitude akin to all males.

Today's Comment: Why is it that men are notorious for wanting to do it on their own? They don't like to ask for directions.

From September 1957 to April 1958 I served as a pastoral intern in a Baptist Church in St. Clair Shores, Michigan. I was an intern under the supervision of Missionary Internship, founded by Dr. R.E. Thompson. Every Friday about fifty of us interns met in a Detroit area Baptist Church. We were together for the day and were encouraged and inspired by four dear servants of God. In addition to Dr. Thompson, a Navigator man helped us to pursue the memorization of scripture. Fred Reinich was the main director and had great input into my life. The fourth leader was Dr. Henry Brandt, a Christian Psychologist, from Flint who drove in to help in the areas of counseling. One day, I had a most valuable one hour session with Dr. Brandt. His insights and counseling have helped me over the last five plus decades. I have since learned that counselors also struggle with issues.

Dr. Brandt has told the story of a time when he and his wife were driving home to Flint, MI. They had come up from the south and when they reached the Ohio Turnpike, Dr. Brandt turned west and headed for Chicago. His wife told him that he was going the wrong way. Dr. Brandt replied that he knew where he was going. After a few minutes on the Ohio Turnpike he noticed a sign stating how many miles it was to Chicago. He says, much to his dismay, that he drove several miles past more Chicago signs trying to figure out how he could get to Detroit without having to make a U-turn.

Men, when you are headed in the wrong direction do you welcome a correction? Would you ever stop and ask for directions? I know it is a humbling thing for men, but as children of God and men of God, let's also be men enough to admit we need help. We do sometimes take a wrong turn.

Today's Golden Nugget of Truth: "The humble He guides in justice, and the humble He teaches His way." Psalm 25:9

Today's Philosophical Tidbit: "God knows the way. He drew the map. He knows the way home." Max Lucado

December 25
The Light Of The World Is Jesus

Today's Smile: Timmy took part in his first Christmas Sunday School program. He was three years old and his mother had worked with him helping him to memorize seven words which he was to recite. Like most mothers of three year olds, she sat on the front pew in order to prompt him, should he forget any of his words.

Well, it happened. He drew a blank unable to remember his line. Timmy's mother leaned forward and said as quietly as she could, "I am the Light of the world." She repeated it, "I am the Light of the world."

He heard her, and with as big a voice as a three year old could muster, he boomed out, "My mother is the light of the world!"

Today's Comment: Today we celebrate the birth of our Savior, the Lord Jesus Christ. The Light of the world! The Light that came into our world to deliver us from darkness.

Larry Locken is a friend and neighbor. We live in the same condominium. He shared in a church service a story which I asked if I could share with you. Larry and his wife Joy were missionaries for 46 years, serving with Word of Life in Germany and Africa. Here is his story, as he shared it with us:

"Colonel James B Irwin was one of 12 astronauts that walked on the moon. Colonel Irwin was a Christian and after his retirement in 1972, he founded the High Flight Foundation, spending his last 20 years as a Goodwill Ambassador for the Prince of Peace. He travelled the world sharing the gospel.

"I was ministering with Word of Life in Germany. We were asked to arrange meetings for James in various parts of Germany and then our quartet accompanied him on the tours. People came by the hundreds. We sang and he shared his moon walk experience and the gospel.

"One day I took Colonel Irwin to Austria for the day where the two of us did some skiing on the Alps. On our return that night, there in front of us was a full moon. What a moment! Just to think that this man sitting beside me had been up there on that moon. I thought of the words which he had often shared in the meetings, 'Jesus walking on the earth is more important than man walking on the moon.' That night those words and that thought took on new meaning in my life."

The Lord Jesus Christ came to our earth that first Christmas, the Light of the world. He was born to die. He came with the purpose of being the sacrifice for your sin and mine, the sin of the whole world. Pray that on this Christmas Day the coming of that Babe may take on new meaning for every one of us. Jesus, the Light of the world!

Today's Golden Nugget of Truth: "And she will bring forth a Son, and you shall call His name Jesus, for He will save His people from their sins." Matthew 1:21

Today's Philosophical Tidbit: "May the Christ of Christmas be the most treasured gift that you ever have or ever will receive. This gift will last forever, for it is the person of Christ, the Eterrnal God." A. Daniel Goldsmith

December 26
Watch Your Manners

*T*oday's Smile: There was a big Boxing Day Sale in a ladies dress shop in Toronto. Natalie was suffering from the flu and so she sent her husband to the ladies store and told him what she wanted him to buy. You'll find it on the first table to the left of the main door. You can't miss it.

When he got there, a crowd of women were milling about the table, grabbing up the bargains. Time and time again, the poor husband tried to get near the counter but was abruptly pushed aside and treated rudely. After about ten minutes of being shoved around, he remembered his college football days and poised himself for a center rush, pushing the women in all directions. No sooner had he gone on the offensive, when he was promptly accosted by the store security. "See here mister, why can't you act like a gentleman?"

"I've been acting like a gentleman for ten minutes," said the battered husband, "but I figured that I would never get my hands on the item that I want until I started acting like some of these woman."

Today's Comment: Well that is not true of most women. Men are equally as ill-mannered and may not just push and shove, but sometimes take to fighting. What is it about human nature that fights to be number one, to get ahead no matter who they trample on, to satisfy the *me first*? The only answer I have is that it is the sinful nature which we have inherited. We've all sinned and failed to measure up to God's standard. We were born sinners and need to repent of our sin and receive Christ as our personal Savior. He alone can transform us and make us more gentlemanly and lady-like. He is the Author of salvation and he can make us new creatures.

Are we only interested in looking out for ourselves? The Lord Jesus Christ will take our old selfish life and make it into a selfless life. We just celebrated His birth yesterday. He was born in human flesh to sacrifice His life and pay the penalty for our sin. That's what Christmas is all about. Let us pray that the Christ of Christmas will be manifested in our lives.

Today's Golden Nugget of Truth: "A new commandment I give to you, that you love one another; as I have loved you, that you also love one another." John 13:34

Today's Philosophical Tidbit: "The word Christian is both a noun and an adjective. We need more *adjective Christians*, more *Christian* Christians, Christians who are more Christian in thought and spirit and deed as well as in name." Vance Havner

December 27
A Changed Life

*T**oday's Smile:* Young Jared was spending Christmas with his grandparents. His grandpa was giving him a tour of their new condominium. Grandpa had been an avid reader all his years and so had one room as a library.

Jared was trying his best to read the titles and authors of some of his books. There were books by Robert Louis Stevenson, James Fenimore Cooper, Adoniram Judson Gordon, and many more. Since he was so young he was having a hard time with these big strange names. Finally he spotted a book that said "Dictionary." "What's this thick book, Gramps? I've never seen such a big book. What's the story about?"

"Well," said his grandpa, "you might say it is a book of short stories," laughing as he said that. "Really, Jared, it is a book of words. Every known word in the English language is written in that book. If you want to know what the word means, or how to spell it, you use this book."

"You mean that some guy sat down and wrote out all of those words so you could know how to spell them? Why didn't he use his computer? My computer has a spell checker. You don't need to know how to spell. You just click the little check mark where it says ABC and it spells the word for you."

Today's Comment: With the passing of time have come many changes. I remember when there were cars that started with a crank. I learned to write in school using a pen nib which we dipped in an ink well. I recall a telephone which was on a party line. In one of my early pastoral ministries, there were 23 other homes on the same telephone line. Yes, I've used a big dictionary to find the correct spelling. There have been so many changes in such a short period of time. All in my lifetime!

How wonderful to see the change that occurs in a short time when one believes the Word of God and surrenders his/her life to the Lord Jesus Christ. Do you remember Charles Colson? He was once known as President Nixon's *hatchet man*. He was imprisoned for obstruction of justice, received Christ as his personal Savior and later founded Prison Fellowship.

In the province of Saskatchewan in recent years there was a man, Serge LeClerc, who was dubbed "Canada's most dangerous criminal." After receiving the Lord Jesus Christ as his personal Savior he became Legislative Secretary for Corrections in Saskatchewan. He went from being a law breaker to being a law maker.

In 2014 I heard Tass Saada share his testimony and how Jesus Christ became his Savior. Taas's life was radically changed from the enjoyment he had in being a sniper and killing people for Yasser Arafat to a fulfilled life, leading a ministry that reaches out to Palestinians and Israelis with the message of hope as found only in Jesus.

A changeless God will change sinners into saints the moment they surrender to Him. Pray that many will come to a saving knowledge of Jesus Christ today.

Today's Golden Nugget of Truth: "Therefore, if anyone is in Christ, he is a new creation, old things have passed away; behold, all things have become new." Second Corinthians 5:17

Today's Philosophical Tidbit: "God's Word has transforming power to radically change a person's life." Ray Ellis

December 28
A Grateful Heart

Today's Smile: It was a few days after Christmas and Lyndon walked a couple of blocks away to visit with his grandma and grandpa. He and his family had celebrated at his grandparents' house on Christmas Eve. On Christmas Day his family went to one of his uncle's place out in the country.

He was telling his grandparents about all the fun they had on Christmas Day playing in the snow. They went tobogganing and also had a sleigh ride. He also told them about the presents that he had received from his aunts and uncles who had gathered there.

Just before he left his grandparents' place he remembered that his mother had reminded him to thank his grandparents' for their Christmas gift. "Thanks, grandma and grandpa, for the harmonica you gave me for Christmas. It's the best Christmas present I ever got."

"I'm glad that you like it," said his grandpa. "Do you know how to play it yet?"

"Oh, I don't play it," said Lyndon. "My mom gives me a dollar each day if I don't play it during the day, and my dad gives me five dollars a week not to play it at night."

Today's Comment: A friend shared that his older brother had given their parents a deep fryer for Christmas. The parents looked at it and thanked their son. Later, the son said to his parents, "You don't seem very excited with my gift."

They replied saying, "Well, you gave us a deep fryer last Christmas." Have you forgotten what you gave last year, or what you received and who gave it?

I think back over eight decades to presents that I have received. There was a harmonica, a drum set, tinker toy (if you don't know what that is, ask a grandparent), ties, books, clothes, money, gift cards, etc. However, there was one gift that I often received. It was a letter from my oldest son. It is a love letter, full of thanks and nice compliments. It has been his way of sharing his heart to those he loves. His siblings also receive one.

Material things are nice, but they don't last. They wear out, they rust, they break and they become obsolete. Over the years we have also outgrown some of them. Others have lost their appeal. Love never fails. It never wears out or becomes outdated. I trust you gave and received "love" this Christmas. Pray as we enter a new year that we will give a gift that lasts, the gift of love.

Today's Golden Nugget of Truth: "Many waters cannot quench love, nor can the floods drown it." Song of Solomon 8:7

Today's Philosophical Tidbit: "If you love someone, put their name in a circle, instead of a heart, because hearts can break, but circles go on forever." Author Unknown

December 29
Setting Boundaries

*T*oday's Smile: Blake, who graduated from university with top honors in computer science, had secured a job with a large software company. He gave his little eight year old sister a computer as a Christmas gift. She was very excited to receive the same, but there had been so much family around that he did not get around to helping her until a few days following Christmas Day.

Finally he went over the manual in detail, cautioning her about opening attachments that she was unfamiliar with and also warning her not to go on the pornographic sites. "These," he said, "will warp your mind and lead you in a downward path. I gave you this computer, praying that you will seek only the good that can be found. There are a number of good Christian sites for children, good music, and I trust that if you subscribe to Facebook, that you will be careful. I want it to be a helpful tool for you, not harmful."

As they were about to type in a password, he received a call from and old friend, so he left her alone for a few minutes. When he returned he discovered that she was ready to type in a password, according to the instructions in the manual. "OK," he said, "let me help you get started. Type in the password you have chosen."

She typed, and typed, and typed. He had never seen anyone take so long to type in a password. "Sis," he said, "what was your password? Nothing is happening."

"I typed, MickeyMinnieGoofyPlutoHueyDeweyLouieDonald Washington."

"That's way too long," he said.

"Well, it says here in the manual that it has to be eight characters and a capital."

Today's Comment: Does your young person have a computer? Do you know what they are viewing? As I write these comments today, I checked and there are over "three billion people, world-wide, accessing the internet. I watched a website as that number increased at the rate of 8 new internet users per second."[1] "35% of all internet downloads are related to pornography. Kids ages 8 to 18 now spend an average of 10 hours and 45 minutes a day seven days a week with media."[2]

Josh McDowell, founder of Josh McDowell Ministry is reaching young people worldwide with the truth and love of Jesus. On his website he has stated: "A perverted morality storm swirls around our kids. With just one keystroke on a smart phone, tablet, or laptop, your child can open up some of the worst pornography and sexually graphic content (1 billion+ pornographic pages) you can imagine, all in private. Just a few decades ago pornographic magazines were sold behind store counters, placed in paper bags, and limited to purchasers 21 years and older. Most adult men didn't even want to be seen carrying such a magazine out of a store. Today pornography is available to anyone, including your kids and teenagers. And it is just one 'private' click away."[3]

So, if you have an 8 year old or young person in your home, are you aware of the seriousness of this demonic invasion into your home? Pray that your child or children will be able to stand strong in face of this horrific storm that is warping the minds and corrupting the morals. It is addictive, worse than any drug. In a loving way, help your young ones to see that pornography is a tool of the Devil.

Today's Golden Nugget of Truth: "Therefore we also, since we are surrounded by so great a cloud of witnesses, let us lay aside every weight, and the sin which so easily ensnares us, and let us run with endurance the race that is set before us." Hebrews 12:1

Today's Philosophical Tidbit: "God keep me pure in money, morals and motives." Written by Philip Howard when he was 15 years old.

December 30
A Critical Spirit

*T*oday's Smile: Tony had just accepted the position of senior pastor at the First Baptist Church. He had opportunity to meet with the former pastor, who was packing up his books and moving his stuff out of his study. The two men sat drinking coffee together, when Franklin, the pastor who had resigned, reached into his pocket and handed Tony three envelopes. "This," said Franklin, "is my little gift for you as you begin your ministry here at First Church. If after a time, you have a problem in the church, take envelope number one and read it. If you have a second major upset, take envelope two and read it and the same with number three."

Tony was extremely happy with his position as senior pastor at First Church. Things went well. He began to wonder why his predecessor gave him the envelopes. He didn't have any problems. He was into his fifth year when he hit a bump. He thought maybe he should open the first envelope and see what Franklin had to say. He did. The note inside that envelope said, "Blame the congregation!"

Well, things eventually settled down. Two years later, another problem surfaced. Tony opened the second envelope. The note in this envelope said, "Blame the deacons!" As so often happens, it wasn't long before he was again experiencing a problem. This time he was the recipient of a lot of criticism. He opened the third envelope. The note said, "Prepare three envelopes!"

Today's Comment: Two days from now and we will begin a new year. As we look back over the past year did we experience any "bumps" along the way? What did we do? Blame our parents, our spouse, our children, our employer, our employee, our neighbor, our pastor, our congregation? Did we look in a mirror? Was the problem something that we initiated? Could we have done better? Could we have taken a different approach? Did we pray or did we criticize?

Did you leave a church, this past year, and you're now attending another church? Was it something the pastor said in that previous church that did not set well with you? Or maybe it was the deacons, or elders; maybe it was a fellow member or friend. So you left your church, believing that you are now in the *right* church. That is permissible. You have the privilege to go elsewhere, just don't go around *bad mouthing* your previous church. True, your previous fellowship may not have pleased you, but as a child of God don't be criticizing it. The church you left may be just what someone else needs. Instead of spewing out poison about the church that you left, spend some time praying for that church. Prayer changes things. Prayer changes churches!

Today's Golden Nugget of Truth: "Do not be rash with your mouth, and let not your heart utter anything hastily before God, for God is in heaven and you on earth; therefore let your words be few." Ecclesiastes 5:2

Today's Philosophical Tidbit: "God never gives us discernment in order that we may criticize, but that we may intercede." Oswald Chambers

December 31
An Ever-Laughing Life

T *oday's Smile:* This is the last day of the year. What can I say? Three hundred and sixty-four smiles in the past, or if it is leap year than you read three hundred and sixty-five smiles. On the other hand you may have received this book in the middle of the year, or last week for a Christmas gift and you haven't read the entire book.

When I had about two thirds of this book written, I became convicted about writing a book of jokes and humor, especially since there is so much sadness in the world that I wrote out every joke that I had ever heard and threw them all into the fireplace and the fire just roared!!!

Today's Comment: Well, I did question continuing, but you know that I didn't burn the manuscript. You are holding the book in your hands. However, there were times when I thought, as I was working on this project, that with so much tragedy and suffering in the world that maybe I shouldn't write such a book. I was encouraged a few months ago to keep writing when I read the book *Trusting God When Life Hurts*.

That book was written by Jim and Linda Penner, who have been friends for a few decades. In their book they shared their journey of seeking God throughout years of chronic, debilitating suffering and pain. Linda has been in constant pain for many years. In the book Jim says: "Anyone who knows me knows that I love humor and find value in it. Life is perpetually heavy and serious in the environment of incessant pain and suffering. At appropriate moments we need to do what we can to lighten the load a bit and that is when I apply something God says in His Word: 'A joyful heart is good medicine, but a crushed spirit dries up the bones.' Proverbs 17:22. One of the things we have learned in this long season of suffering is to distinguish between what we should take seriously and what we should not."[1]

I don't know who said it, but someone said it well: "Laughter is a wonderful coping devise we're given to help us enjoy life's still waters to their fullest and successfully traverse the dangerous currents. Humor is something I can get serious about. It is nothing less than an extravagant gift to be both enjoyed and shared."

As we are about to leave this old year and enter a new one, you may be wondering what is ahead. The story has been told of some men who were in a storm on a leaky old ship. One of them asked the captain, "Are we safe?" He said, "Well, the boilers are weak and may explode at any moment. The ship is taking on water. To be very honest with you, we may go up, or we may go down, but at any rate, we are going on."

Adrian Rogers said at the close of a year: "Jesus may come; we may go up. We may die, and go down and then up, but at any rate, we are going on."

I pray that as you enter the New Year that you can say that your spirit has been lifted, your day brightened and your future doesn't look quite so gloomy. I trust that this book has help a little.

Today's Golden Nugget of Truth: "Then our mouth was filled with laughter, and our tongue with singing. Then they said among the nations, the Lord has done great things for them. The Lord has done great things for us, whereof we are glad." Psalm 126:2, 3

Today's Philosophical Tidbit: "May you have an ever-laughing life!" John Coulombe

END NOTES

INTRODUCTION
1. Charles R. Swindoll, *Laugh Again* (Word Publishing, Dallas, TX, 1992), p 9

January 17
1. http://billygraham.org/story/the-story-behind-billy-grahams-first-sermon/

January 31
1. https://www.christiancourier.com/articles/1200-how-to-read-the-book-nine-rules-for-effective-bible-reading

February 8
1. Charles R. Swindoll, *Laugh Again* (Word Publishing, Dallas, TX, 1992), p 20-21

March 1
1. Paul Estabrooks, *Daily Inspiration From The Lion's Den* (Open Doors International, Inc. Santa Ana, CA, 2012), January 26

March 5
1. http://www.dts.edu/read/take-crazy-out-of-busy/

March 6
1. Grady Wilson, *Count It All Joy*, (Broadman Press, Nashville, TN, 1984), p 138

March 8
1. http://www.intouch.org/you/article-archive/content/topic/seeking_god_s_guidance_article#.VJdrFcFAA

March 28
1. November, 2004; www.PreachingToday.com

May 2
1. Vance Havner, *The Best of Vance Havner*, (Copyright Fleming H. Revell Company 1969, reprinted 1980 by Baker Book House, Grand Rapids, MI with permission of copyright owner), p 62-63

May 6
1. Garth & Merv Rosell, *Shoe-Leather Faith*, (Bruce Publishing Company, Saint Paul, MN 1960), Item #93

May 13
1. www.eaec.org/desk/joe_wright_prayer.htm

May 22
1. W. E. Thorn, *A Bit Of Honey,* (Zondervan Publishing House, Grand Rapids, MI 1964) p 22

June 8
1. Anne Graham Lotz, *The Joy Of My Heart,* (Paragraph from an email devotional), October 9, 2014

June 18
1. Mark Lee, *Humor Is No Laughing Matter,* (Horizon House Publishers, Beaverlodge, AB 1981), p 171

June 24
1. *www.ifad.org/rpr2011/report/e/rpr2011.*
2. *mic.com/.../45-surprising-facts-about-extreme-poverty-around-the-world*
3. *thp.org/knowledge-center/know-your-world-facts-about-hunger-poverty/*

June 26
1. Grady Wilson, *Count It all Joy*, (Broadman Press, Nashville, TN, 1984), p 93

July 2
1. David Jeremiah, *Medicine For The Soul, Volume One*

July 23
1. Norman B. Rohrer, *A Life Surprised,* (Tyndale House Publishers, Inc. Wheaton, IL 1981), p 127-128

July 27
1. Permission given by Ray Olson to share this story

August 1
1. Jack Hyles, *From Vapor To Floods,* (Hyles-Anderson Publishers, Hammond, IN, 1974) p 390

August 3
1. Bruce Metzger 1951, *Jesus and Others and You* (The Lorain County Free-Net Chapel, North Central, OH 2012)

August 4
1. Grady Wilson, *Count It All Joy,* (Broadman Press, Nashville, TN, 1984), p 151

August 27
1. *http://www.preachit.org/newsletter.cfm?record=136&mode= 274* August 11, 2009

August 29
1. Paul Estabrooks, *Daily Inspiration From The Lion's Den,* (Open Doors International, Santa Ana, CA 2013)
2. Adrian Rogers, *Love Worth Finding - Daily Devotionals,* March 14, 2013

October 2
1. Albert Runge, *A Brooklyn Jew Meets Jesus,* (Christian Publications, Camp Hill, PA, 2001), p 68

October 3
1. Ibid, p 69
2. http://www.gty.org/resources/questions/QA191

October 8
1. http://www.sunnyskyz.com/good-news/470/noah-s-ark-has-been-found-why-are-they-keeping-us-in-the-dark-

2. http://worldnewsdailyreport.com/red-sea-archaeologists-discover-remains-of-egyptian-army-from-the-biblical-exodus/

October 14
1. http://www.plasticsurgery.org/news/past-press-releases/2013-archives/14-million-cosmetic-plastic-surgery-procedures-performed-in-2012.html
2. http://www.worldwatch.org/node/764 8 billion on cosmetics
3. http://www.aboutmissions.org/statistics.html 11.4 billion given to foreign missions

October 23
1. Paul Estabrooks, *Daily Inspiration From The Lion's Den,* (Open Doors International, Santa Ana, CA 2013) January 14

October 27
1. Adapted from a sermon by Dr. Maurice R. Irvin. Used by permission.

October 29
1. http://drjamesdobson.org/Solid-Answers/Answers?a=2ab633a5-708a-4352-b7a1-38f6e8dbc568
2. http://drjamesdobson.org/Solid-Answers/Answers?a=28460daa-b016-49a4-9283-d1e8714a4c5b#sthash.lrLBHu4W.dpuf

November 3
1. www.foxbusiness.comApril16/12

November 15
1. Norman B. Rohrer, *A Life Surprised,* (Tyndale House Publishers, Inc. Wheaton, IL 1981), p 10-11

November 16
1. http://www.whoisgodblog.com/bruised-but-not-broken.html

November 19
1. http://www.nairaland.com/746723/famous-atheists-last-words-before
2. http://raptureintheairnow.com/?topic=last-words-of-saints-and-of-the-sinners

November 24
1. https://www.opendoorsusa.org/christian-persecution/

November 26
1. Oswald J. Smith, *The Savior Can Solve Every Problem,* (Copyright 1932 by B. D. Ackley. Renewal 1960 by The Rodeheaver Company, owner)

December 1
1. https://www.lawdepot.ca/articles/The_Importance_of_a_Last_ Will_and_Testament.html
2. http://retirehappy.ca/too-many-canadians-have-no-will/

December 4
1. http://www.ontarioimmigration.ca/OI/en/living/OI_HOW_ LIVE _TORONTO.html
2. en.wikipedia.org/wiki/amsterdam

December 29
1. www.internetlivestats.com
2. www.webroot.com/ca/en
3. www.josh.org

December 31
1. Jim & Linda Penner, Trusting God When Life Hurts" (Jim & Linda Penner, Abbotsford, BC 2014), p 79

INDEX

Today's Smile

February 3
July 14

BUTCHER:
August 13
November 23

CARE GROUP:
November 12

CELL PHONE:
January 10

CEO / MANAGER:
January 2
January 5
January 27
February 16
February 25
March 24
May 1
June 9
June 10
June 29
July 11
July 31
August 17
September 17
October 16
October 30
November 10

CHEF:
January 27

CHILDREN:
January 4
January 31
February 23
April 9

May 12
May 23
May 30
June 1
July 2
July 5
July 9
July 18
September 6
September 19
September 20
September 24
October 12
October 29
December 10
December 22
December 25
December 27

CHURCH:
January 4
January 29
March 23
October 6
October 24

CHOIR:
April 10

CIVIL SERVANTS:
May 9

CLERK:
January 25
March 28
April 28
June 30
August 17
August 21

September 8
September 17

COMPUTER:
    January 21
    July 25
    December 29

CONCERT:
    November 28

CONSTRUCTION:
    June 13
    June 14

COUNSELLOR:
    October 23

COUNTRY CHURCH:
    January 31
    March 15

COUNTRY STORE:
    August 16

COURTSHIP:
    February 11
    February 12
    February 29
    March 17
    April 17
    June 3
    September 3
    December 16

CRUISE:
    September 18

CUSTODIAN:
    January 31
    November 17

December 31

CUSTOMS OFFICER:
    June 6

DATING:
    May 20
    December 20

DEACONS:
    March 15
    August 7

DELIVERIES:
    March 26
    April 24
    July 10

DENOMINATIONS:
    September 29

DENTIST:
    October 25

DICTIONARY:
    December 27

DIET:
    January 1
    January 18
    March 8
    April 4
    August 24

DINING:
    January 13
    January 26
    March 10
    December 22

DIVORCE:

November 27

DOCTOR:
    January 9
    January 14
    January 24
    February 5
    February 15
    February 18
    February 21
    March 20
    April 12
    June 23
    September 6
    October 27

DOGS:
    September 7

DRIFTER:
    August 28

DRUNKARD:
    August 4
    October 9
    October 24

ENGAGEMENT:
    June 3

ENGINEER:
    October 28

EPIGRAPHER:
    March 31

EQUESTRIAN:
    September 2

EVANGELIST:
    February 24

March 6
March 25
May 18
July 23

FAMILY:
    January 31
    February 7
    December 22
    December 23

FARMER/RANCHER:
    January 29
    March 30
    April 2
    April 15
    April 16
    April 18
    May 3
    May 21
    August 26
    September 14
    October 2
    October 3
    November 18
    December 18

FATHER:
    May 8
    June 5
    June 16
    June 22
    July 5
    September 24
    December 1

FIREFIGHTER:
    August 3
    August 31

FIRST RESPONDER:
   January 24
   August 31

FISHERMEN:
   January 6
   May 15
   July 28
   August 22

FLIGHT ATT:
   February 28
   July 6
   October 18
   November 30

FLYING:
   May 4
   July 5
   July 8
   July 19
   October 17
   November 11
   November 30

FOOTBALL:
   October 21

FRIENDS:
   January 25
   March 4
   April 21
   July 3
   August 9
   September 7

FRUIT MARKET:
   June 30

GOLFER:
   May 13
   June 19
   June 23
   September 5

GOVERNMENT:
   January 22
   April 20
   June 21
   July 1
   November 7

GRANDCHILDREN:
   July 17

GRANDFATHER:
   December 20
   December 27

GRANDMOTHER:
   July 17
   August 3
   August 30
   December 13

GRANDPARENTS:
   November 25
   December 28

HOMELESS:
   November 24

HONEYMOONERS:
   July 7
   July 22
   December 6

HORSE:
   September 2

HOSPITAL:
  July 13

HUMORIST:
  March 12

HUNTERS:
  September 21
  October 17
  October 20
  October 28
  November 22
  November 29

HUSBAND / WIFE:
  January 2
  January 21
  January 25
  January 26
  January 27
  February 2
  February 4
  February 13
  March 7
  April 6
  April 13
  April 27
  May 28
  June 11
  June 27
  July 24
  August 2
  August 8
  August 23
  August 29
  September 2
  September 18
  September 23
  October 13

October 14
October 31
November 26

JEWISH:
  January 18

JOB INTERVIEW:
  January 27
  June 9
  November 1

LAWYER:
  January 14
  March 21
  May 3
  May 24

LETTER CARRIER:
  June 12
  November 4

MAGICIAN:
  July 20
  August 1

MARINES:
  November 11

MAYOR:
  April 19
  December 17

MECHANIC:
  January 25
  April 12
  August 28

METEROLOGIST:
  August 5

MISSIONARY:
May 13
May 29

MOTHER:
February 23
May 10
May 11
May 12
March 12
June 7

LIBRAIAN:
November 13

MOTHER-IN-LAW:
June 11

MUSIC:
April 10

MUSICIAN:
May 14

NEIGHBORS:
January 26
May 17
November 3
November 25

NEWLY MARRIED:
June 15
July 22
November 21

NEWSPAPER:
December 5

NEWS REPORTER:
February 24
March 31
September 26

NURSE:
January 7
April 5
September 28

NURSERY SCHOOL:
October 11

ORDERLY:
August 14

PARAMETIC:
January 24

PARROT:
August 25
October 26

PASTOR:
January 15
January 17
January 23
January 31
February 6
February 8
February 22
March 5
March 13
March 16
March 18
April 3
April 9
April 29
May 2
May 22
May 29
May 30
July 26
August 6
August 7

August 8
August 18
September 1
September 11
September 12
September 16
September 22
September 30
October 5
December 7
December 30

PHARMACIST:
January 23

PICNIC:
July 16

PLUMBER:
May 23
November 18

POLICE:
January 24
February 17
February 19
April 22
May 19
July 16
August 11
September 4
September 13
October 31
November 28

PORTER:
September 9

PRE-SCHOOLER:
October 29

PRESIDENT:
July 4

PRIEST:
January 11
January 15
January 24
January 30
February 26
March 14
June 18
April 8
November 16

PRINTER:
December 9

PRISONER:
January 12
March 1

PROFESSOR:
January 20
February 22
March 29
April 19
July 27
September 10
October 28
November 6
November 15
November 17
December 14

PSYCHIATRIST:
March 3
October 28
November 14

QUIZ:

January 8
March 27

RECEPTIONIST:
January 19
June 12

RECIPE:
October 4

RED CROSS:
January 24

SAILORS:
June 2

SALESPERSON:
June 24
June 28
June 29

SCIENTIST:
October 19

SECRETARY:
January 19
February 1
May 27

SENATOR:
November 8

SENIOR:
January 20
January 21
January 23
March 21
March 23
April 13
October 27

SHEPHERD:
May 14

SHOPPER:
March 22
June 17
July 12
August 2
December 8
December 26

SINGLE MOM:
January 4
March 10
April 7

SPEAKER:
March 12
July 21
September 27

STORY TELLER:
July 15

STUDENTS:
February 10
March 2
March 11
March 13
March 29
April 25
June 4
June 8
June 25
August 27
October 2
October 3
October 7
November 2
November 13

November 17
November 20
December 3
December 21

SUNDAY SCHOOL:
January 4
February 9
April 7
May 15
August 18

SURVEYOR:
May 21

TAVERN:
October 6

TAXES:
July 1

TAXI DRIVER:
June 25
November 19

TEACHER:
February 20
March 19
March 27
April 13
May 6
May 10
May 26
June 1
June 20
September 25
December 2

TEENAGER:
January 16

TELEGRAM:
August 15

THERAPIST:
March 9

THIEF:
August 10

TOUR GUIDE:
July 13

TREASURER:
January 29

TRUCK DRIVER:
March 26

TWINS:
February 18
March 3

USHER:
January 25

VENTRILOQUIST:
August 13

VETERINARIAN:
January 9

WAITER/WAITRESS:
February 27
October 8
December 4

WEDDING:
June 26
August 15

WIDOW:
October 26
July 30

Today's Comment

ABILITIES:
June 13

ABUNDANCE:
December 23

ACCEPTANCE:
February 12
October 19

ADVERTISE:
April 8

ADVICE:
January 9

AGING:
April 13
October 27
November 5
December 8

AMEN:
August 8

APPEARANCE:
October 18

APPETITE:
October 4
October 14

APPOINTMENTS:
April 21

APPRECIATION:
October 1

ASSUMPTIONS:
February 28

ASSURANCE:

June 21

ATTENTIVE:
March 25
July 8

ATTITUDE:
December 17

ATTRACTIVE:
June 22

BEGINNER:
June 9

BEHAVIOUR:
January 11

BENEVOLENCE:
January 24

BIBLE:
February 20
February 26
May 2
May 26
June 5
August 18
October 26
December 14

BLAMELESS:
October 24

BLAMING OTHERS:
April 8
July 17
August 12
November 4

BLENDED FAMILY:
July 20

BORN AGAIN:
August 4
August 6
August 25

BORROWING:
November 3

BREVITY:
April 15

CANTANKEROUS:
October 31

CARING:
March 20
March 21
August 3

CENSORSHIP:
July 25

CHARACTER:
March 31

CHRISTIAN LIFE:
February 17
March 14
March 26
April 10
April 14
April 21
April 28
April 29
May 29
July 11
August 11
August 14
September 6
September 13
September 17
September 28
October 10

December 21

CHURCH:
June 2
June 19

CHURCH MINISTRY:
June 29

CLARITY:
May 14

COINCIDENTAL:
May 8

COMMITMENT:
April 23
June 12
October 21

COMMUNICATION:
January 23
June 8

COMPLAINING:
January 30
February 4
July 6
July 30
October 13

COMPLIMENT:
January 13
May 22

CONCENTRATION:
July 12

CONFIDENTIAL:
June 20

CONSIDERATE:
June 30

CONTENTMENT:
March 19

CONTROL:
July 25

CRITICISM:
October 13
November 16
December 30

DEAF:
March 11

DEATH:
January 18
September 1

DEBT:
November 3

DECEPTION:
January 10
February 27
March 9
March 17
April 1
April 2
June 10
August 28

DECISION:
December 20

DEMONIC:
October 3
November 24

DENIAL:
August 17

DEVOTIONS:
July 27

DILIGENCE:
April 23

DISABILITY:
September 5
September 7

DISAGREEABLE
August 5

DISCIPLINE:
October 29
December 10

DISCONTENT:
March 19

DISCOURAGED:
December 5

DISHONESTY:
March 28
November 23
December 3

DISOBEDIENCE:
December 2

DISTRACTED:
June 12

DIVISIONS:
January 15
March 23

DREAMS:
February 13

DRUNKENESS:
September 16
September 25
October 9

EMBARRASSMENT:

February 12

GOSPEL:
April 9
December 25

GOSSIP:
October 5
November 2

GUIDANCE:
January 9
January 31
July 14
July 16

GULLIBLE:
March 9

HANDWRITING:
January 23

HARD WORK:
June 29

HEALTHY:
February 5

HEAVEN:
February 15
May 18
September 2
December 12

HELPFUL:
July 18

HONESTY:
January 19
March 28

HONORED:
May 11

HOSPITALITY:
July 26

HUMILITY:
June 9
August 3
September 14
September 24
October 17
November 10

HUMOR:
May 27
December 31

HURTING:
November 27

IMPATIENCE:
March 26

INFERIORITY:
April 5

INNOCENCE:
July 5

INSTRUCTIONS:
May 28

INTERRUPTIONS:
January 14
August 6

INVESTING:
November 1

JOKES:
August 13
November 19

JUDGMENT:
February 18
February 19

February 23

MISINFORMED:
October 13

MISINTERPRETATE:
May 21

MISJUDGE:
January 5

MISSIONS:
March 7
May 7
July 18
December 4

MISTAKE:
January 3
June 10
December 9
December 24

MISUNDERSTAND:
January 4
January 21
April 25
August 20
October 12

MONEY:
January 16
May 31

MUSIC:
March 18

OBEDIENT:
November 22

OPINION:
June 25
October 28

OPTIMISTIC:
March 3
October 20

PARENTING:
April 27

PATIENCE:
January 12
June 30
July 13
July 30
September 20
December 21

PEACEFUL:
June 15

PENALTY:
December 2

PERSECUTION:
March 1
March 7
October 23
November 24

PERSONALITY:
May 12

PESSIMISTIC:
March 3
October 20

PORNOGRAPHY:
December 29

POVERTY:
June 24

PRAYER:
January 27
February 8
February 9

REVENGE:
April 22
April 29

REWARDS:
March 30

RIDICULED:
September 10

RUDENESS:
October 25

SACRIFICE:
November 11

SALVATION:
August 25
September 19
December 27

SATISFACTION:
June 6
August 26
November 6

SECOND COMING:
February 6
May 20

SELF-CENTERED:
August 3

SENSITIVE:
November 28

SICKNESS:
October 27

SINFUL:
January 7

SINGING:
December 22

SLEEPLESS:
May 17

SPEAKER:
February 16

SPEECH:
January 8
February 24
March 4
March 6
March 10
April 19
August 21

SPEEDING:
September 4

STEALING:
January 19

STEWARDS:
May 9

SUBTITUTES:
December 6

SUPERIORITY:
April 5

SURRENDER:
March 8

TEACHING:
January 4
February 7
May 10
July 9
July 16

TEMPTATION:
May 19
May 23

THANKFUL:
    February 2
    April 7
    April 12
    August 8
    November 13
    November 25

THINKING:
    January 22

TIPPING:
    September 9

TITHING:
    January 29
    August 27

TRUST:
    August 1

TRUTHFUL:
    March 22
    June 17
    July 28
    October 8

UNDERSTANDING:
    June 28
    July 2

UNFRIENDLY:
    September 11

VARIETY:
    November 21

VISION:
    March 21

VOLUNTEER:
    April 18
    December 18

WAITING:
    July 13

WAR:
    June 6

WISDOM:
    January 20

WITNESSING:
    May 3
    May 24
    July 19
    July 23
    August 22
    September 9
    November 15
    December 25

WORRY:
    February 1
    June 15
    October 7

APPENDIX "A"

WHAT THEN

When the great factory plants of our cities
Have turned out their last finished works,
When our merchants have sold their last product,
And sent home the last of the clerks;
When our banks have transacted their business,
And paid out the last dividend;
When the Judge of the earth calls a reckoning,
And asks for a balance, WHAT THEN?

When the church choir has sung its last anthem,
And the preacher has made his last prayer;
When the people have heard their last sermon,
And the sound has died out on the air;
When the Bible lies closed on the pulpit,
And the pews are all empty of men,
When each one stands facing his record,
And the great book is opened, WHAT THEN?

When the actors have played their last drama,
And the mimic has made his last fun,
When the film has flashed its last picture,
And the billboard displayed its last run;
When the crowds seeking pleasure have vanished,
And gone out in the darkness again,
When the trumpet of ages is sounded,

And we all stand before Him, WHAT THEN?
When the bugle call sinks into silence,
And the long marching columns stand still;
When the captain repeats his last orders,
And they've captured the last fort and hill;
When the flag has been hauled from the mast-head,
And peace seems to reign among men,
When those who rejected the Savior
Are asked for a reason, WHAT THEN?

Author Unknown

APPENDIX "B"

HOW TO GET TO HEAVEN

A friend who lived in Calgary, Alberta and who was deeply in love with that city used to say wherever he went, that if you don't think you will make it to heaven, by all means visit Calgary. When I lived in Calgary, I was told that heaven was just one step beyond Abbotsford, BC

Some think that Calgary is next best to heaven, others think that Abbotsford is. They are both great cities. I've lived in both cities. They've both been called "God's Country." However, neither one is heaven. But there is a heaven, and it's a real place. The question is "How do we get to the real heaven?"

When we moved from Alberta to BC we had to sort our "stuff." We had a house to sell and a house to buy. We had to find a bank and secure a mortgage. We had to pack and unpack, disconnect and connect utilities, licenses, insurance, health care changes, etc.

What do we have to do to get to heaven from British Columbia? Some people think that they have to sort "stuff." They hope that by cleaning up their act, or doing good that God will accept them. The Bible is clear on this point. Performing good works, sacrificing things, improving your life, looking better, paying your dues, etc., will not reserve a place for you in heaven. "All our works are as filthy rags." (Isaiah 64:6}

God tells us simply that we all fail to measure up (Romans 3:23). We are sinners. No amount of good works will enable us to settle into a new home in heaven. God says in His Word (The Bible) that it is not our works, (Ephesians 2:8, 9) good though they may be, that gives us title deed to a place in heaven. Jesus Christ died for our sins. He paid the price demanded. He paid with His own life.

We don't have to go through a realtor and buy a place in heaven. God has gone to prepare a place for us. No mortgage will be needed. Jesus paid for it. The question is, "How do we qualify?" Enter in by the door. Jesus Christ is that door (John 10:9). There is only one way to get to heaven from BC (or where you are). It is not in doing good. It is not in being religious. It is not in buying our way in. It is through Jesus Christ. He is the entrance into heaven. He is the ONLY way (Acts 4:12). All roads may have led to Rome, but there is only one road to heaven.

Are you on that road? Your travel has been paid for by Jesus Christ, but you must reach out and by faith receive what He has done for you. You need to know that God loves you and wants that you should experience peace now, and be assured of eternal life.

Do you want to be sure that you know where you're going when you die? Then tell God (pray): "Dear Lord Jesus, I know that I am a sinner. I have been trusting in my own good works. I realize now, that is not the way into heaven and life everlasting. You alone are the way. I believe that You died on the cross for my sin. I repent of my sin. I open the door of my life and invite You to come in and be my Lord and Saviour. Help me to follow You and live for You the rest of my life. I thank You for hearing my prayer." Amen.

The Bible says, "Whosoever shall call upon the Name of the Lord shall be saved." Romans10:13. If you prayed that prayer, tell someone. Seek out the help of a pastor or Christian friend, someone that will help you grow spiritually. I trust that I will meet you in heaven.

A. Daniel Goldsmith

More info: **www.truthmedia.com\talk**
or **www.greatcommissionnetwork.com**

JOKES QUOTES & ANECDOTES

Made Especially For Citizens With Seniority
By A. Daniel Goldsmith

JOKES QUOTES &ANECDOTES

MADE ESPECIALLY FOR CITIZENS WITH SENIORITY

A. DANIEL GOLDSMITH

It has often been said that laughter is the best medicine. This is a book that proves that old adage. Within the pages of this book is a collection of humor and trivia with senior citizens in mind. As readers devour this treasure chest of seniors' wit and wisdom, they will find themselves laughing right along with the author.

In view of the fact that there are many physical and emotional issues at this stage of life, this book suggests laughter as the best remedy to any and all ailments from which readers may suffer.

"Dan Goldsmith has compiled a volume of pure joy. . . Keep it close when your long hair has given way to a longing for hair. . . I'd take this book over Prozac any day." **Phil Callaway, Speaker and Author of "Laughing Matters." Three Hills, AB**

"Danny Goldsmith and I were young together as boys in Ontario. Now we are older and live far apart, but still friends who love to share memories, and to laugh. . . Danny's book will help you to say thanks for the gift of laughter. . ." **Dr. Leighton Ford, President, Leighton Ford Ministries, Charlotte, NC**

"A wonderful resource of quips and funny stories. . . You will thoroughly enjoy this treasure chest of senior's wit and wisdom." **Rev. Allen Powles, Pastor to Seniors and Adult Ministries, Beulah Alliance Church, Edmonton, AB**

Order this book at **www.xulonpress.com/bookstore** or at a Christian Book Store, online book supplier, or as an e-book.

CPSIA information can be obtained at www.ICGtesting.com
Printed in the USA
LVOW04s0059080715

445325LV00014B/113/P